BIRDS OF PREY: SENSEI & STUDENT

BIRDS OF PREY: SENSEI & STUDENT

Gail Simone — writer

Ed Benes Michael Golden Joe Bennett Cliff Richards — pencillers

Alex Lei Ed Benes Ruy Jose Mike Manley Scott Hanna Michael Golden — inkers

Hi-Fi — colorist

Jared K. Fletcher Rob Leigh Nick Napolitano — letterers

Ed Benes with Alex Lei Dan Brereton Greg Land with Jay Leisten and Matt Ryan — original series covers

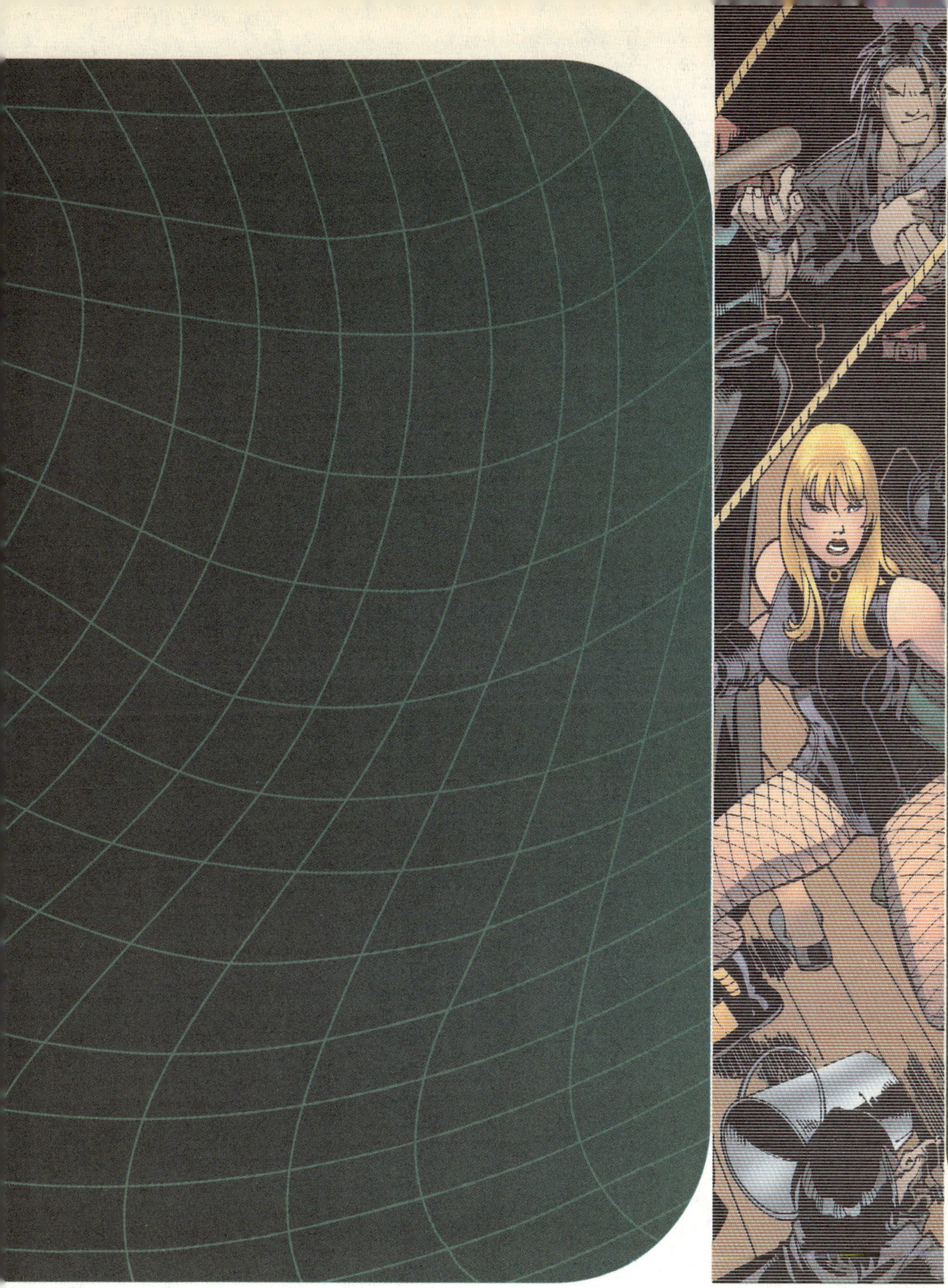

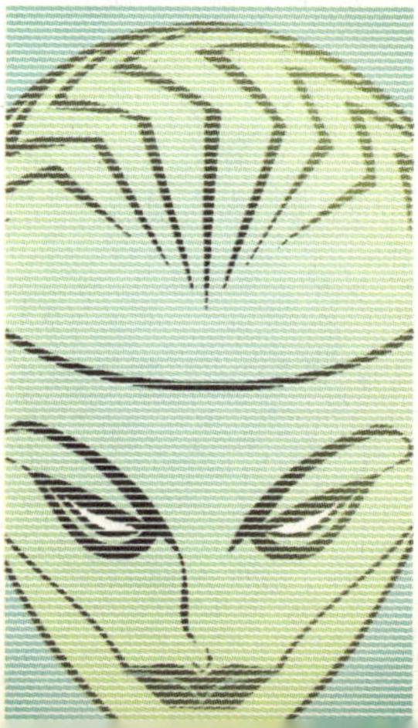

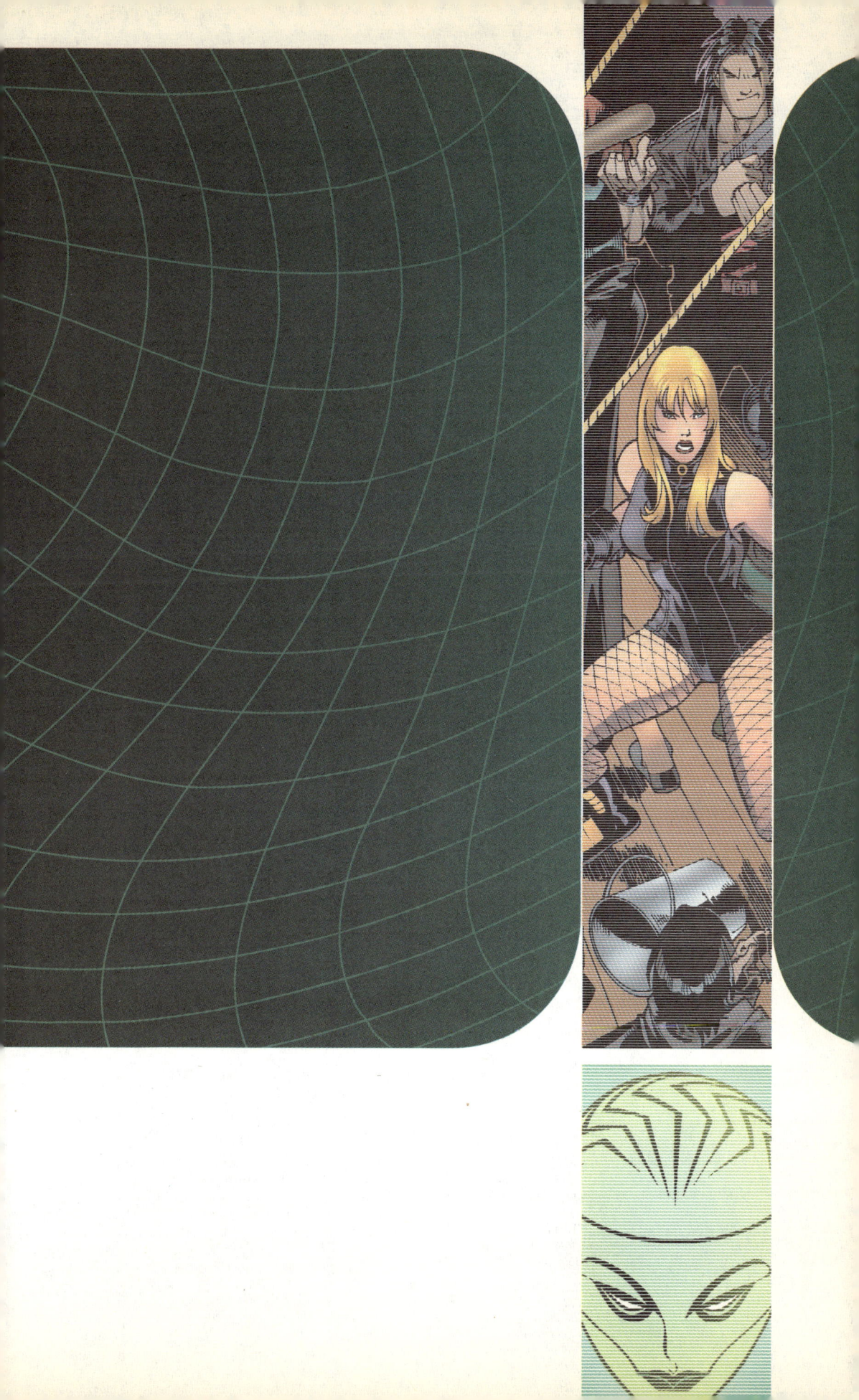

Dan DiDio	VP-Executive Editor
Lysa Hawkins Joan Hilty	Editors-original series
Harvey Richards	Assistant Editor-original series
Anton Kawasaki	Editor-collected edition
Robbin Brosterman	Senior Art Director
Paul Levitz	President & Publisher
Georg Brewer	VP-Design & Retail Product Development
Richard Bruning	Senior VP-Creative Director
Patrick Caldon	Senior VP-Finance & Operations
Chris Caramalis	VP-Finance
Terri Cunningham	VP-Managing Editor
Alison Gill	VP-Manufacturing
Rich Johnson	VP-Book Trade Sales
Hank Kanalz	VP-General Manager, WildStorm
Lillian Laserson	Senior VP & General Counsel
Jim Lee	Editorial Director-WildStorm
David McKillips	VP-Advertising & Custom Publishing
John Nee	VP-Business Development
Gregory Noveck	Senior VP-Creative Affairs
Cheryl Rubin	Senior VP-Brand Management
Bob Wayne	VP-Sales & Marketing

BIRDS OF PREY: SENSEI & STUDENT
Published by DC Comics. Cover and compilation copyright © 2004 DC Comics. All Rights Reserved.

Originally published in single magazine form in BIRDS OF PREY #62-68. Copyright © 2004 DC Comics. All Rights Reserved. All characters, their distinctive likenesses and related elements featured in this publication are trademarks of DC Comics. The stories, characters and incidents featured in this publication are entirely fictional. DC Comics does not read or accept unsolicited submissions of ideas, stories or artwork.

DC Comics, 1700 Broadway, New York, NY 10019
A Warner Bros. Entertainment Company
Printed in Canada. Second Printing.
ISBN: 1-4012-0434-1
ISBN 13: 978-1-4012-0434-1

Cover illustration by Greg Land and Matt Ryan with Justin Ponsor.
All covers colored by Hi-Fi and Justin Ponsor.

C A S T   O F   C H A R A C T E R S

O R A C L E

The niece and adopted daughter of Gotham City Police Commissioner James Gordon, Barbara Gordon was entranced by her uncle's clandestine associations with Gotham's mysterious guardian Batman. Inspired by the Dark Knight to create her *own* costumed identity, Barbara began aiding and abetting Batman's war on crime as Batgirl. But a bullet from the psychotic Joker ended all that. Now paralyzed from the waist down, Barbara nevertheless refuses to live a sedentary life in a wheelchair. With a vast computer network and her own photographic memory, Barbara Gordon has become the all-seeing Oracle — information broker to costumed crime fighters. And no longer content to remain on the sidelines of crime-fighting, Oracle is itching to take a more *proactive* role in troubleshooting global crises.

B L A C K   C A N A R Y

Dinah Lance grew up in the shadow of the legendary Justice Society of America, inheriting the role of Black Canary from her well-intentioned but domineering mother. Armed with a super-powered sonic cry and a mastery of several martial arts, Dinah helped found the JSA's successor, the Justice League of America. When her relationship with Oliver Queen — Green Arrow — soured, Dinah left the Emerald Archer to blaze her own path. Now, with little direction, Dinah strives to rediscover what the mantle of Black Canary means to her and to the world.

H U N T R E S S

The sole surviving member of a mob family murdered by rival factions of the city's Mafioso, young Helena Bertinelli was forced to live among Sicilian relatives, swearing revenge on the men who carried out her family's execution. Trained to fight by her cousin, and armed with a crossbow and knife, Helena returned to Gotham as the Huntress — determined to dismantle the organization to which she was once bound by blood. Now one of Gotham's vigilantes known to use more extreme methods in crime-fighting, the Huntress has yet to gain the full trust of Oracle.

L A D Y   S H I V A

Sandra Woosan dedicated her life to mastering the martial arts, exploring the more spiritual side of combat. She eventually took the name Lady Shiva, and became a creature of intellect and spirituality. To finance her studies, Shiva became a mercenary, ignoring the moral implications of her actions in favor of perfecting her art. She is now known around the world as a nearly unbeatable combatant.

C H E S H I R E

Cheshire is a highly skilled mercenary who lives by her own code of ethics. Besides being skilled in all forms of martial arts, she is also an expert in the field of poisons, and often coats her razor-sharp artificial fingernails with powerful toxins. Years ago she had a union with Roy Harper, the hero known as Arsenal, and gave birth to a daughter, Lian — who is currently in Harper's custody.

S A V A N T

For someone whose physical and mental abilities equal those of the Birds, Savant is ripe with potential — but lacks a real identity of his own. After trying to prove himself and his abilities by drawing the Birds into an elaborate trap, Savant was defeated and imprisoned. But he soon escaped and is currently at large....

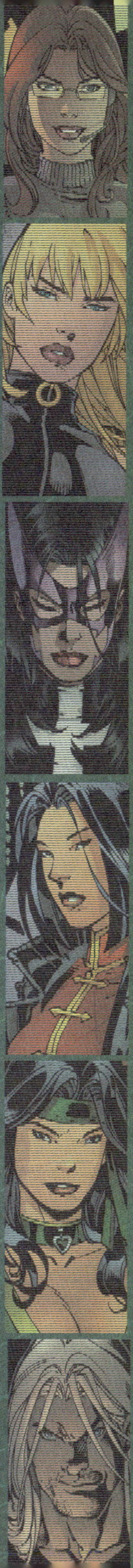

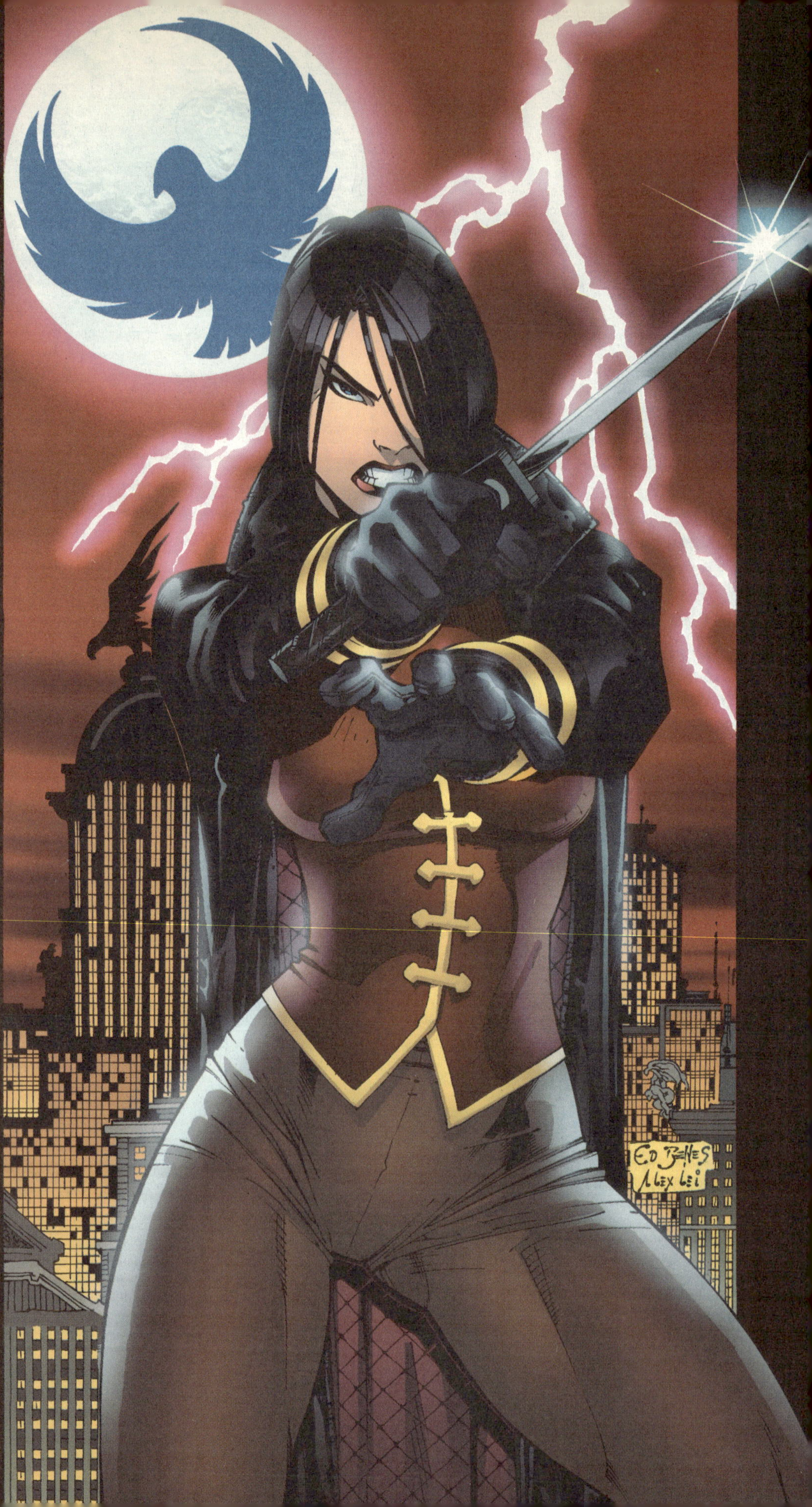
ED BENES
Alex Lei

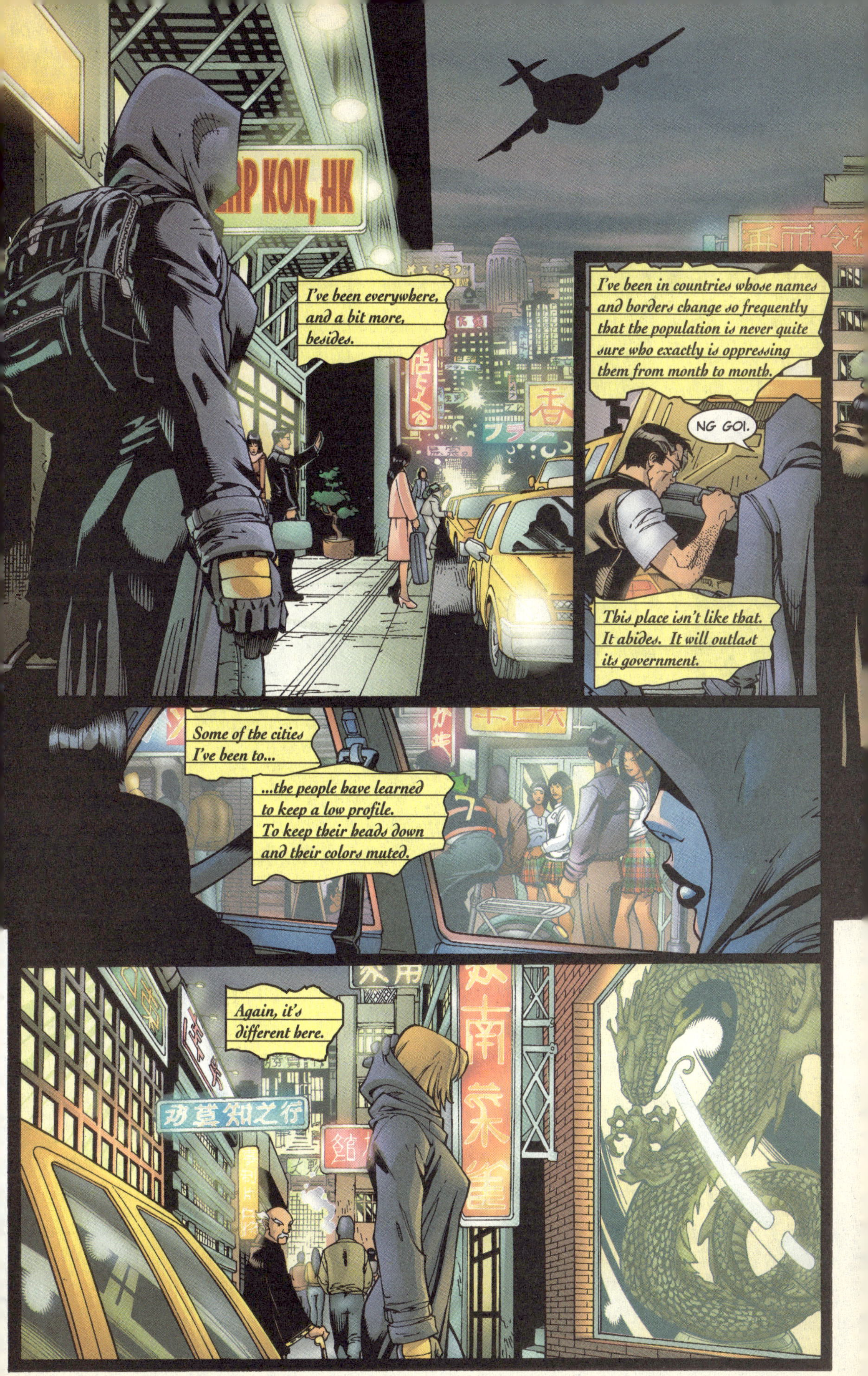
MONG KOK, HK
I've been everywhere, and a bit more, besides.
I've been in countries whose names and borders change so frequently that the population is never quite sure who exactly is oppressing them from month to month.
NG GOI.
This place isn't like that. It abides. It will outlast its government.
Some of the cities I've been to...
...the people have learned to keep a low profile. To keep their heads down and their colors muted.
Again, it's different here.

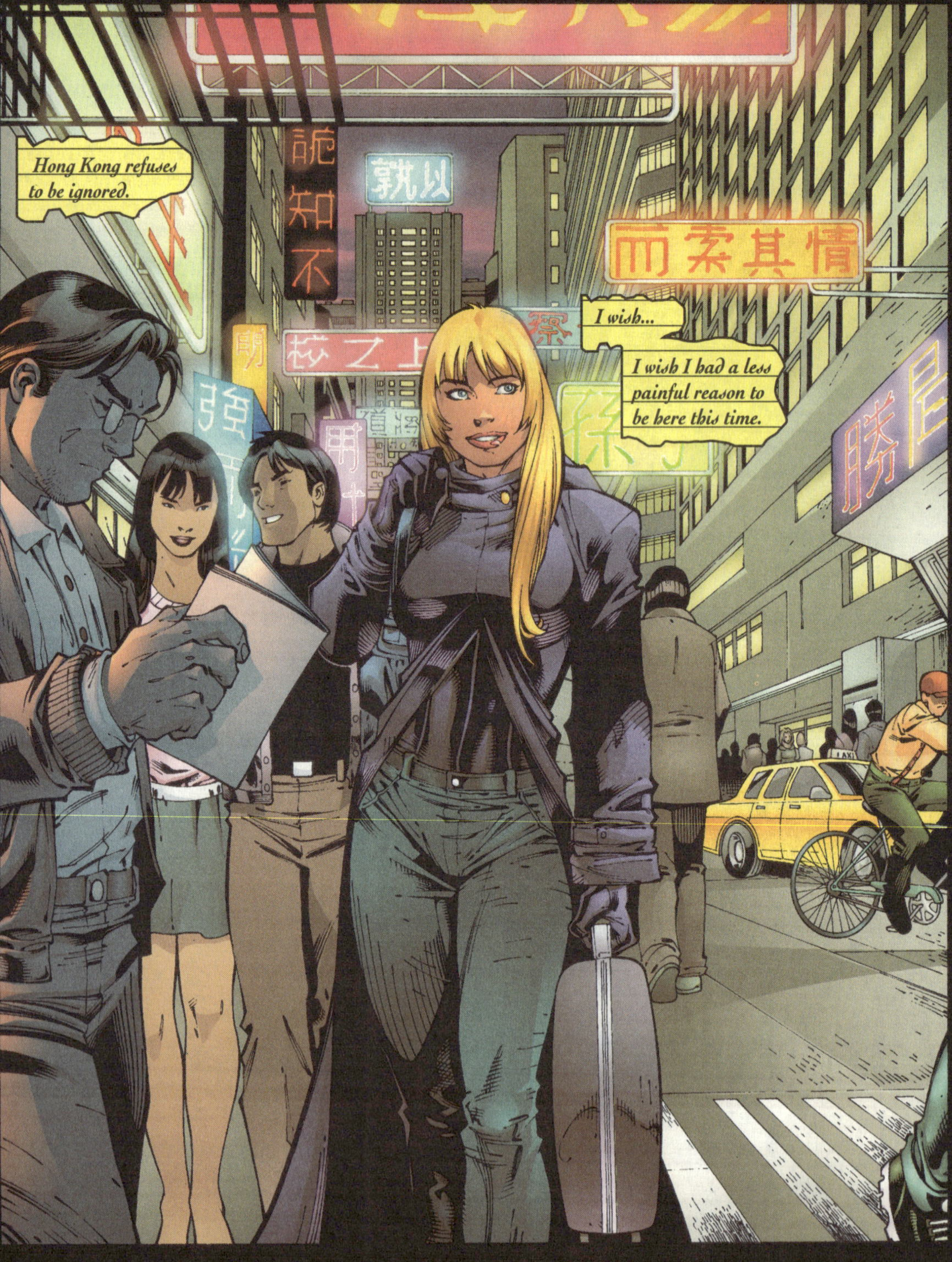
Hong Kong refuses to be ignored.
I wish...
I wish I had a less painful reason to be here this time.

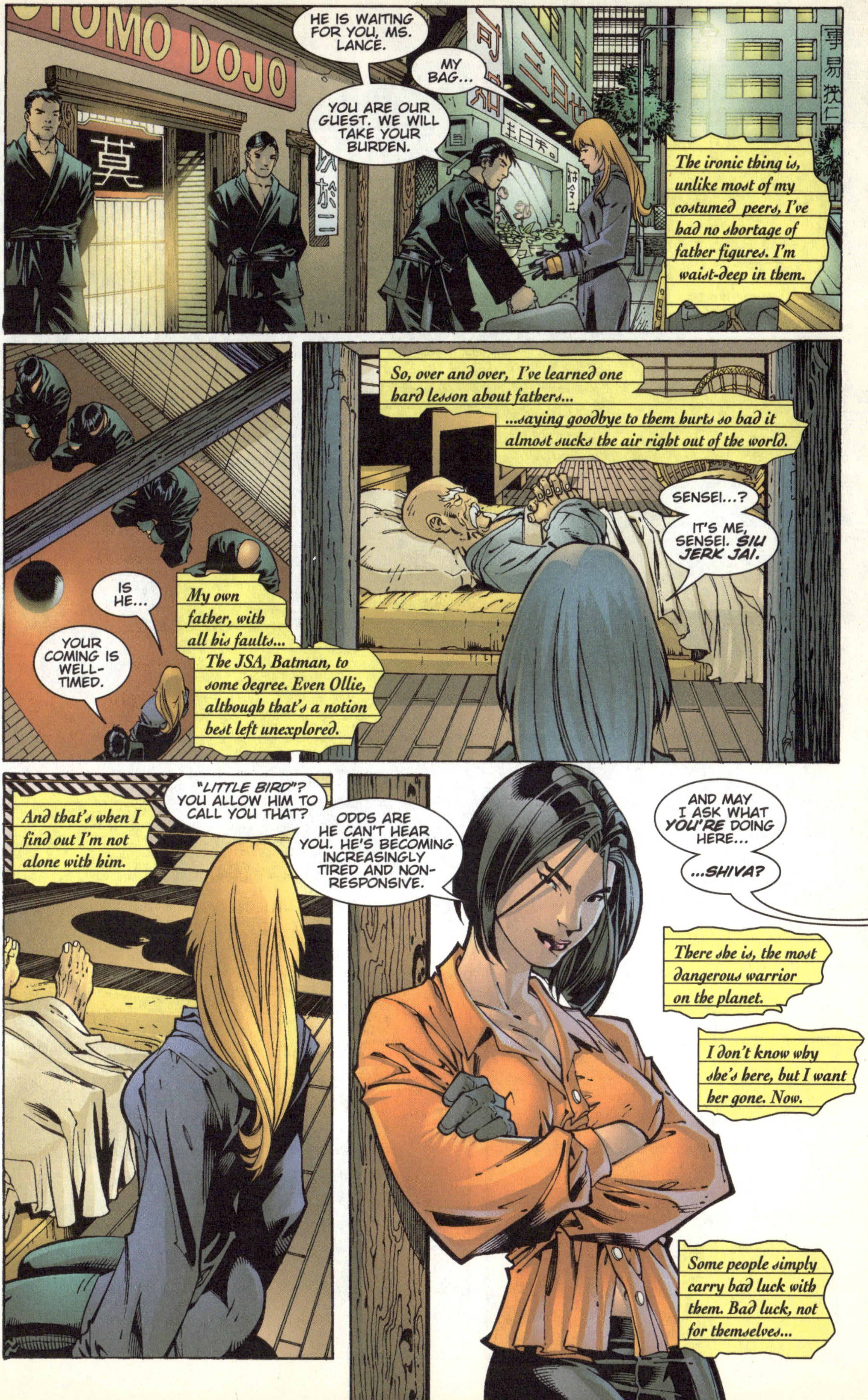
OTOMO DOJO
HE IS WAITING FOR YOU, MS. LANCE.
MY BAG...
YOU ARE OUR GUEST. WE WILL TAKE YOUR BURDEN.
The ironic thing is, unlike most of my costumed peers, I've had no shortage of father figures. I'm waist-deep in them.
IS HE...
YOUR COMING IS WELL-TIMED.
My own father, with all his faults...
The JSA, Batman, to some degree. Even Ollie, although that's a notion best left unexplored.
So, over and over, I've learned one hard lesson about fathers...
...saying goodbye to them hurts so bad it almost sucks the air right out of the world.
SENSEI...?
IT'S ME, SENSEI. SIU JERK JAI.
And that's when I find out I'm not alone with him.
"LITTLE BIRD"? YOU ALLOW HIM TO CALL YOU THAT?
ODDS ARE HE CAN'T HEAR YOU. HE'S BECOMING INCREASINGLY TIRED AND NON-RESPONSIVE.
AND MAY I ASK WHAT YOU'RE DOING HERE...
...SHIVA?
There she is, the most dangerous warrior on the planet.
I don't know why she's here, but I want her gone. Now.
Some people simply carry bad luck with them. Bad luck, not for themselves...

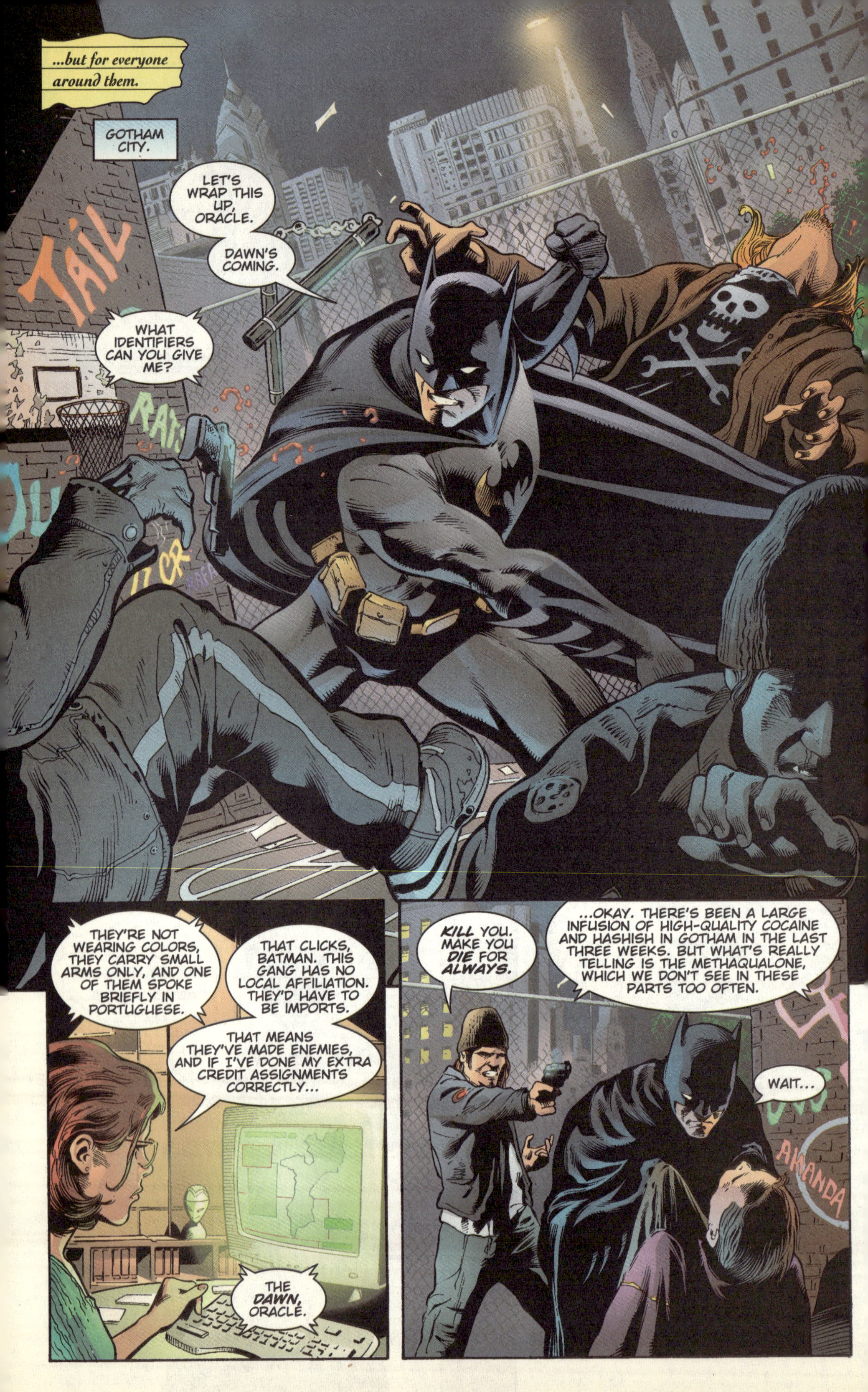
...but for everyone around them.
GOTHAM CITY.
LET'S WRAP THIS UP, ORACLE.
DAWN'S COMING.
WHAT IDENTIFIERS CAN YOU GIVE ME?
THEY'RE NOT WEARING COLORS, THEY CARRY SMALL ARMS ONLY, AND ONE OF THEM SPOKE BRIEFLY IN PORTUGUESE.
THAT CLICKS, BATMAN. THIS GANG HAS NO LOCAL AFFILIATION. THEY'D HAVE TO BE IMPORTS.
THAT MEANS THEY'VE MADE ENEMIES, AND IF I'VE DONE MY EXTRA CREDIT ASSIGNMENTS CORRECTLY...
THE DAWN, ORACLE.
KILL YOU. MAKE YOU DIE FOR ALWAYS.
...OKAY. THERE'S BEEN A LARGE INFUSION OF HIGH-QUALITY COCAINE AND HASHISH IN GOTHAM IN THE LAST THREE WEEKS. BUT WHAT'S REALLY TELLING IS THE METHAQUALONE, WHICH WE DON'T SEE IN THESE PARTS TOO OFTEN.
WAIT...

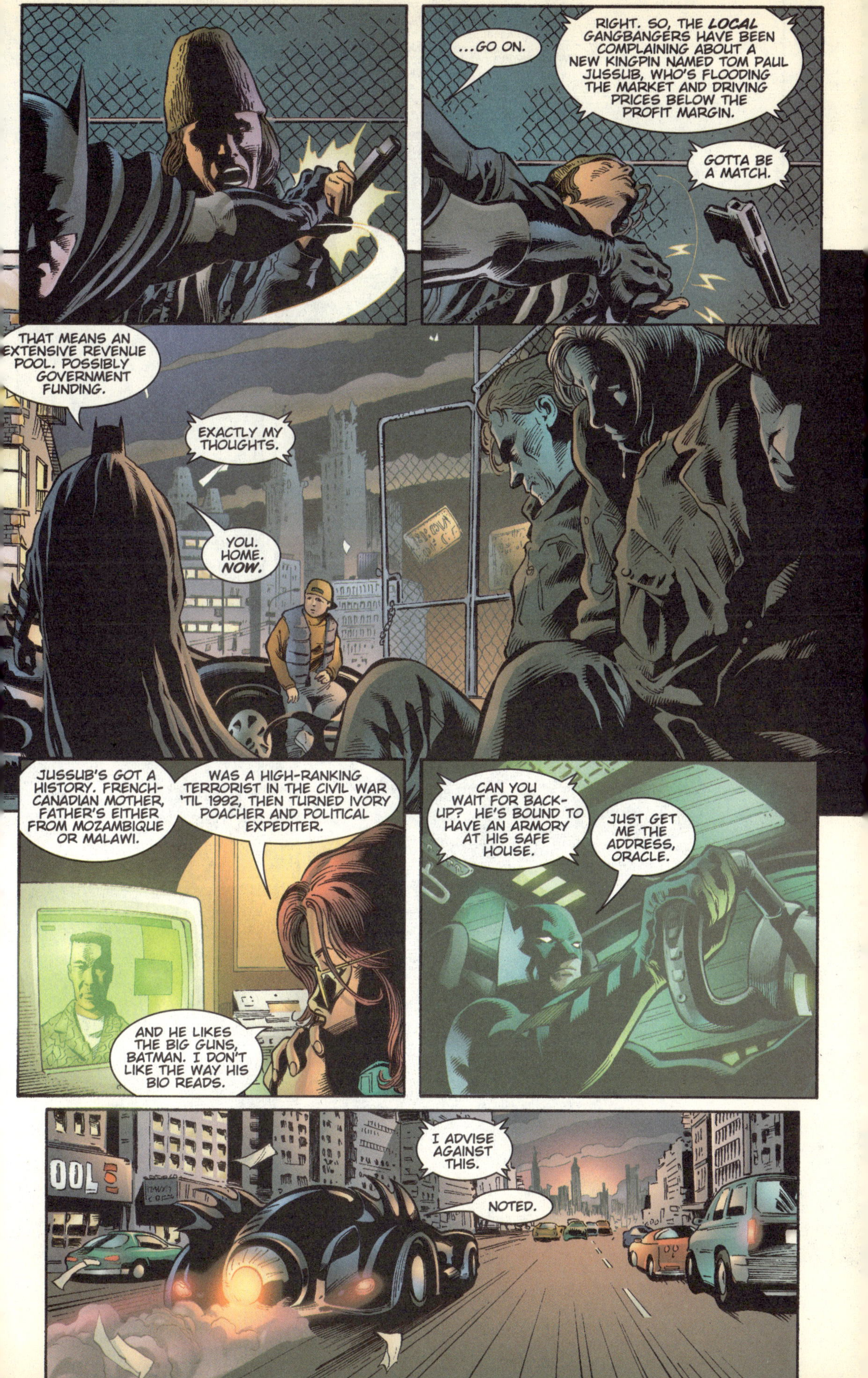
...GO ON.
RIGHT. SO, THE LOCAL GANGBANGERS HAVE BEEN COMPLAINING ABOUT A NEW KINGPIN NAMED TOM PAUL JUSSUB, WHO'S FLOODING THE MARKET AND DRIVING PRICES BELOW THE PROFIT MARGIN.
GOTTA BE A MATCH.
THAT MEANS AN EXTENSIVE REVENUE POOL. POSSIBLY GOVERNMENT FUNDING.
EXACTLY MY THOUGHTS.
YOU. HOME. NOW.
JUSSUB'S GOT A HISTORY. FRENCH-CANADIAN MOTHER, FATHER'S EITHER FROM MOZAMBIQUE OR MALAWI.
WAS A HIGH-RANKING TERRORIST IN THE CIVIL WAR 'TIL 1992, THEN TURNED IVORY POACHER AND POLITICAL EXPEDITER.
AND HE LIKES THE BIG GUNS, BATMAN. I DON'T LIKE THE WAY HIS BIO READS.
CAN YOU WAIT FOR BACK-UP? HE'S BOUND TO HAVE AN ARMORY AT HIS SAFE HOUSE.
JUST GET ME THE ADDRESS, ORACLE.
I ADVISE AGAINST THIS.
NOTED.

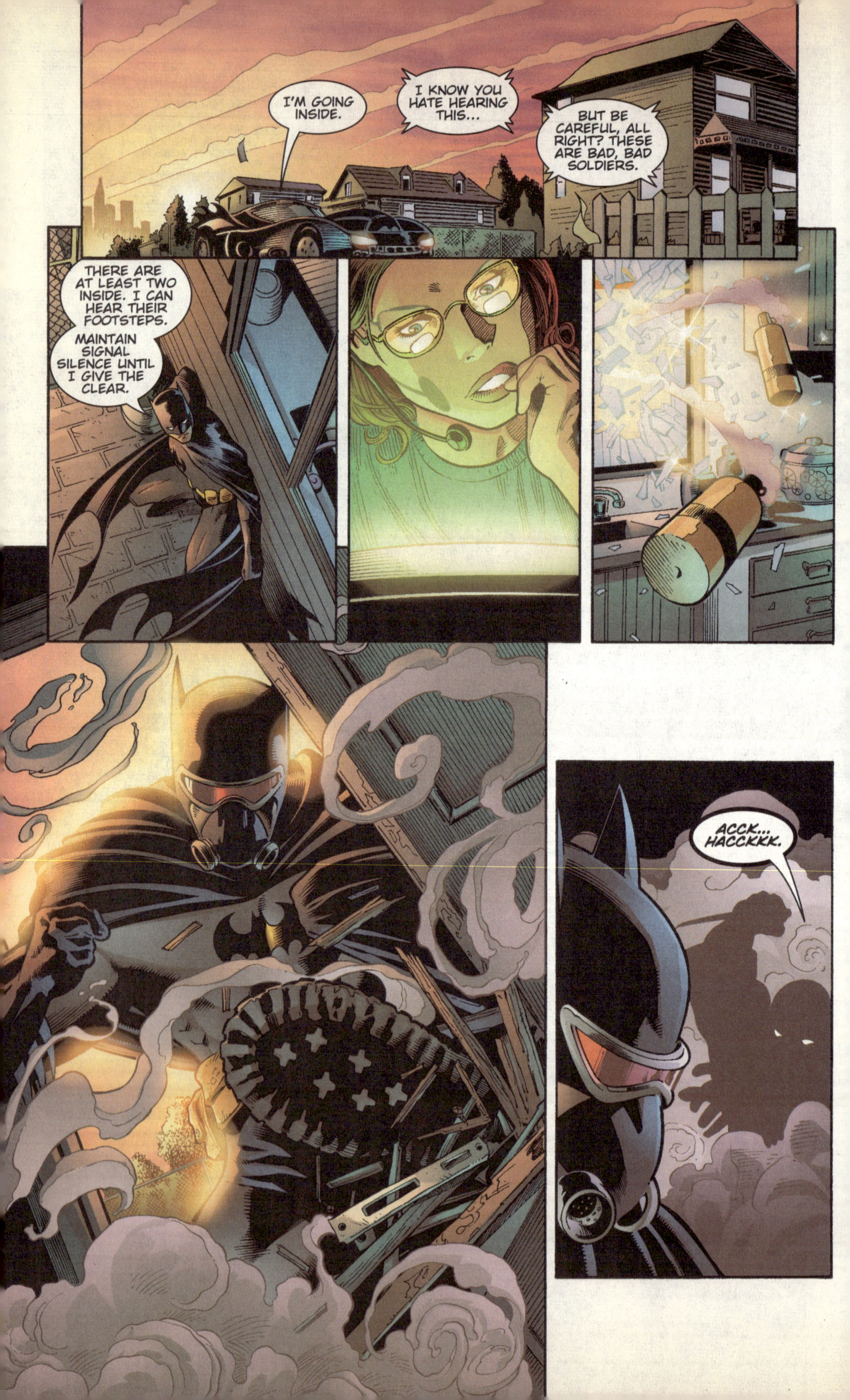
I'M GOING INSIDE.
I KNOW YOU HATE HEARING THIS...
BUT BE CAREFUL, ALL RIGHT? THESE ARE BAD, BAD SOLDIERS.
THERE ARE AT LEAST TWO INSIDE. I CAN HEAR THEIR FOOTSTEPS.
MAINTAIN SIGNAL SILENCE UNTIL I GIVE THE CLEAR.
ACCK... HACCKKK.

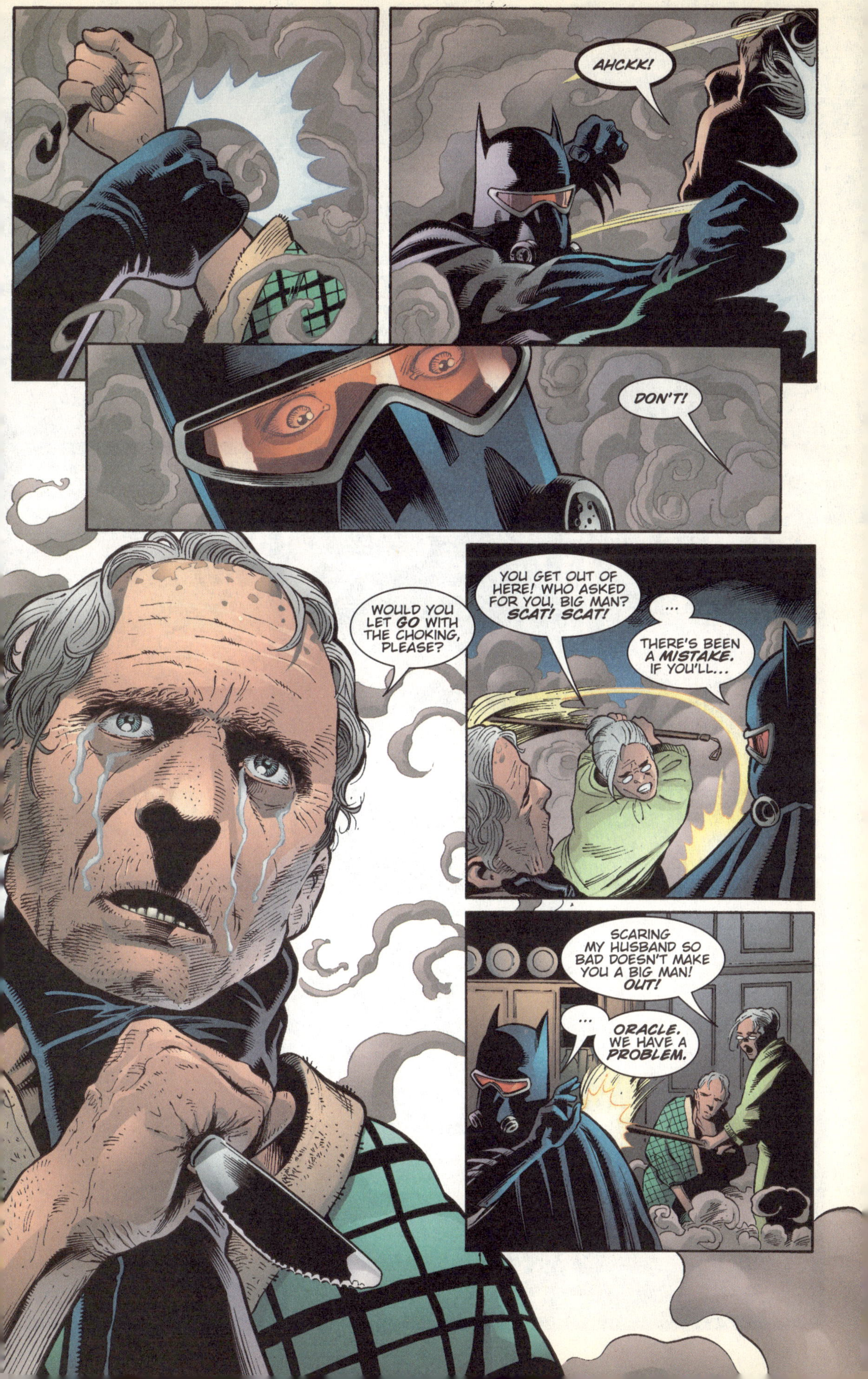
AHCKK!
DON'T!
WOULD YOU LET GO WITH THE CHOKING, PLEASE?
YOU GET OUT OF HERE! WHO ASKED FOR YOU, BIG MAN? SCAT! SCAT!
...
THERE'S BEEN A MISTAKE. IF YOU'LL...
SCARING MY HUSBAND SO BAD DOESN'T MAKE YOU A BIG MAN! OUT!
...
ORACLE. WE HAVE A PROBLEM.

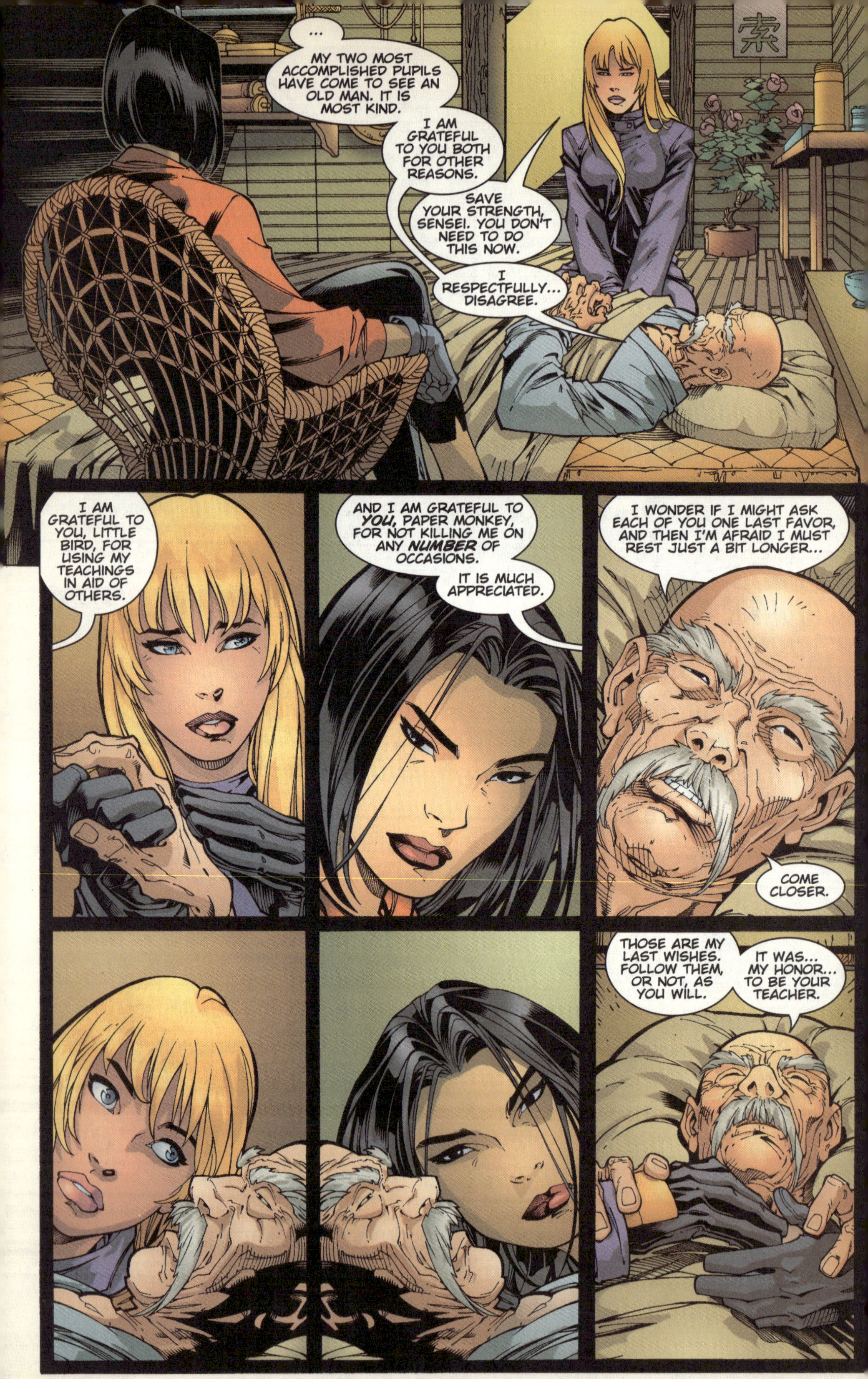
...
MY TWO MOST ACCOMPLISHED PUPILS HAVE COME TO SEE AN OLD MAN. IT IS MOST KIND.
I AM GRATEFUL TO YOU BOTH FOR OTHER REASONS.
SAVE YOUR STRENGTH, SENSEI. YOU DON'T NEED TO DO THIS NOW.
I RESPECTFULLY... DISAGREE.
I AM GRATEFUL TO YOU, LITTLE BIRD, FOR USING MY TEACHINGS IN AID OF OTHERS.
AND I AM GRATEFUL TO *YOU,* PAPER MONKEY, FOR NOT KILLING ME ON ANY *NUMBER* OF OCCASIONS.
IT IS MUCH APPRECIATED.
I WONDER IF I MIGHT ASK EACH OF YOU ONE LAST FAVOR, AND THEN I'M AFRAID I MUST REST JUST A BIT LONGER...
COME CLOSER.
THOSE ARE MY LAST WISHES. FOLLOW THEM, OR NOT, AS YOU WILL.
IT WAS... MY HONOR... TO BE YOUR TEACHER.

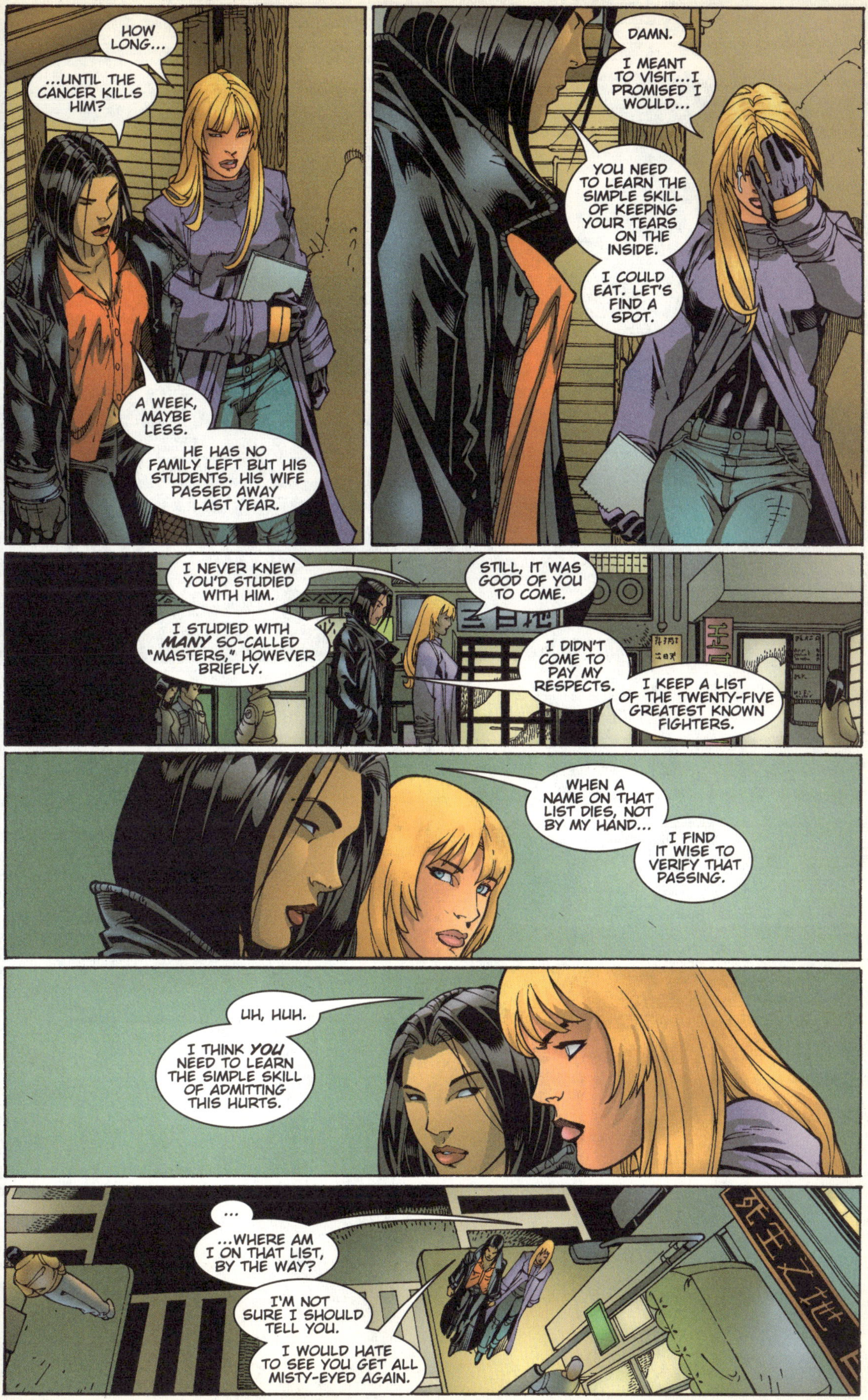
HOW LONG...
...UNTIL THE CANCER KILLS HIM?
A WEEK, MAYBE LESS.
HE HAS NO FAMILY LEFT BUT HIS STUDENTS. HIS WIFE PASSED AWAY LAST YEAR.
DAMN.
I MEANT TO VISIT...I PROMISED I WOULD...
YOU NEED TO LEARN THE SIMPLE SKILL OF KEEPING YOUR TEARS ON THE INSIDE.
I COULD EAT. LET'S FIND A SPOT.
I NEVER KNEW YOU'D STUDIED WITH HIM.
I STUDIED WITH *MANY* SO-CALLED "MASTERS," HOWEVER BRIEFLY.
STILL, IT WAS GOOD OF YOU TO COME.
I DIDN'T COME TO PAY MY RESPECTS.
I KEEP A LIST OF THE TWENTY-FIVE GREATEST KNOWN FIGHTERS.
WHEN A NAME ON THAT LIST DIES, NOT BY MY HAND...
I FIND IT WISE TO VERIFY THAT PASSING.
UH, HUH.
I THINK *YOU* NEED TO LEARN THE SIMPLE SKILL OF ADMITTING THIS HURTS.
...
...WHERE AM I ON THAT LIST, BY THE WAY?
I'M NOT SURE I SHOULD TELL YOU.
I WOULD HATE TO SEE YOU GET ALL MISTY-EYED AGAIN.

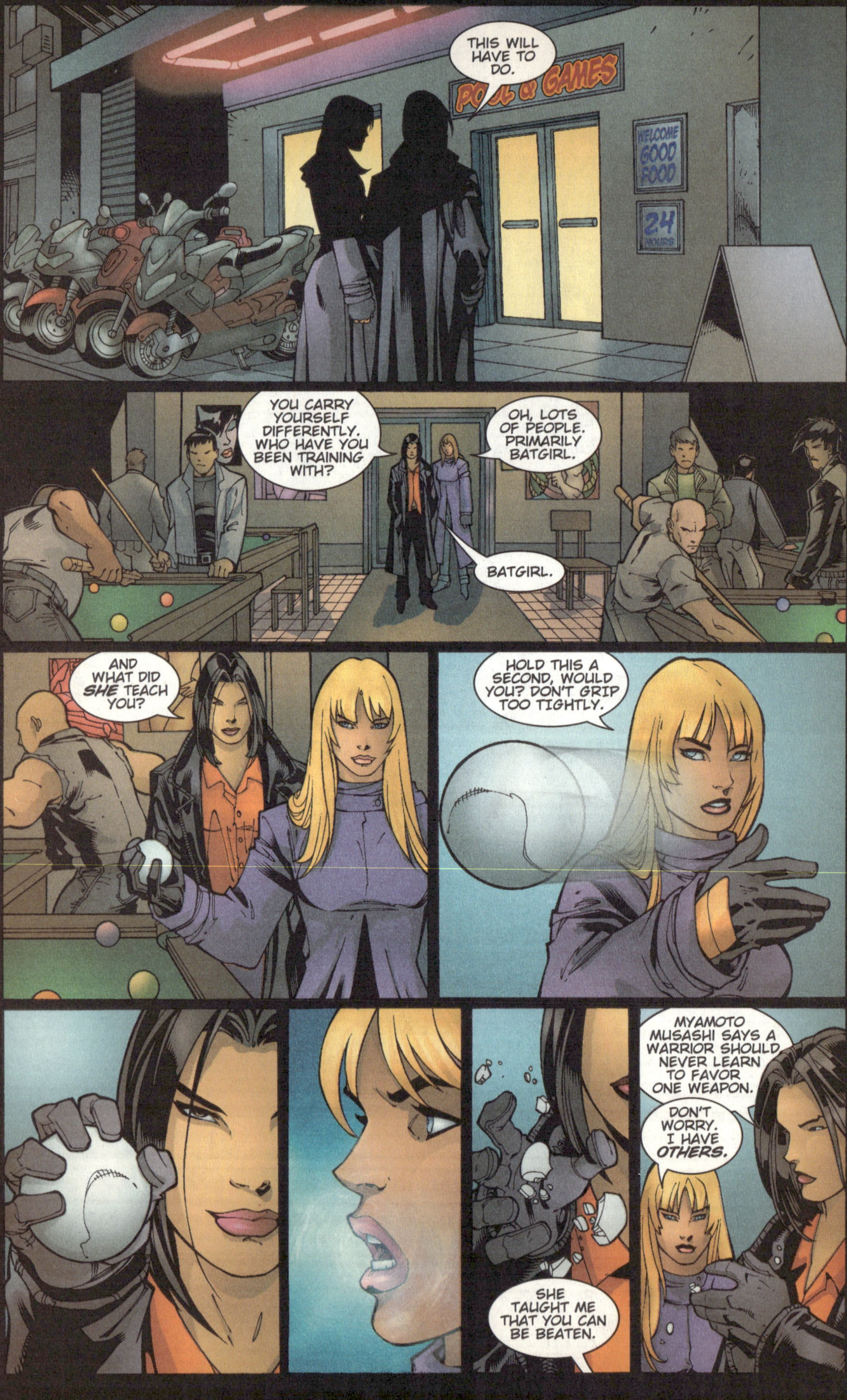
THIS WILL HAVE TO DO.
POOL & GAMES
WELCOME GOOD FOOD
24 HOURS
YOU CARRY YOURSELF DIFFERENTLY. WHO HAVE YOU BEEN TRAINING WITH?
OH, LOTS OF PEOPLE. PRIMARILY BATGIRL.
BATGIRL.
AND WHAT DID SHE TEACH YOU?
HOLD THIS A SECOND, WOULD YOU? DON'T GRIP TOO TIGHTLY.
MYAMOTO MUSASHI SAYS A WARRIOR SHOULD NEVER LEARN TO FAVOR ONE WEAPON.
DON'T WORRY. I HAVE OTHERS.
SHE TAUGHT ME THAT YOU CAN BE BEATEN.

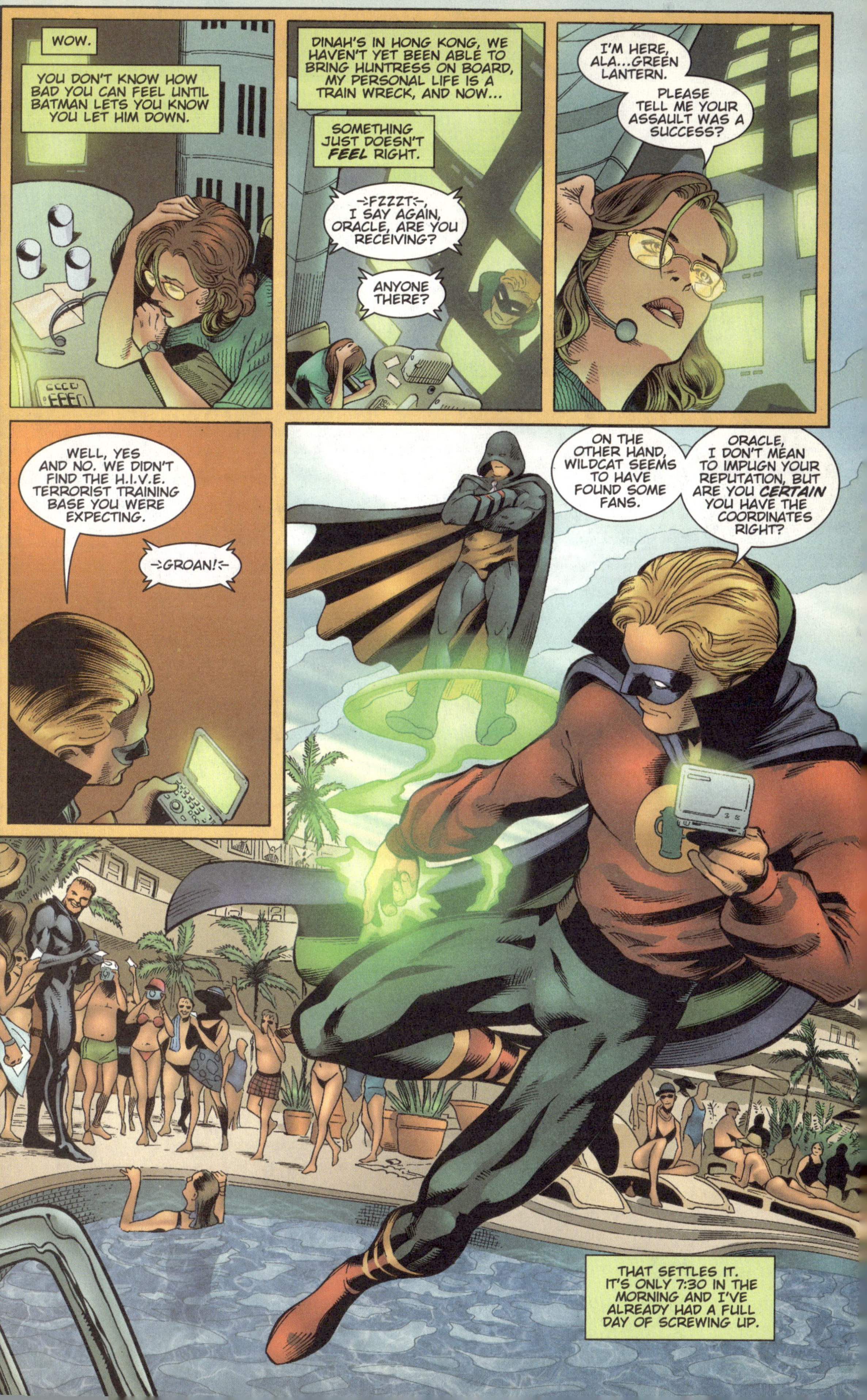

WOW.
YOU DON'T KNOW HOW BAD YOU CAN FEEL UNTIL BATMAN LETS YOU KNOW YOU LET HIM DOWN.
DINAH'S IN HONG KONG, WE HAVEN'T YET BEEN ABLE TO BRING HUNTRESS ON BOARD, MY PERSONAL LIFE IS A TRAIN WRECK, AND NOW...
SOMETHING JUST DOESN'T FEEL RIGHT.
-FZZZT-, I SAY AGAIN, ORACLE, ARE YOU RECEIVING?
ANYONE THERE?
I'M HERE, ALA...GREEN LANTERN.
PLEASE TELL ME YOUR ASSAULT WAS A SUCCESS?
WELL, YES AND NO. WE DIDN'T FIND THE H.I.V.E. TERRORIST TRAINING BASE YOU WERE EXPECTING.
-GROAN!-
ON THE OTHER HAND, WILDCAT SEEMS TO HAVE FOUND SOME FANS.
ORACLE, I DON'T MEAN TO IMPUGN YOUR REPUTATION, BUT ARE YOU CERTAIN YOU HAVE THE COORDINATES RIGHT?
THAT SETTLES IT. IT'S ONLY 7:30 IN THE MORNING AND I'VE ALREADY HAD A FULL DAY OF SCREWING UP.

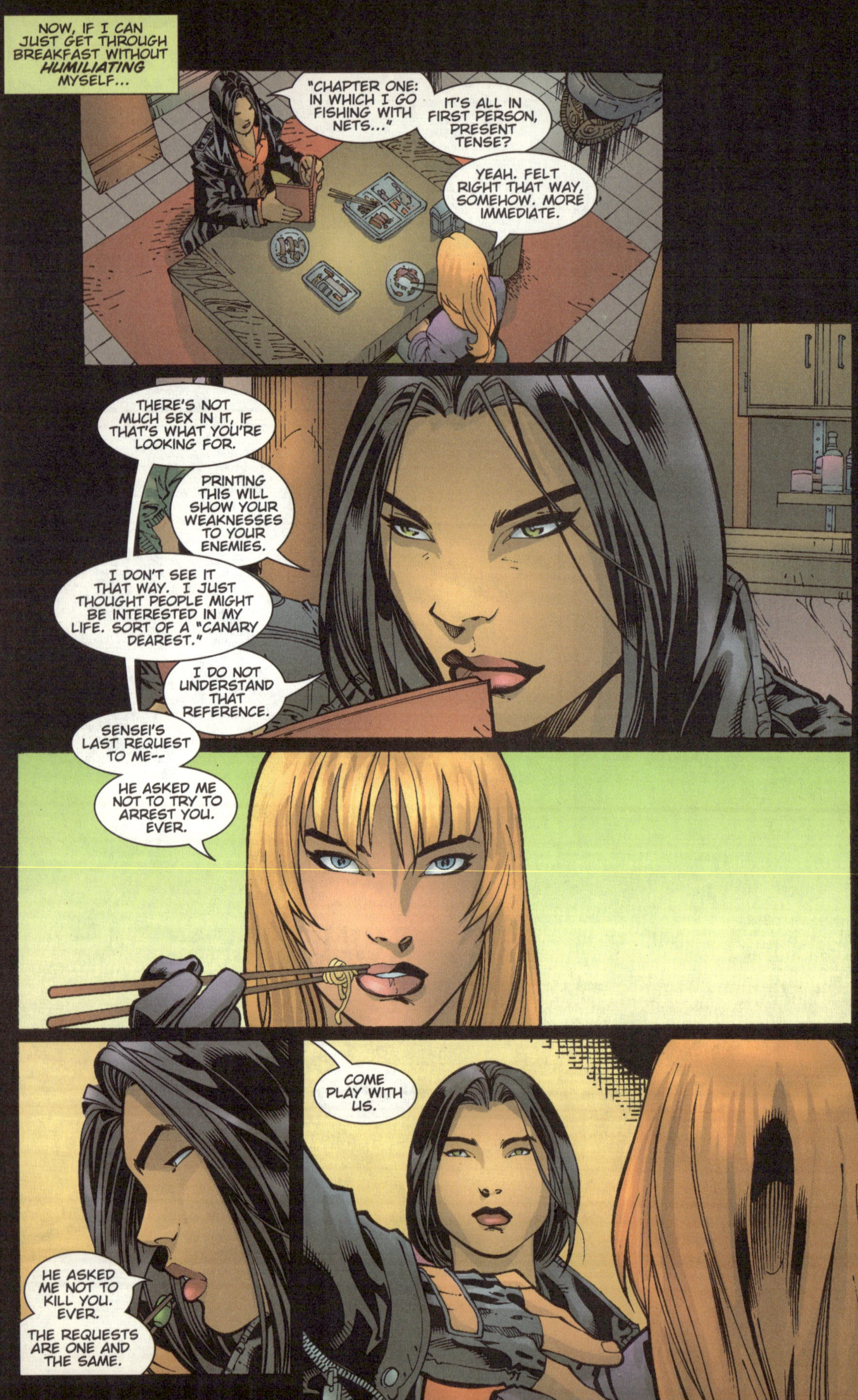
NOW, IF I CAN JUST GET THROUGH BREAKFAST WITHOUT *HUMILIATING* MYSELF...
"CHAPTER ONE: IN WHICH I GO FISHING WITH NETS..."
IT'S ALL IN FIRST PERSON, PRESENT TENSE?
YEAH. FELT RIGHT THAT WAY, SOMEHOW. MORE IMMEDIATE.
THERE'S NOT MUCH SEX IN IT, IF THAT'S WHAT YOU'RE LOOKING FOR.
PRINTING THIS WILL SHOW YOUR WEAKNESSES TO YOUR ENEMIES.
I DON'T SEE IT THAT WAY. I JUST THOUGHT PEOPLE MIGHT BE INTERESTED IN MY LIFE. SORT OF A "CANARY DEAREST."
I DO NOT UNDERSTAND THAT REFERENCE.
SENSEI'S LAST REQUEST TO ME--
HE ASKED ME NOT TO TRY TO ARREST YOU. EVER.
HE ASKED ME NOT TO KILL YOU. EVER.
THE REQUESTS ARE ONE AND THE SAME.
COME PLAY WITH US.

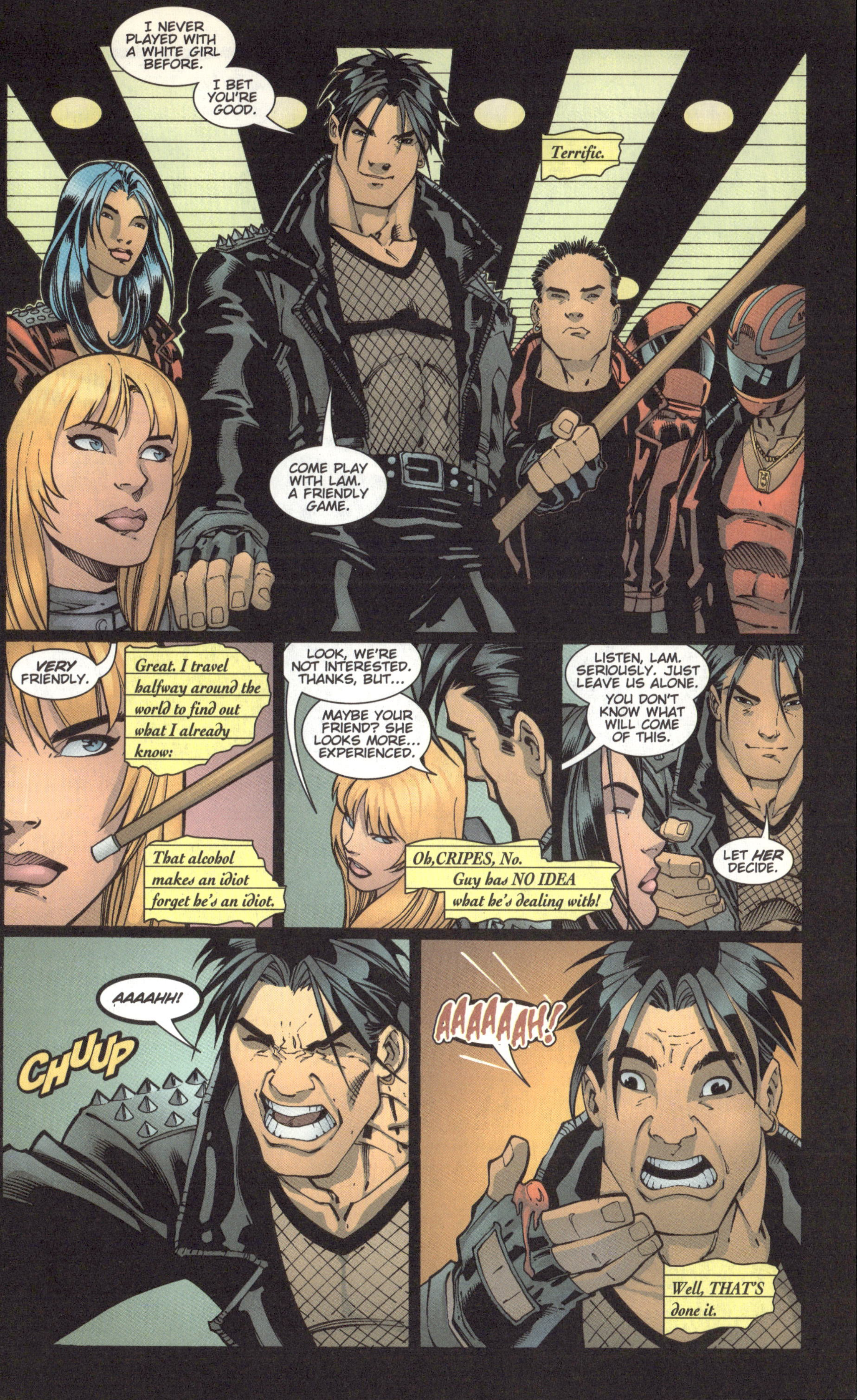
I NEVER PLAYED WITH A WHITE GIRL BEFORE.
I BET YOU'RE GOOD.
Terrific.
COME PLAY WITH LAM. A FRIENDLY GAME.
VERY FRIENDLY.
Great. I travel halfway around the world to find out what I already know:
That alcohol makes an idiot forget he's an idiot.
LOOK, WE'RE NOT INTERESTED. THANKS, BUT...
MAYBE YOUR FRIEND? SHE LOOKS MORE... EXPERIENCED.
Oh, CRIPES, No. Guy has NO IDEA what he's dealing with!
LISTEN, LAM. SERIOUSLY. JUST LEAVE US ALONE. YOU DON'T KNOW WHAT WILL COME OF THIS.
LET HER DECIDE.
AAAAHH!
CHUUP
AAAAAAH!
Well, THAT'S done it.

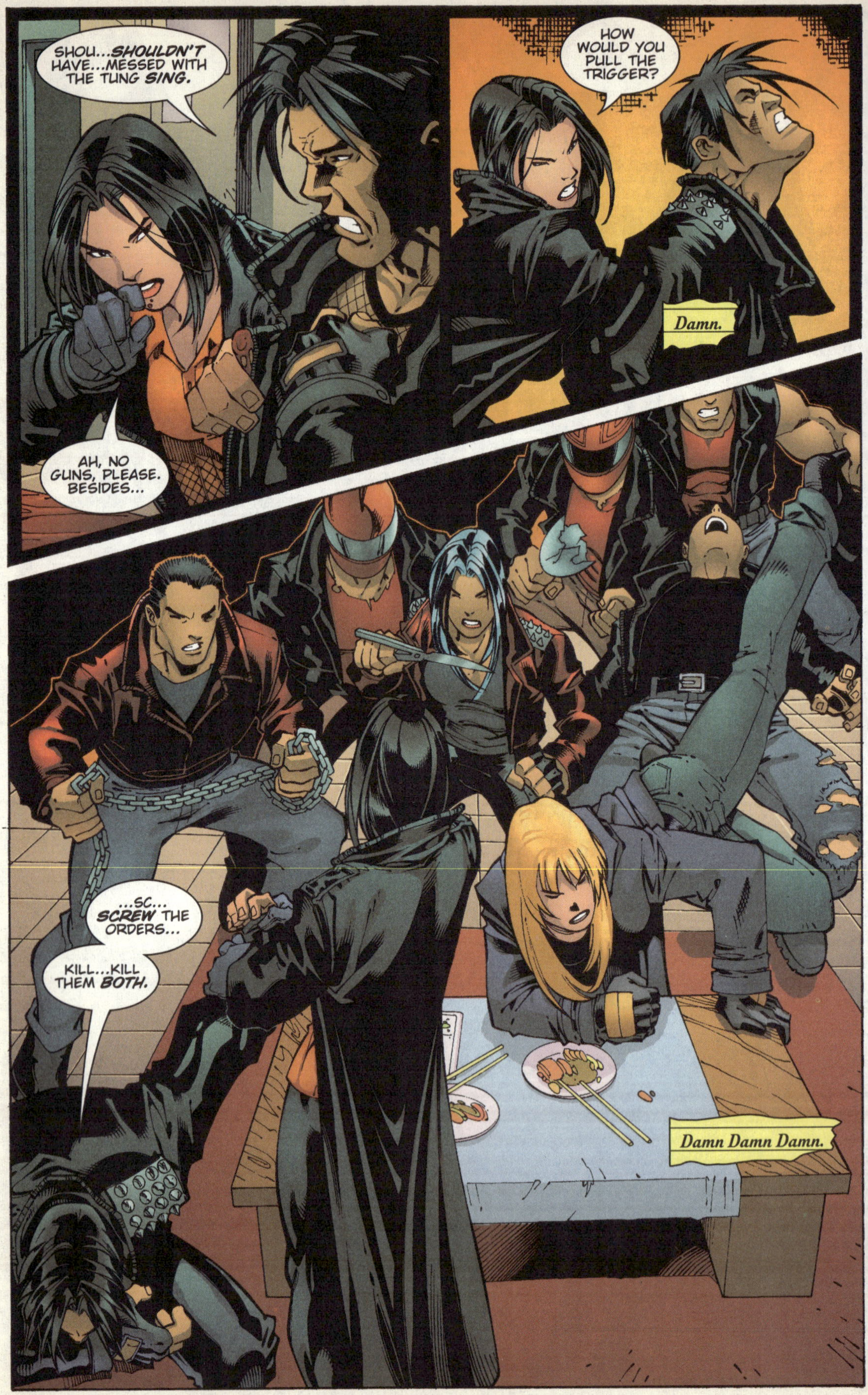
SHOU...SHOULDN'T HAVE...MESSED WITH THE TUNG SING.
AH, NO GUNS, PLEASE. BESIDES...
HOW WOULD YOU PULL THE TRIGGER?
Damn.
...SC... SCREW THE ORDERS...
KILL...KILL THEM BOTH.
Damn Damn Damn.

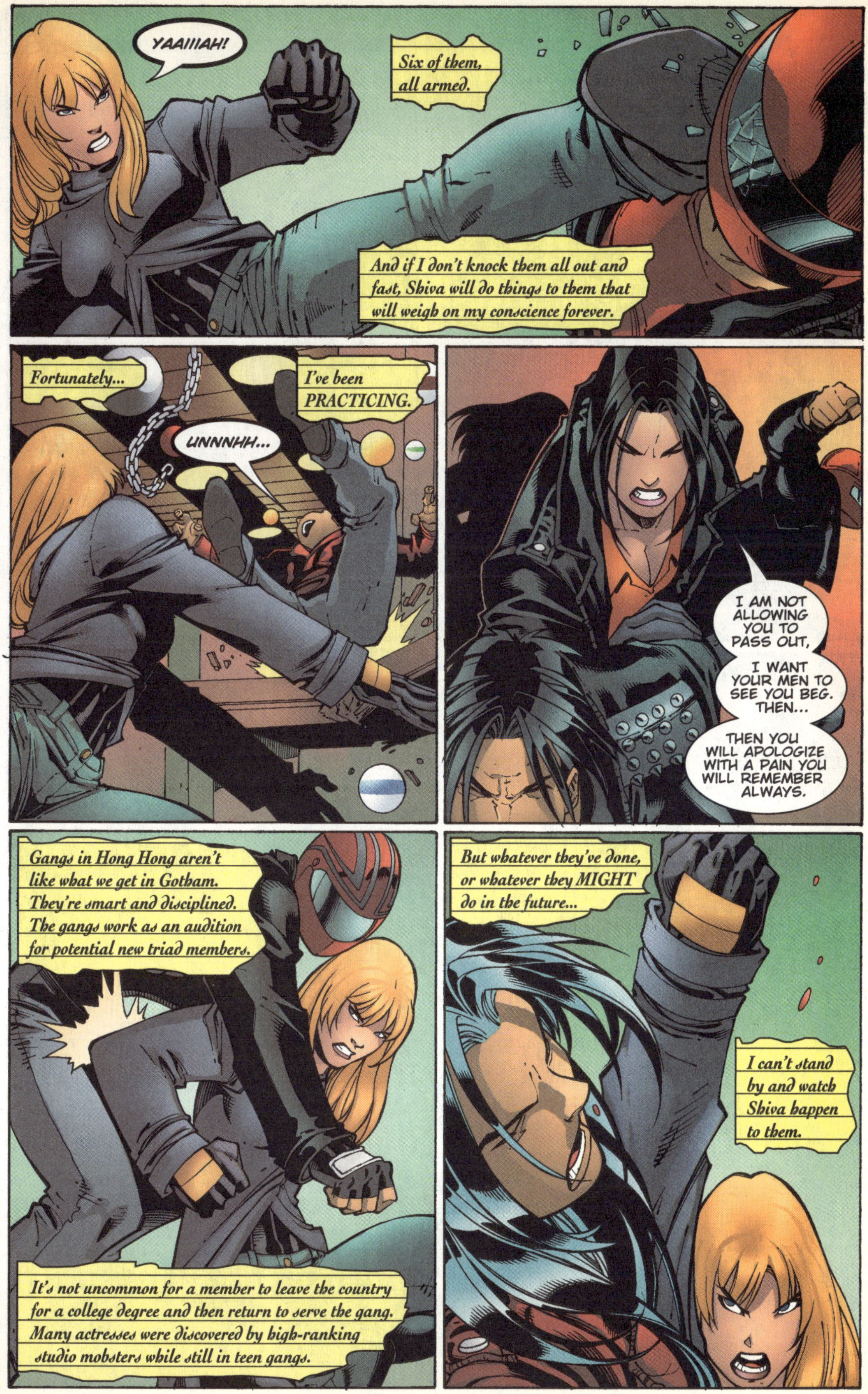
YAAIIIAH!
Six of them, all armed.
And if I don't knock them all out and fast, Shiva will do things to them that will weigh on my conscience forever.
Fortunately...
I've been PRACTICING.
UNNNHH...
I AM NOT ALLOWING YOU TO PASS OUT,
I WANT YOUR MEN TO SEE YOU BEG. THEN...
THEN YOU WILL APOLOGIZE WITH A PAIN YOU WILL REMEMBER ALWAYS.
Gangs in Hong Hong aren't like what we get in Gotham. They're smart and disciplined. The gangs work as an audition for potential new triad members.
It's not uncommon for a member to leave the country for a college degree and then return to serve the gang. Many actresses were discovered by high-ranking studio mobsters while still in teen gangs.
But whatever they've done, or whatever they MIGHT do in the future...
I can't stand by and watch Shiva happen to them.

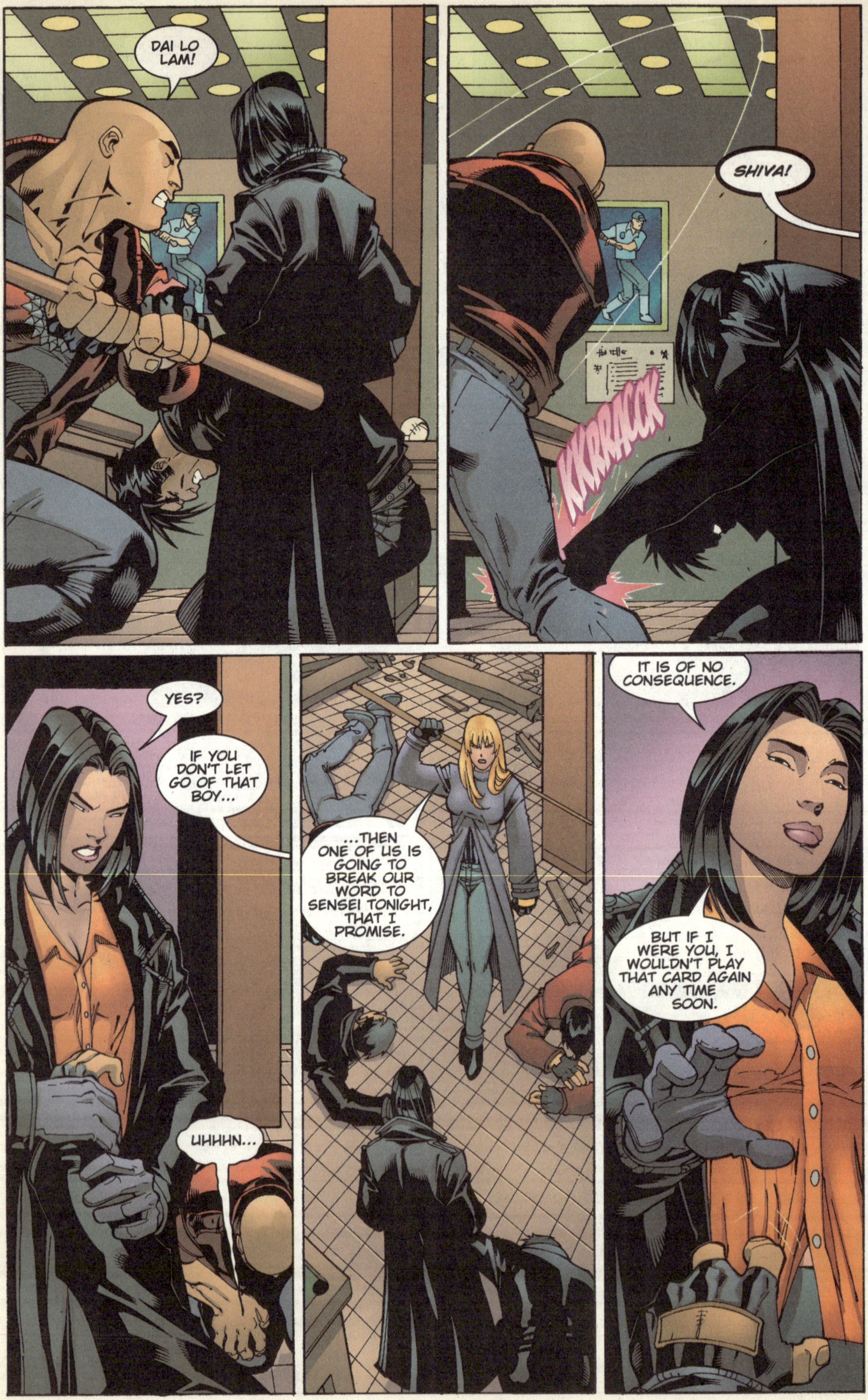
DAI LO LAM!
SHIVA!
KKRRAKCK
YES?
IF YOU DON'T LET GO OF THAT BOY...
...THEN ONE OF US IS GOING TO BREAK OUR WORD TO SENSEI TONIGHT, THAT I PROMISE.
UHHHN...
IT IS OF NO CONSEQUENCE.
BUT IF I WERE YOU, I WOULDN'T PLAY THAT CARD AGAIN ANY TIME SOON.

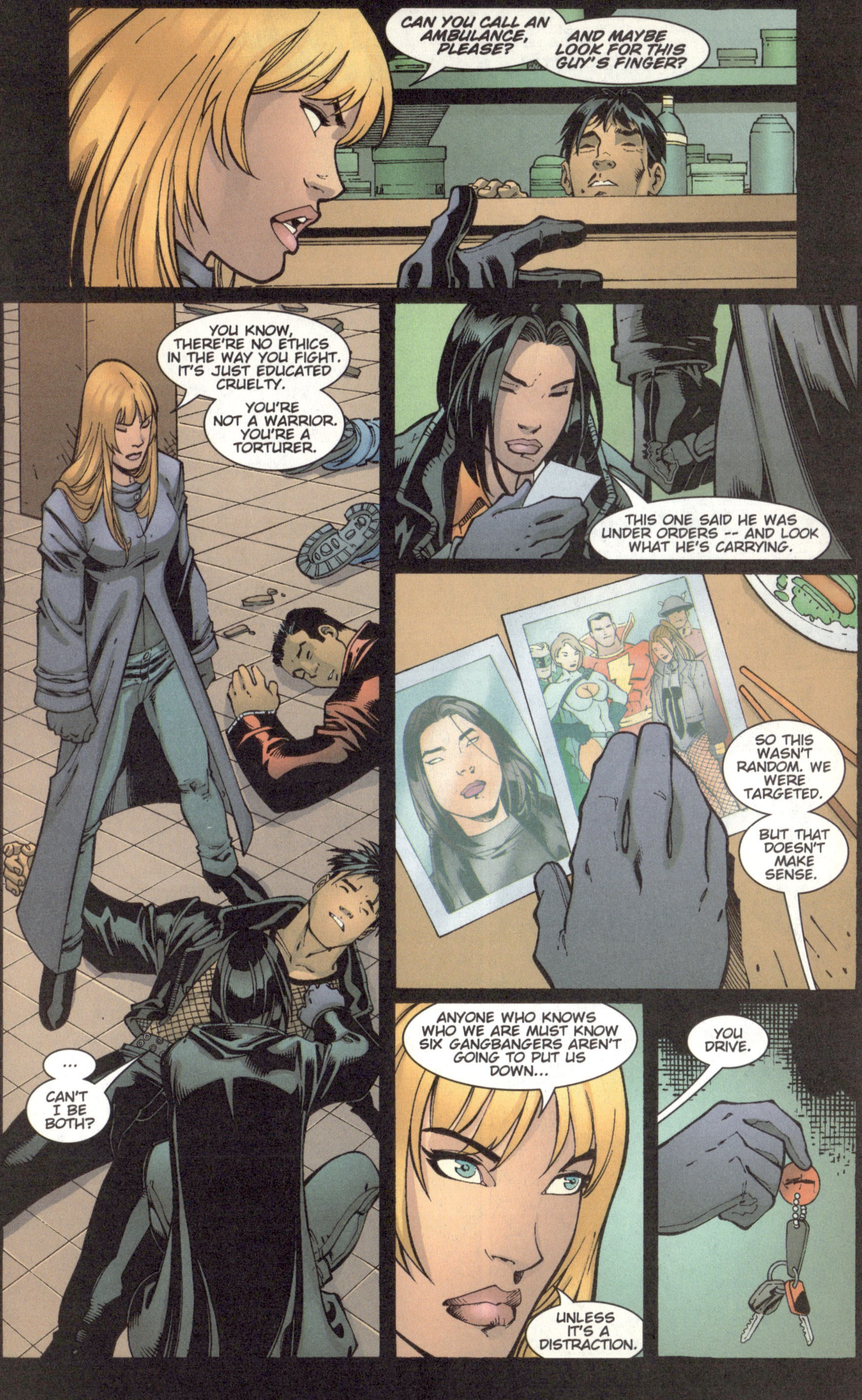
CAN YOU CALL AN AMBULANCE, PLEASE?
AND MAYBE LOOK FOR THIS GUY'S FINGER?
YOU KNOW, THERE'RE NO ETHICS IN THE WAY YOU FIGHT. IT'S JUST EDUCATED CRUELTY.
YOU'RE NOT A WARRIOR. YOU'RE A TORTURER.
... CAN'T I BE BOTH?
THIS ONE SAID HE WAS UNDER ORDERS -- AND LOOK WHAT HE'S CARRYING.
SO THIS WASN'T RANDOM. WE WERE TARGETED.
BUT THAT DOESN'T MAKE SENSE.
ANYONE WHO KNOWS WHO WE ARE MUST KNOW SIX GANGBANGERS AREN'T GOING TO PUT US DOWN...
UNLESS IT'S A DISTRACTION.
YOU DRIVE.

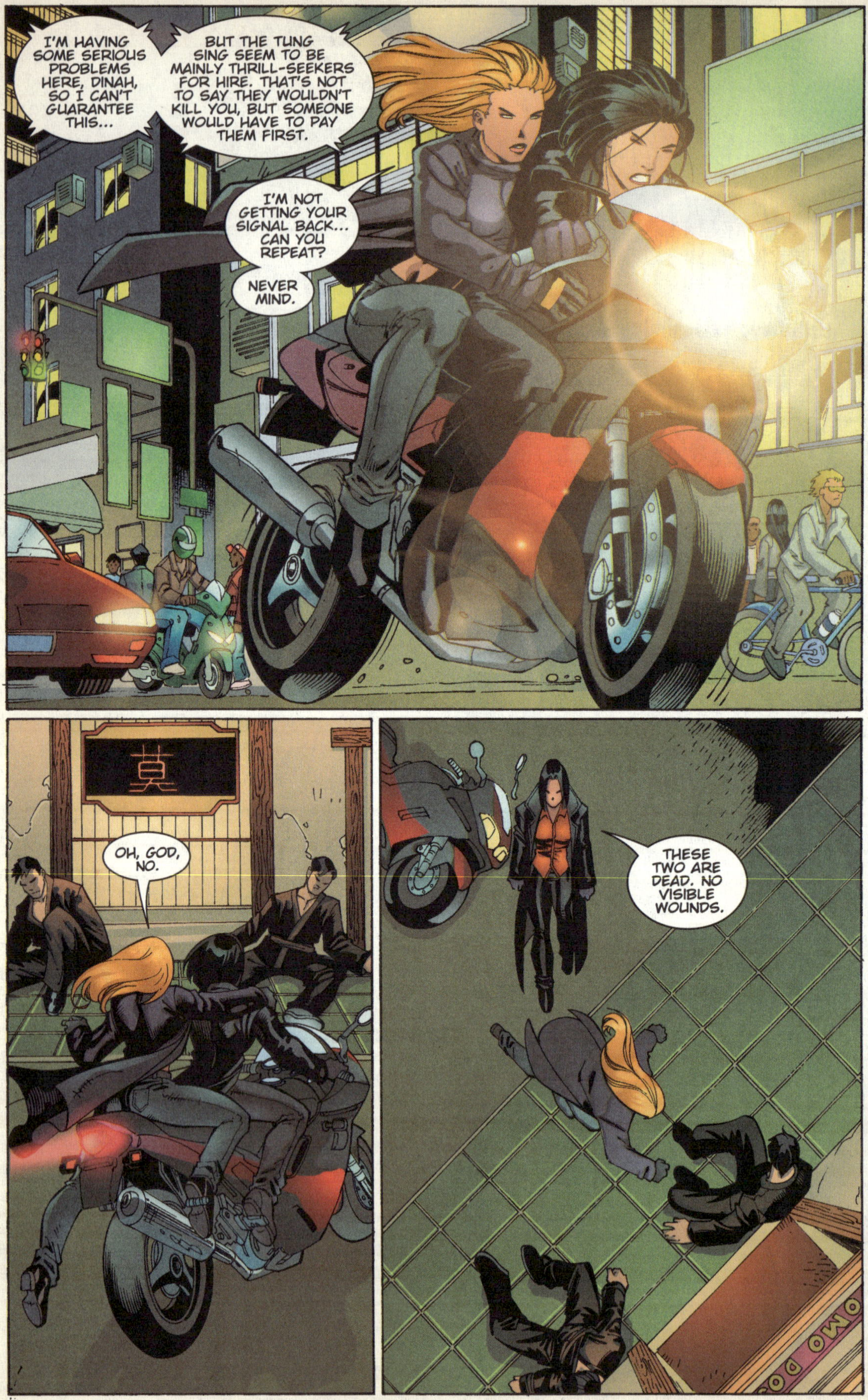
I'M HAVING SOME SERIOUS PROBLEMS HERE, DINAH, SO I CAN'T GUARANTEE THIS...
BUT THE TUNG SING SEEM TO BE MAINLY THRILL-SEEKERS FOR HIRE. THAT'S NOT TO SAY THEY WOULDN'T KILL YOU, BUT SOMEONE WOULD HAVE TO PAY THEM FIRST.
I'M NOT GETTING YOUR SIGNAL BACK... CAN YOU REPEAT?
NEVER MIND.
OH, GOD, NO.
THESE TWO ARE DEAD. NO VISIBLE WOUNDS.

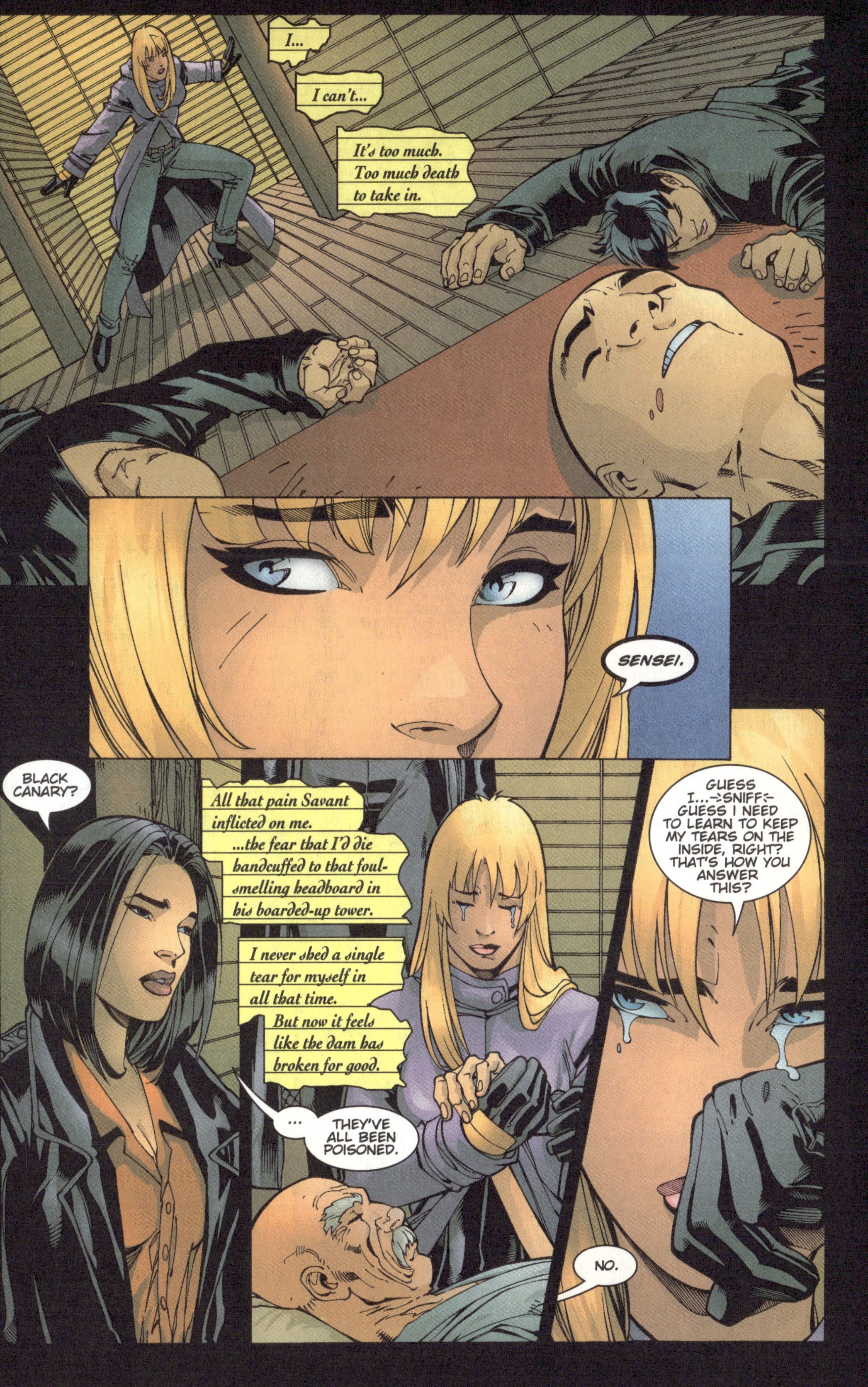

I...
I can't...
It's too much. Too much death to take in.
SENSEI.
BLACK CANARY?
All that pain Savant inflicted on me.
...the fear that I'd die handcuffed to that foul-smelling headboard in his boarded-up tower.
I never shed a single tear for myself in all that time.
But now it feels like the dam has broken for good.
...
THEY'VE ALL BEEN POISONED.
GUESS I... -SNIFF- GUESS I NEED TO LEARN TO KEEP MY TEARS ON THE INSIDE, RIGHT? THAT'S HOW YOU ANSWER THIS?
NO.

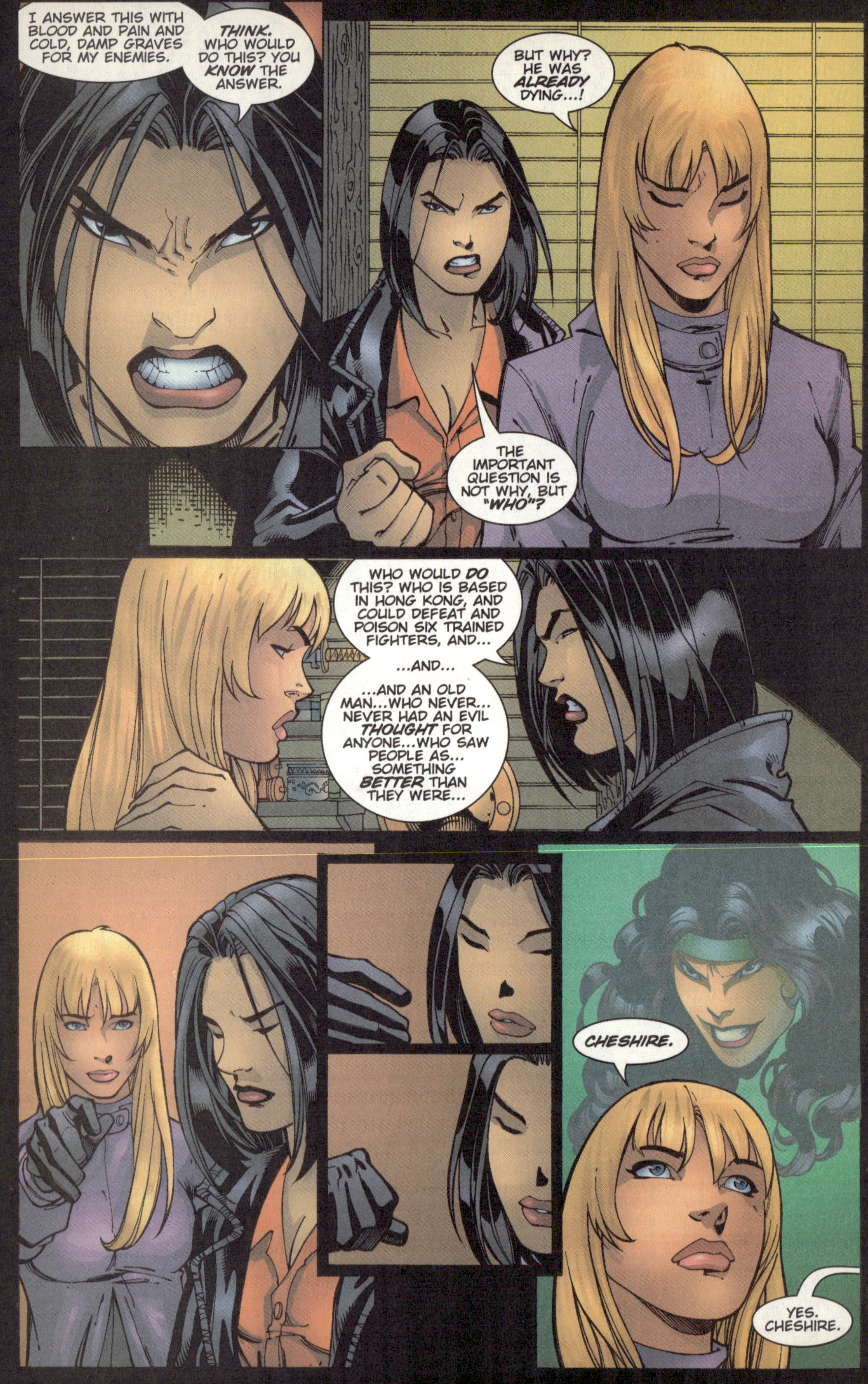
I ANSWER THIS WITH BLOOD AND PAIN AND COLD, DAMP GRAVES FOR MY ENEMIES.
THINK. WHO WOULD DO THIS? YOU KNOW THE ANSWER.
BUT WHY? HE WAS ALREADY DYING...!
THE IMPORTANT QUESTION IS NOT WHY, BUT "WHO"?
WHO WOULD DO THIS? WHO IS BASED IN HONG KONG, AND COULD DEFEAT AND POISON SIX TRAINED FIGHTERS, AND...
...AND...
...AND AN OLD MAN...WHO NEVER... NEVER HAD AN EVIL THOUGHT FOR ANYONE...WHO SAW PEOPLE AS... SOMETHING BETTER THAN THEY WERE...
CHESHIRE.
YES. CHESHIRE.

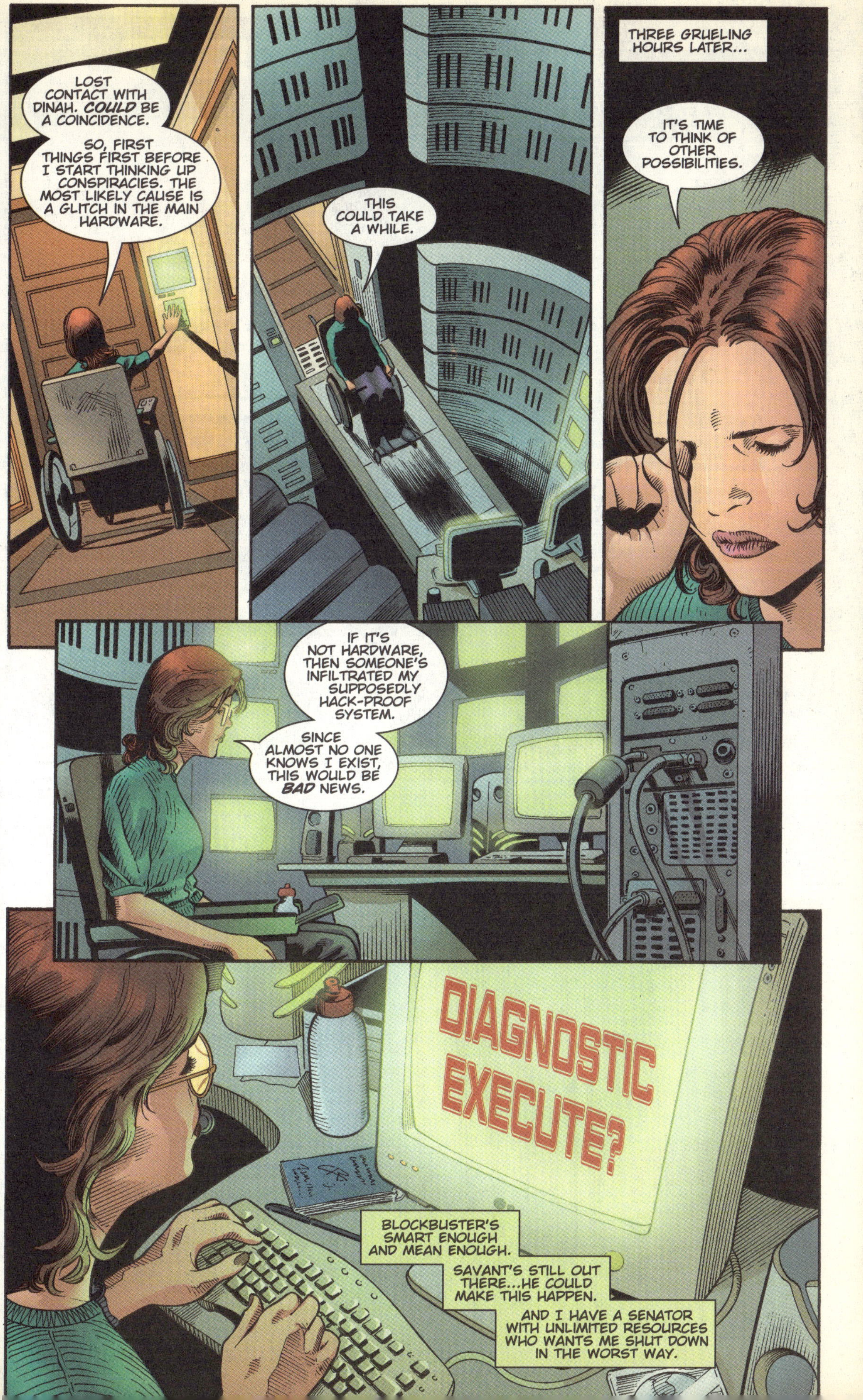
LOST CONTACT WITH DINAH. COULD BE A COINCIDENCE.
SO, FIRST THINGS FIRST BEFORE I START THINKING UP CONSPIRACIES. THE MOST LIKELY CAUSE IS A GLITCH IN THE MAIN HARDWARE.
THIS COULD TAKE A WHILE.
THREE GRUELING HOURS LATER...
IT'S TIME TO THINK OF OTHER POSSIBILITIES.
IF IT'S NOT HARDWARE, THEN SOMEONE'S INFILTRATED MY SUPPOSEDLY HACK-PROOF SYSTEM.
SINCE ALMOST NO ONE KNOWS I EXIST, THIS WOULD BE BAD NEWS.
DIAGNOSTIC EXECUTE?
BLOCKBUSTER'S SMART ENOUGH AND MEAN ENOUGH.
SAVANT'S STILL OUT THERE...HE COULD MAKE THIS HAPPEN.
AND I HAVE A SENATOR WITH UNLIMITED RESOURCES WHO WANTS ME SHUT DOWN IN THE WORST WAY.

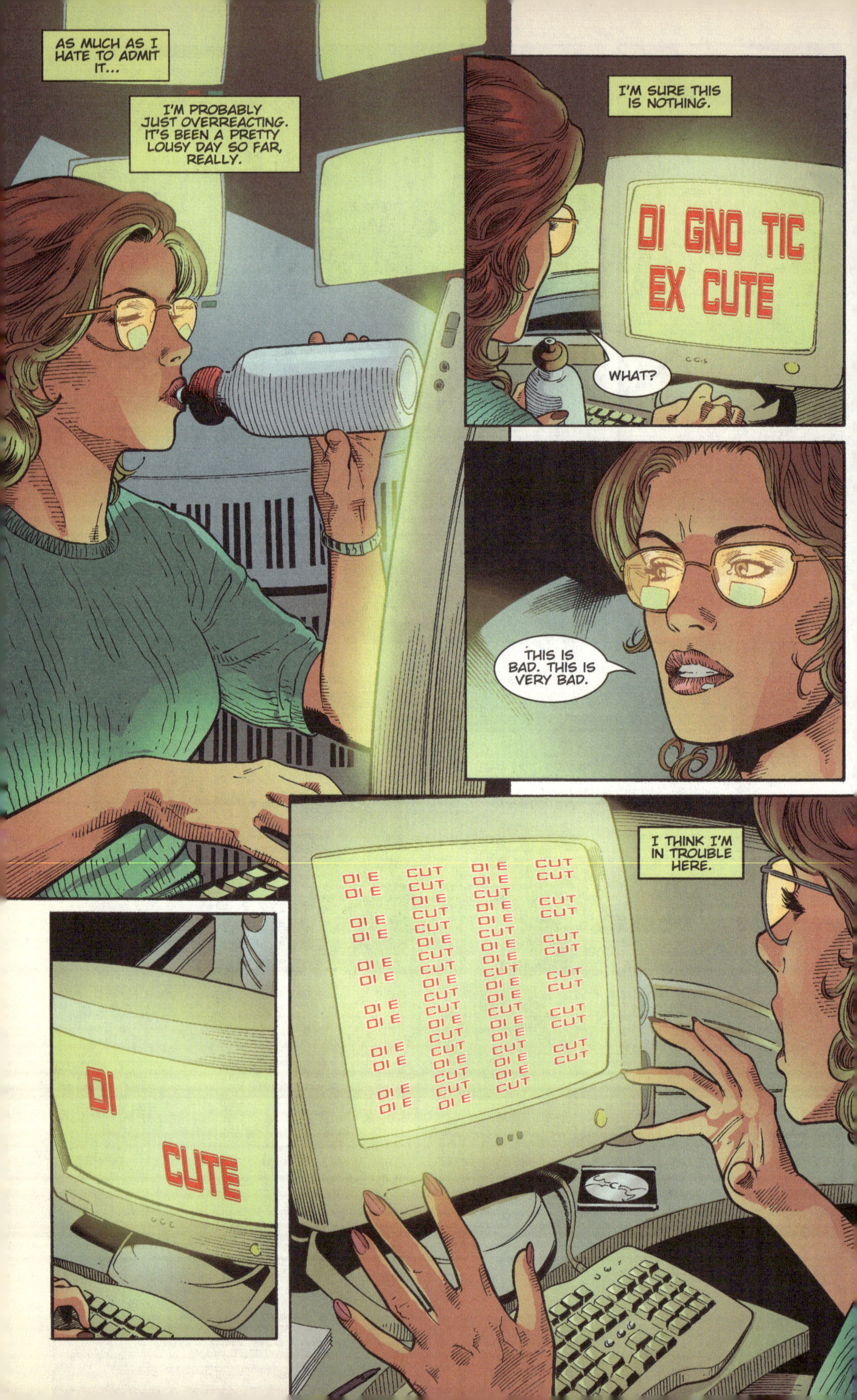
AS MUCH AS I HATE TO ADMIT IT...
I'M PROBABLY JUST OVERREACTING. IT'S BEEN A PRETTY LOUSY DAY SO FAR, REALLY.
I'M SURE THIS IS NOTHING.
DI GNO TIC EX CUTE
WHAT?
THIS IS BAD. THIS IS VERY BAD.
I THINK I'M IN TROUBLE HERE.
DI E CUT DI E CUT
DI CUTE

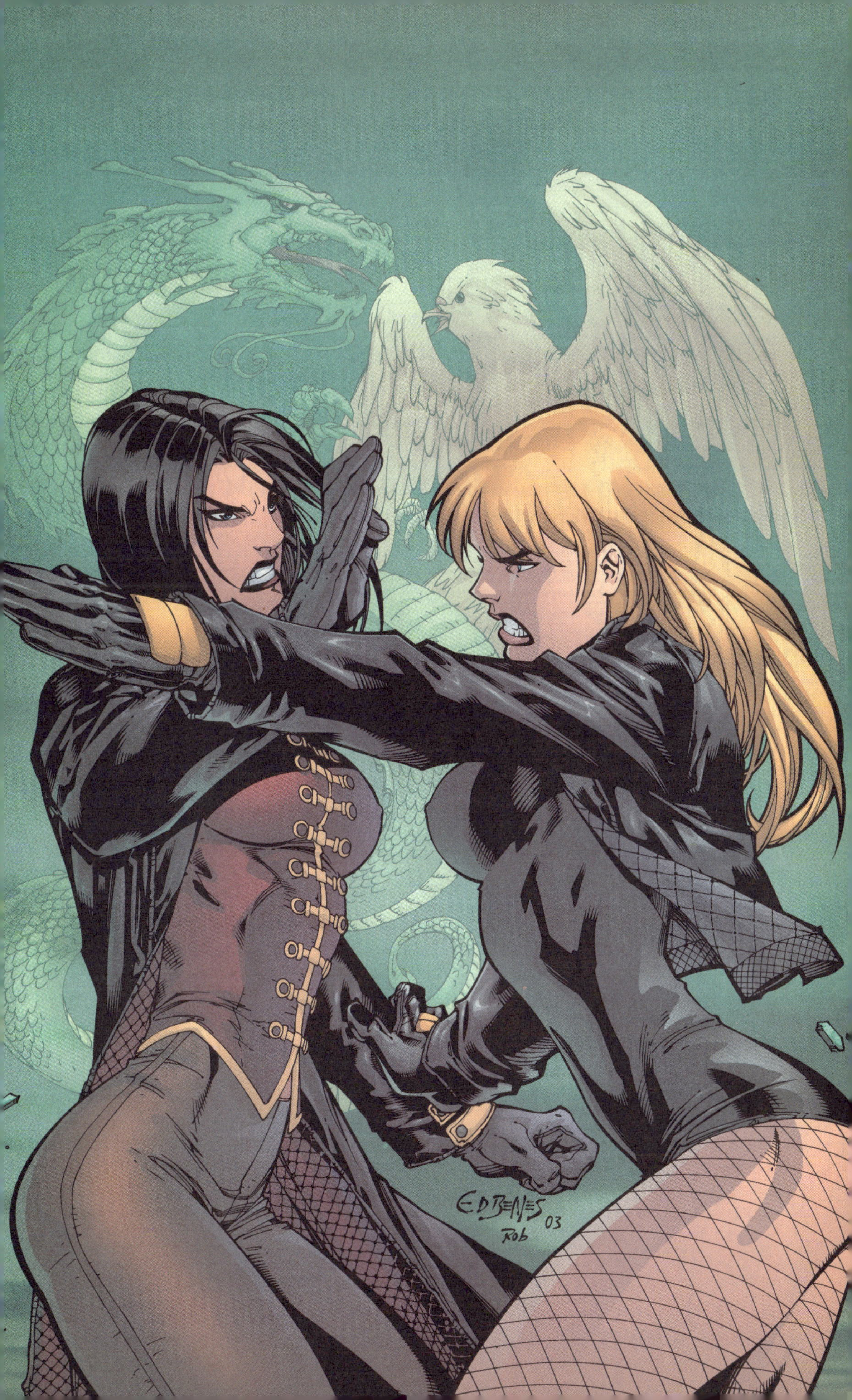
ED BENES 03
Rob

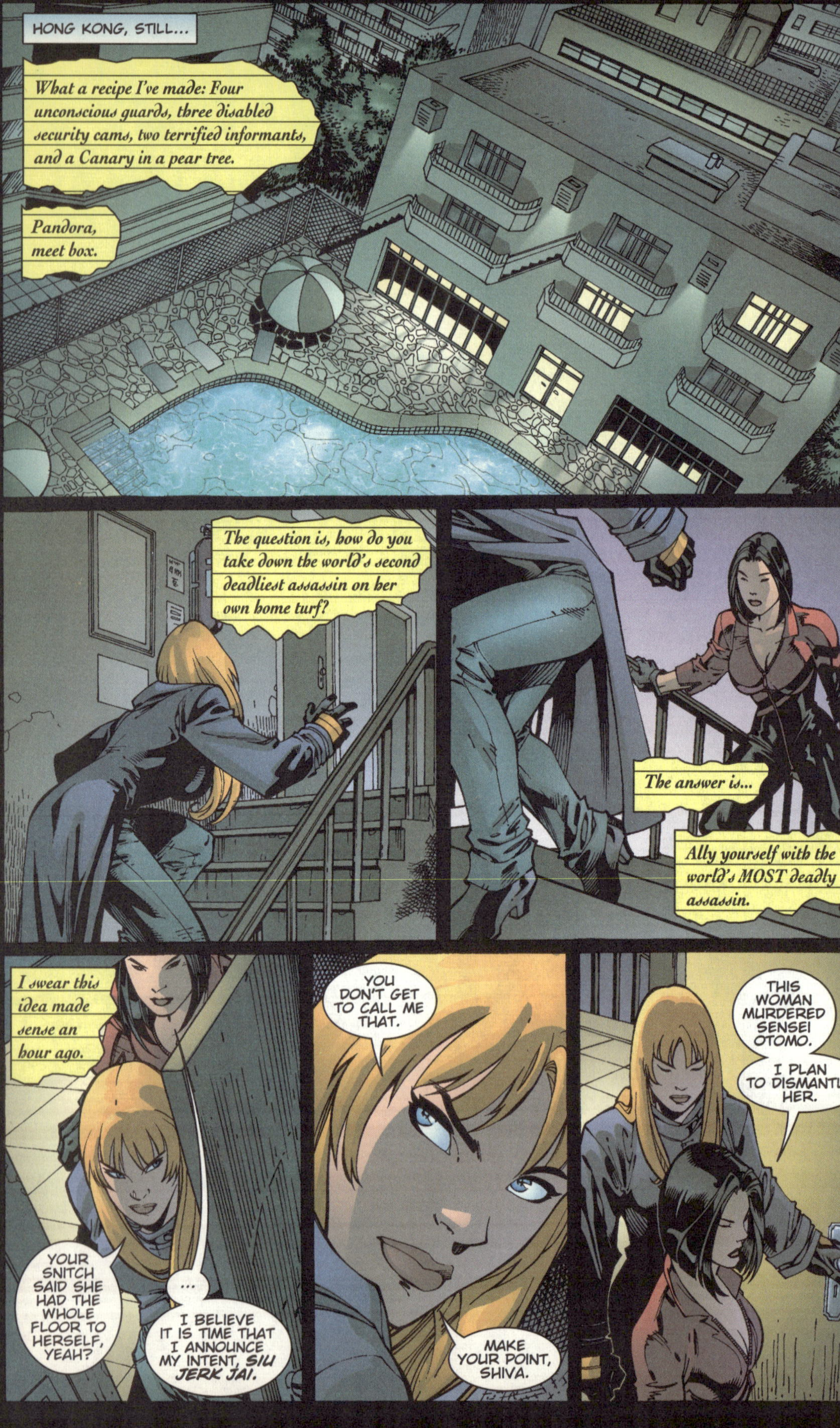
HONG KONG, STILL...
What a recipe I've made: Four unconscious guards, three disabled security cams, two terrified informants, and a Canary in a pear tree.
Pandora, meet box.
The question is, how do you take down the world's second deadliest assassin on her own home turf?
The answer is...
Ally yourself with the world's MOST deadly assassin.
I swear this idea made sense an hour ago.
YOUR SNITCH SAID SHE HAD THE WHOLE FLOOR TO HERSELF, YEAH?
...
I BELIEVE IT IS TIME THAT I ANNOUNCE MY INTENT, SIU JERK JAI.
YOU DON'T GET TO CALL ME THAT.
MAKE YOUR POINT, SHIVA.
THIS WOMAN MURDERED SENSEI OTOMO.
I PLAN TO DISMANTLE HER.

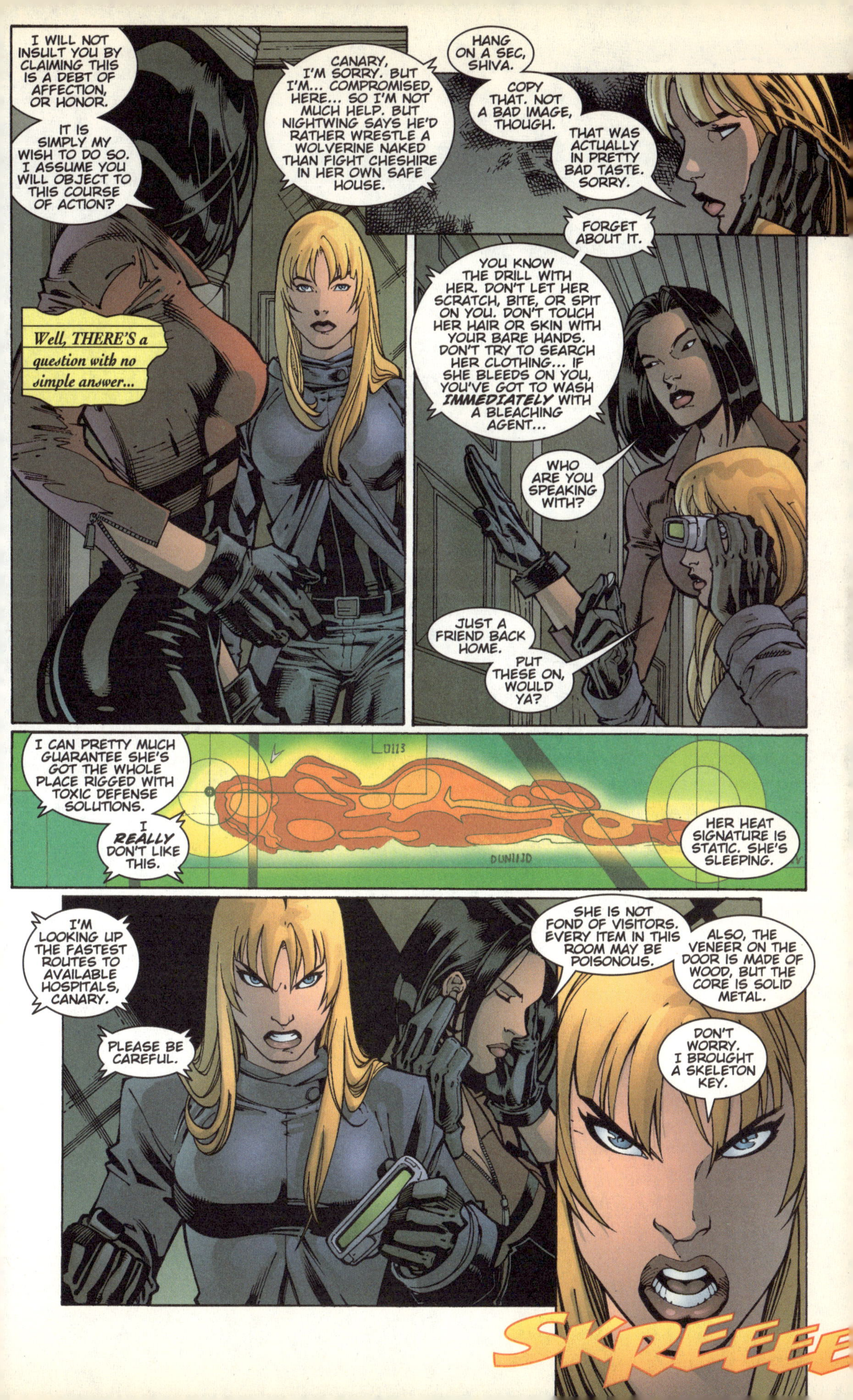
I WILL NOT INSULT YOU BY CLAIMING THIS IS A DEBT OF AFFECTION, OR HONOR.
IT IS SIMPLY MY WISH TO DO SO. I ASSUME YOU WILL OBJECT TO THIS COURSE OF ACTION?
CANARY, I'M SORRY. BUT I'M... COMPROMISED, HERE... SO I'M NOT MUCH HELP. BUT NIGHTWING SAYS HE'D RATHER WRESTLE A WOLVERINE NAKED THAN FIGHT CHESHIRE IN HER OWN SAFE HOUSE.
Well, THERE'S a question with no simple answer...
HANG ON A SEC, SHIVA.
COPY THAT. NOT A BAD IMAGE, THOUGH.
THAT WAS ACTUALLY IN PRETTY BAD TASTE. SORRY.
FORGET ABOUT IT.
YOU KNOW THE DRILL WITH HER. DON'T LET HER SCRATCH, BITE, OR SPIT ON YOU. DON'T TOUCH HER HAIR OR SKIN WITH YOUR BARE HANDS. DON'T TRY TO SEARCH HER CLOTHING... IF SHE BLEEDS ON YOU, YOU'VE GOT TO WASH IMMEDIATELY WITH A BLEACHING AGENT...
WHO ARE YOU SPEAKING WITH?
JUST A FRIEND BACK HOME.
PUT THESE ON, WOULD YA?
I CAN PRETTY MUCH GUARANTEE SHE'S GOT THE WHOLE PLACE RIGGED WITH TOXIC DEFENSE SOLUTIONS.
I REALLY DON'T LIKE THIS.
HER HEAT SIGNATURE IS STATIC. SHE'S SLEEPING.
I'M LOOKING UP THE FASTEST ROUTES TO AVAILABLE HOSPITALS, CANARY.
PLEASE BE CAREFUL.
SHE IS NOT FOND OF VISITORS. EVERY ITEM IN THIS ROOM MAY BE POISONOUS.
ALSO, THE VENEER ON THE DOOR IS MADE OF WOOD, BUT THE CORE IS SOLID METAL.
DON'T WORRY. I BROUGHT A SKELETON KEY.
SKREEEEE

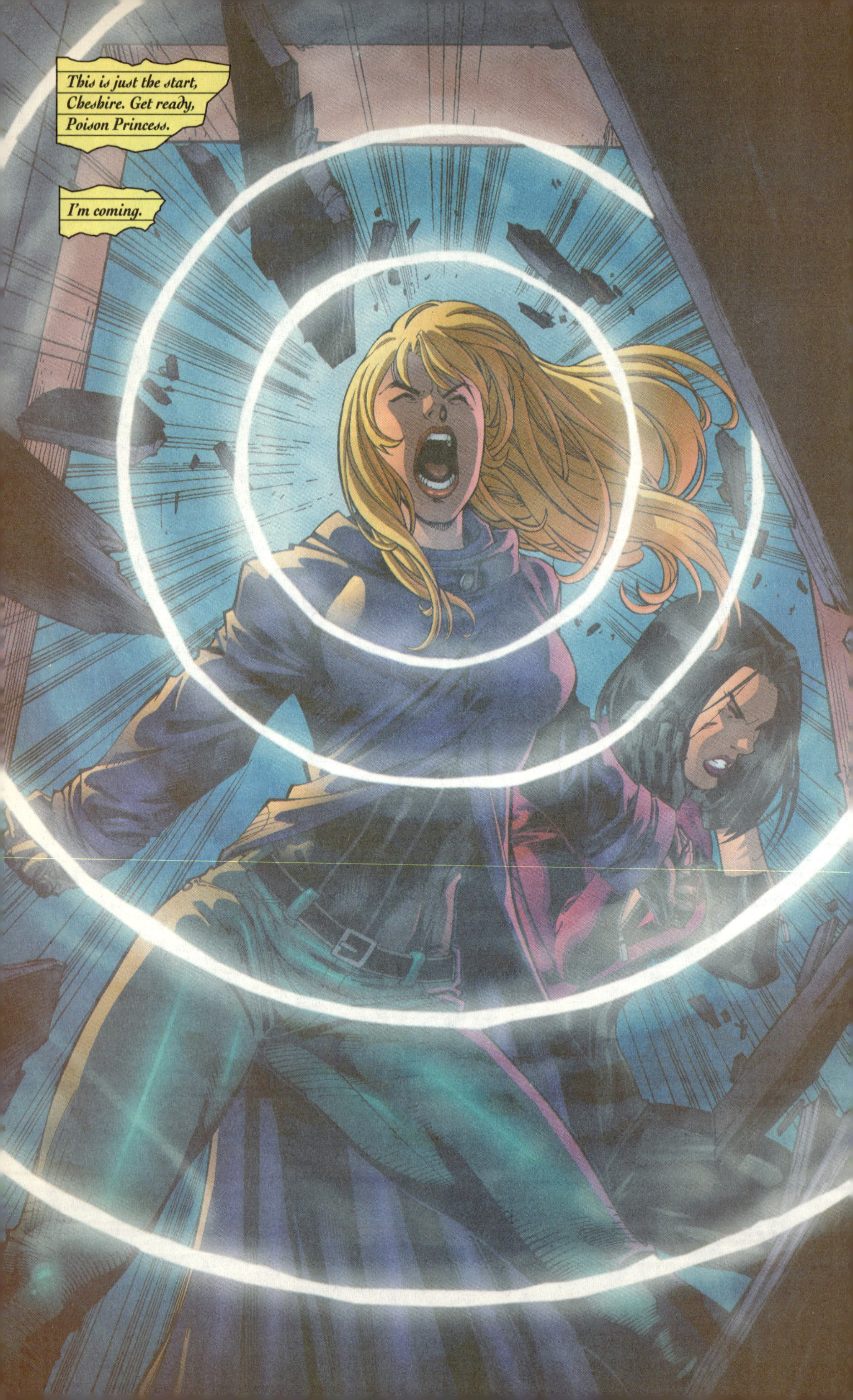
This is just the start, Cheshire. Get ready, Poison Princess.
I'm coming.

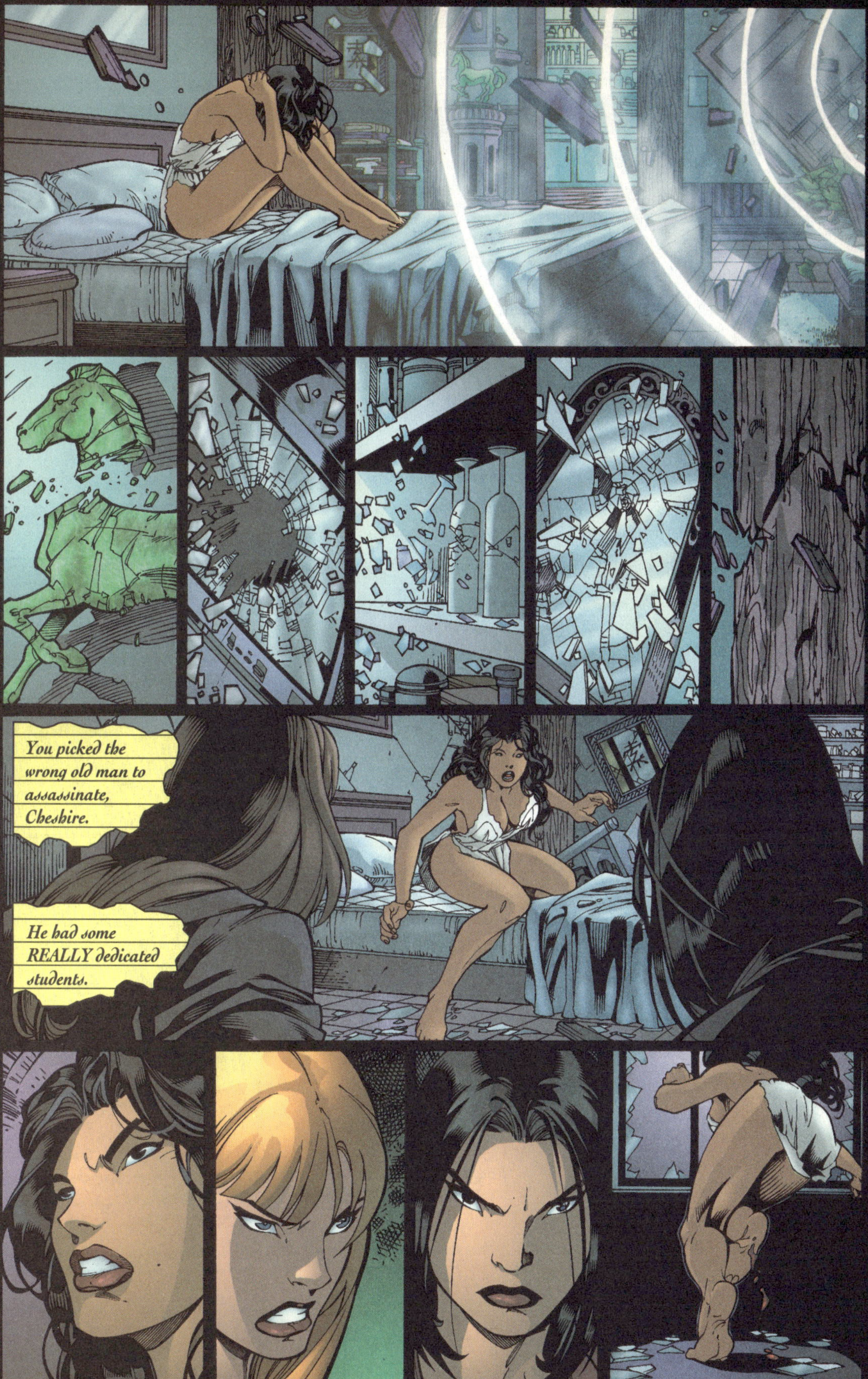
You picked the wrong old man to assassinate, Cheshire.
He had some REALLY dedicated students.

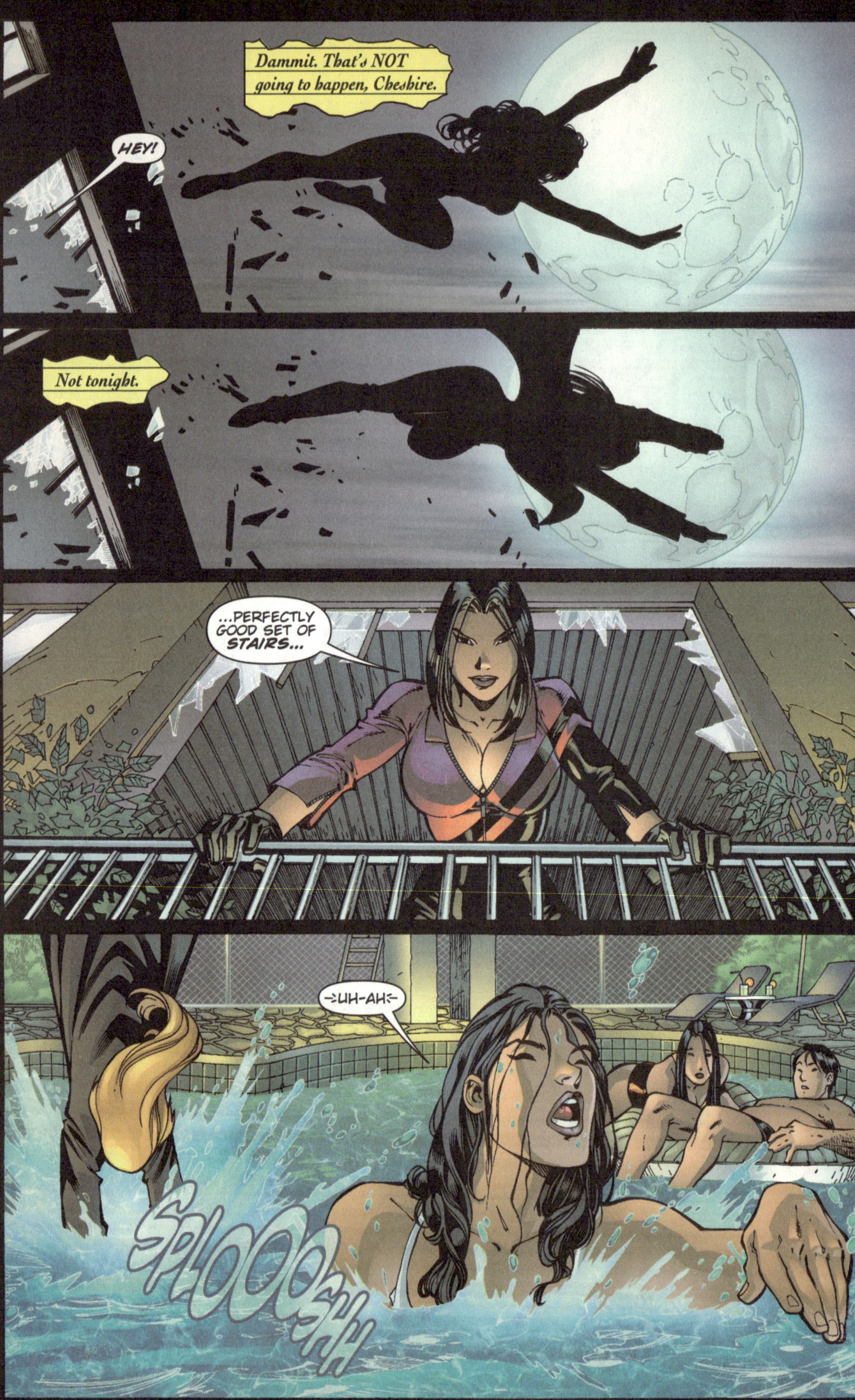
Dammit. That's NOT going to happen, Cheshire.
HEY!
Not tonight.
...PERFECTLY GOOD SET OF STAIRS...
-UH-AH-
SPLOOOSHH

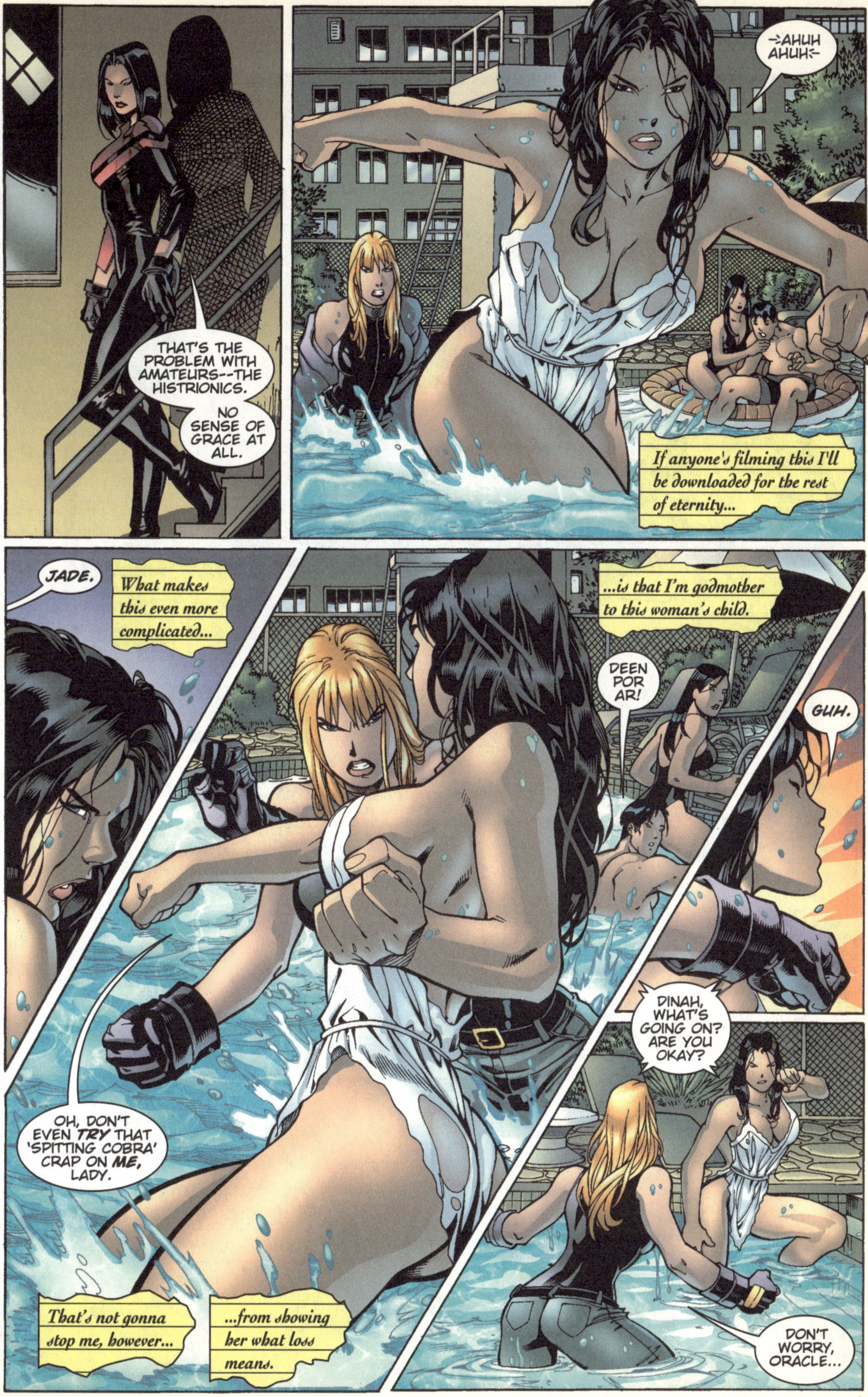
THAT'S THE PROBLEM WITH AMATEURS--THE HISTRIONICS.
NO SENSE OF GRACE AT ALL.
-AHUH AHUH-
If anyone's filming this I'll be downloaded for the rest of eternity...
JADE.
What makes this even more complicated...
...is that I'm godmother to this woman's child.
DEEN POR AR!
GUH.
OH, DON'T EVEN TRY THAT 'SPITTING COBRA' CRAP ON ME, LADY.
That's not gonna stop me, however...
...from showing her what loss means.
DINAH, WHAT'S GOING ON? ARE YOU OKAY?
DON'T WORRY, ORACLE...

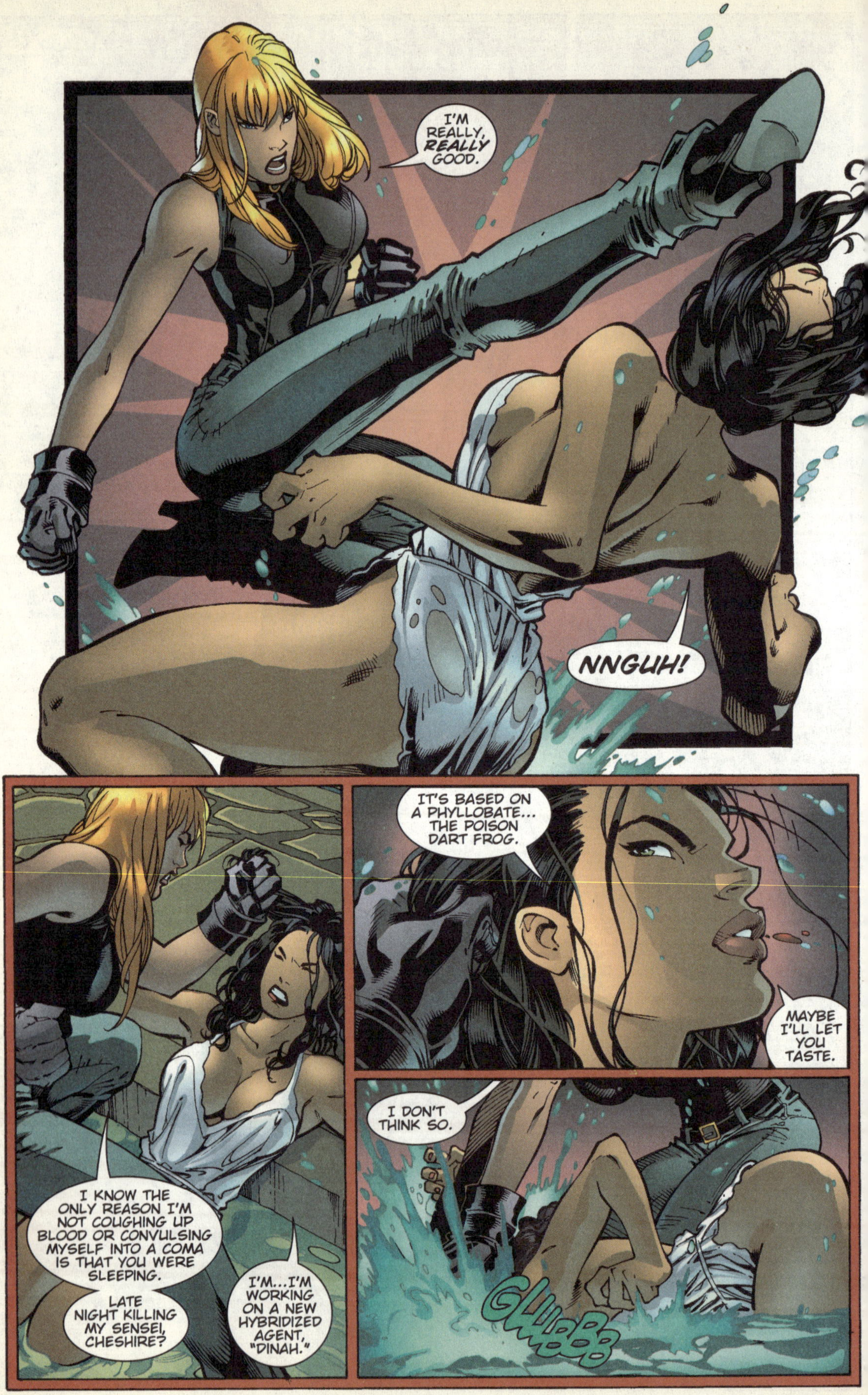

I'M REALLY, *REALLY* GOOD.
NNGUH!
I KNOW THE ONLY REASON I'M NOT COUGHING UP BLOOD OR CONVULSING MYSELF INTO A COMA IS THAT YOU WERE SLEEPING.
LATE NIGHT KILLING MY SENSEI, CHESHIRE?
I'M...I'M WORKING ON A NEW HYBRIDIZED AGENT, "DINAH."
IT'S BASED ON A PHYLLOBATE... THE POISON DART FROG.
MAYBE I'LL LET YOU TASTE.
I DON'T THINK SO.
GLUBBB

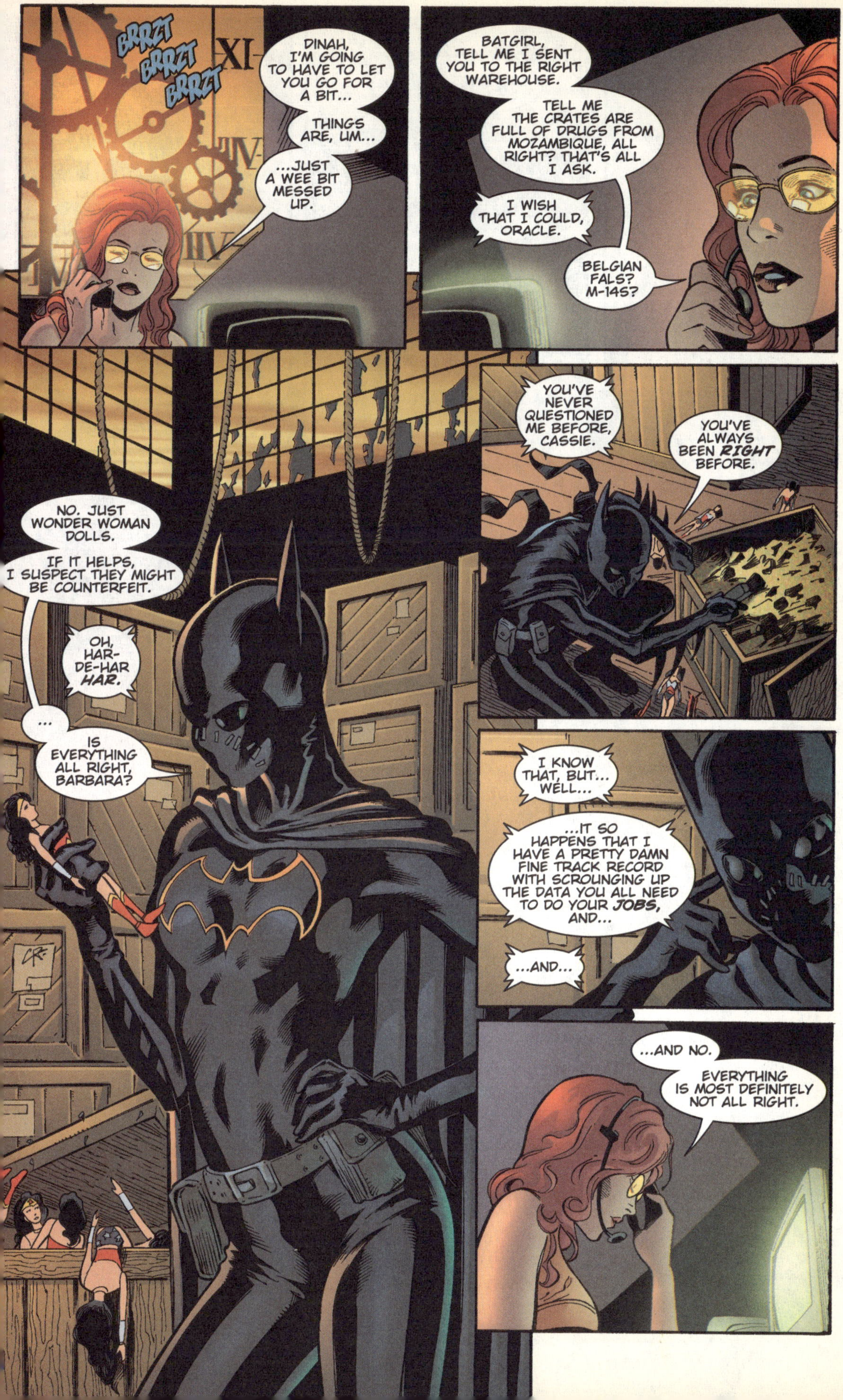
BRRZT BRRZT BRRZT
DINAH, I'M GOING TO HAVE TO LET YOU GO FOR A BIT...
THINGS ARE, UM...
...JUST A WEE BIT MESSED UP.
BATGIRL, TELL ME I SENT YOU TO THE RIGHT WAREHOUSE.
TELL ME THE CRATES ARE FULL OF DRUGS FROM MOZAMBIQUE, ALL RIGHT? THAT'S ALL I ASK.
I WISH THAT I COULD, ORACLE.
BELGIAN FALS? M-145?
NO. JUST WONDER WOMAN DOLLS.
IF IT HELPS, I SUSPECT THEY MIGHT BE COUNTERFEIT.
OH, HAR-DE-HAR HAR.
...
IS EVERYTHING ALL RIGHT, BARBARA?
YOU'VE NEVER QUESTIONED ME BEFORE, CASSIE.
YOU'VE ALWAYS BEEN RIGHT BEFORE.
I KNOW THAT, BUT... WELL...
...IT SO HAPPENS THAT I HAVE A PRETTY DAMN FINE TRACK RECORD WITH SCROUNGING UP THE DATA YOU ALL NEED TO DO YOUR JOBS, AND...
...AND...
...AND NO.
EVERYTHING IS MOST DEFINITELY NOT ALL RIGHT.

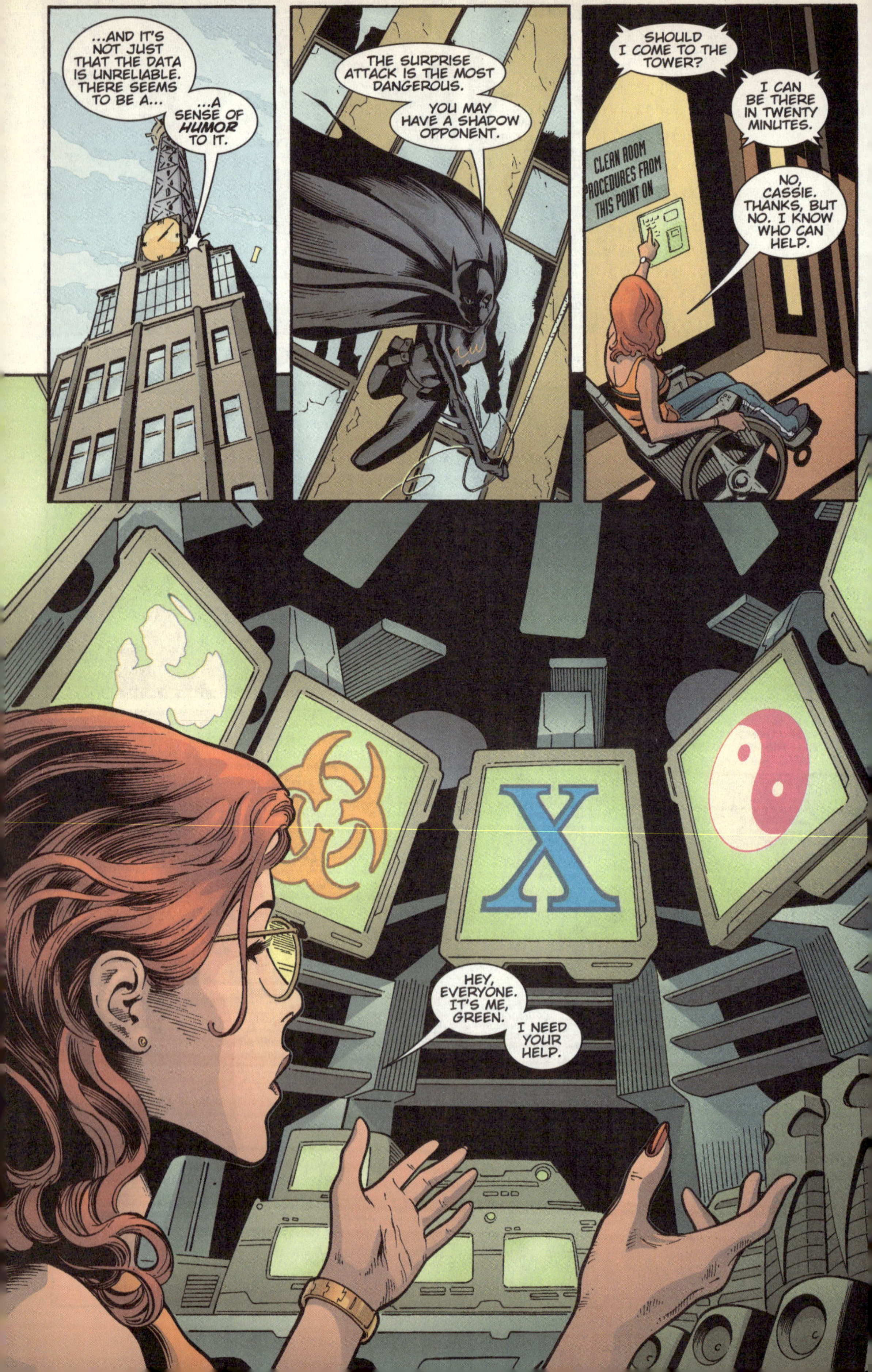
...AND IT'S NOT JUST THAT THE DATA IS UNRELIABLE. THERE SEEMS TO BE A...
...A SENSE OF *HUMOR* TO IT.
THE SURPRISE ATTACK IS THE MOST DANGEROUS.
YOU MAY HAVE A SHADOW OPPONENT.
SHOULD I COME TO THE TOWER?
I CAN BE THERE IN TWENTY MINUTES.
CLEAN ROOM PROCEDURES FROM THIS POINT ON
NO, CASSIE. THANKS, BUT NO. I KNOW WHO CAN HELP.
X
HEY, EVERYONE. IT'S ME, GREEN.
I NEED YOUR HELP.

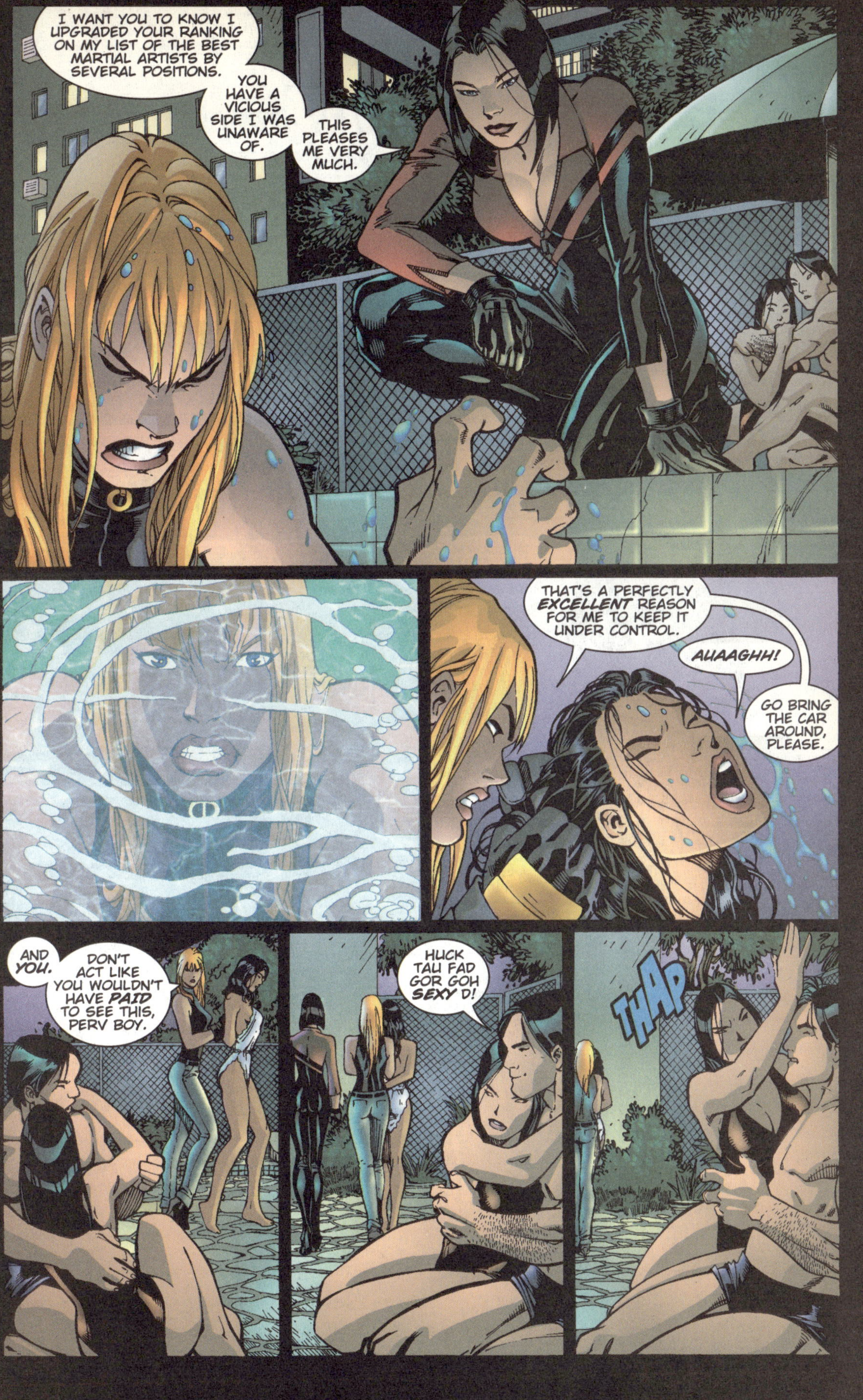
I WANT YOU TO KNOW I UPGRADED YOUR RANKING ON MY LIST OF THE BEST MARTIAL ARTISTS BY SEVERAL POSITIONS.
YOU HAVE A VICIOUS SIDE I WAS UNAWARE OF.
THIS PLEASES ME VERY MUCH.
THAT'S A PERFECTLY EXCELLENT REASON FOR ME TO KEEP IT UNDER CONTROL.
AUAAGHH!
GO BRING THE CAR AROUND, PLEASE.
AND YOU.
DON'T ACT LIKE YOU WOULDN'T HAVE PAID TO SEE THIS, PERV BOY.
HUCK TAU FAD GOR GOH SEXY D!
THAP

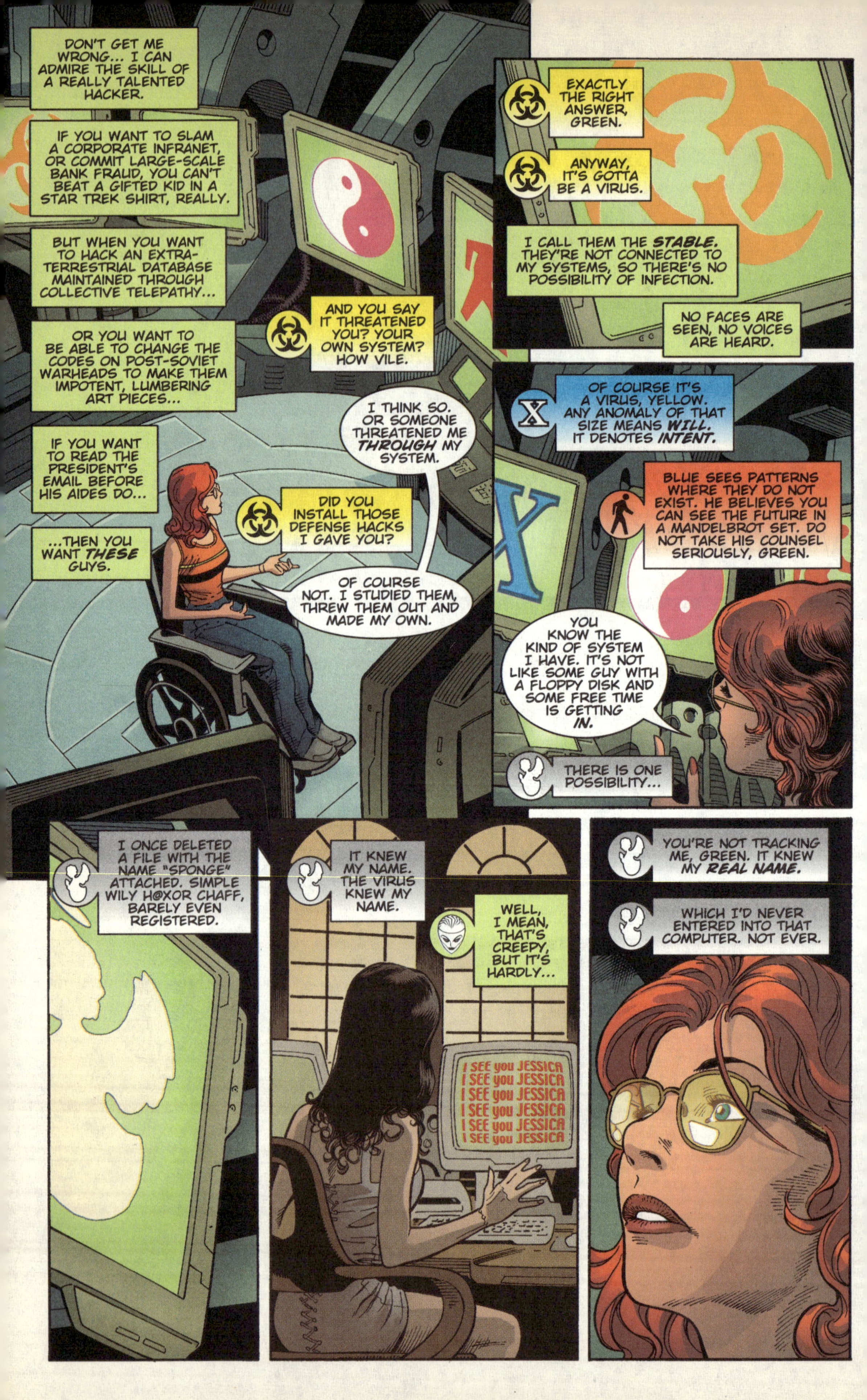
DON'T GET ME WRONG... I CAN ADMIRE THE SKILL OF A REALLY TALENTED HACKER.
IF YOU WANT TO SLAM A CORPORATE INFRANET, OR COMMIT LARGE-SCALE BANK FRAUD, YOU CAN'T BEAT A GIFTED KID IN A STAR TREK SHIRT, REALLY.
BUT WHEN YOU WANT TO HACK AN EXTRA-TERRESTRIAL DATABASE MAINTAINED THROUGH COLLECTIVE TELEPATHY...
OR YOU WANT TO BE ABLE TO CHANGE THE CODES ON POST-SOVIET WARHEADS TO MAKE THEM IMPOTENT, LUMBERING ART PIECES...
IF YOU WANT TO READ THE PRESIDENT'S EMAIL BEFORE HIS AIDES DO...
...THEN YOU WANT *THESE* GUYS.
AND YOU SAY IT THREATENED YOU? YOUR OWN SYSTEM? HOW VILE.
I THINK SO. OR SOMEONE THREATENED ME *THROUGH* MY SYSTEM.
DID YOU INSTALL THOSE DEFENSE HACKS I GAVE YOU?
OF COURSE NOT. I STUDIED THEM, THREW THEM OUT AND MADE MY OWN.
EXACTLY THE RIGHT ANSWER, GREEN.
ANYWAY, IT'S GOTTA BE A VIRUS.
I CALL THEM THE *STABLE*. THEY'RE NOT CONNECTED TO MY SYSTEMS, SO THERE'S NO POSSIBILITY OF INFECTION.
NO FACES ARE SEEN, NO VOICES ARE HEARD.
OF COURSE IT'S A VIRUS, YELLOW. ANY ANOMALY OF THAT SIZE MEANS *WILL*. IT DENOTES *INTENT*.
BLUE SEES PATTERNS WHERE THEY DO NOT EXIST. HE BELIEVES YOU CAN SEE THE FUTURE IN A MANDELBROT SET. DO NOT TAKE HIS COUNSEL SERIOUSLY, GREEN.
YOU KNOW THE KIND OF SYSTEM I HAVE. IT'S NOT LIKE SOME GUY WITH A FLOPPY DISK AND SOME FREE TIME IS GETTING *IN*.
THERE IS ONE POSSIBILITY...
I ONCE DELETED A FILE WITH THE NAME "SPONGE" ATTACHED. SIMPLE WILY H@XOR CHAFF, BARELY EVEN REGISTERED.
IT KNEW MY NAME. THE VIRUS KNEW MY NAME.
WELL, I MEAN, THAT'S CREEPY, BUT IT'S HARDLY...
I SEE you JESSICA
I SEE you JESSICA
I SEE you JESSICA
I SEE you JESSICA
I SEE you JESSICA
I SEE you JESSICA
YOU'RE NOT TRACKING ME, GREEN. IT KNEW MY *REAL NAME*.
WHICH I'D NEVER ENTERED INTO THAT COMPUTER. NOT EVER.

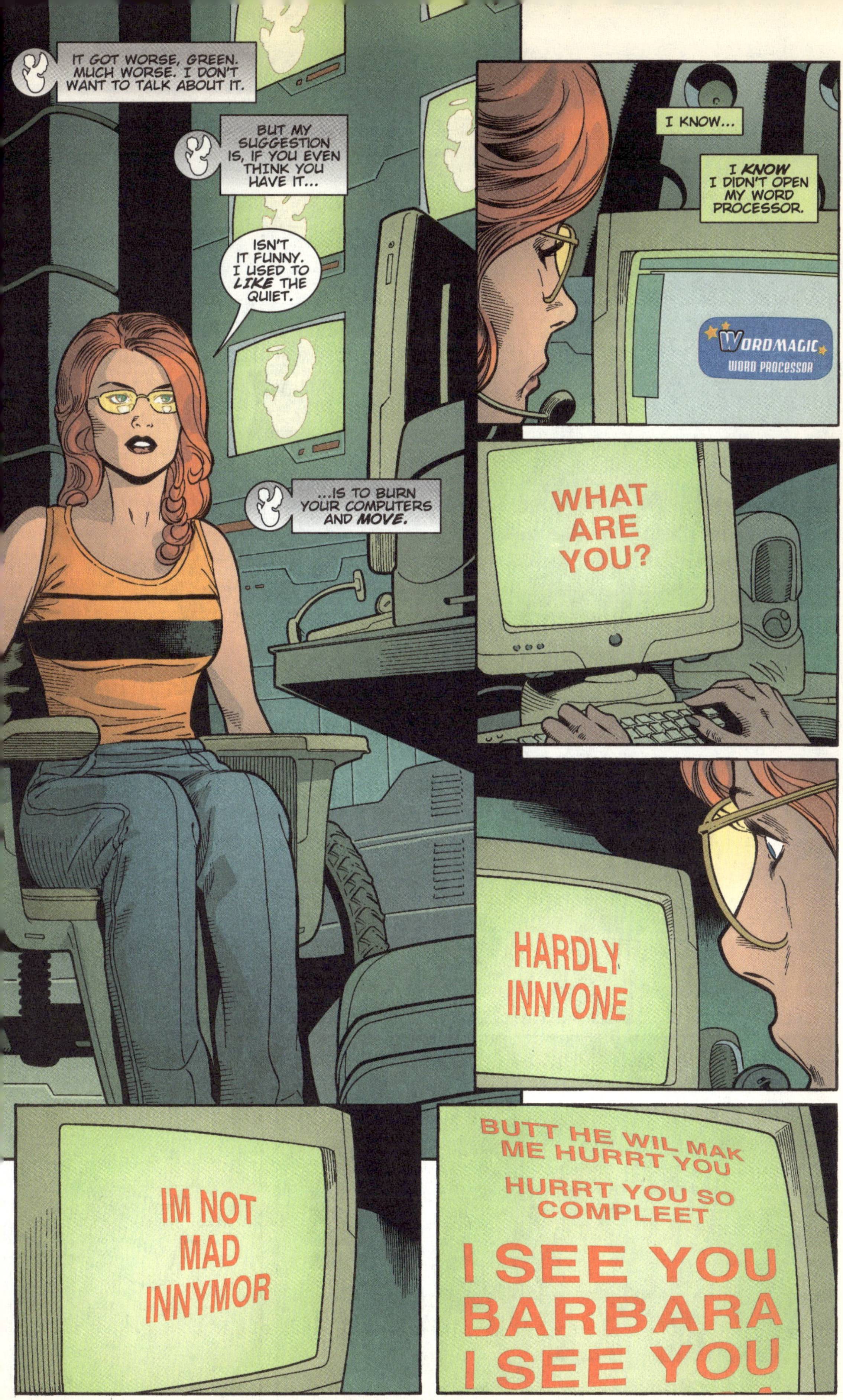
IT GOT WORSE, GREEN. MUCH WORSE. I DON'T WANT TO TALK ABOUT IT.
BUT MY SUGGESTION IS, IF YOU EVEN THINK YOU HAVE IT...
ISN'T IT FUNNY. I USED TO *LIKE* THE QUIET.
...IS TO BURN YOUR COMPUTERS AND *MOVE.*
I KNOW...
I *KNOW* I DIDN'T OPEN MY WORD PROCESSOR.
WORDMAGIC
WORD PROCESSOR
WHAT ARE YOU?
HARDLY INNYONE
IM NOT MAD INNYMOR
BUTT HE WIL MAK ME HURRT YOU
HURRT YOU SO COMPLEET
I SEE YOU BARBARA I SEE YOU

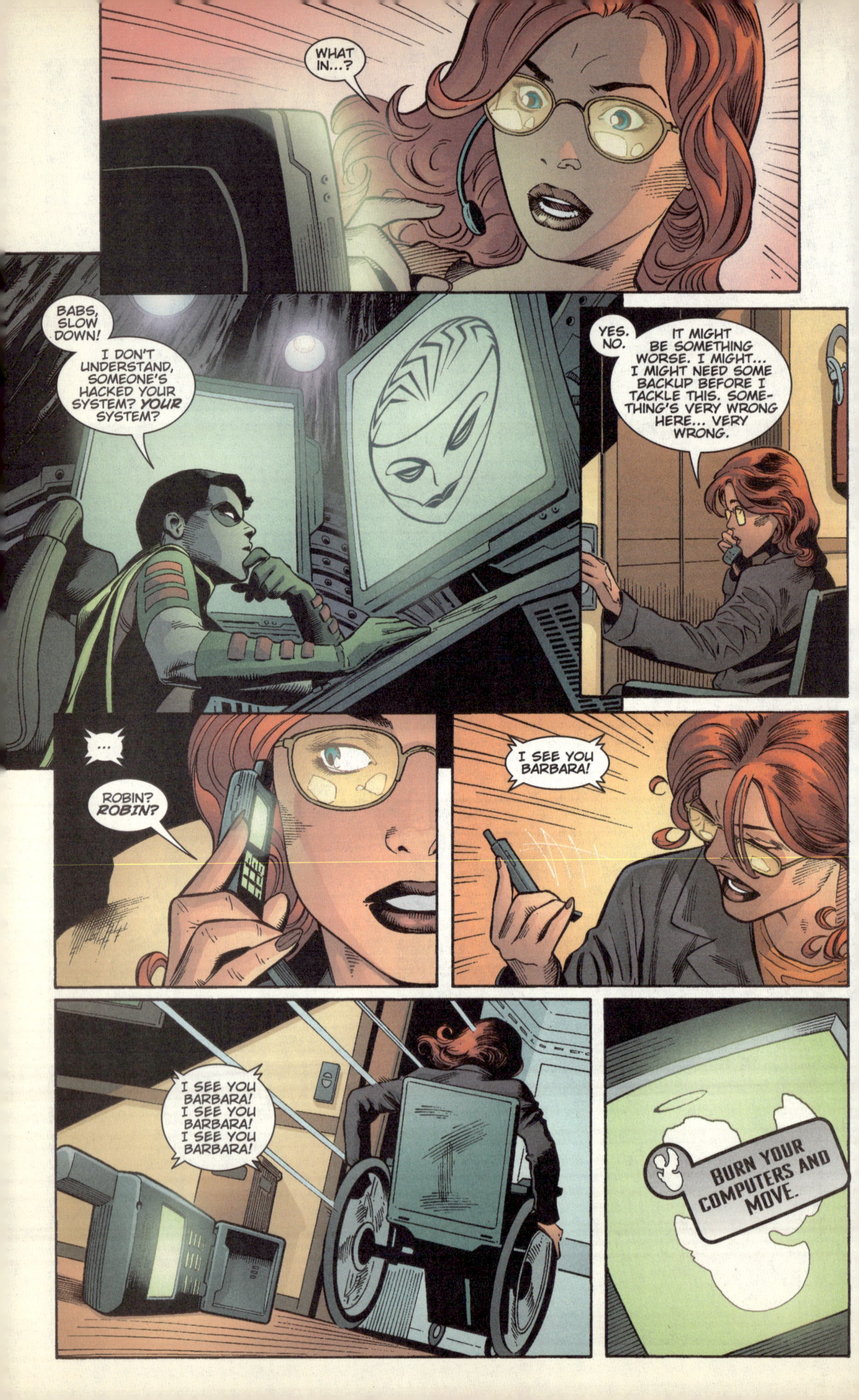
WHAT IN...?
BABS, SLOW DOWN!
I DON'T UNDERSTAND, SOMEONE'S HACKED YOUR SYSTEM? *YOUR* SYSTEM?
YES. NO.
IT MIGHT BE SOMETHING WORSE. I MIGHT... I MIGHT NEED SOME BACKUP BEFORE I TACKLE THIS. SOMETHING'S VERY WRONG HERE... VERY WRONG.
...
ROBIN? *ROBIN?*
I SEE YOU BARBARA!
I SEE YOU BARBARA! I SEE YOU BARBARA! I SEE YOU BARBARA!
BURN YOUR COMPUTERS AND MOVE.

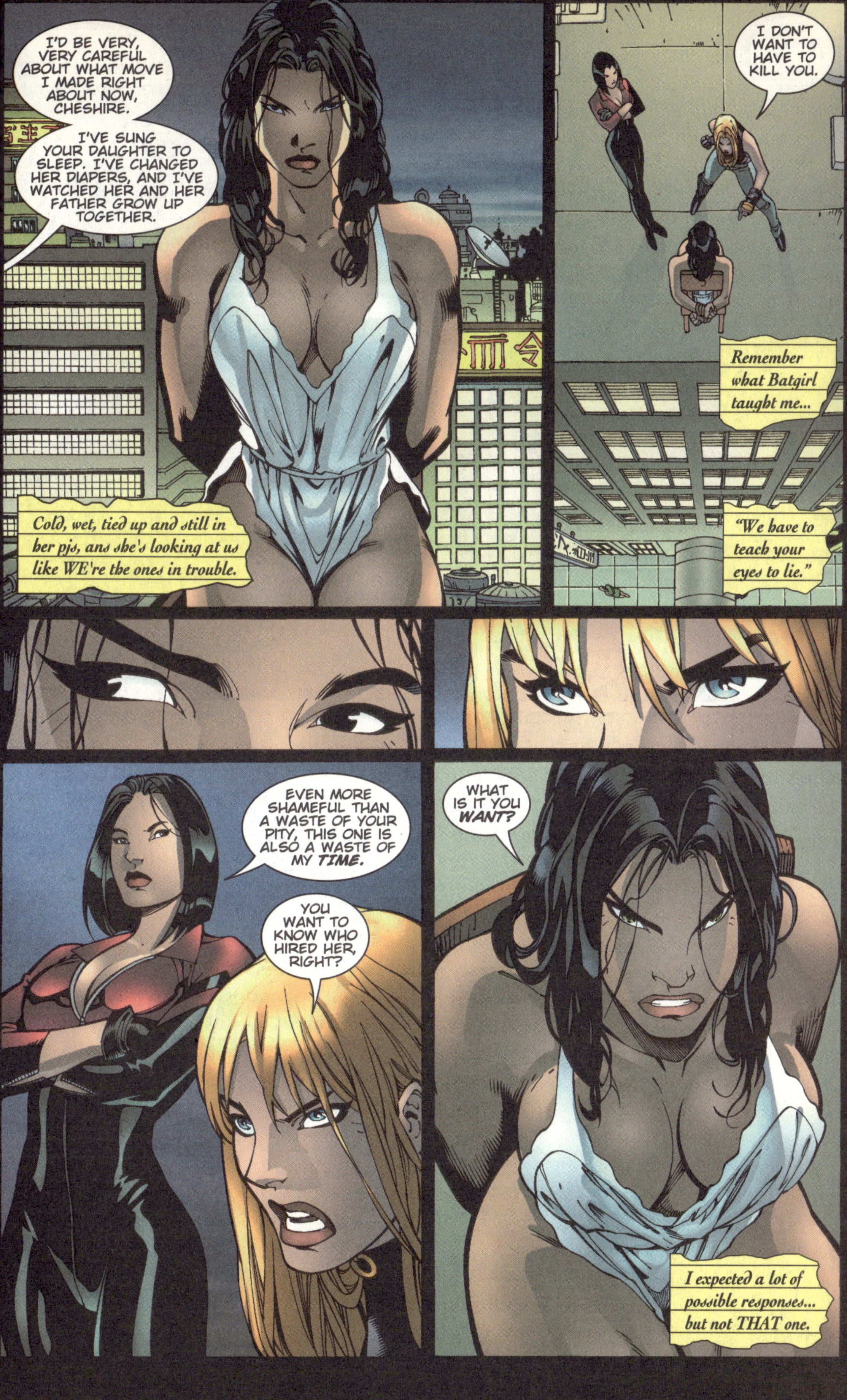

I'D BE VERY, VERY CAREFUL ABOUT WHAT MOVE I MADE RIGHT ABOUT NOW, CHESHIRE.
I'VE SUNG YOUR DAUGHTER TO SLEEP. I'VE CHANGED HER DIAPERS, AND I'VE WATCHED HER AND HER FATHER GROW UP TOGETHER.
Cold, wet, tied up and still in her pjs, ans she's looking at us like WE're the ones in trouble.
I DON'T WANT TO HAVE TO KILL YOU.
Remember what Batgirl taught me...
"We have to teach your eyes to lie."
EVEN MORE SHAMEFUL THAN A WASTE OF YOUR PITY, THIS ONE IS ALSO A WASTE OF MY TIME.
YOU WANT TO KNOW WHO HIRED HER, RIGHT?
WHAT IS IT YOU WANT?
I expected a lot of possible responses... but not THAT one.

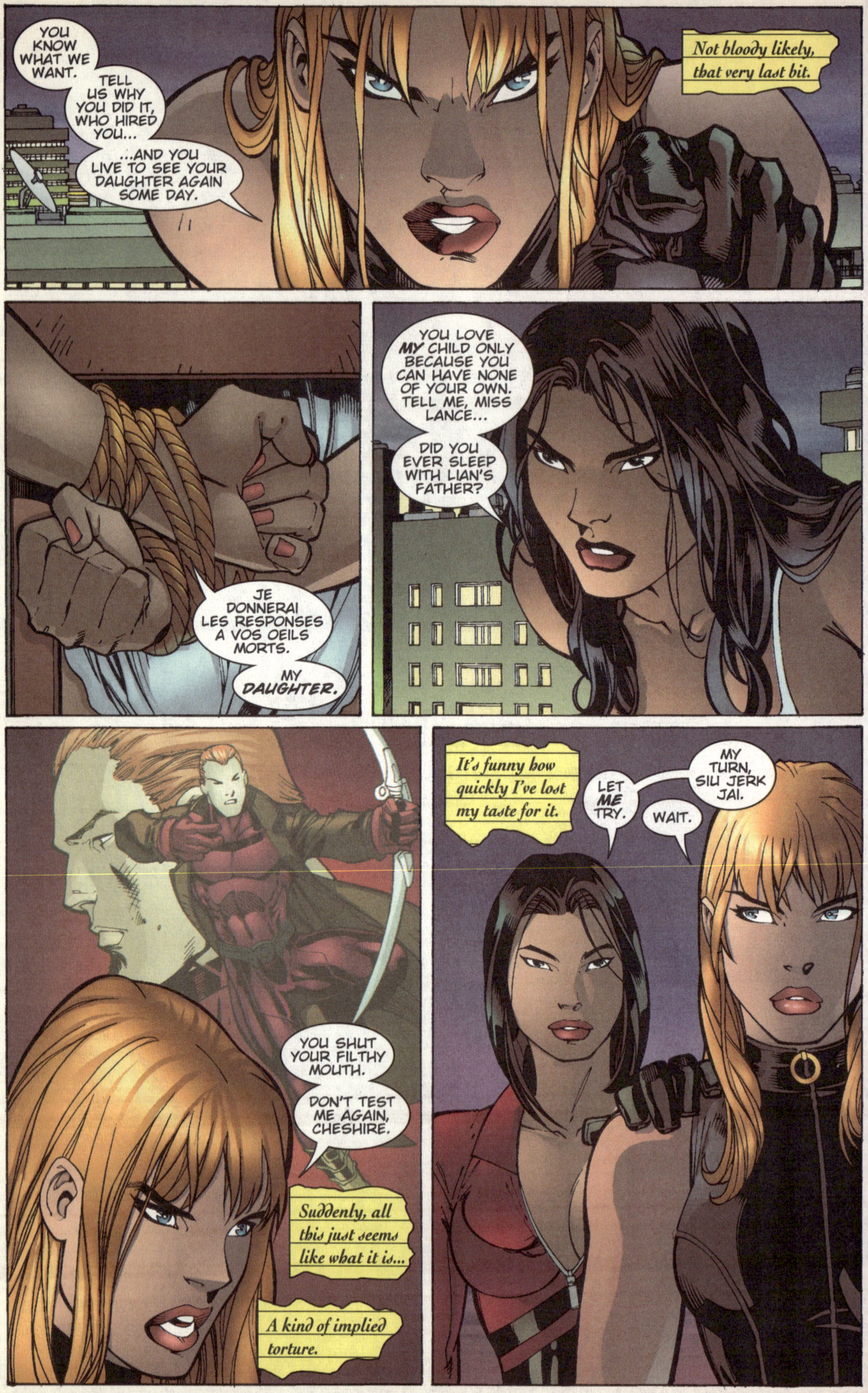
YOU KNOW WHAT WE WANT.
TELL US WHY YOU DID IT, WHO HIRED YOU...
...AND YOU LIVE TO SEE YOUR DAUGHTER AGAIN SOME DAY.
Not bloody likely, that very last bit.
YOU LOVE MY CHILD ONLY BECAUSE YOU CAN HAVE NONE OF YOUR OWN. TELL ME, MISS LANCE...
DID YOU EVER SLEEP WITH LIAN'S FATHER?
JE DONNERAI LES RESPONSES A VOS OEILS MORTS.
MY DAUGHTER.
YOU SHUT YOUR FILTHY MOUTH.
DON'T TEST ME AGAIN, CHESHIRE.
Suddenly, all this just seems like what it is...
A kind of implied torture.
It's funny how quickly I've lost my taste for it.
LET ME TRY.
MY TURN, SIU JERK JAI.
WAIT.

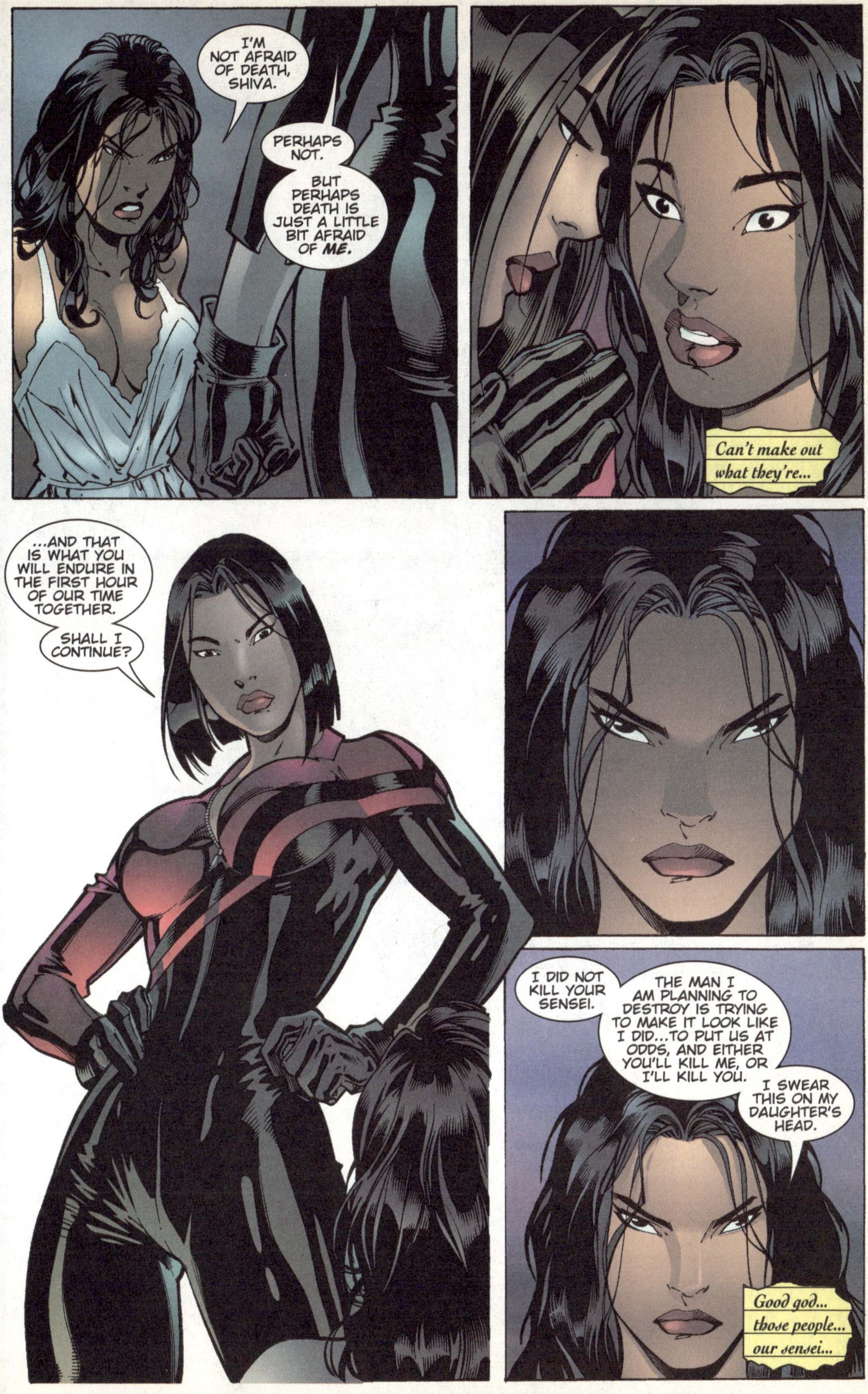
I'M NOT AFRAID OF DEATH, SHIVA.
PERHAPS NOT.
BUT PERHAPS DEATH IS JUST A LITTLE BIT AFRAID OF *ME.*
Can't make out what they're...
...AND THAT IS WHAT YOU WILL ENDURE IN THE FIRST HOUR OF OUR TIME TOGETHER.
SHALL I CONTINUE?
I DID NOT KILL YOUR SENSEI.
THE MAN I AM PLANNING TO DESTROY IS TRYING TO MAKE IT LOOK LIKE I DID...TO PUT US AT ODDS, AND EITHER YOU'LL KILL ME, OR I'LL KILL YOU.
I SWEAR THIS ON MY DAUGHTER'S HEAD.
Good god... those people... our sensei...

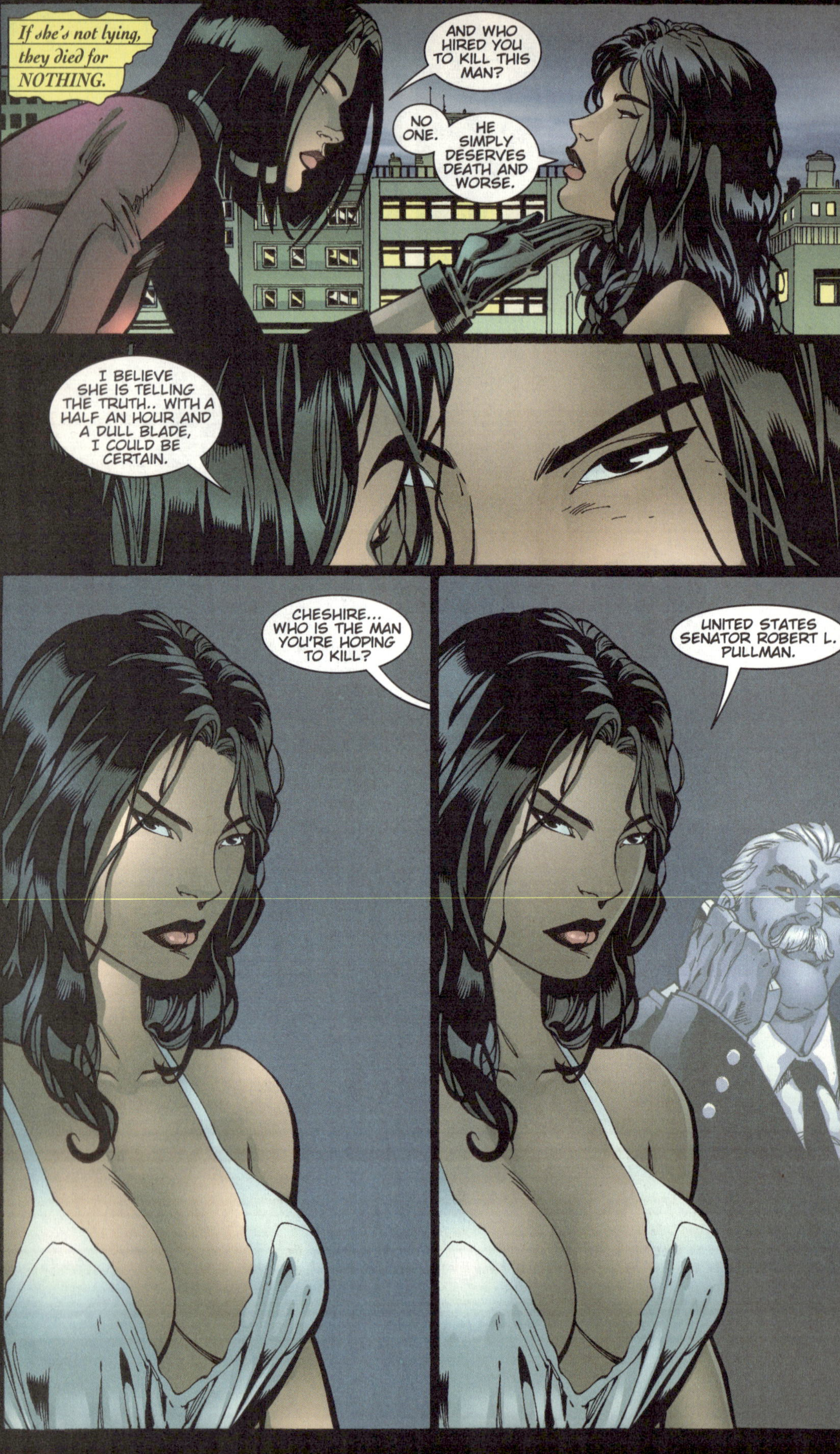

If she's not lying, they died for NOTHING.
AND WHO HIRED YOU TO KILL THIS MAN?
NO ONE.
HE SIMPLY DESERVES DEATH AND WORSE.
I BELIEVE SHE IS TELLING THE TRUTH.. WITH A HALF AN HOUR AND A DULL BLADE, I COULD BE CERTAIN.
CHESHIRE... WHO IS THE MAN YOU'RE HOPING TO KILL?
UNITED STATES SENATOR ROBERT L. PULLMAN.

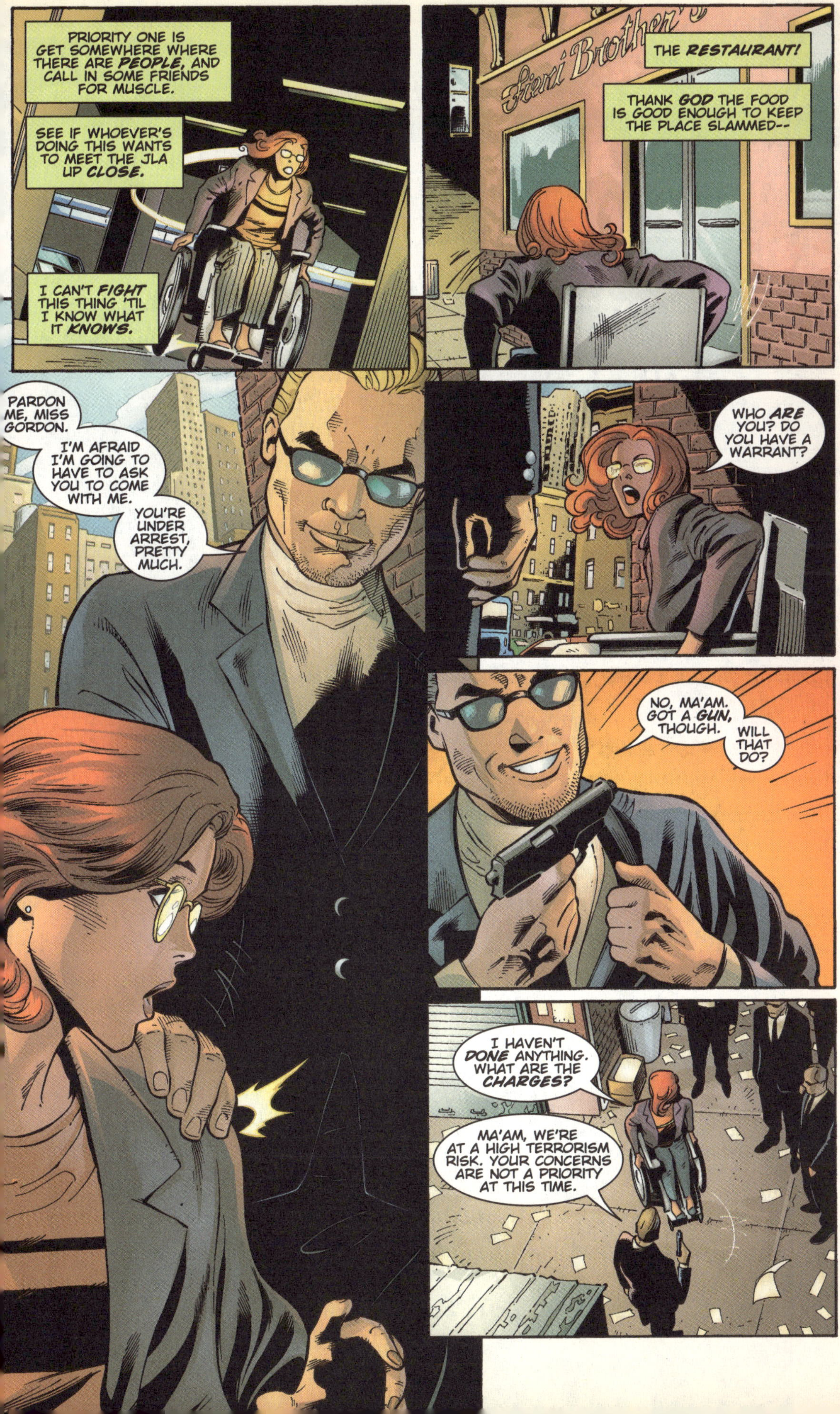

PRIORITY ONE IS GET SOMEWHERE WHERE THERE ARE PEOPLE, AND CALL IN SOME FRIENDS FOR MUSCLE.
SEE IF WHOEVER'S DOING THIS WANTS TO MEET THE JLA UP CLOSE.
I CAN'T FIGHT THIS THING 'TIL I KNOW WHAT IT KNOWS.
Fieri Brother's
THE RESTAURANT!
THANK GOD THE FOOD IS GOOD ENOUGH TO KEEP THE PLACE SLAMMED--
PARDON ME, MISS GORDON.
I'M AFRAID I'M GOING TO HAVE TO ASK YOU TO COME WITH ME.
YOU'RE UNDER ARREST, PRETTY MUCH.
WHO ARE YOU? DO YOU HAVE A WARRANT?
NO, MA'AM. GOT A GUN, THOUGH.
WILL THAT DO?
I HAVEN'T DONE ANYTHING. WHAT ARE THE CHARGES?
MA'AM, WE'RE AT A HIGH TERRORISM RISK. YOUR CONCERNS ARE NOT A PRIORITY AT THIS TIME.

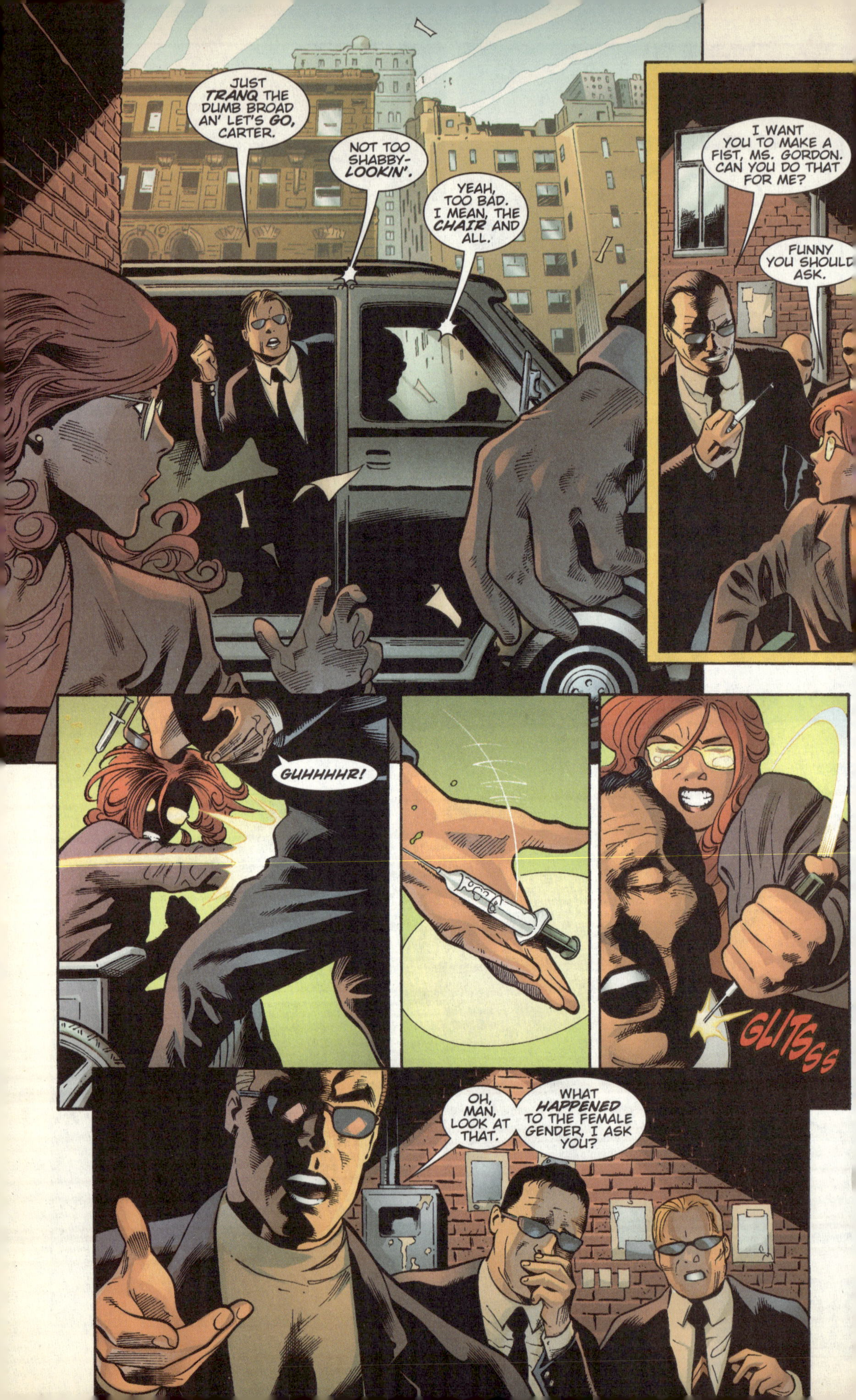
JUST TRANQ THE DUMB BROAD AN' LET'S GO, CARTER.
NOT TOO SHABBY-LOOKIN'.
YEAH, TOO BAD. I MEAN, THE CHAIR AND ALL.
I WANT YOU TO MAKE A FIST, MS. GORDON. CAN YOU DO THAT FOR ME?
FUNNY YOU SHOULD ASK.
GUHHHHR!
GLITSSS
OH, MAN, LOOK AT THAT.
WHAT HAPPENED TO THE FEMALE GENDER, I ASK YOU?

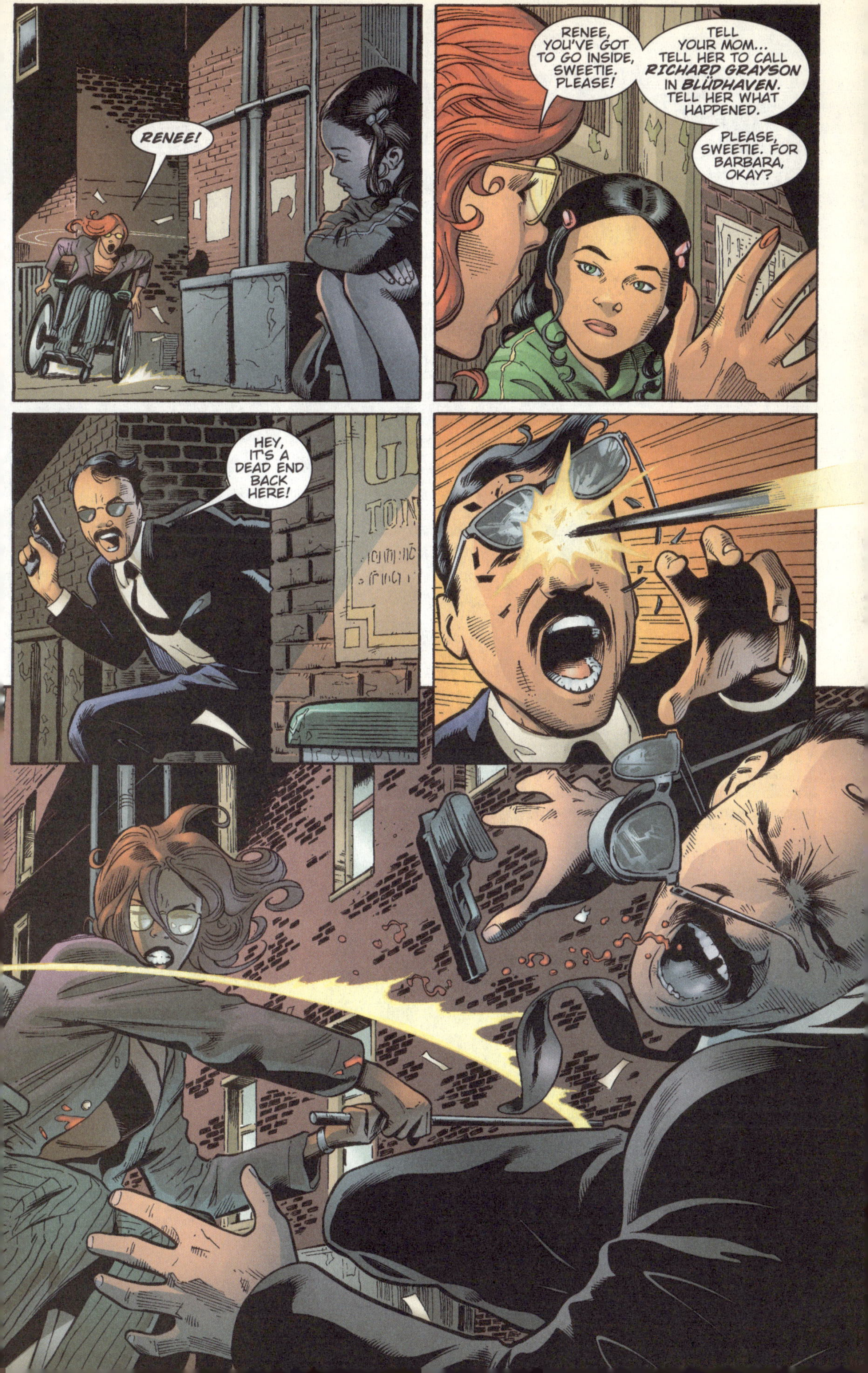
RENEE!
RENEE, YOU'VE GOT TO GO INSIDE, SWEETIE. PLEASE!
TELL YOUR MOM... TELL HER TO CALL RICHARD GRAYSON IN BLÜDHAVEN. TELL HER WHAT HAPPENED.
PLEASE, SWEETIE. FOR BARBARA, OKAY?
HEY, IT'S A DEAD END BACK HERE!

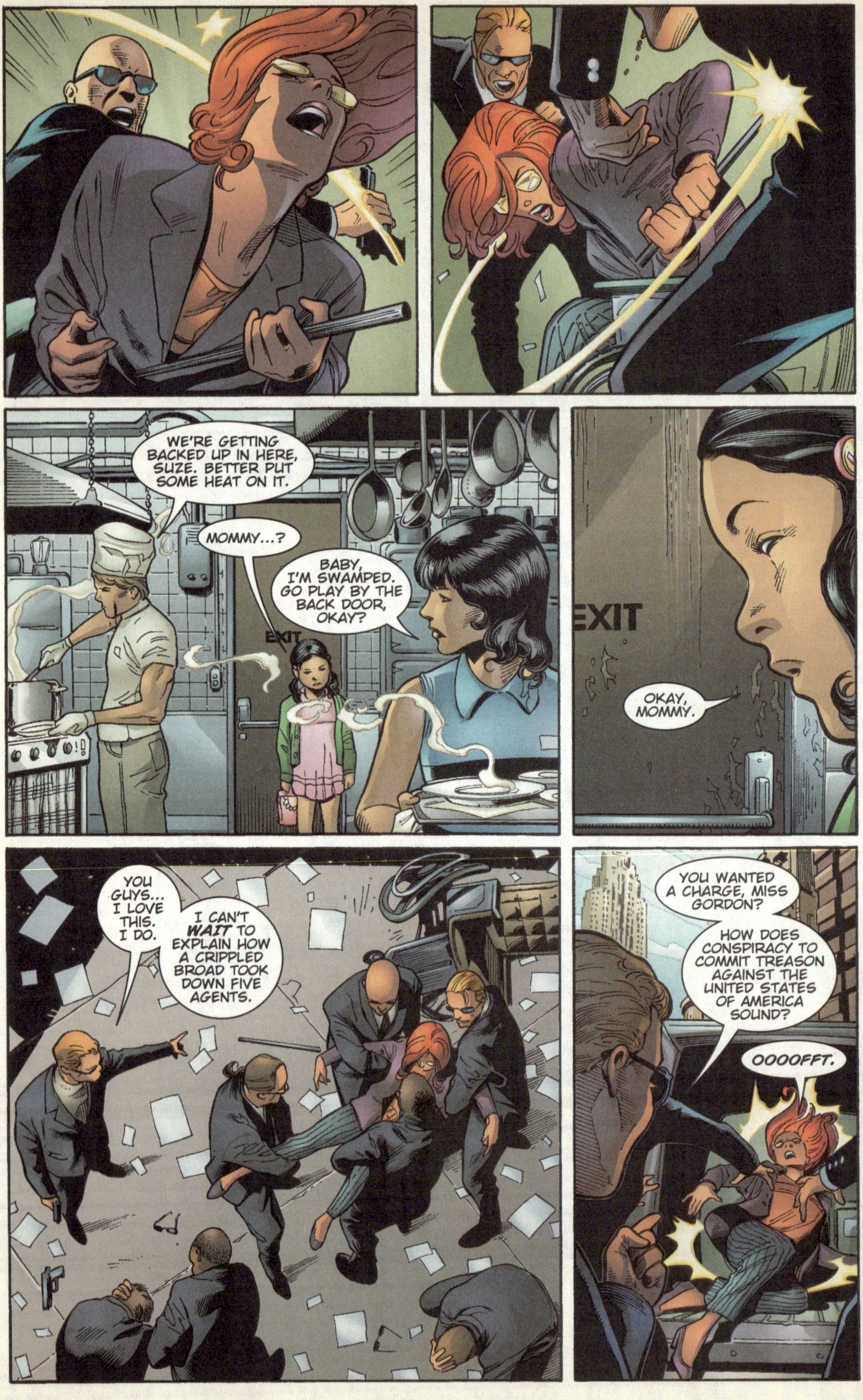
WE'RE GETTING BACKED UP IN HERE, SUZE. BETTER PUT SOME HEAT ON IT.
MOMMY...?
BABY, I'M SWAMPED. GO PLAY BY THE BACK DOOR, OKAY?
EXIT
EXIT
OKAY, MOMMY.
YOU GUYS... I LOVE THIS. I DO.
I CAN'T *WAIT* TO EXPLAIN HOW A CRIPPLED BROAD TOOK DOWN FIVE AGENTS.
YOU WANTED A CHARGE, MISS GORDON?
HOW DOES CONSPIRACY TO COMMIT TREASON AGAINST THE UNITED STATES OF AMERICA SOUND?
OOOOFFT.

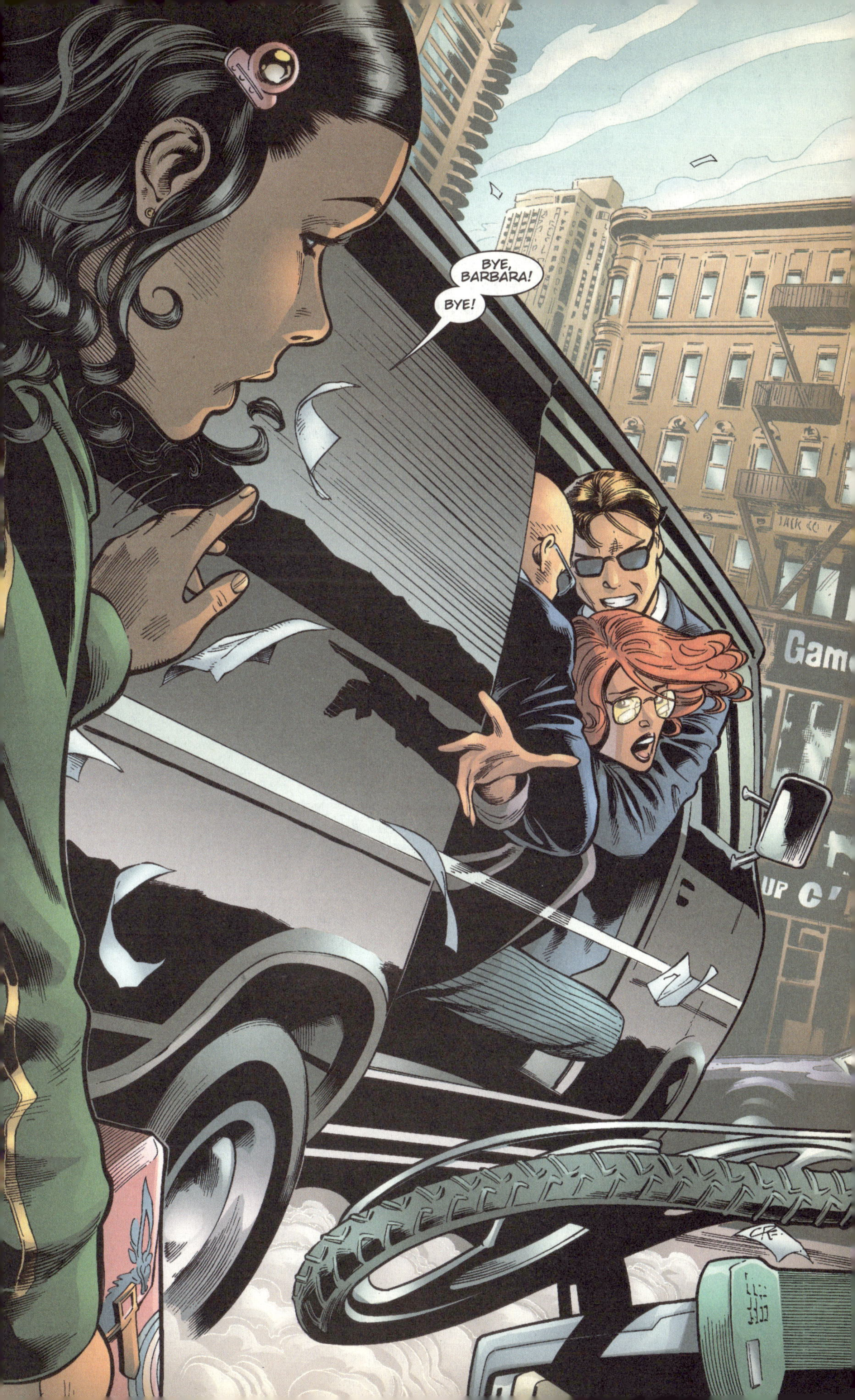
BYE, BARBARA!
BYE!

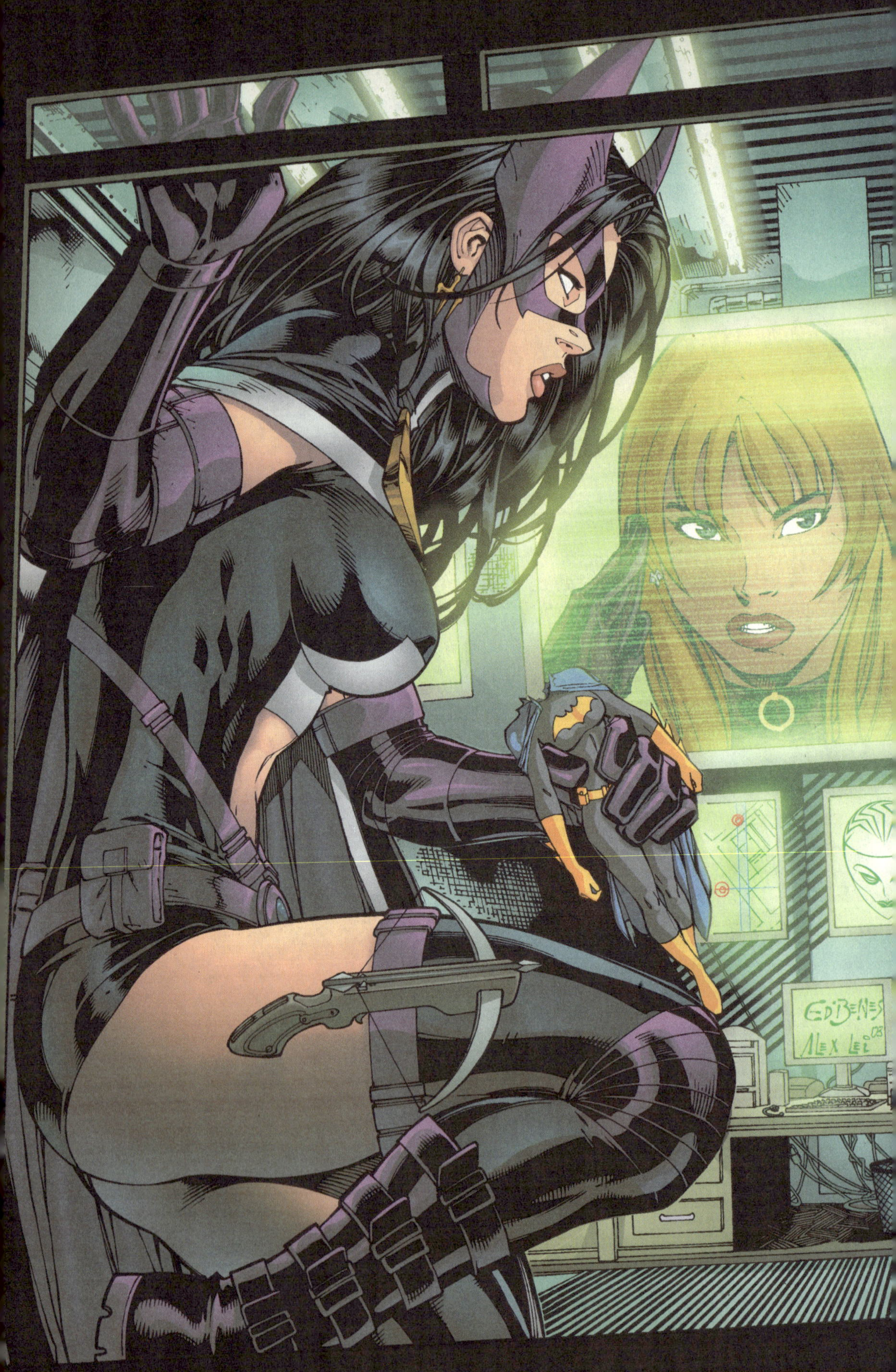
ED BENES
ALEX LEI 03

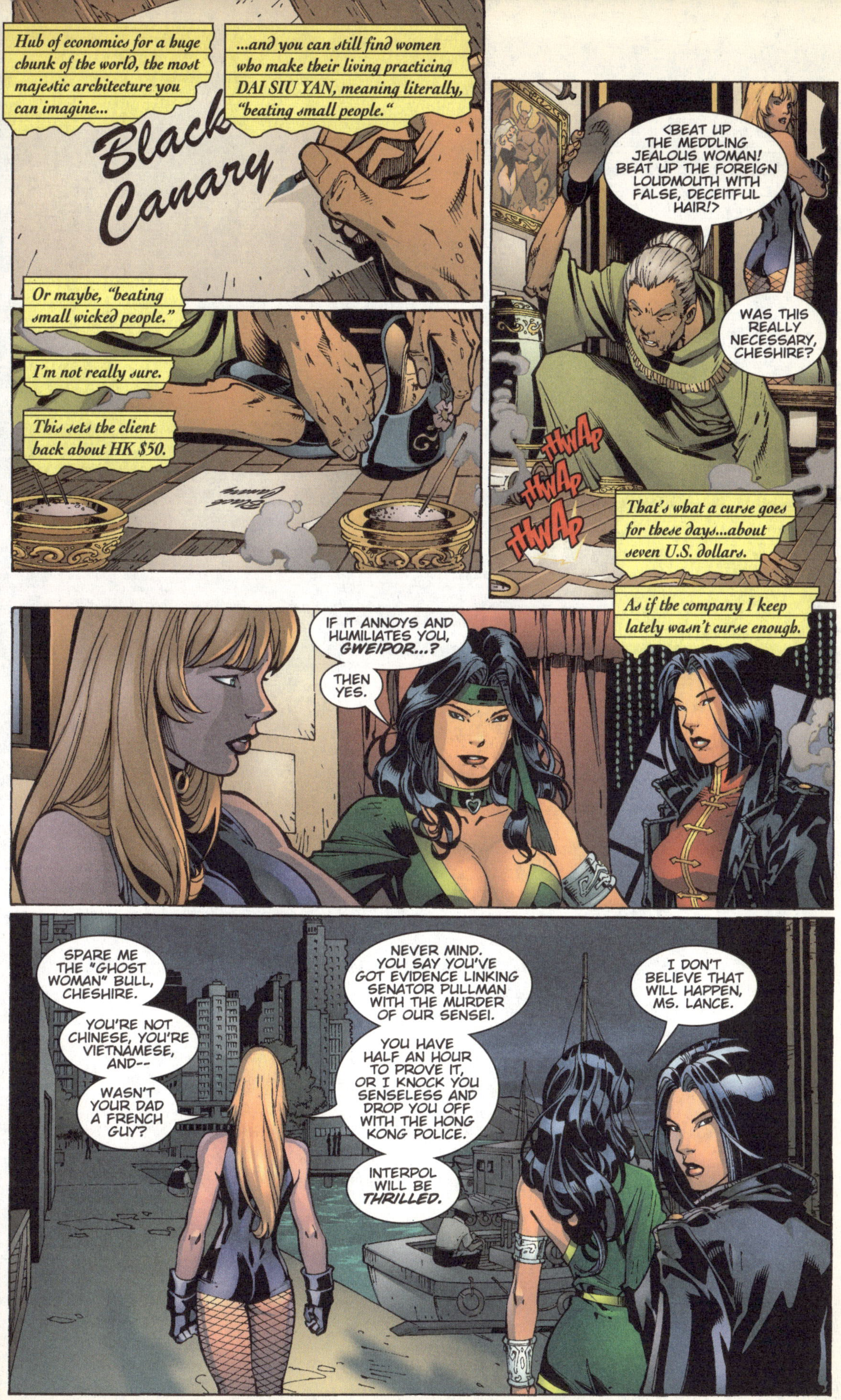
Hub of economics for a huge chunk of the world, the most majestic architecture you can imagine...
...and you can still find women who make their living practicing DAI SIU YAN, meaning literally, "beating small people."
Black Canary
<BEAT UP THE MEDDLING JEALOUS WOMAN! BEAT UP THE FOREIGN LOUDMOUTH WITH FALSE, DECEITFUL HAIR!>
Or maybe, "beating small wicked people."
I'm not really sure.
This sets the client back about HK $50.
WAS THIS REALLY NECESSARY, CHESHIRE?
THWAP THWAP THWAP
That's what a curse goes for these days...about seven U.S. dollars.
As if the company I keep lately wasn't curse enough.
IF IT ANNOYS AND HUMILIATES YOU, GWEIPOR...?
THEN YES.
SPARE ME THE "GHOST WOMAN" BULL, CHESHIRE.
YOU'RE NOT CHINESE, YOU'RE VIETNAMESE, AND--
WASN'T YOUR DAD A FRENCH GUY?
NEVER MIND. YOU SAY YOU'VE GOT EVIDENCE LINKING SENATOR PULLMAN WITH THE MURDER OF OUR SENSEI.
YOU HAVE HALF AN HOUR TO PROVE IT, OR I KNOCK YOU SENSELESS AND DROP YOU OFF WITH THE HONG KONG POLICE.
INTERPOL WILL BE THRILLED.
I DON'T BELIEVE THAT WILL HAPPEN, MS. LANCE.

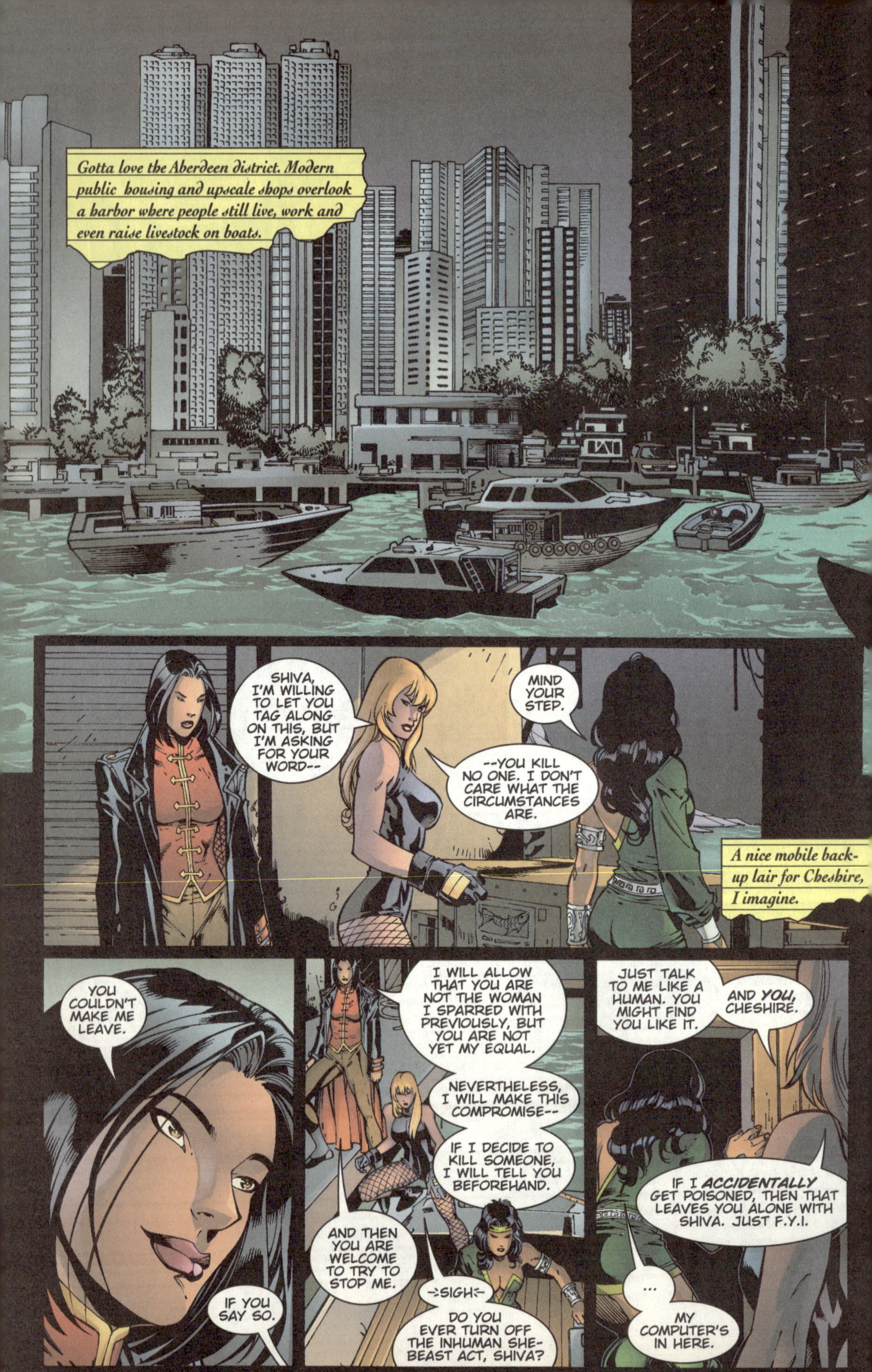
Gotta love the Aberdeen district. Modern public housing and upscale shops overlook a harbor where people still live, work and even raise livestock on boats.
SHIVA, I'M WILLING TO LET YOU TAG ALONG ON THIS, BUT I'M ASKING FOR YOUR WORD--
MIND YOUR STEP.
--YOU KILL NO ONE. I DON'T CARE WHAT THE CIRCUMSTANCES ARE.
A nice mobile back-up lair for Cheshire, I imagine.
YOU COULDN'T MAKE ME LEAVE.
IF YOU SAY SO.
I WILL ALLOW THAT YOU ARE NOT THE WOMAN I SPARRED WITH PREVIOUSLY, BUT YOU ARE NOT YET MY EQUAL.
NEVERTHELESS, I WILL MAKE THIS COMPROMISE--
IF I DECIDE TO KILL SOMEONE, I WILL TELL YOU BEFOREHAND.
AND THEN YOU ARE WELCOME TO TRY TO STOP ME.
-SIGH-
DO YOU EVER TURN OFF THE INHUMAN SHE-BEAST ACT, SHIVA?
JUST TALK TO ME LIKE A HUMAN. YOU MIGHT FIND YOU LIKE IT.
AND YOU, CHESHIRE.
IF I ACCIDENTALLY GET POISONED, THEN THAT LEAVES YOU ALONE WITH SHIVA. JUST F.Y.I.
...
MY COMPUTER'S IN HERE.

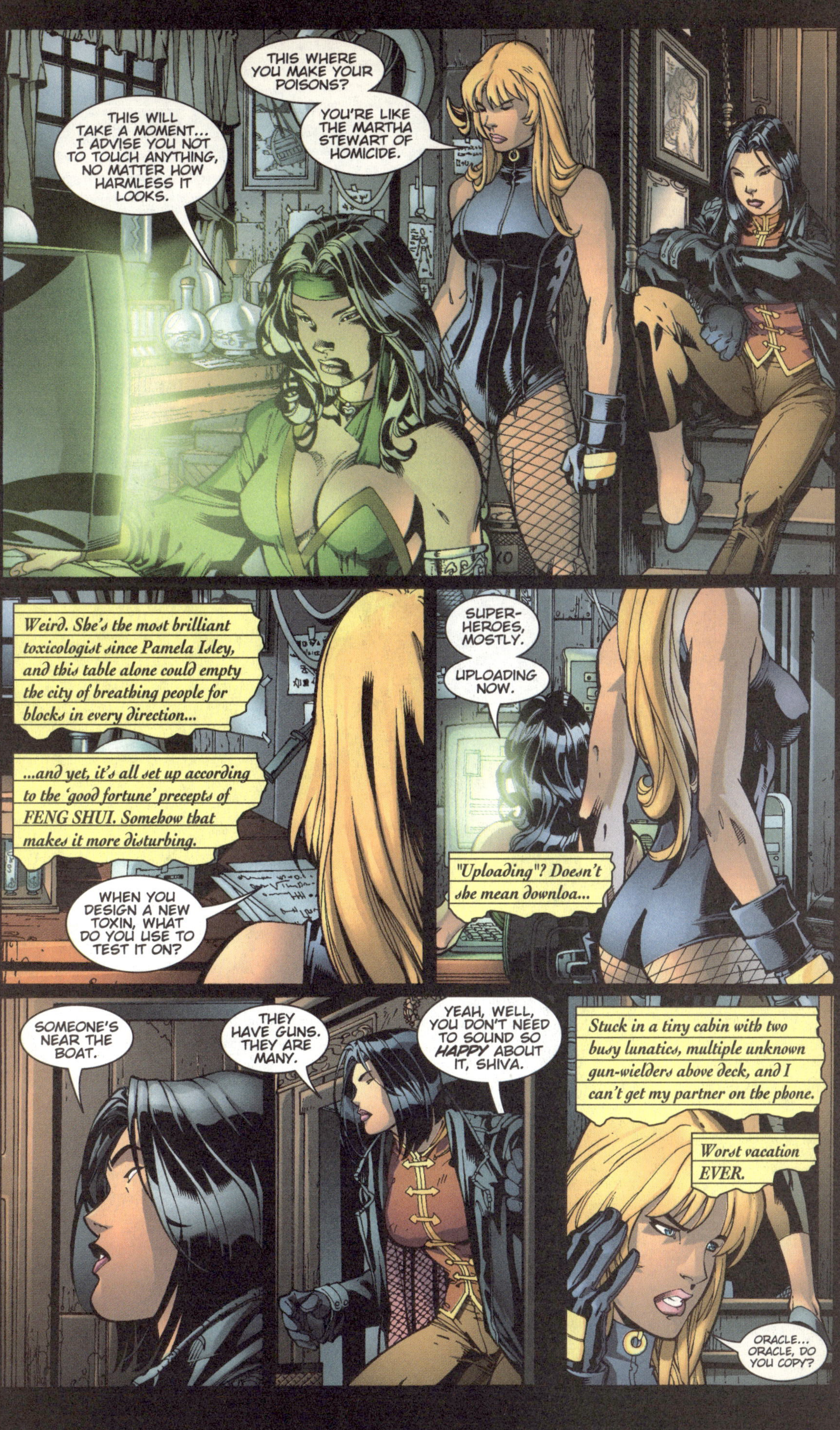
THIS WILL TAKE A MOMENT... I ADVISE YOU NOT TO TOUCH ANYTHING, NO MATTER HOW HARMLESS IT LOOKS.
THIS WHERE YOU MAKE YOUR POISONS?
YOU'RE LIKE THE MARTHA STEWART OF HOMICIDE.
Weird. She's the most brilliant toxicologist since Pamela Isley, and this table alone could empty the city of breathing people for blocks in every direction...
...and yet, it's all set up according to the 'good fortune' precepts of FENG SHUI. Somehow that makes it more disturbing.
WHEN YOU DESIGN A NEW TOXIN, WHAT DO YOU USE TO TEST IT ON?
SUPER-HEROES, MOSTLY.
UPLOADING NOW.
"Uploading"? Doesn't she mean downloa...
SOMEONE'S NEAR THE BOAT.
THEY HAVE GUNS. THEY ARE MANY.
YEAH, WELL, YOU DON'T NEED TO SOUND SO HAPPY ABOUT IT, SHIVA.
Stuck in a tiny cabin with two busy lunatics, multiple unknown gun-wielders above deck, and I can't get my partner on the phone.
Worst vacation EVER.
ORACLE... ORACLE, DO YOU COPY?

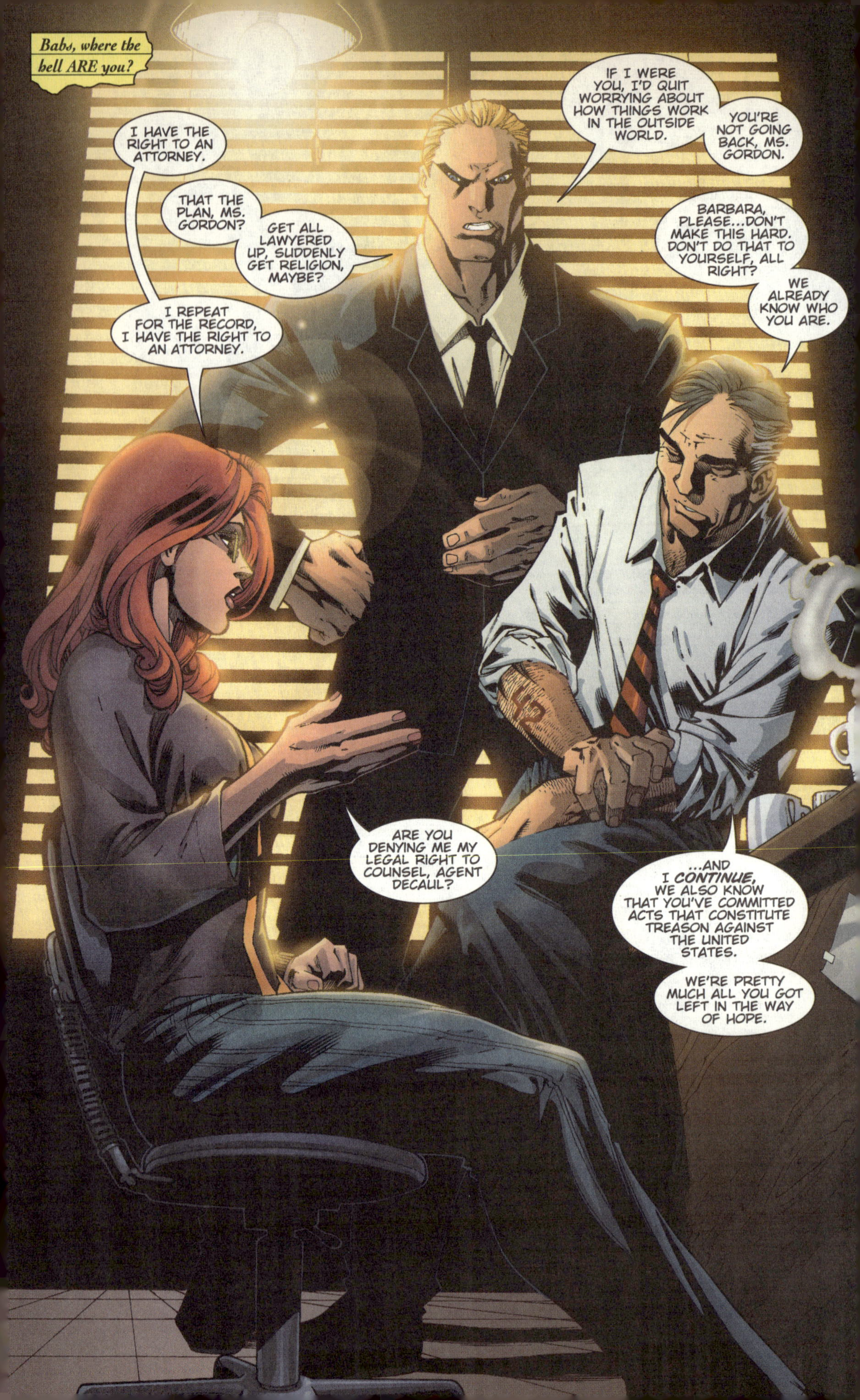
Babs, where the hell ARE you?
I HAVE THE RIGHT TO AN ATTORNEY.
THAT THE PLAN, MS. GORDON?
GET ALL LAWYERED UP, SUDDENLY GET RELIGION, MAYBE?
I REPEAT FOR THE RECORD, I HAVE THE RIGHT TO AN ATTORNEY.
IF I WERE YOU, I'D QUIT WORRYING ABOUT HOW THINGS WORK IN THE OUTSIDE WORLD.
YOU'RE NOT GOING BACK, MS. GORDON.
BARBARA, PLEASE...DON'T MAKE THIS HARD. DON'T DO THAT TO YOURSELF, ALL RIGHT?
WE ALREADY KNOW WHO YOU ARE.
ARE YOU DENYING ME MY LEGAL RIGHT TO COUNSEL, AGENT DECAUL?
...AND I CONTINUE, WE ALSO KNOW THAT YOU'VE COMMITTED ACTS THAT CONSTITUTE TREASON AGAINST THE UNITED STATES.
WE'RE PRETTY MUCH ALL YOU GOT LEFT IN THE WAY OF HOPE.

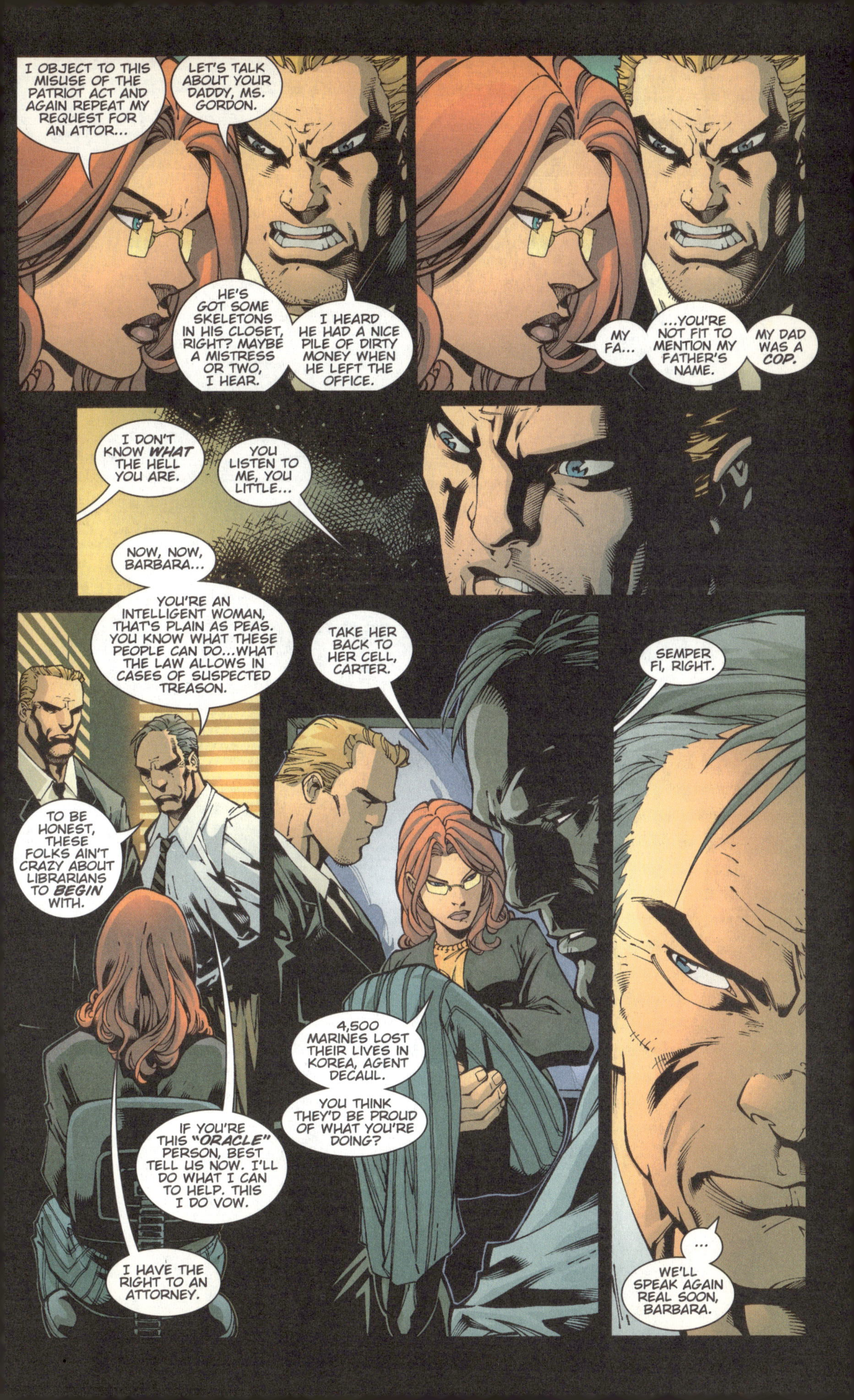

I OBJECT TO THIS MISUSE OF THE PATRIOT ACT AND AGAIN REPEAT MY REQUEST FOR AN ATTOR...
LET'S TALK ABOUT YOUR DADDY, MS. GORDON.
HE'S GOT SOME SKELETONS IN HIS CLOSET, RIGHT? MAYBE A MISTRESS OR TWO, I HEAR.
I HEARD HE HAD A NICE PILE OF DIRTY MONEY WHEN HE LEFT THE OFFICE.
MY FA...
...YOU'RE NOT FIT TO MENTION MY FATHER'S NAME.
MY DAD WAS A *COP.*
I DON'T KNOW *WHAT* THE HELL YOU ARE.
YOU LISTEN TO ME, YOU LITTLE...
NOW, NOW, BARBARA...
YOU'RE AN INTELLIGENT WOMAN, THAT'S PLAIN AS PEAS. YOU KNOW WHAT THESE PEOPLE CAN DO...WHAT THE LAW ALLOWS IN CASES OF SUSPECTED TREASON.
TO BE HONEST, THESE FOLKS AIN'T CRAZY ABOUT LIBRARIANS TO *BEGIN* WITH.
IF YOU'RE THIS *"ORACLE"* PERSON, BEST TELL US NOW. I'LL DO WHAT I CAN TO HELP. THIS I DO VOW.
I HAVE THE RIGHT TO AN ATTORNEY.
TAKE HER BACK TO HER CELL, CARTER.
4,500 MARINES LOST THEIR LIVES IN KOREA, AGENT DECAUL.
YOU THINK THEY'D BE PROUD OF WHAT YOU'RE DOING?
SEMPER FI, RIGHT.
...
WE'LL SPEAK AGAIN REAL SOON, BARBARA.

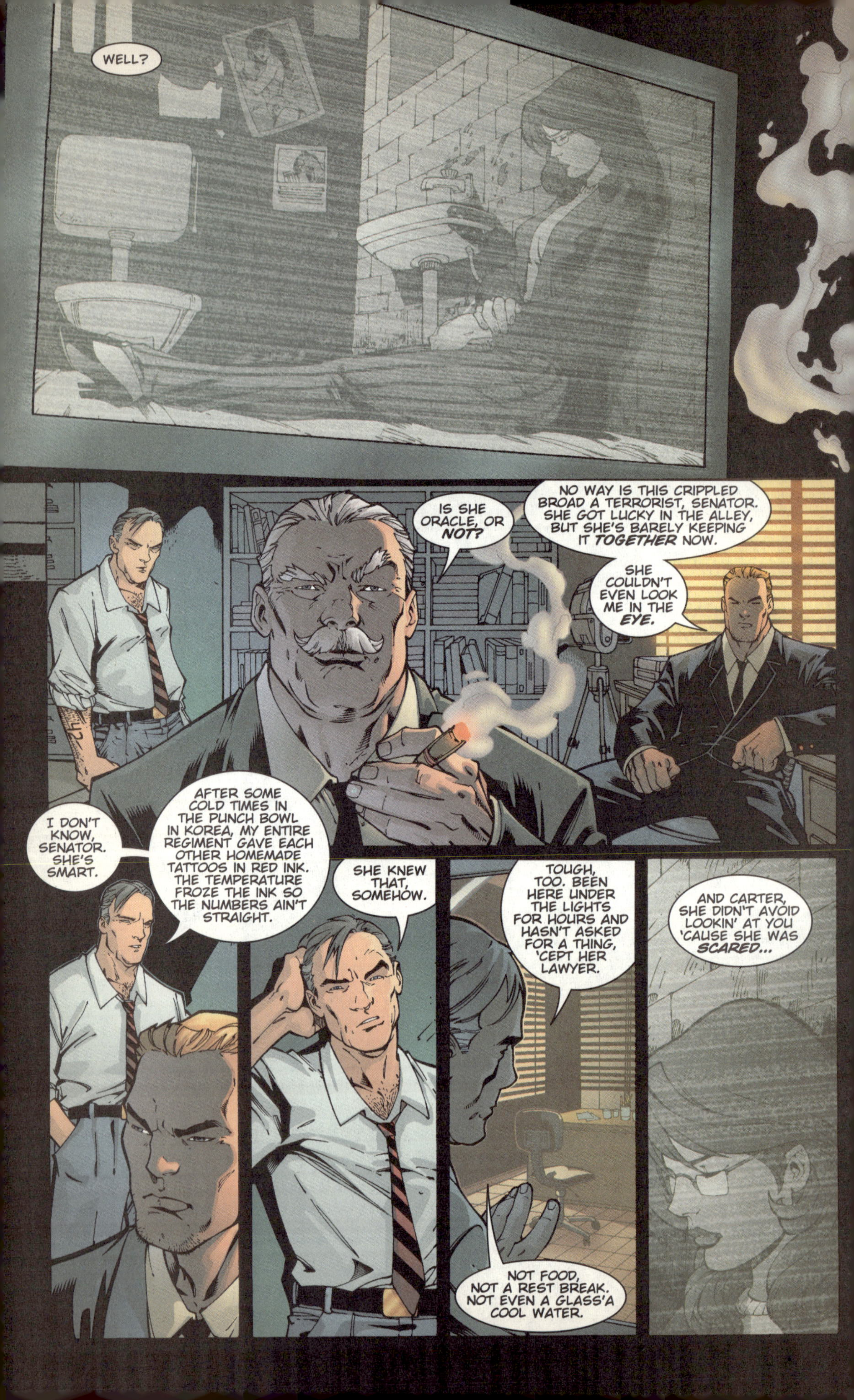
WELL?
IS SHE ORACLE, OR NOT?
NO WAY IS THIS CRIPPLED BROAD A TERRORIST, SENATOR. SHE GOT LUCKY IN THE ALLEY, BUT SHE'S BARELY KEEPING IT TOGETHER NOW.
SHE COULDN'T EVEN LOOK ME IN THE EYE.
I DON'T KNOW, SENATOR. SHE'S SMART.
AFTER SOME COLD TIMES IN THE PUNCH BOWL IN KOREA, MY ENTIRE REGIMENT GAVE EACH OTHER HOMEMADE TATTOOS IN RED INK. THE TEMPERATURE FROZE THE INK SO THE NUMBERS AIN'T STRAIGHT.
SHE KNEW THAT, SOMEHOW.
TOUGH, TOO. BEEN HERE UNDER THE LIGHTS FOR HOURS AND HASN'T ASKED FOR A THING, 'CEPT HER LAWYER.
NOT FOOD, NOT A REST BREAK. NOT EVEN A GLASS'A COOL WATER.
AND CARTER, SHE DIDN'T AVOID LOOKIN' AT YOU 'CAUSE SHE WAS SCARED...

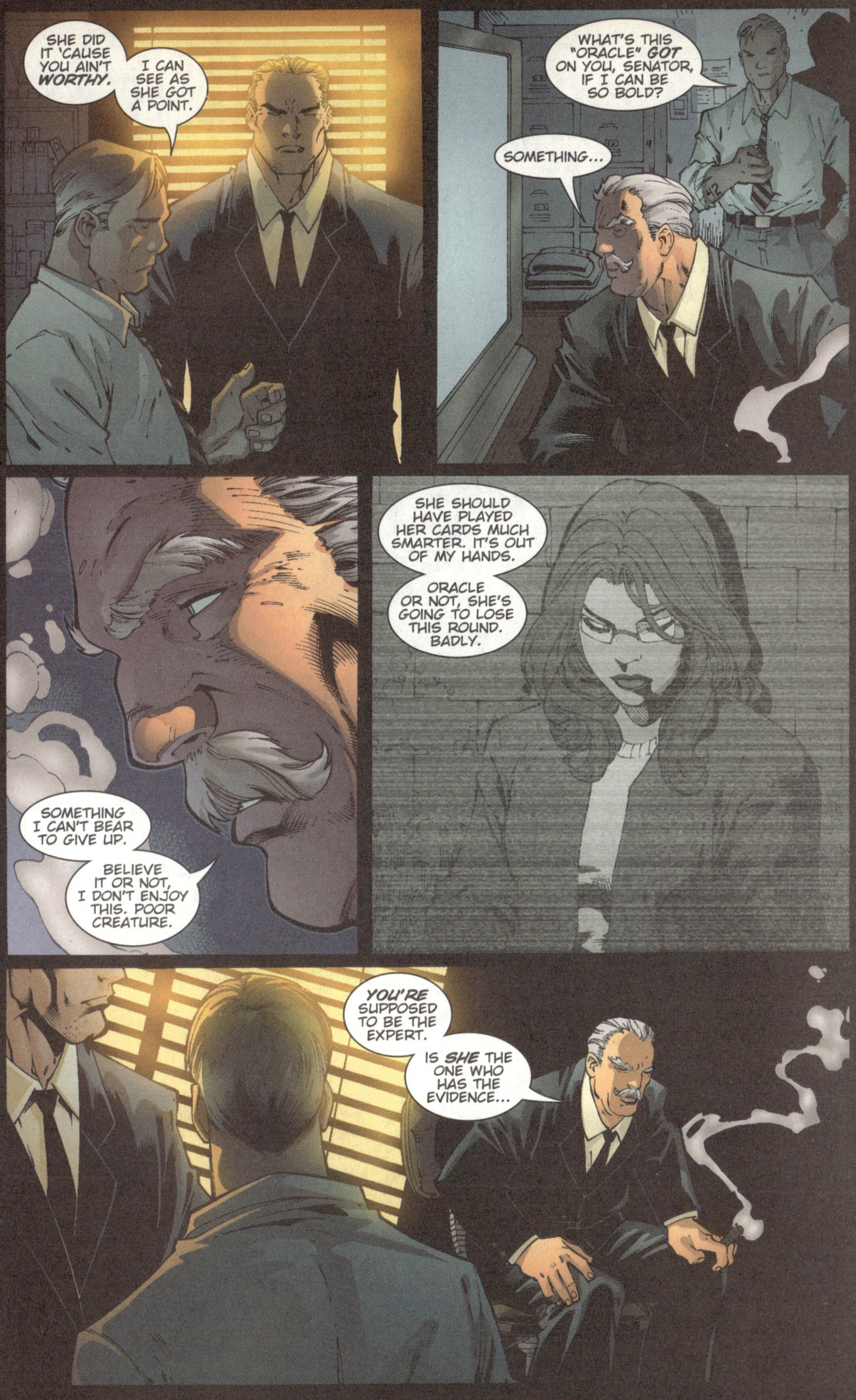
SHE DID IT 'CAUSE YOU AIN'T **WORTHY.**
I CAN SEE AS SHE GOT A POINT.
WHAT'S THIS "ORACLE" **GOT** ON YOU, SENATOR, IF I CAN BE SO BOLD?
SOMETHING...
SOMETHING I CAN'T BEAR TO GIVE UP.
BELIEVE IT OR NOT, I DON'T ENJOY THIS. POOR CREATURE.
SHE SHOULD HAVE PLAYED HER CARDS MUCH SMARTER. IT'S OUT OF MY HANDS.
ORACLE OR NOT, SHE'S GOING TO LOSE THIS ROUND. BADLY.
YOU'RE SUPPOSED TO BE THE EXPERT.
IS ***SHE*** THE ONE WHO HAS THE EVIDENCE...

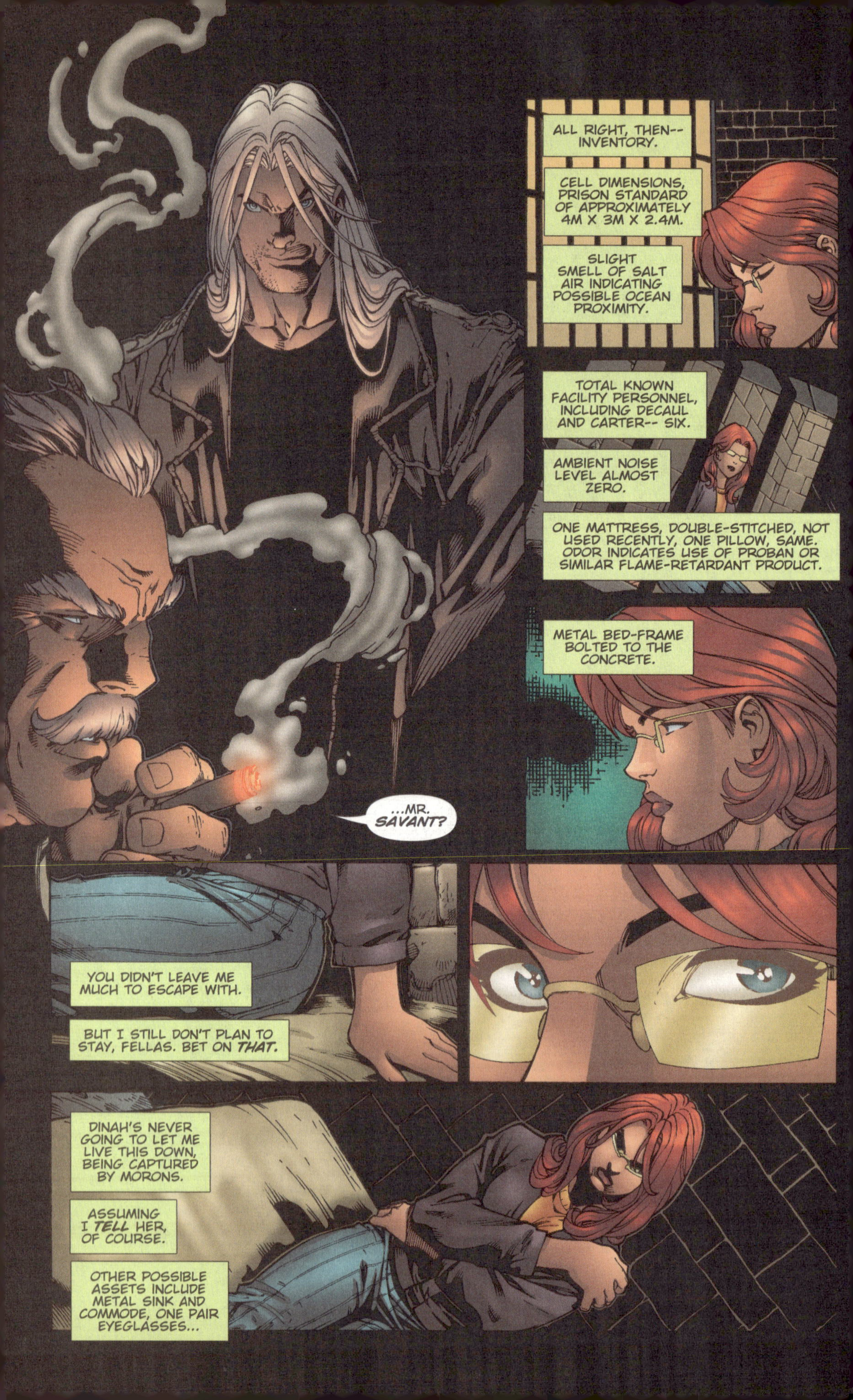
ALL RIGHT, THEN-- INVENTORY.
CELL DIMENSIONS, PRISON STANDARD OF APPROXIMATELY 4M X 3M X 2.4M.
SLIGHT SMELL OF SALT AIR INDICATING POSSIBLE OCEAN PROXIMITY.
TOTAL KNOWN FACILITY PERSONNEL, INCLUDING DECAUL AND CARTER-- SIX.
AMBIENT NOISE LEVEL ALMOST ZERO.
ONE MATTRESS, DOUBLE-STITCHED, NOT USED RECENTLY, ONE PILLOW, SAME. ODOR INDICATES USE OF PROBAN OR SIMILAR FLAME-RETARDANT PRODUCT.
METAL BED-FRAME BOLTED TO THE CONCRETE.
...MR. SAVANT?
YOU DIDN'T LEAVE ME MUCH TO ESCAPE WITH.
BUT I STILL DON'T PLAN TO STAY, FELLAS. BET ON THAT.
DINAH'S NEVER GOING TO LET ME LIVE THIS DOWN, BEING CAPTURED BY MORONS.
ASSUMING I TELL HER, OF COURSE.
OTHER POSSIBLE ASSETS INCLUDE METAL SINK AND COMMODE, ONE PAIR EYEGLASSES...

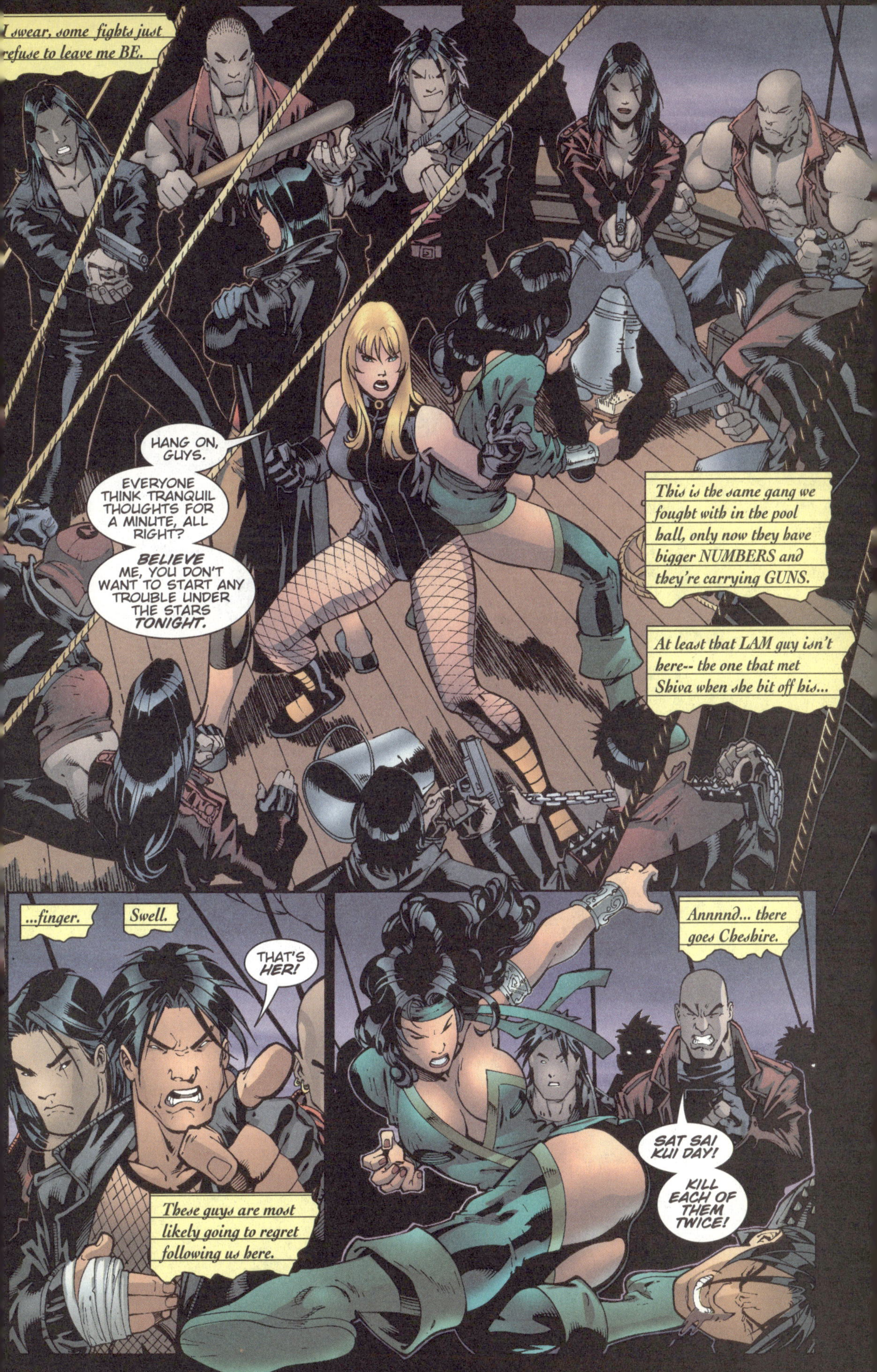

I swear, some fights just refuse to leave me BE.
HANG ON, GUYS.
EVERYONE THINK TRANQUIL THOUGHTS FOR A MINUTE, ALL RIGHT?
BELIEVE ME, YOU DON'T WANT TO START ANY TROUBLE UNDER THE STARS TONIGHT.
This is the same gang we fought with in the pool hall, only now they have bigger NUMBERS and they're carrying GUNS.
At least that LAM guy isn't here-- the one that met Shiva when she bit off his...
...finger.
Swell.
THAT'S HER!
These guys are most likely going to regret following us here.
Annnnd... there goes Cheshire.
SAT SAI KUI DAY!
KILL EACH OF THEM TWICE!

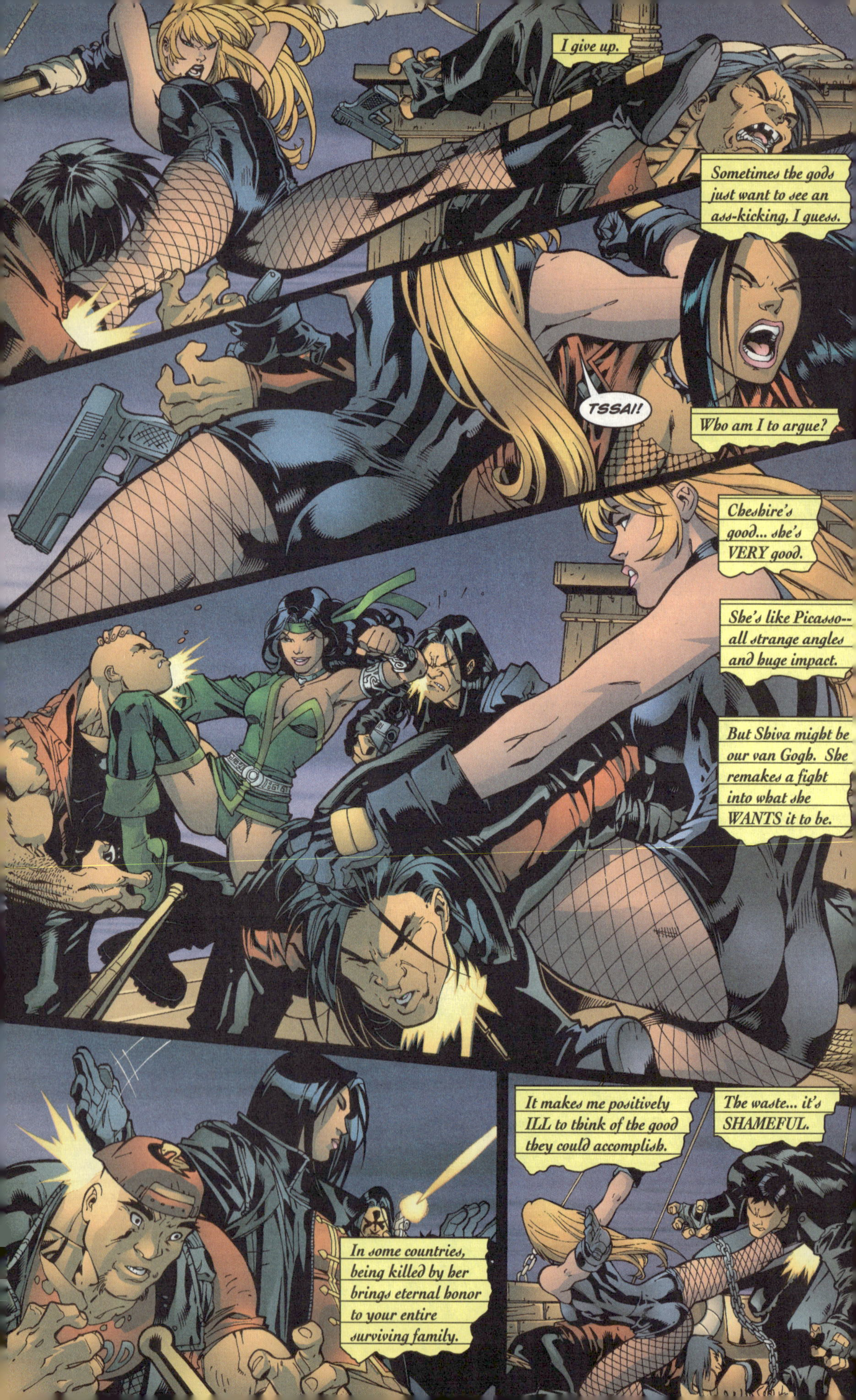
I give up.
Sometimes the gods just want to see an ass-kicking, I guess.
TSSAI!
Who am I to argue?
Cheshire's good... she's VERY good.
She's like Picasso--all strange angles and huge impact.
But Shiva might be our van Gogh. She remakes a fight into what she WANTS it to be.
In some countries, being killed by her brings eternal honor to your entire surviving family.
It makes me positively ILL to think of the good they could accomplish.
The waste... it's SHAMEFUL.

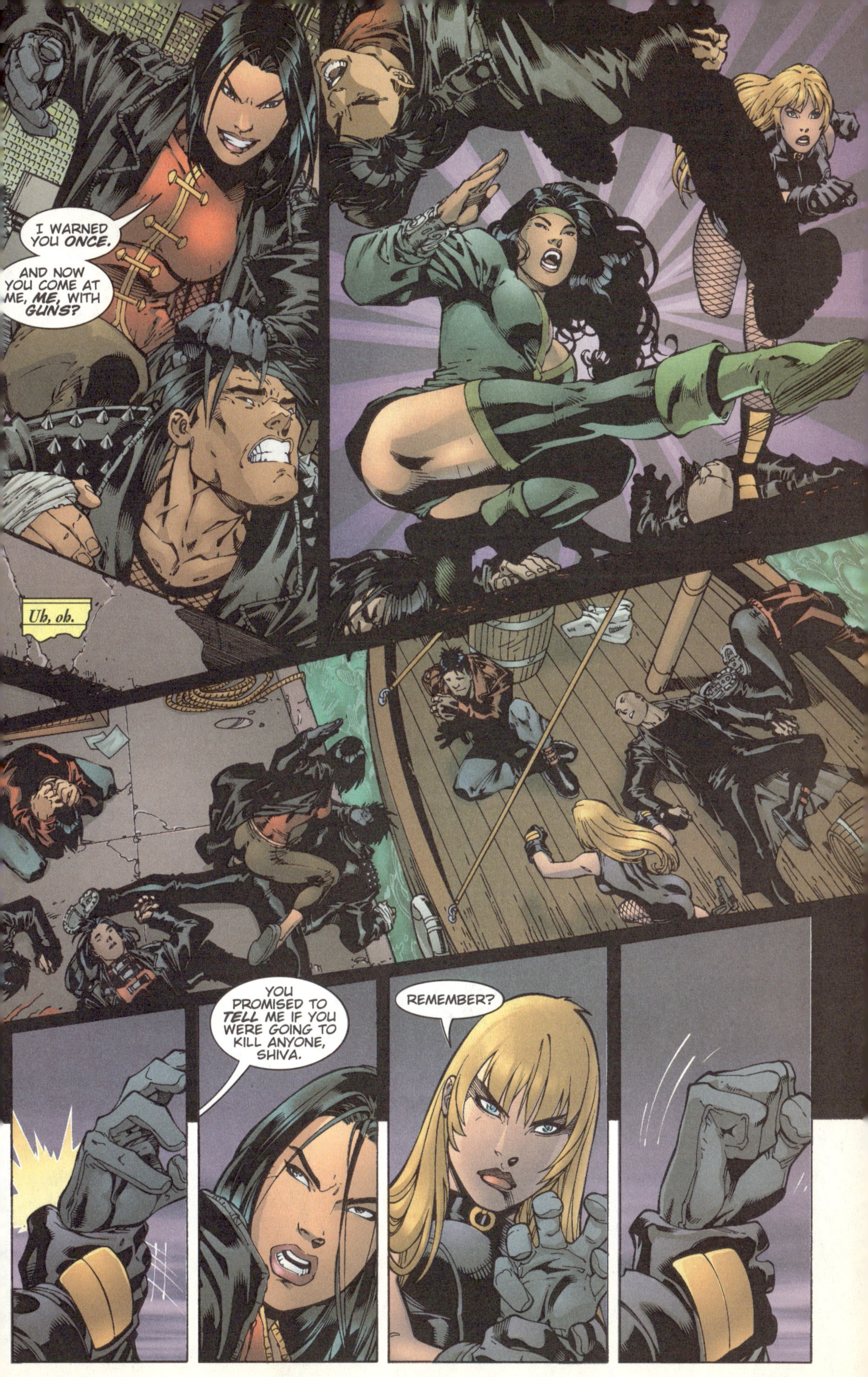
I WARNED YOU *ONCE.*
AND NOW YOU COME AT ME, ***ME,*** WITH ***GUNS?***
Uh, oh.
YOU PROMISED TO ***TELL*** ME IF YOU WERE GOING TO KILL ANYONE, SHIVA.
REMEMBER?

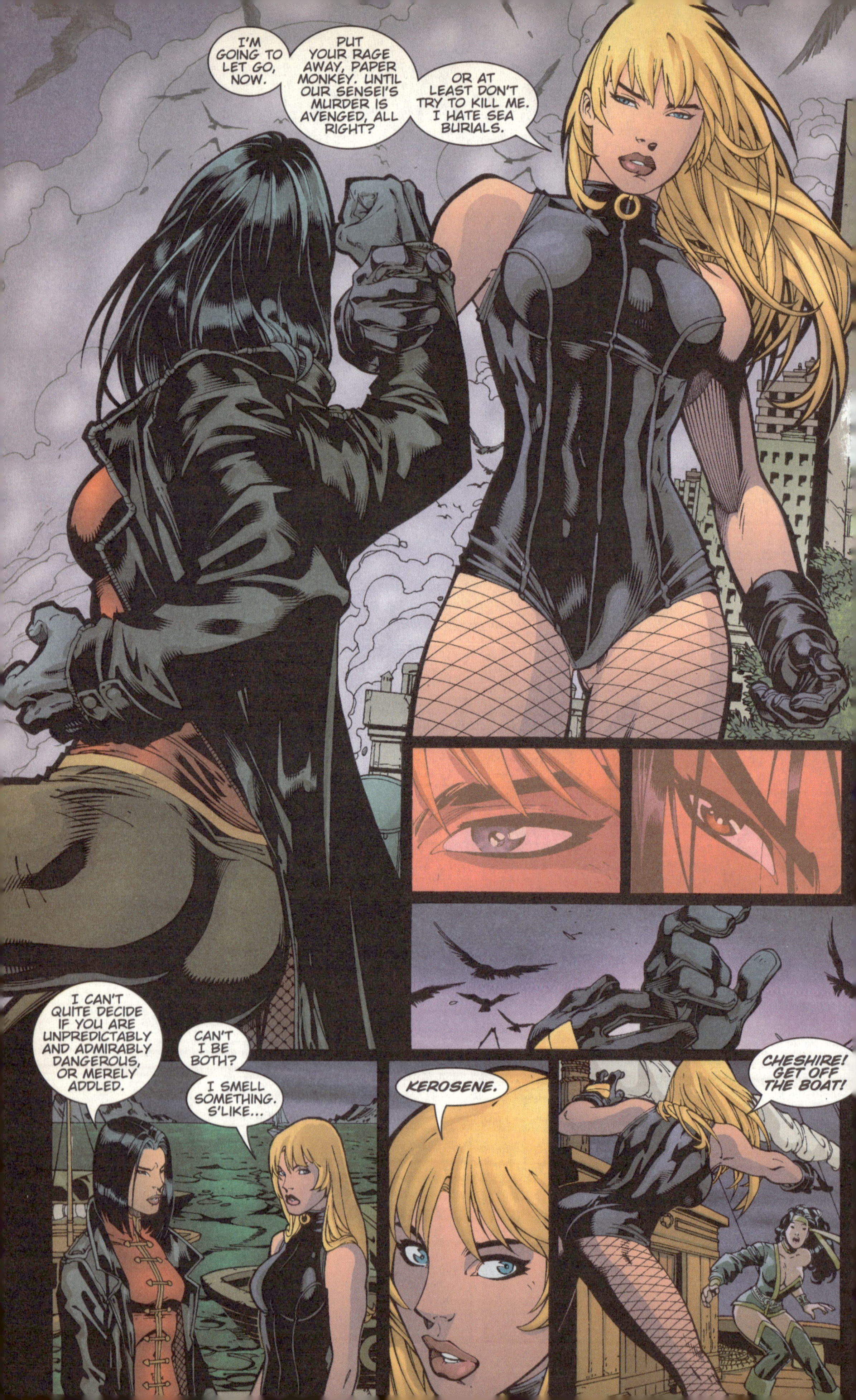

I'M GOING TO LET GO, NOW.
PUT YOUR RAGE AWAY, PAPER MONKEY. UNTIL OUR SENSEI'S MURDER IS AVENGED, ALL RIGHT?
OR AT LEAST DON'T TRY TO KILL ME. I HATE SEA BURIALS.
I CAN'T QUITE DECIDE IF YOU ARE UNPREDICTABLY AND ADMIRABLY DANGEROUS, OR MERELY ADDLED.
CAN'T I BE BOTH?
I SMELL SOMETHING. S'LIKE...
KEROSENE.
CHESHIRE! GET OFF THE BOAT!

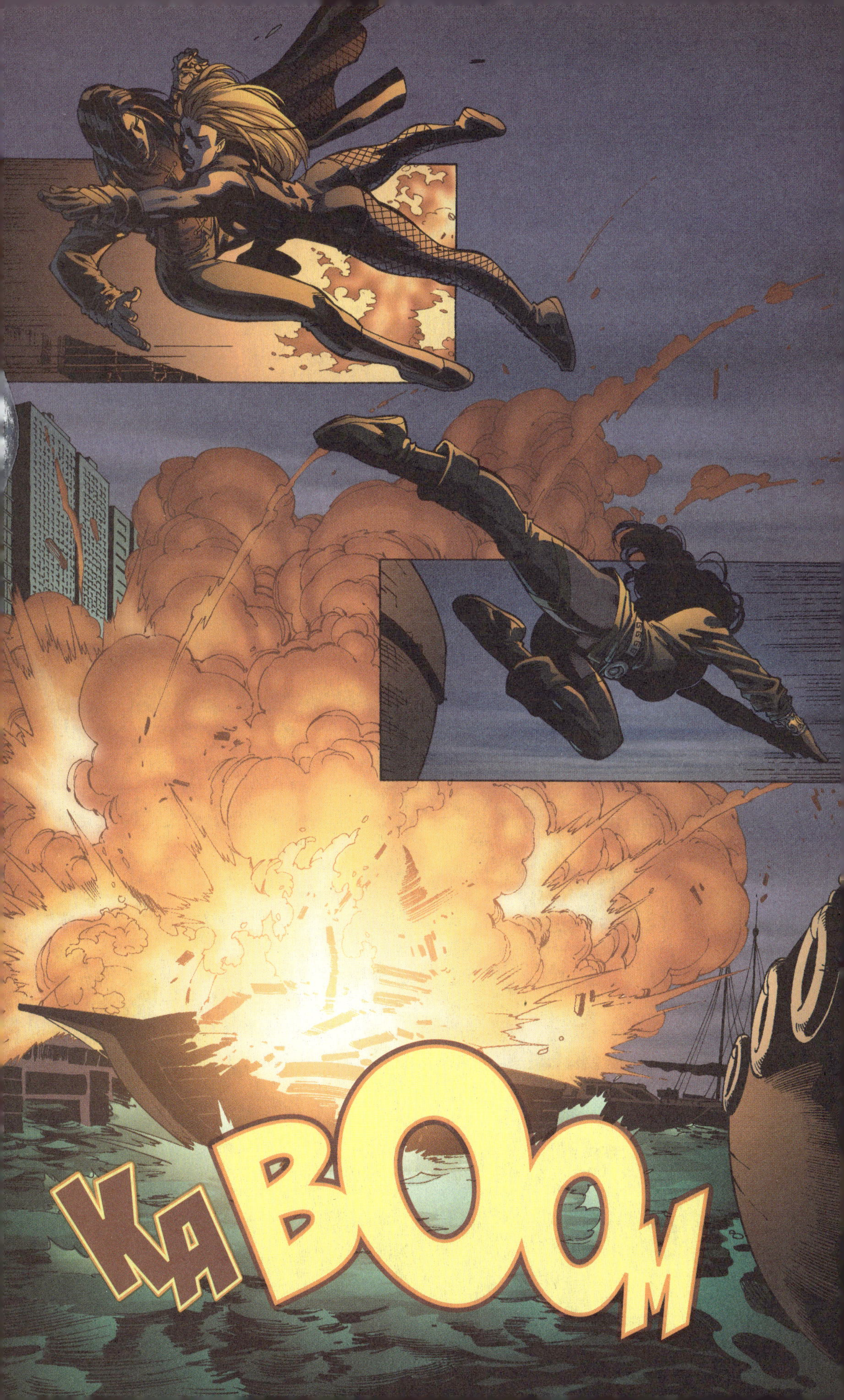
KABOOM

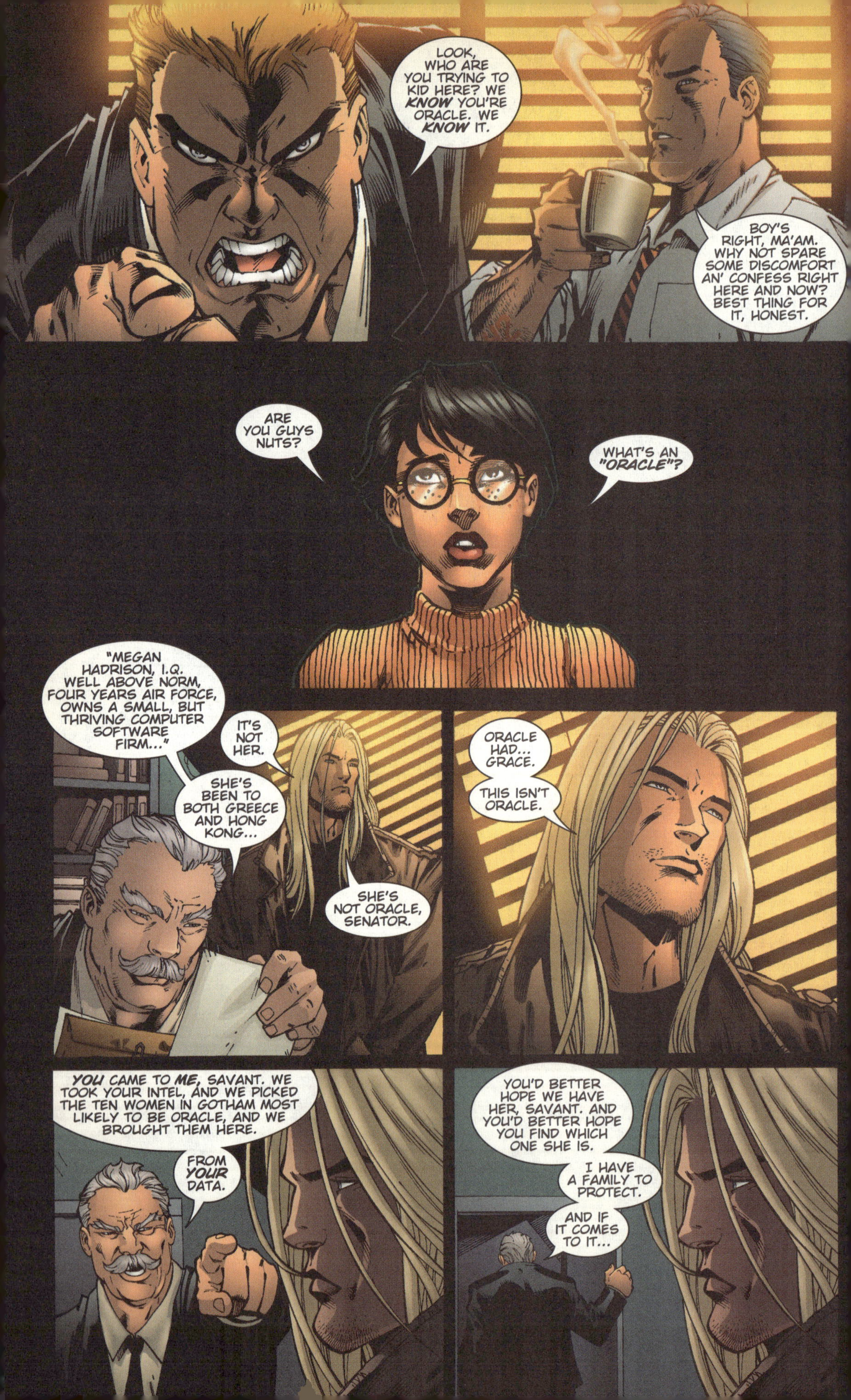
LOOK, WHO ARE YOU TRYING TO KID HERE? WE KNOW YOU'RE ORACLE. WE KNOW IT.
BOY'S RIGHT, MA'AM. WHY NOT SPARE SOME DISCOMFORT AN' CONFESS RIGHT HERE AND NOW? BEST THING FOR IT, HONEST.
ARE YOU GUYS NUTS?
WHAT'S AN "ORACLE"?
"MEGAN HADRISON, I.Q. WELL ABOVE NORM, FOUR YEARS AIR FORCE, OWNS A SMALL, BUT THRIVING COMPUTER SOFTWARE FIRM..."
IT'S NOT HER.
SHE'S BEEN TO BOTH GREECE AND HONG KONG...
SHE'S NOT ORACLE, SENATOR.
ORACLE HAD... GRACE.
THIS ISN'T ORACLE.
YOU CAME TO ME, SAVANT. WE TOOK YOUR INTEL, AND WE PICKED THE TEN WOMEN IN GOTHAM MOST LIKELY TO BE ORACLE, AND WE BROUGHT THEM HERE.
FROM YOUR DATA.
YOU'D BETTER HOPE WE HAVE HER, SAVANT. AND YOU'D BETTER HOPE YOU FIND WHICH ONE SHE IS.
I HAVE A FAMILY TO PROTECT.
AND IF IT COMES TO IT...

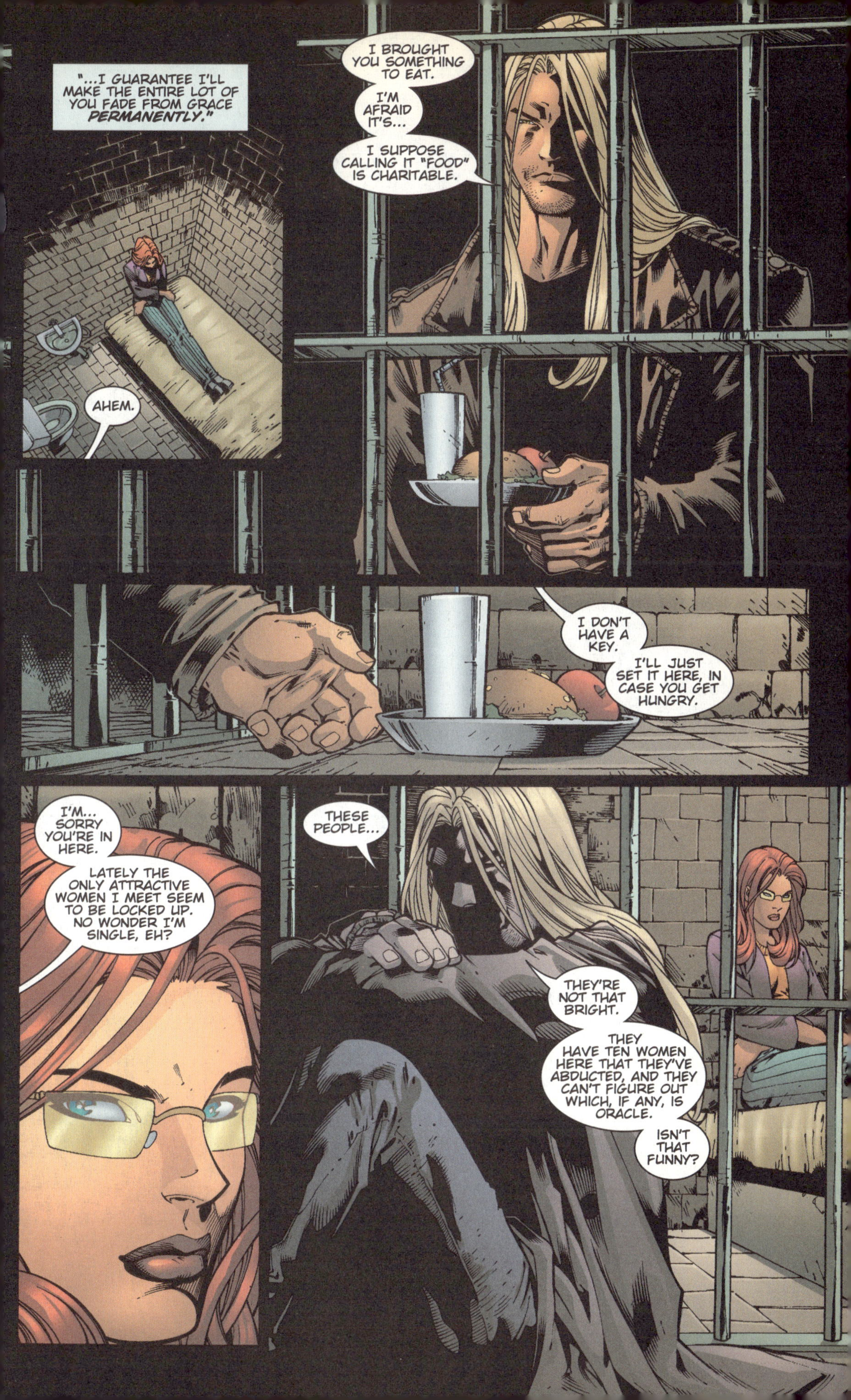
"...I GUARANTEE I'LL MAKE THE ENTIRE LOT OF YOU FADE FROM GRACE *PERMANENTLY.*"
AHEM.
I BROUGHT YOU SOMETHING TO EAT.
I'M AFRAID IT'S...
I SUPPOSE CALLING IT "FOOD" IS CHARITABLE.
I DON'T HAVE A KEY.
I'LL JUST SET IT HERE, IN CASE YOU GET HUNGRY.
I'M... SORRY YOU'RE IN HERE.
LATELY THE ONLY ATTRACTIVE WOMEN I MEET SEEM TO BE LOCKED UP. NO WONDER I'M SINGLE, EH?
THESE PEOPLE...
THEY'RE NOT THAT BRIGHT.
THEY HAVE TEN WOMEN HERE THAT THEY'VE ABDUCTED, AND THEY CAN'T FIGURE OUT WHICH, IF ANY, IS ORACLE.
ISN'T THAT FUNNY?

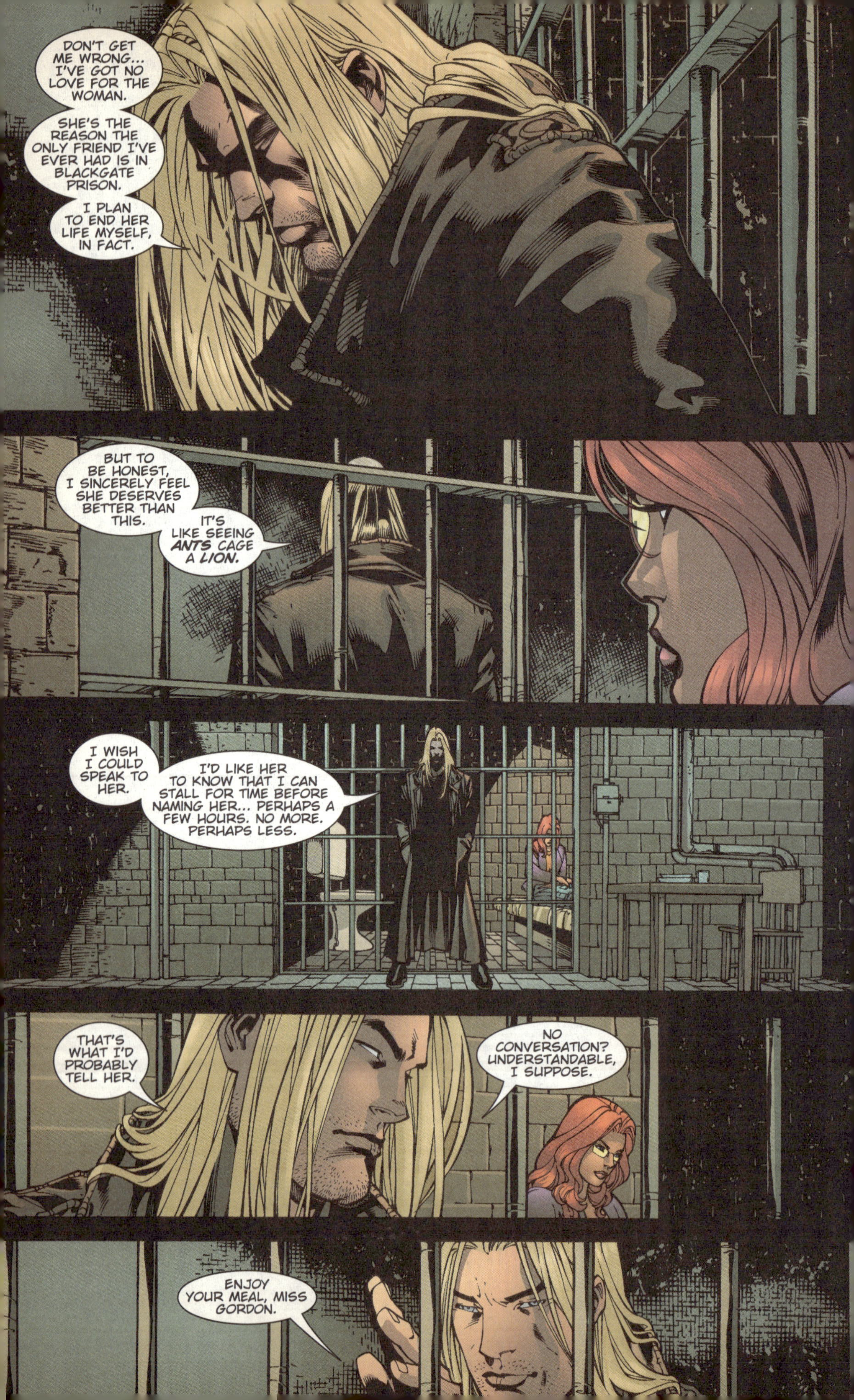
DON'T GET ME WRONG... I'VE GOT NO LOVE FOR THE WOMAN.
SHE'S THE REASON THE ONLY FRIEND I'VE EVER HAD IS IN BLACKGATE PRISON.
I PLAN TO END HER LIFE MYSELF, IN FACT.
BUT TO BE HONEST, I SINCERELY FEEL SHE DESERVES BETTER THAN THIS.
IT'S LIKE SEEING **ANTS** CAGE A **LION.**
I WISH I COULD SPEAK TO HER.
I'D LIKE HER TO KNOW THAT I CAN STALL FOR TIME BEFORE NAMING HER... PERHAPS A FEW HOURS. NO MORE. PERHAPS LESS.
THAT'S WHAT I'D PROBABLY TELL HER.
NO CONVERSATION? UNDERSTANDABLE, I SUPPOSE.
ENJOY YOUR MEAL, MISS GORDON.

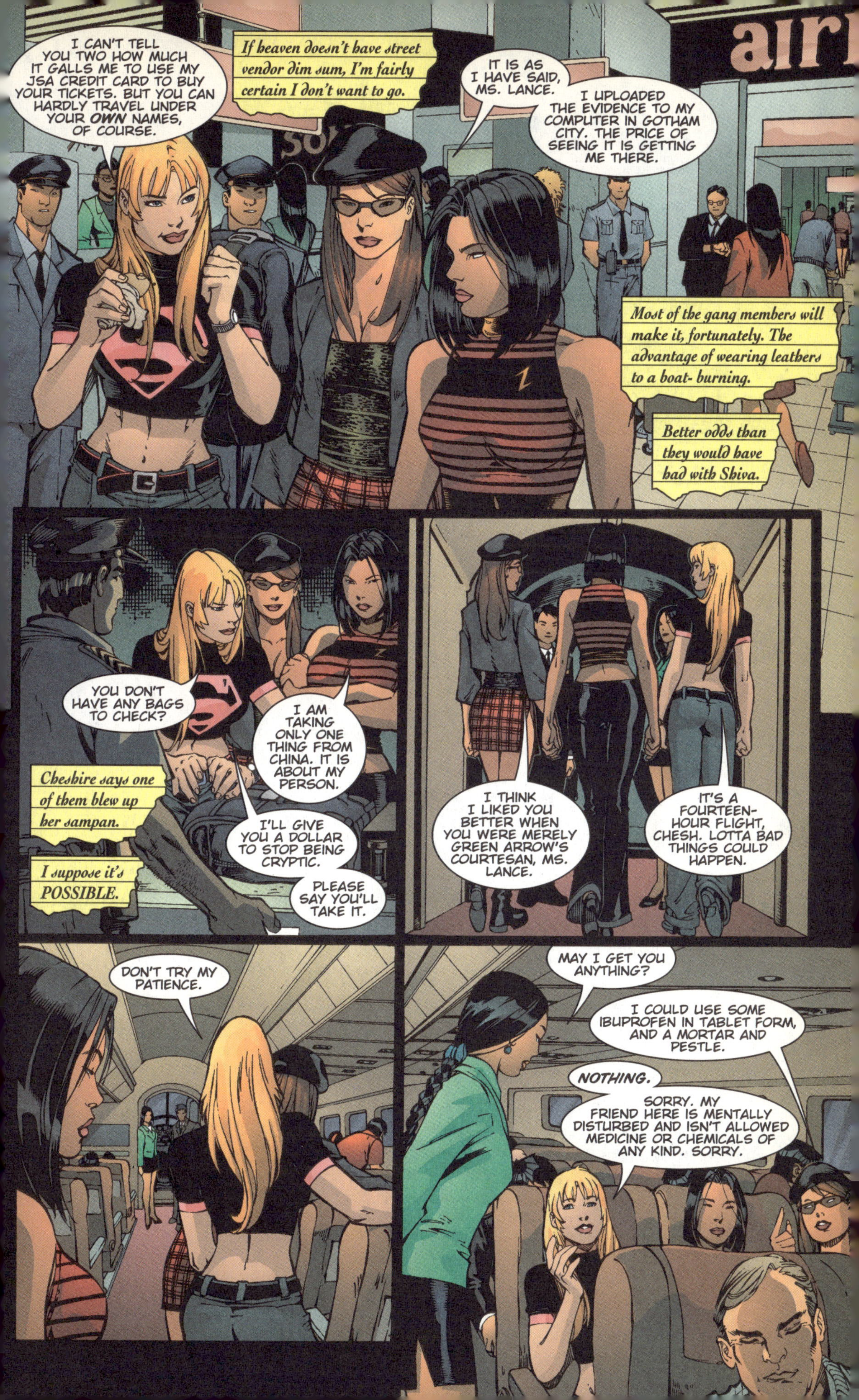
I CAN'T TELL YOU TWO HOW MUCH IT GALLS ME TO USE MY JSA CREDIT CARD TO BUY YOUR TICKETS. BUT YOU CAN HARDLY TRAVEL UNDER YOUR *OWN* NAMES, OF COURSE.
If heaven doesn't have street vendor dim sum, I'm fairly certain I don't want to go.
IT IS AS I HAVE SAID, MS. LANCE.
I UPLOADED THE EVIDENCE TO MY COMPUTER IN GOTHAM CITY. THE PRICE OF SEEING IT IS GETTING ME THERE.
air
Most of the gang members will make it, fortunately. The advantage of wearing leathers to a boat-burning.
Better odds than they would have had with Shiva.
YOU DON'T HAVE ANY BAGS TO CHECK?
I AM TAKING ONLY ONE THING FROM CHINA. IT IS ABOUT MY PERSON.
Cheshire says one of them blew up her sampan.
I'LL GIVE YOU A DOLLAR TO STOP BEING CRYPTIC.
I suppose it's POSSIBLE.
PLEASE SAY YOU'LL TAKE IT.
I THINK I LIKED YOU BETTER WHEN YOU WERE MERELY GREEN ARROW'S COURTESAN, MS. LANCE.
IT'S A FOURTEEN-HOUR FLIGHT, CHESH. LOTTA BAD THINGS COULD HAPPEN.
DON'T TRY MY PATIENCE.
MAY I GET YOU ANYTHING?
I COULD USE SOME IBUPROFEN IN TABLET FORM, AND A MORTAR AND PESTLE.
NOTHING.
SORRY. MY FRIEND HERE IS MENTALLY DISTURBED AND ISN'T ALLOWED MEDICINE OR CHEMICALS OF ANY KIND. SORRY.

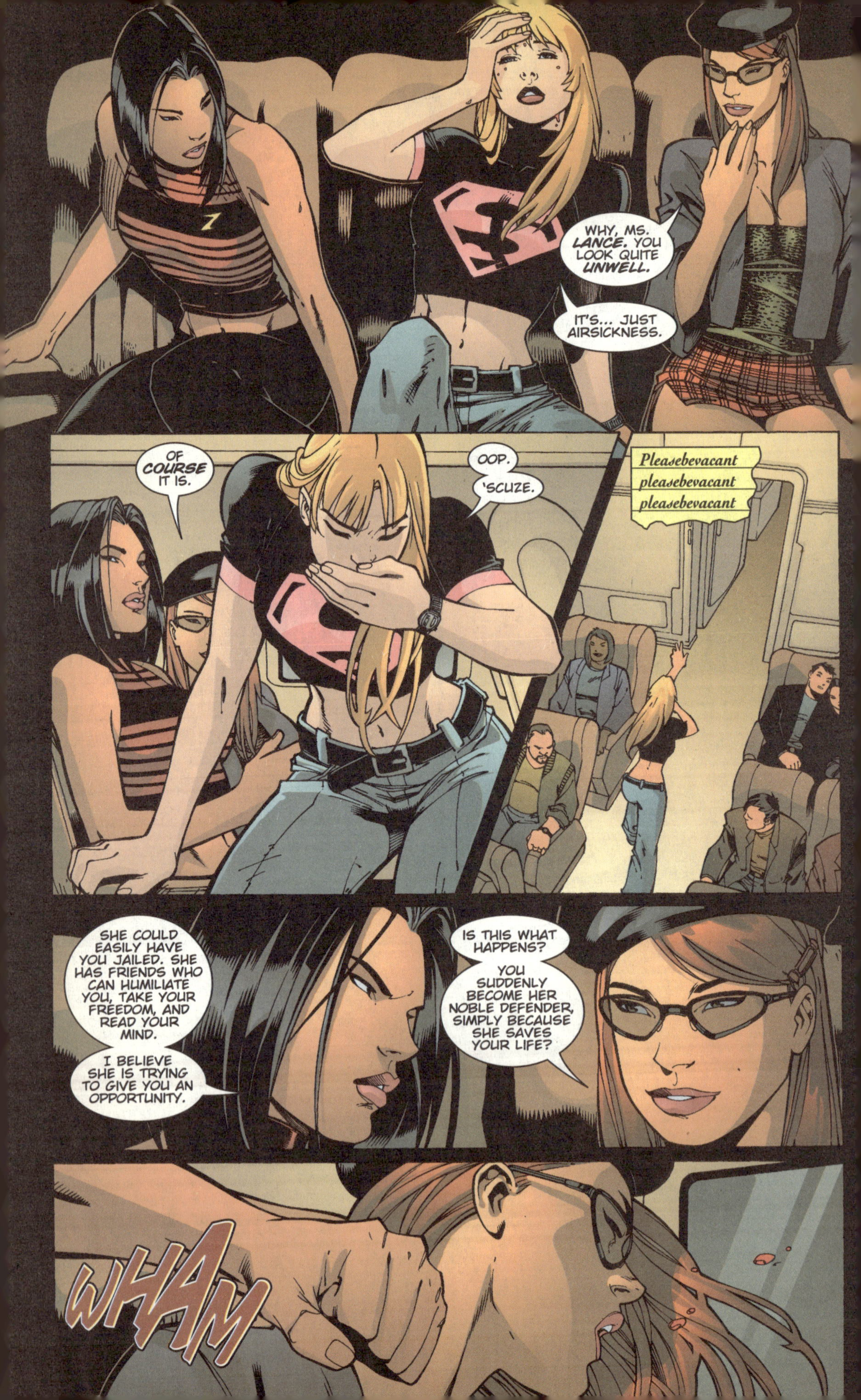
WHY, MS. LANCE. YOU LOOK QUITE UNWELL.
IT'S... JUST AIRSICKNESS.
OF COURSE IT IS.
OOP.
'SCUZE.
Pleasebevacant
pleasebevacant
pleasebevacant
SHE COULD EASILY HAVE YOU JAILED. SHE HAS FRIENDS WHO CAN HUMILIATE YOU, TAKE YOUR FREEDOM, AND READ YOUR MIND.
I BELIEVE SHE IS TRYING TO GIVE YOU AN OPPORTUNITY.
IS THIS WHAT HAPPENS?
YOU SUDDENLY BECOME HER NOBLE DEFENDER, SIMPLY BECAUSE SHE SAVES YOUR LIFE?
WHAM

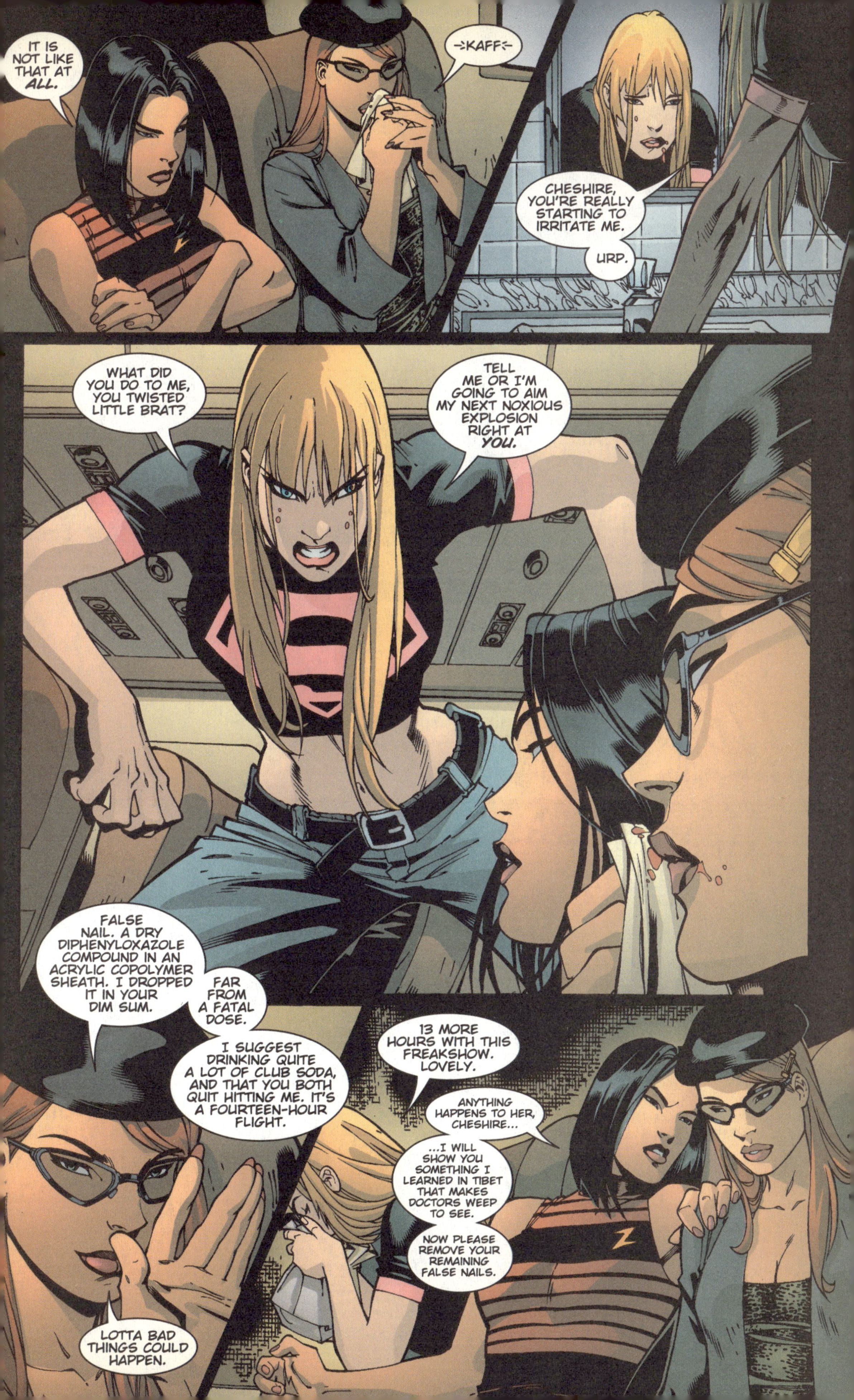
IT IS NOT LIKE THAT AT ALL.
-KAFF-
CHESHIRE, YOU'RE REALLY STARTING TO IRRITATE ME.
URP.
WHAT DID YOU DO TO ME, YOU TWISTED LITTLE BRAT?
TELL ME OR I'M GOING TO AIM MY NEXT NOXIOUS EXPLOSION RIGHT AT YOU.
FALSE NAIL. A DRY DIPHENYLOXAZOLE COMPOUND IN AN ACRYLIC COPOLYMER SHEATH. I DROPPED IT IN YOUR DIM SUM.
FAR FROM A FATAL DOSE.
I SUGGEST DRINKING QUITE A LOT OF CLUB SODA, AND THAT YOU BOTH QUIT HITTING ME. IT'S A FOURTEEN-HOUR FLIGHT.
LOTTA BAD THINGS COULD HAPPEN.
13 MORE HOURS WITH THIS FREAKSHOW. LOVELY.
ANYTHING HAPPENS TO HER, CHESHIRE...
...I WILL SHOW YOU SOMETHING I LEARNED IN TIBET THAT MAKES DOCTORS WEEP TO SEE.
NOW PLEASE REMOVE YOUR REMAINING FALSE NAILS.

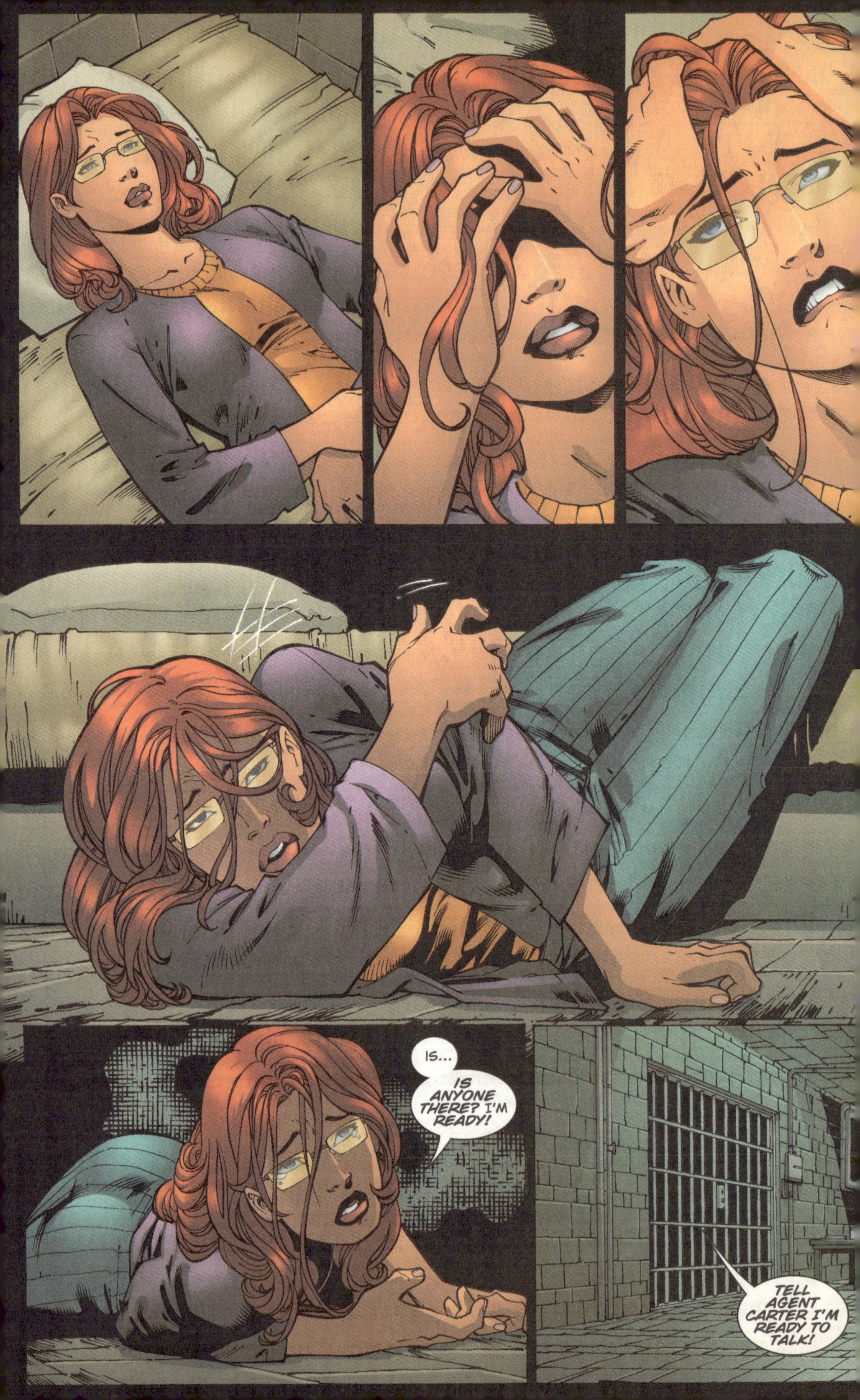
IS...
IS ANYONE THERE? I'M READY!
TELL AGENT CARTER I'M READY TO TALK!

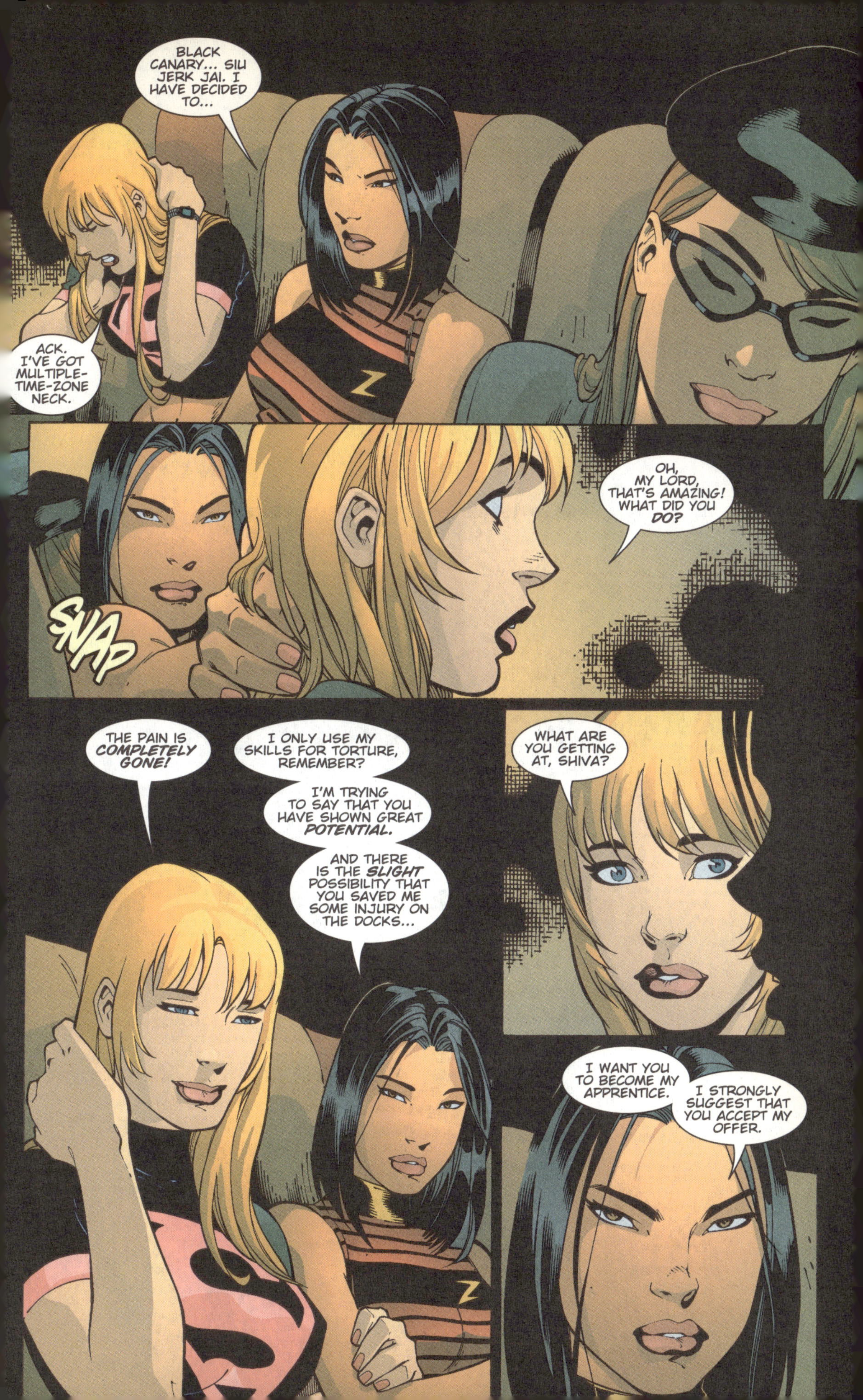
BLACK CANARY... SIU JERK JAI. I HAVE DECIDED TO...
ACK. I'VE GOT MULTIPLE-TIME-ZONE NECK.
SNAP
OH, MY LORD, THAT'S AMAZING! WHAT DID YOU *DO?*
THE PAIN IS *COMPLETELY GONE!*
I ONLY USE MY SKILLS FOR TORTURE, REMEMBER?
I'M TRYING TO SAY THAT YOU HAVE SHOWN GREAT *POTENTIAL.*
AND THERE IS THE *SLIGHT* POSSIBILITY THAT YOU SAVED ME SOME INJURY ON THE DOCKS...
WHAT ARE YOU GETTING AT, SHIVA?
I WANT YOU TO BECOME MY APPRENTICE.
I STRONGLY SUGGEST THAT YOU ACCEPT MY OFFER.

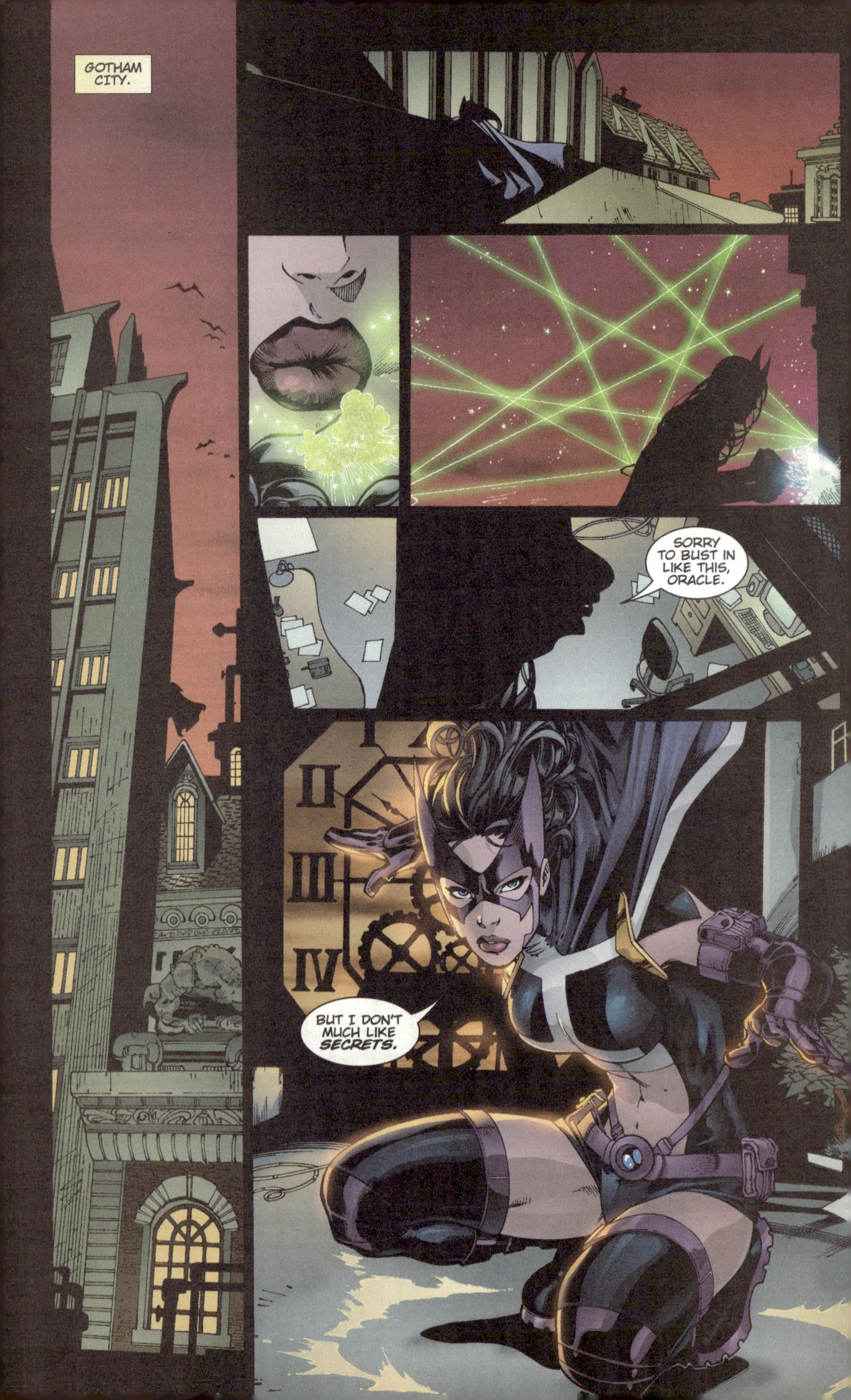
GOTHAM CITY.
SORRY TO BUST IN LIKE THIS, ORACLE.
BUT I DON'T MUCH LIKE SECRETS.

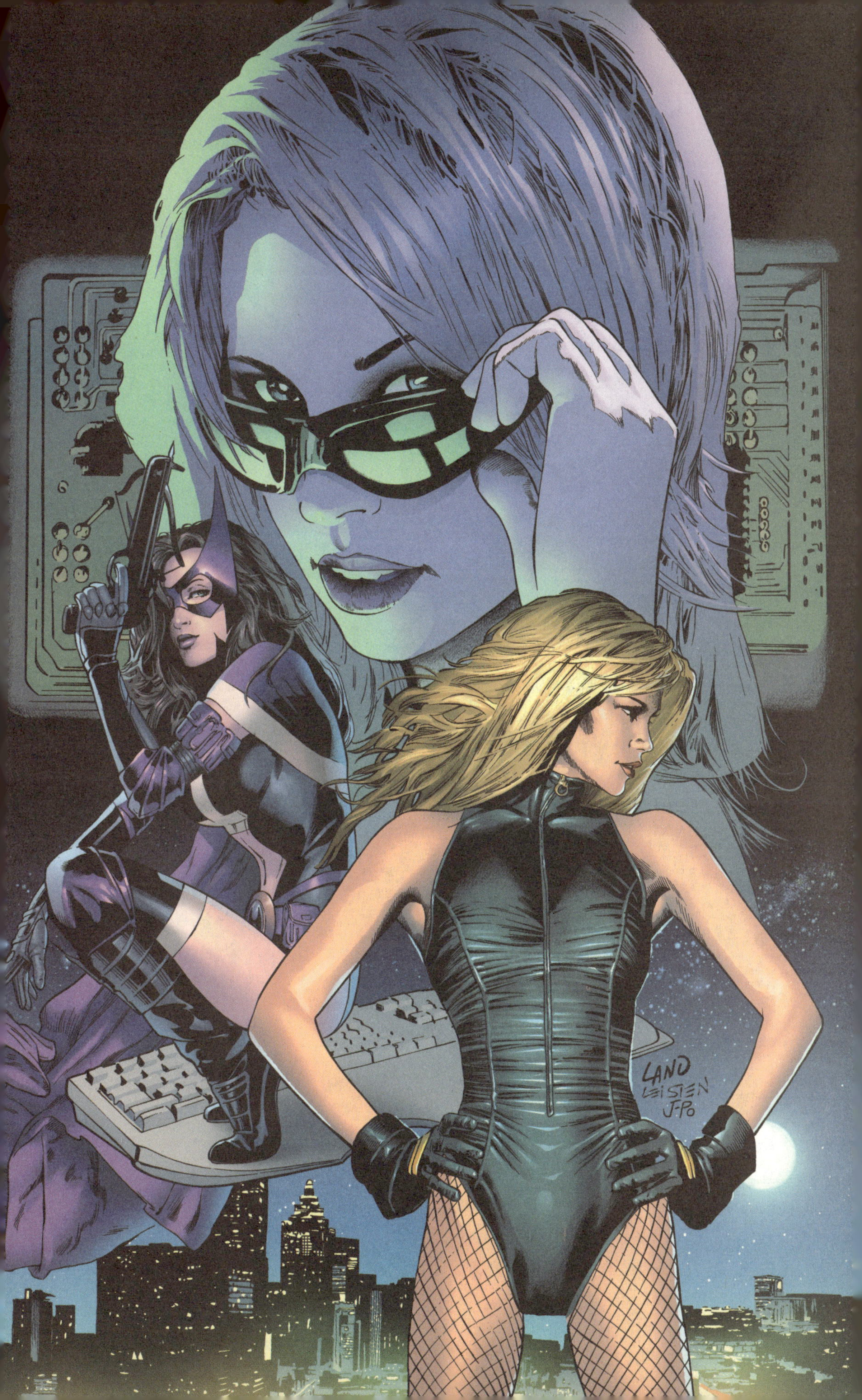
LAND
LEISEN
J-Po

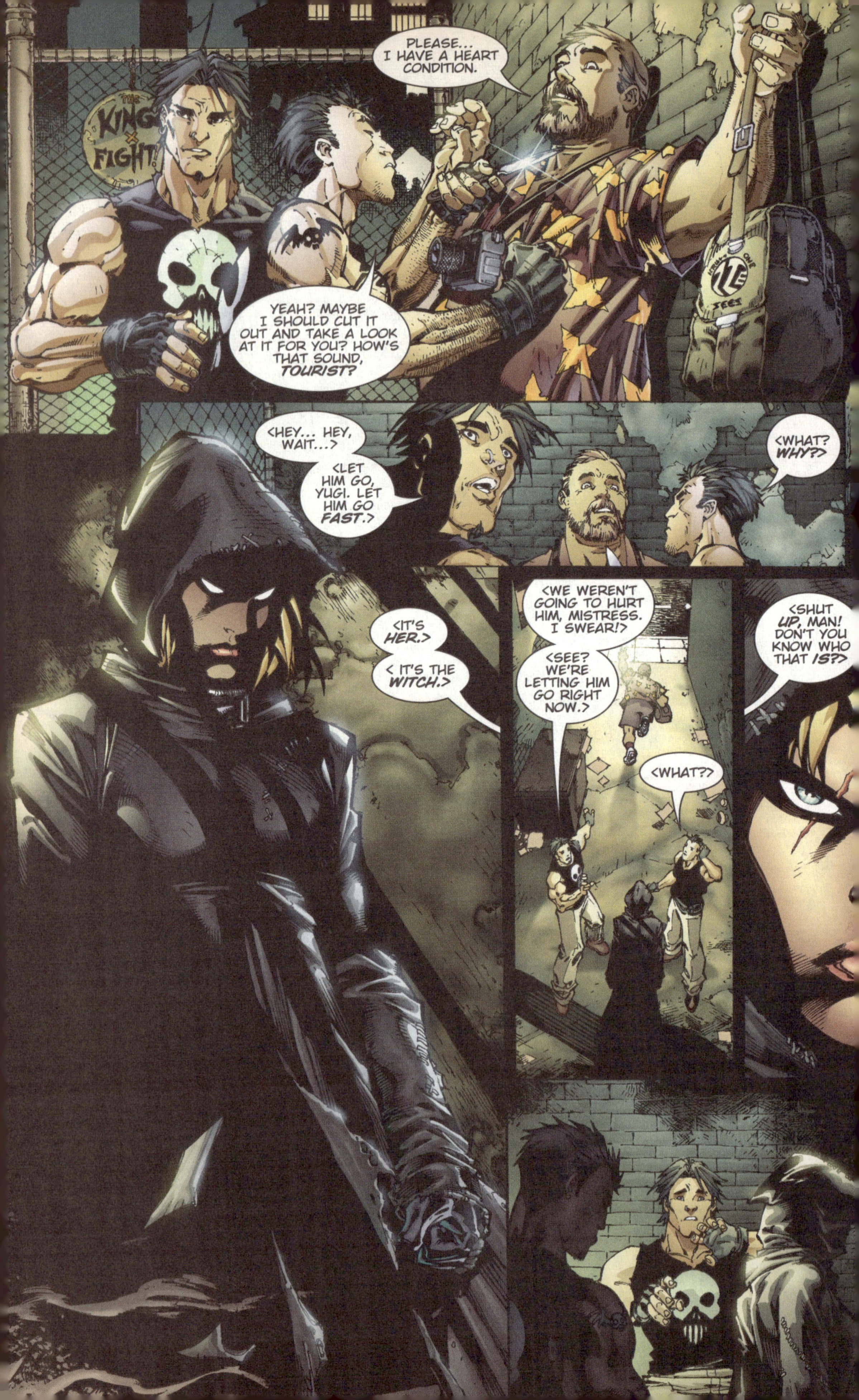

THE KING × FIGHT!
PLEASE... I HAVE A HEART CONDITION.
YEAH? MAYBE I SHOULD CUT IT OUT AND TAKE A LOOK AT IT FOR YOU? HOW'S THAT SOUND, *TOURIST?*
<HEY... HEY, WAIT...>
<LET HIM GO, YUGI. LET HIM GO *FAST*.>
<WHAT? *WHY?*>
<IT'S *HER*.>
< IT'S THE *WITCH*.>
<WE WEREN'T GOING TO HURT HIM, MISTRESS. I SWEAR!>
<SEE? WE'RE LETTING HIM GO RIGHT NOW.>
<WHAT??>
<SHUT *UP*, MAN! DON'T YOU KNOW WHO THAT *IS*?>

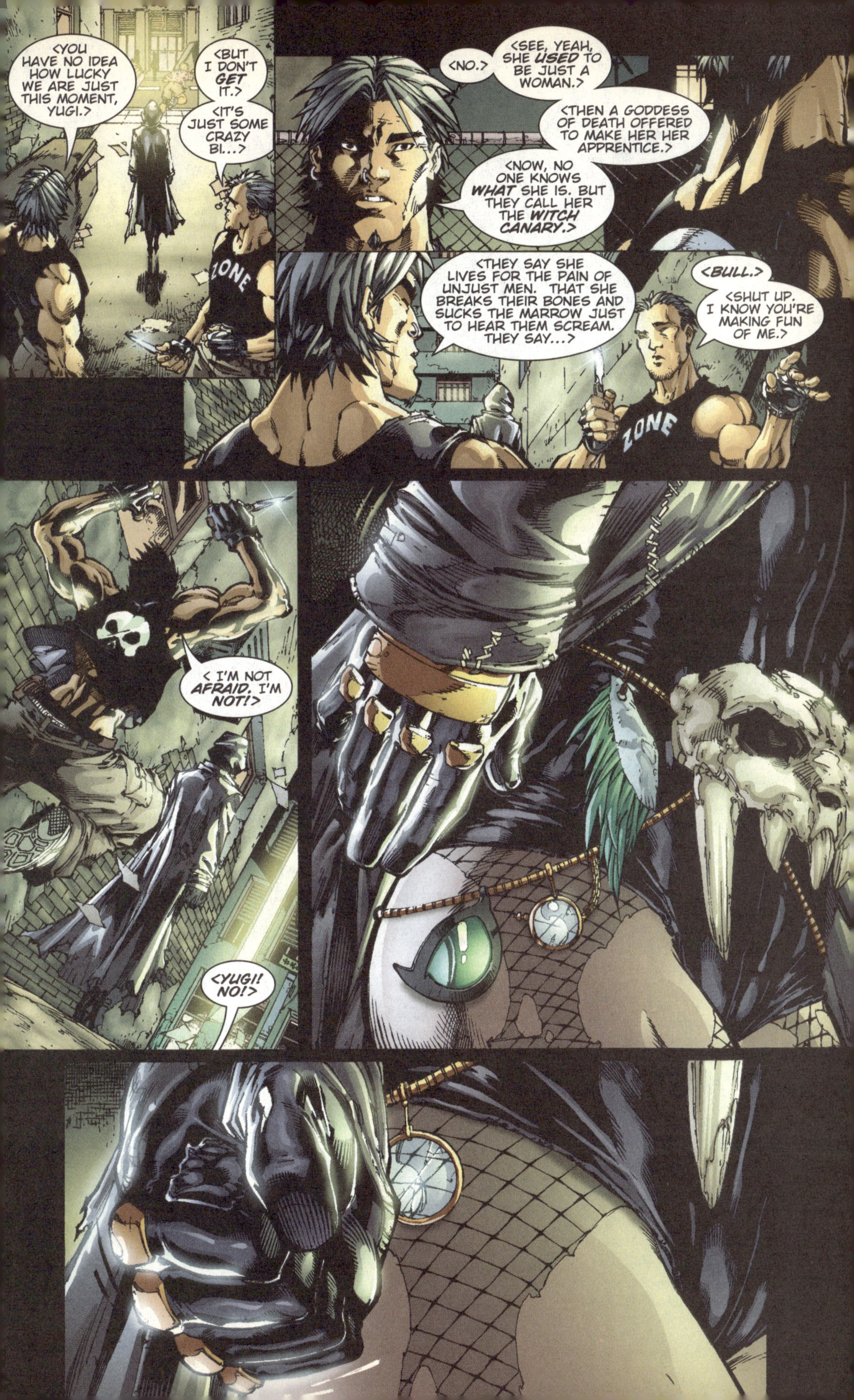
<YOU HAVE NO IDEA HOW LUCKY WE ARE JUST THIS MOMENT, YUGI.>
<BUT I DON'T *GET* IT.>
<IT'S JUST SOME CRAZY BI...>
<NO.>
<SEE, YEAH, SHE *USED* TO BE JUST A WOMAN.>
<THEN A GODDESS OF DEATH OFFERED TO MAKE HER HER APPRENTICE.>
<NOW, NO ONE KNOWS *WHAT* SHE IS. BUT THEY CALL HER THE *WITCH CANARY*.>
<THEY SAY SHE LIVES FOR THE PAIN OF UNJUST MEN. THAT SHE BREAKS THEIR BONES AND SUCKS THE MARROW JUST TO HEAR THEM SCREAM. THEY SAY...>
<*BULL*.>
<SHUT UP. I KNOW YOU'RE MAKING FUN OF ME.>
< I'M NOT *AFRAID*. I'M *NOT*!>
<*YUGI! NO!*>

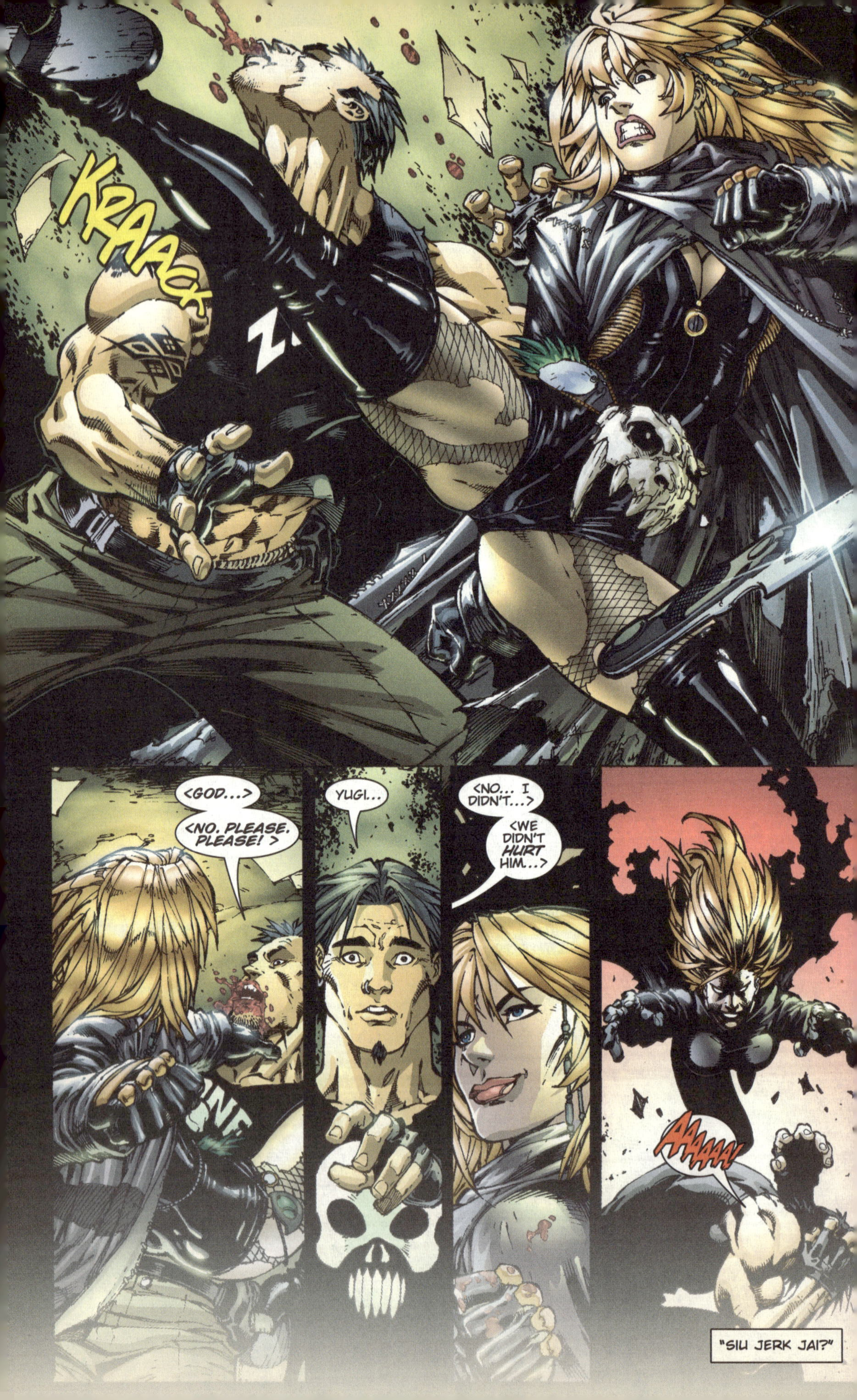
KRAAACK
<GOD...>
<NO. PLEASE. PLEASE! >
YUGI...
<NO... I DIDN'T...>
<WE DIDN'T HURT HIM...>
AAAAAA!
"SIU JERK JAI?"

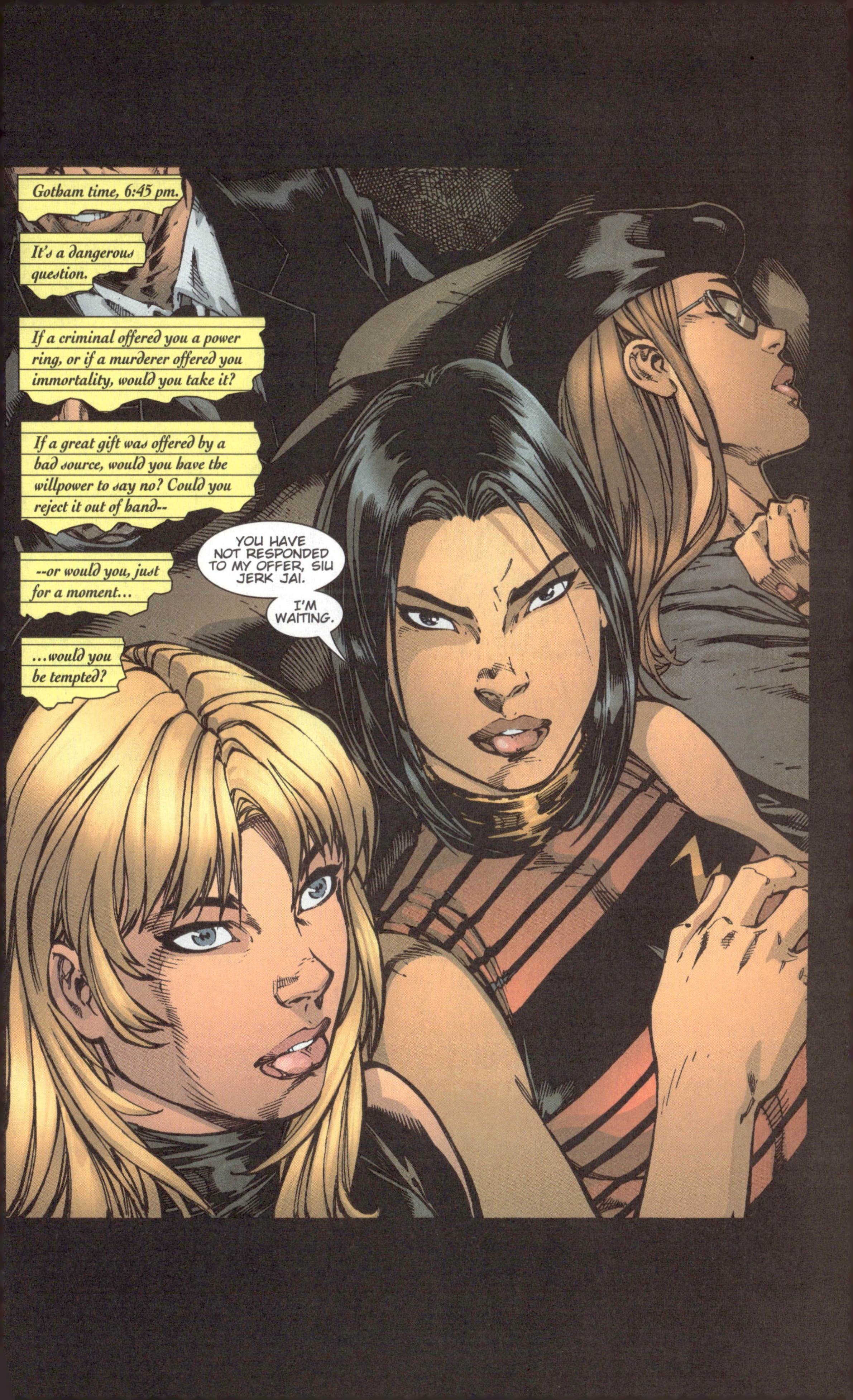
Gotham time, 6:45 pm.
It's a dangerous question.
If a criminal offered you a power ring, or if a murderer offered you immortality, would you take it?
If a great gift was offered by a bad source, would you have the willpower to say no? Could you reject it out of hand--
--or would you, just for a moment...
...would you be tempted?
YOU HAVE NOT RESPONDED TO MY OFFER, SIU JERK JAI.
I'M WAITING.

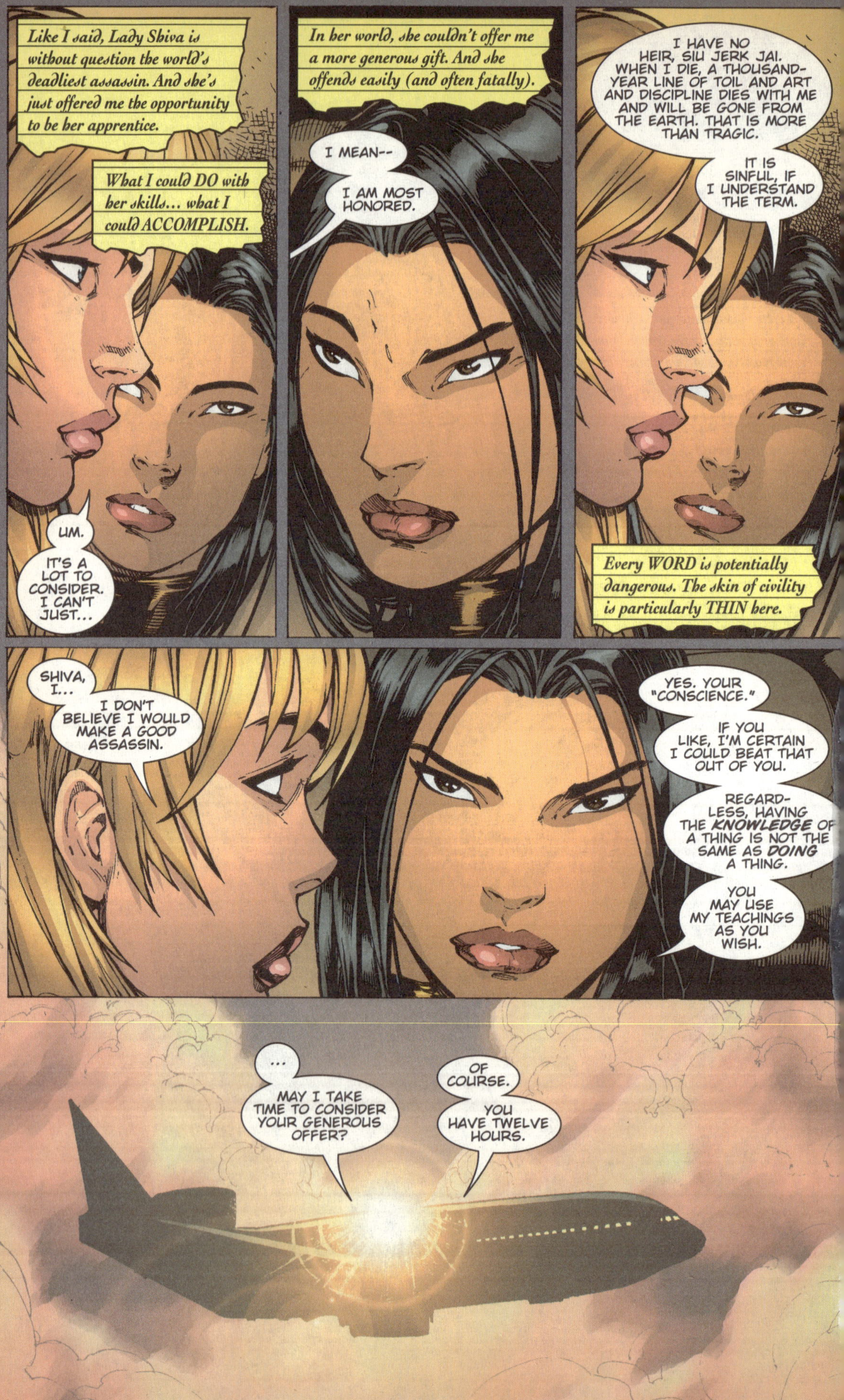
Like I said, Lady Shiva is without question the world's deadliest assassin. And she's just offered me the opportunity to be her apprentice.
What I could DO with her skills... what I could ACCOMPLISH.
UM.
IT'S A LOT TO CONSIDER. I CAN'T JUST...
In her world, she couldn't offer me a more generous gift. And she offends easily (and often fatally).
I MEAN--
I AM MOST HONORED.
I HAVE NO HEIR, SIU JERK JAI. WHEN I DIE, A THOUSAND-YEAR LINE OF TOIL AND ART AND DISCIPLINE DIES WITH ME AND WILL BE GONE FROM THE EARTH. THAT IS MORE THAN TRAGIC.
IT IS SINFUL, IF I UNDERSTAND THE TERM.
Every WORD is potentially dangerous. The skin of civility is particularly THIN here.
SHIVA, I...
I DON'T BELIEVE I WOULD MAKE A GOOD ASSASSIN.
YES. YOUR "CONSCIENCE."
IF YOU LIKE, I'M CERTAIN I COULD BEAT THAT OUT OF YOU.
REGARD-LESS, HAVING THE KNOWLEDGE OF A THING IS NOT THE SAME AS DOING A THING.
YOU MAY USE MY TEACHINGS AS YOU WISH.
...
MAY I TAKE TIME TO CONSIDER YOUR GENEROUS OFFER?
OF COURSE.
YOU HAVE TWELVE HOURS.

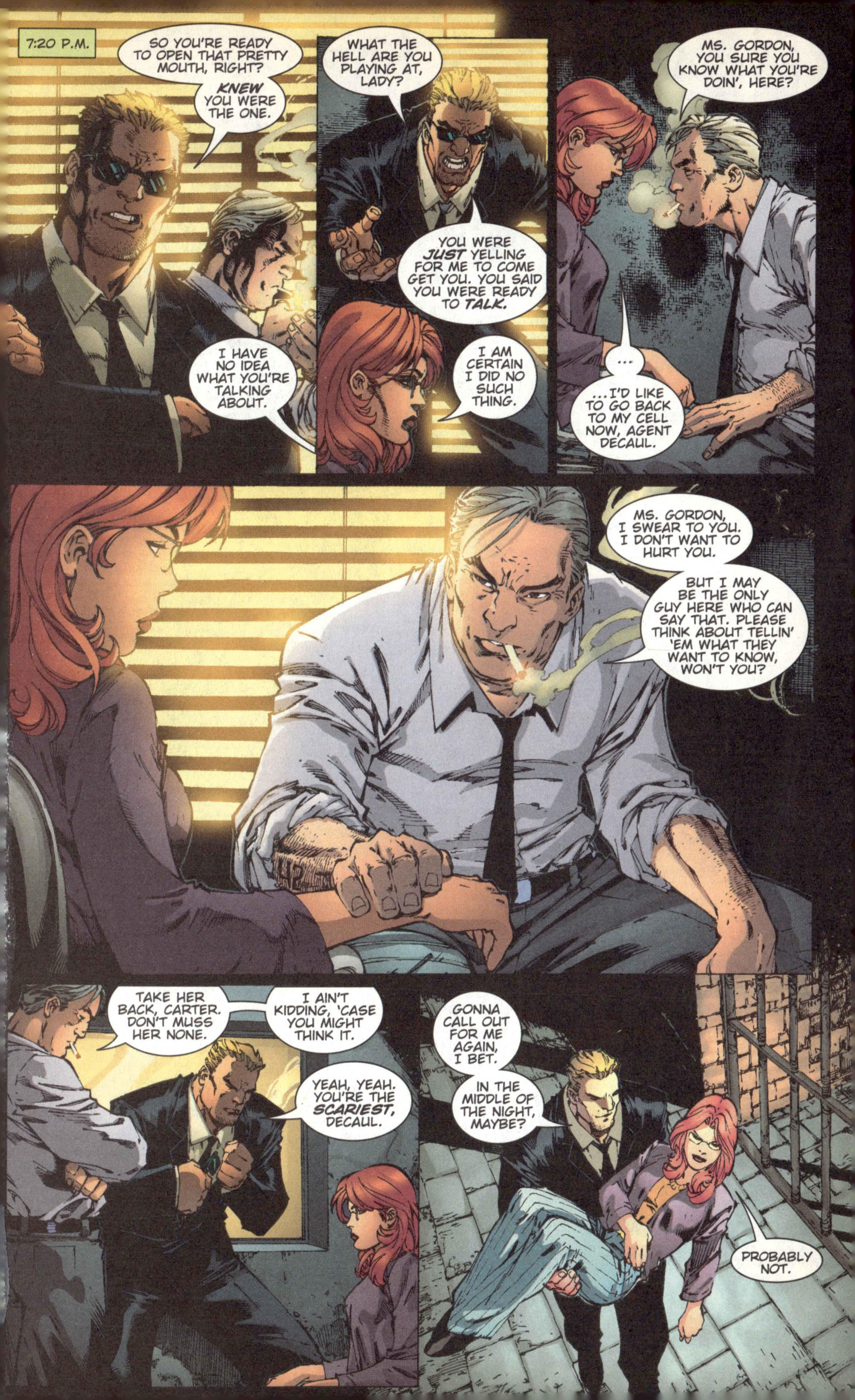
7:20 P.M.
SO YOU'RE READY TO OPEN THAT PRETTY MOUTH, RIGHT? KNEW YOU WERE THE ONE.
I HAVE NO IDEA WHAT YOU'RE TALKING ABOUT.
WHAT THE HELL ARE YOU PLAYING AT, LADY?
YOU WERE JUST YELLING FOR ME TO COME GET YOU. YOU SAID YOU WERE READY TO TALK.
I AM CERTAIN I DID NO SUCH THING.
MS. GORDON, YOU SURE YOU KNOW WHAT YOU'RE DOIN', HERE?
...
...I'D LIKE TO GO BACK TO MY CELL NOW, AGENT DECAUL.
MS. GORDON, I SWEAR TO YOU. I DON'T WANT TO HURT YOU.
BUT I MAY BE THE ONLY GUY HERE WHO CAN SAY THAT. PLEASE THINK ABOUT TELLIN' 'EM WHAT THEY WANT TO KNOW, WON'T YOU?
TAKE HER BACK, CARTER. DON'T MUSS HER NONE.
I AIN'T KIDDING, 'CASE YOU MIGHT THINK IT.
YEAH, YEAH. YOU'RE THE SCARIEST, DECAUL.
GONNA CALL OUT FOR ME AGAIN, I BET.
IN THE MIDDLE OF THE NIGHT, MAYBE?
PROBABLY NOT.

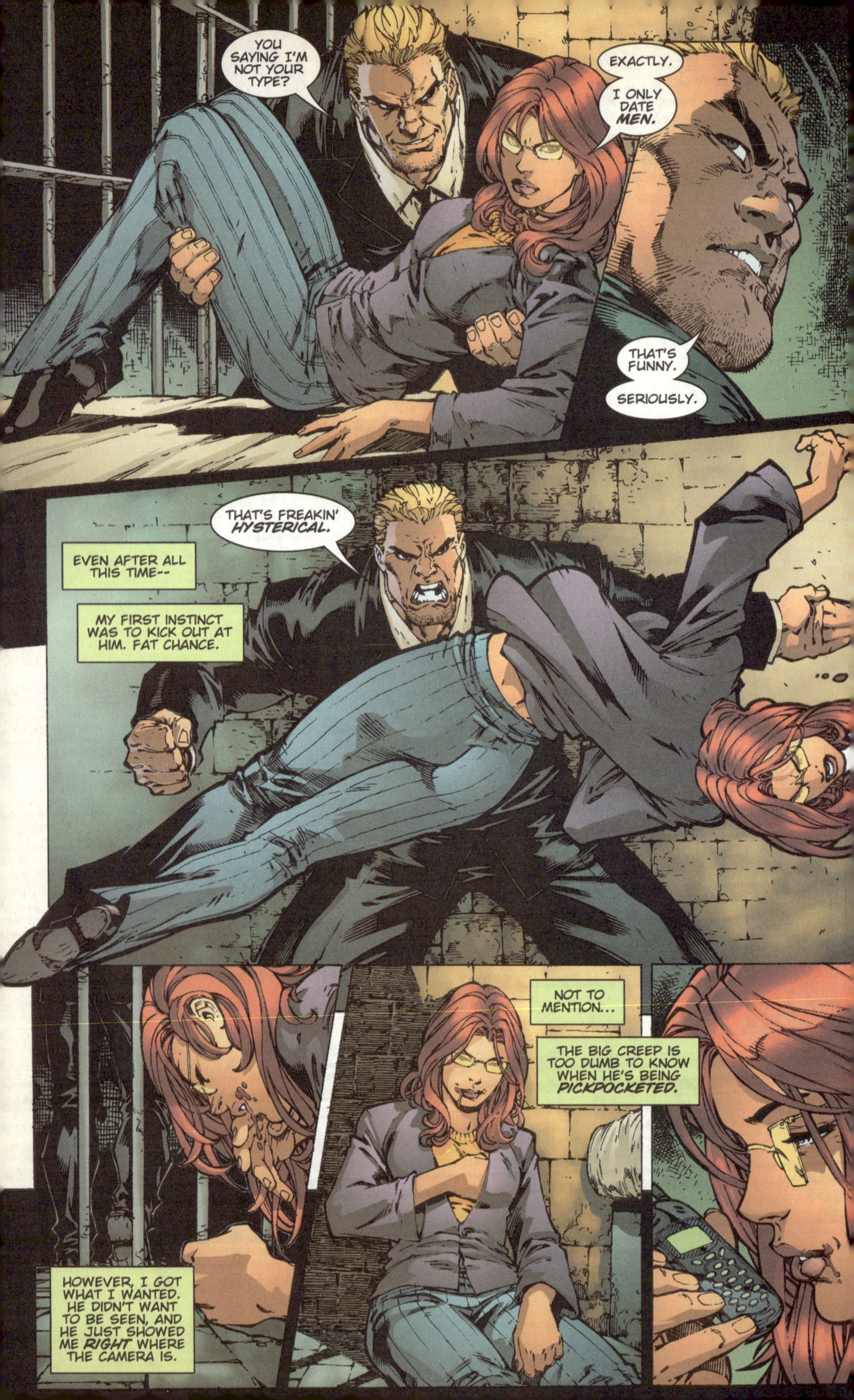

YOU SAYING I'M NOT YOUR TYPE?
EXACTLY.
I ONLY DATE *MEN.*
THAT'S FUNNY.
SERIOUSLY.
THAT'S FREAKIN' *HYSTERICAL.*
EVEN AFTER ALL THIS TIME--
MY FIRST INSTINCT WAS TO KICK OUT AT HIM. FAT CHANCE.
NOT TO MENTION...
THE BIG CREEP IS TOO DUMB TO KNOW WHEN HE'S BEING *PICKPOCKETED.*
HOWEVER, I GOT WHAT I WANTED. HE DIDN'T WANT TO BE SEEN, AND HE JUST SHOWED ME *RIGHT* WHERE THE CAMERA IS.

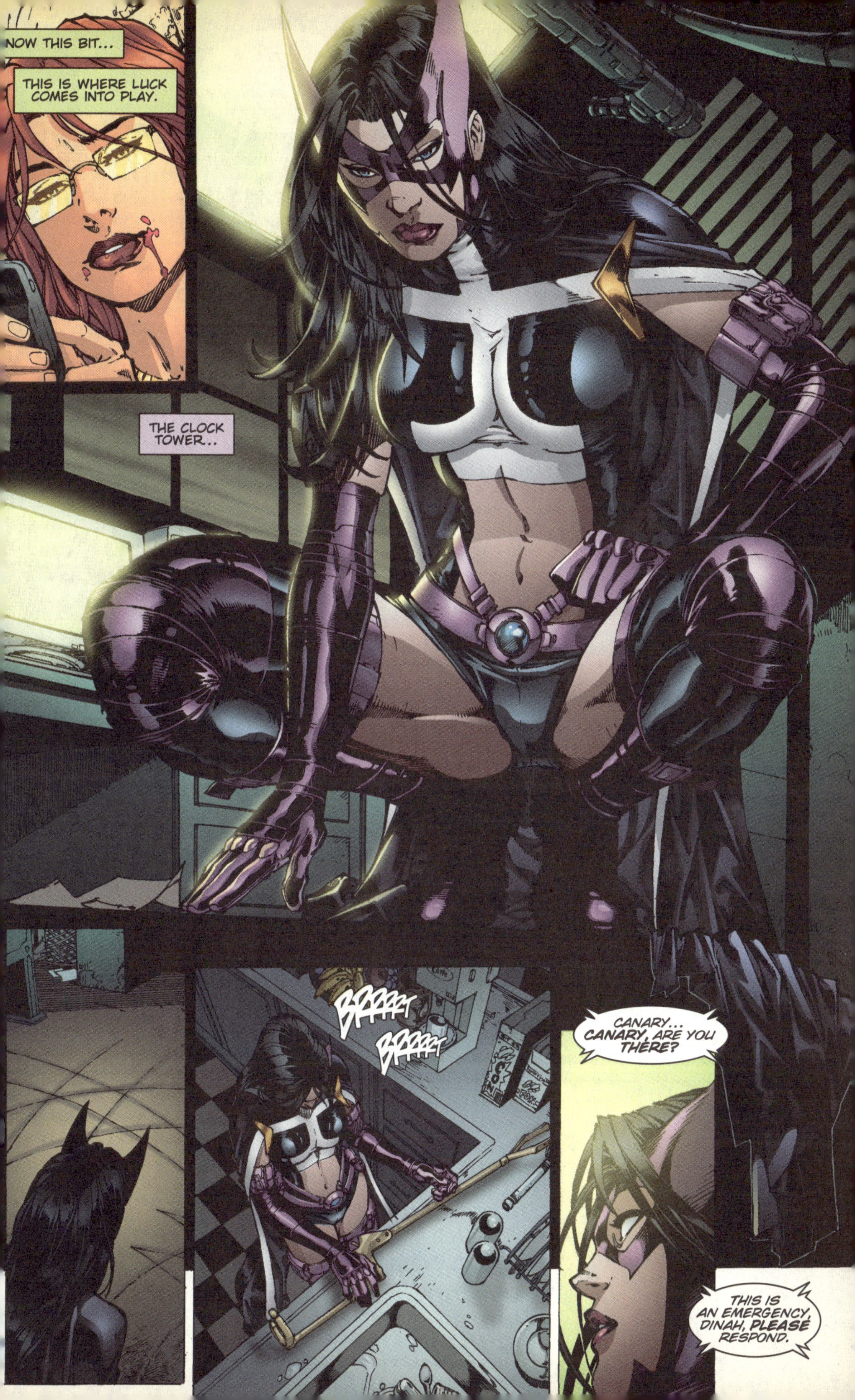

NOW THIS BIT...
THIS IS WHERE LUCK COMES INTO PLAY.
THE CLOCK TOWER..
BRRRRT
BRRRRT
CANARY... CANARY, ARE YOU THERE?
THIS IS AN EMERGENCY, DINAH, PLEASE RESPOND.

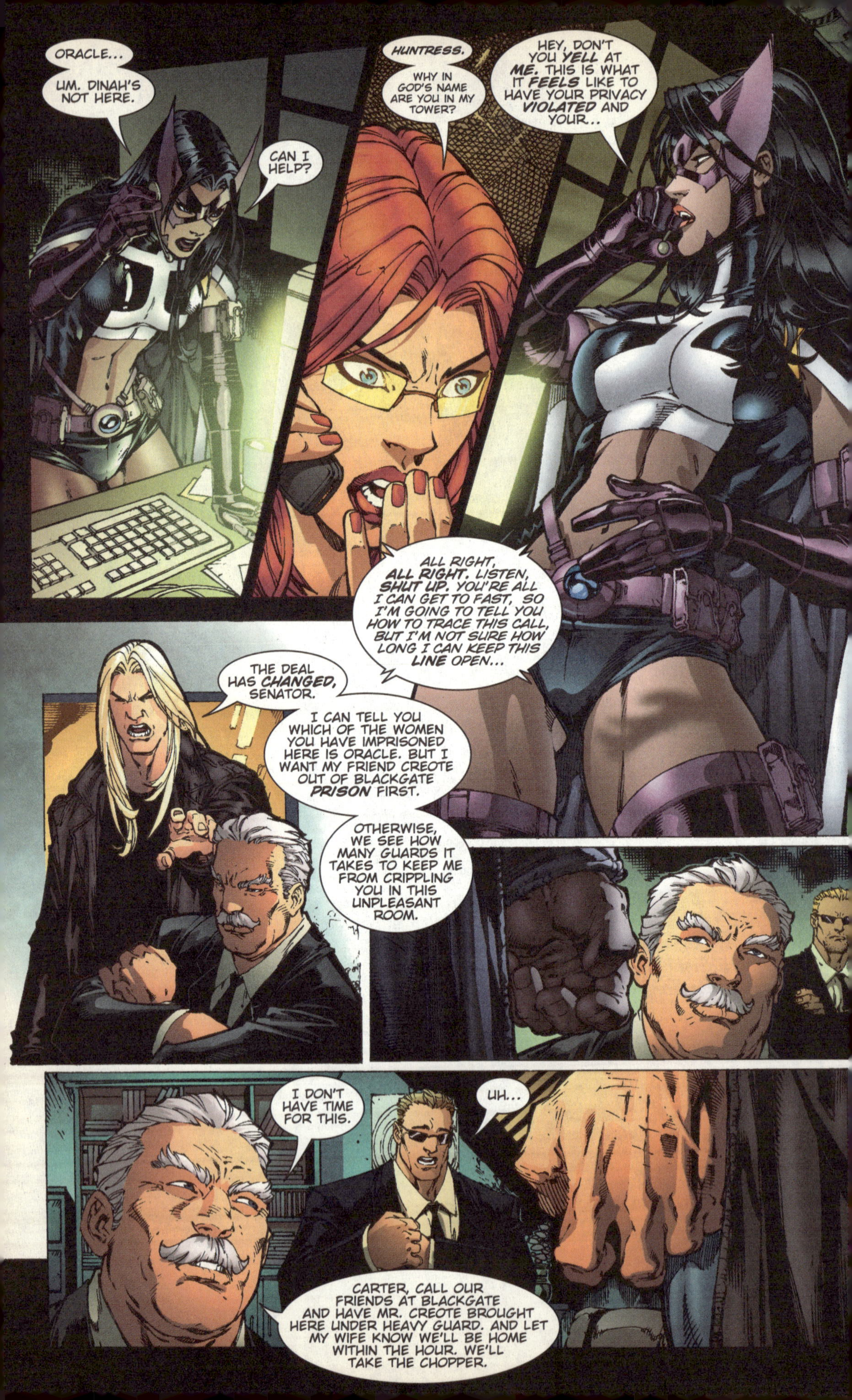
ORACLE...
UM. DINAH'S NOT HERE.
CAN I HELP?
HUNTRESS.
WHY IN GOD'S NAME ARE YOU IN MY TOWER?
HEY, DON'T YOU YELL AT ME. THIS IS WHAT IT FEELS LIKE TO HAVE YOUR PRIVACY VIOLATED AND YOUR...
ALL RIGHT, ALL RIGHT. LISTEN, SHUT UP. YOU'RE ALL I CAN GET TO FAST, SO I'M GOING TO TELL YOU HOW TO TRACE THIS CALL, BUT I'M NOT SURE HOW LONG I CAN KEEP THIS LINE OPEN...
THE DEAL HAS CHANGED, SENATOR.
I CAN TELL YOU WHICH OF THE WOMEN YOU HAVE IMPRISONED HERE IS ORACLE. BUT I WANT MY FRIEND CREOTE OUT OF BLACKGATE PRISON FIRST.
OTHERWISE, WE SEE HOW MANY GUARDS IT TAKES TO KEEP ME FROM CRIPPLING YOU IN THIS UNPLEASANT ROOM.
I DON'T HAVE TIME FOR THIS.
UH...
CARTER, CALL OUR FRIENDS AT BLACKGATE AND HAVE MR. CREOTE BROUGHT HERE UNDER HEAVY GUARD. AND LET MY WIFE KNOW WE'LL BE HOME WITHIN THE HOUR. WE'LL TAKE THE CHOPPER.

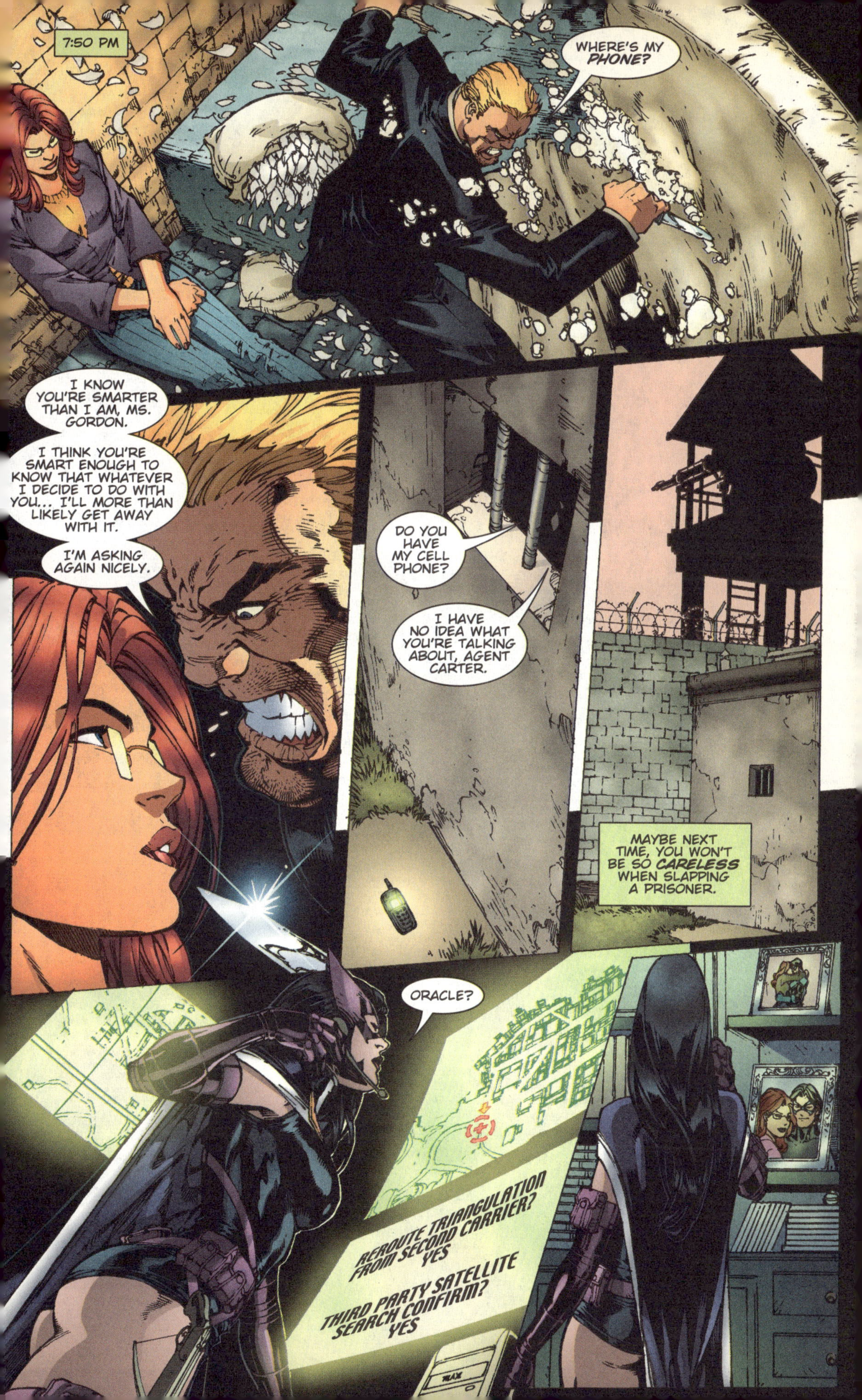
7:50 PM
WHERE'S MY PHONE?
I KNOW YOU'RE SMARTER THAN I AM, MS. GORDON.
I THINK YOU'RE SMART ENOUGH TO KNOW THAT WHATEVER I DECIDE TO DO WITH YOU... I'LL MORE THAN LIKELY GET AWAY WITH IT.
I'M ASKING AGAIN NICELY.
DO YOU HAVE MY CELL PHONE?
I HAVE NO IDEA WHAT YOU'RE TALKING ABOUT, AGENT CARTER.
MAYBE NEXT TIME, YOU WON'T BE SO CARELESS WHEN SLAPPING A PRISONER.
ORACLE?
REROUTE TRIANGULATION FROM SECOND CARRIER? YES
THIRD PARTY SATELLITE SEARCH CONFIRM? YES

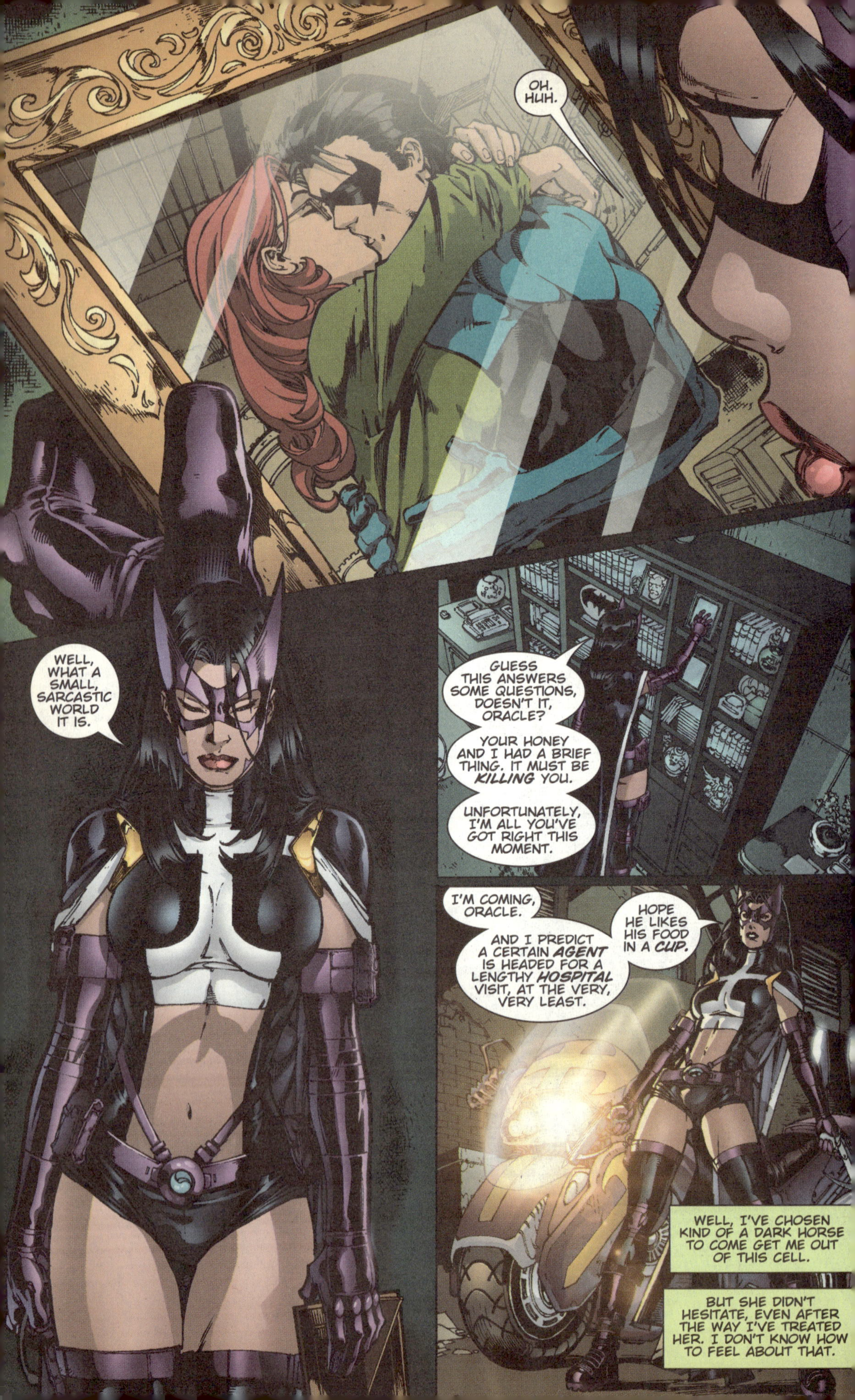
OH. HUH.
WELL, WHAT A SMALL, SARCASTIC WORLD IT IS.
GUESS THIS ANSWERS SOME QUESTIONS, DOESN'T IT, ORACLE?
YOUR HONEY AND I HAD A BRIEF THING. IT MUST BE KILLING YOU.
UNFORTUNATELY, I'M ALL YOU'VE GOT RIGHT THIS MOMENT.
I'M COMING, ORACLE.
AND I PREDICT A CERTAIN AGENT IS HEADED FOR A LENGTHY HOSPITAL VISIT, AT THE VERY, VERY LEAST.
HOPE HE LIKES HIS FOOD IN A CUP.
WELL, I'VE CHOSEN KIND OF A DARK HORSE TO COME GET ME OUT OF THIS CELL.
BUT SHE DIDN'T HESITATE, EVEN AFTER THE WAY I'VE TREATED HER. I DON'T KNOW HOW TO FEEL ABOUT THAT.

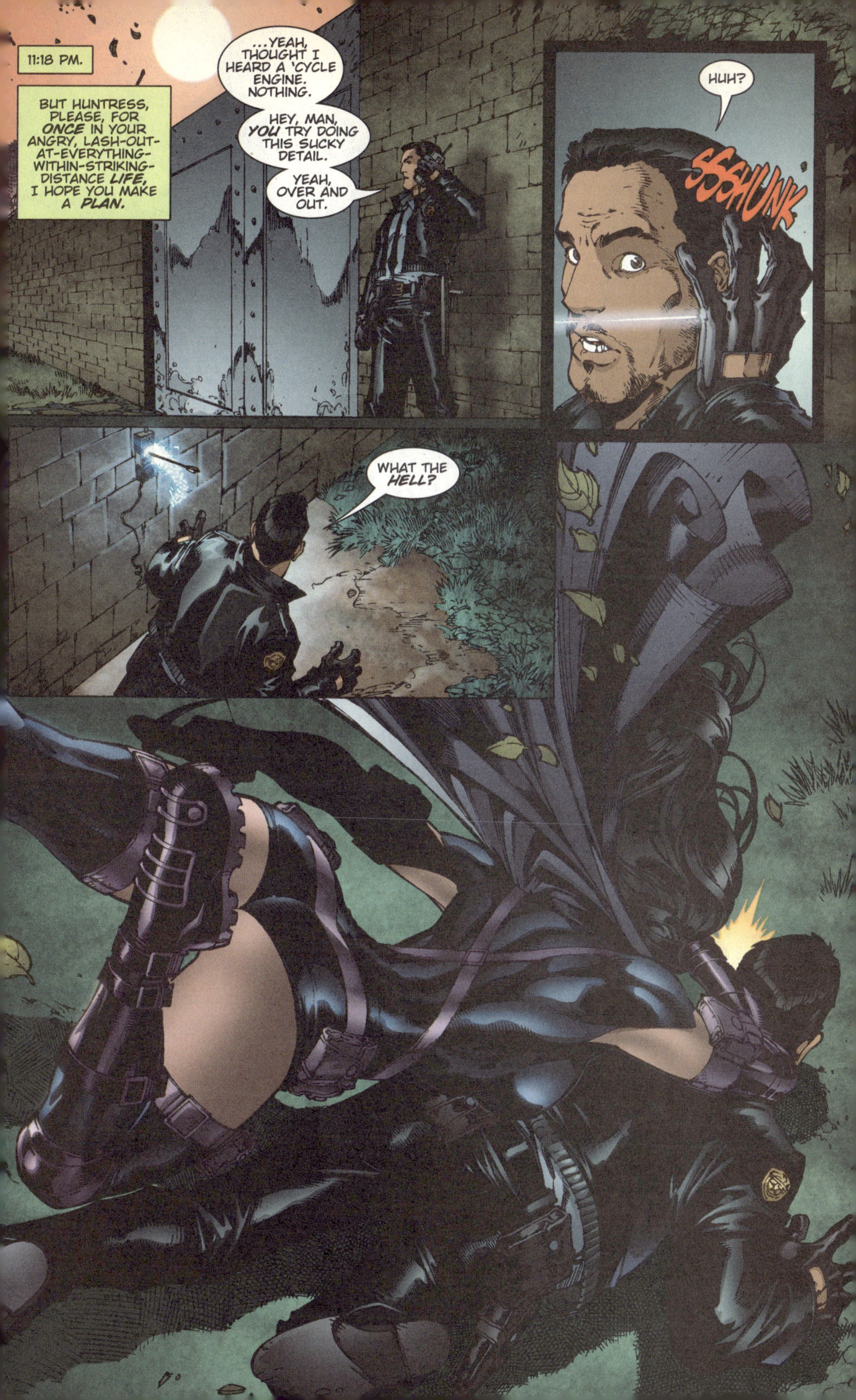

11:18 PM.
BUT HUNTRESS, PLEASE, FOR ONCE IN YOUR ANGRY, LASH-OUT-AT-EVERYTHING-WITHIN-STRIKING-DISTANCE LIFE, I HOPE YOU MAKE A PLAN.
...YEAH, THOUGHT I HEARD A 'CYCLE ENGINE. NOTHING.
HEY, MAN, YOU TRY DOING THIS SUCKY DETAIL.
YEAH, OVER AND OUT.
HUH?
SSSHUNK
WHAT THE HELL?

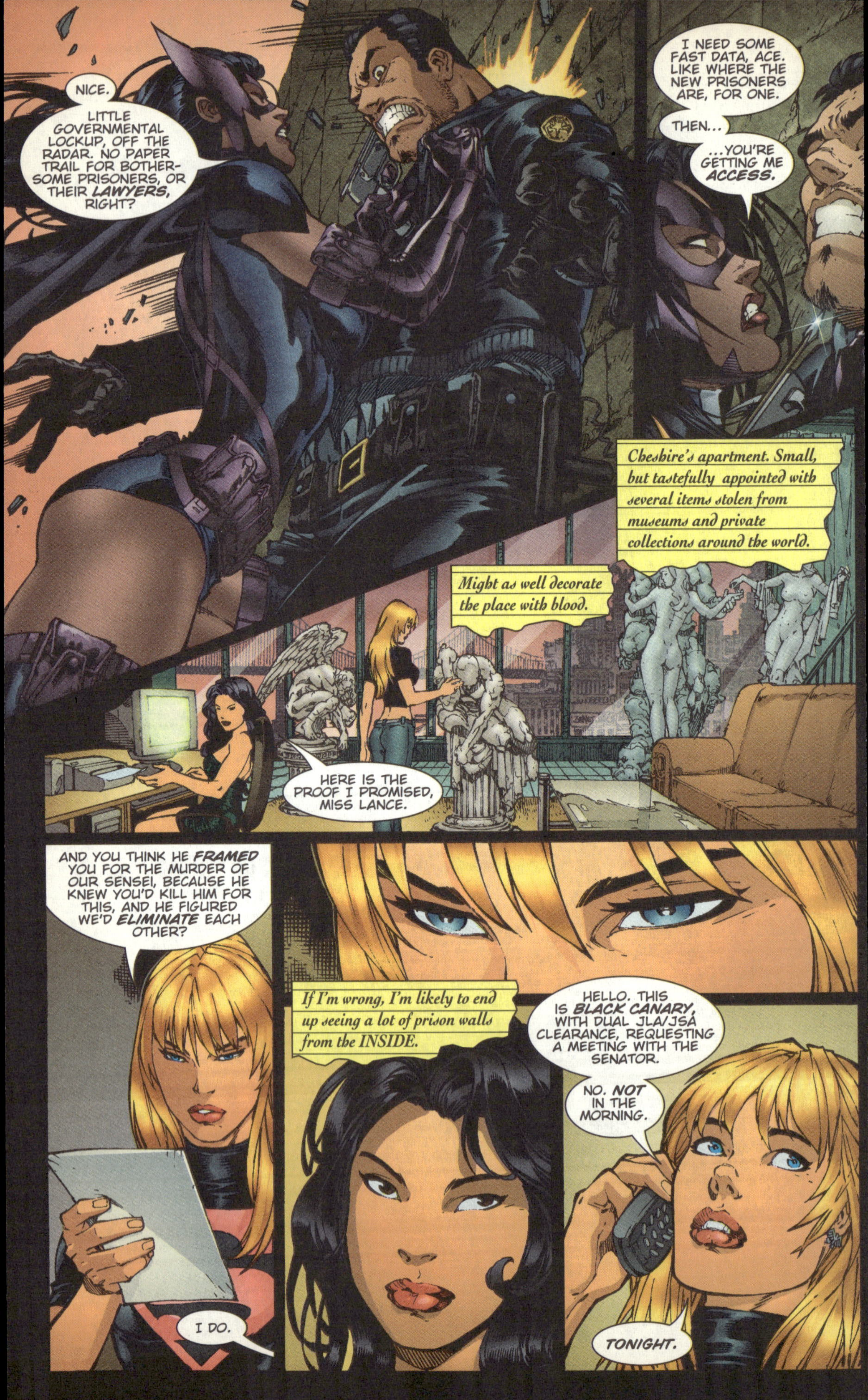
NICE.
LITTLE GOVERNMENTAL LOCKUP, OFF THE RADAR. NO PAPER TRAIL FOR BOTHER-SOME PRISONERS, OR THEIR *LAWYERS*, RIGHT?
I NEED SOME FAST DATA, ACE. LIKE WHERE THE NEW PRISONERS ARE, FOR ONE.
THEN...
...YOU'RE GETTING ME *ACCESS.*
Cheshire's apartment. Small, but tastefully appointed with several items stolen from museums and private collections around the world.
Might as well decorate the place with blood.
HERE IS THE PROOF I PROMISED, MISS LANCE.
AND YOU THINK HE *FRAMED* YOU FOR THE MURDER OF OUR SENSEI, BECAUSE HE KNEW YOU'D KILL HIM FOR THIS, AND HE FIGURED WE'D *ELIMINATE* EACH OTHER?
I DO.
If I'm wrong, I'm likely to end up seeing a lot of prison walls from the INSIDE.
HELLO. THIS IS *BLACK CANARY,* WITH DUAL JLA/JSA CLEARANCE, REQUESTING A MEETING WITH THE SENATOR.
NO. *NOT* IN THE MORNING.
TONIGHT.

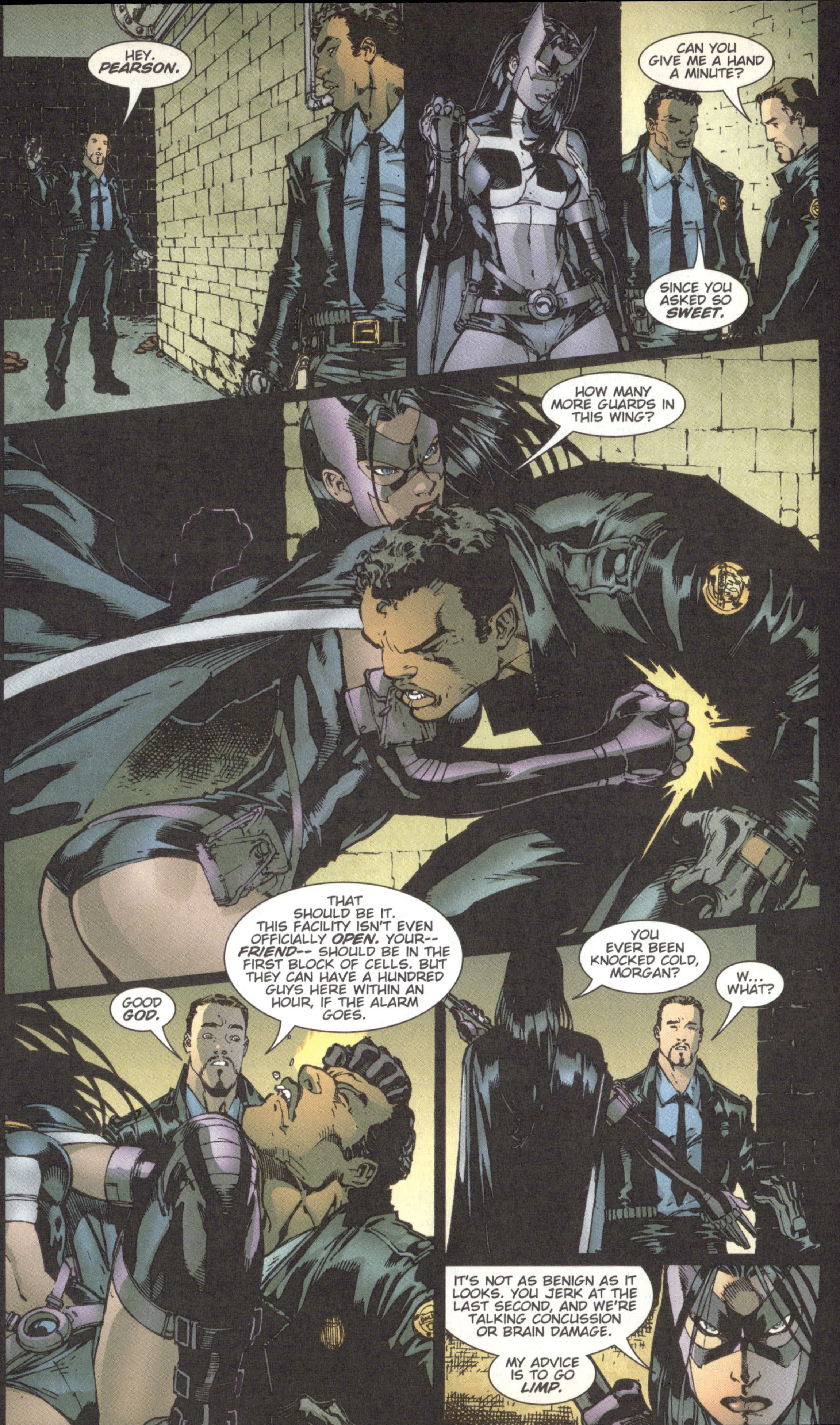
HEY. PEARSON.
CAN YOU GIVE ME A HAND A MINUTE?
SINCE YOU ASKED SO SWEET.
HOW MANY MORE GUARDS IN THIS WING?
THAT SHOULD BE IT. THIS FACILITY ISN'T EVEN OFFICIALLY OPEN. YOUR-- FRIEND-- SHOULD BE IN THE FIRST BLOCK OF CELLS. BUT THEY CAN HAVE A HUNDRED GUYS HERE WITHIN AN HOUR, IF THE ALARM GOES.
GOOD GOD.
YOU EVER BEEN KNOCKED COLD, MORGAN?
W... WHAT?
IT'S NOT AS BENIGN AS IT LOOKS. YOU JERK AT THE LAST SECOND, AND WE'RE TALKING CONCUSSION OR BRAIN DAMAGE.
MY ADVICE IS TO GO LIMP.

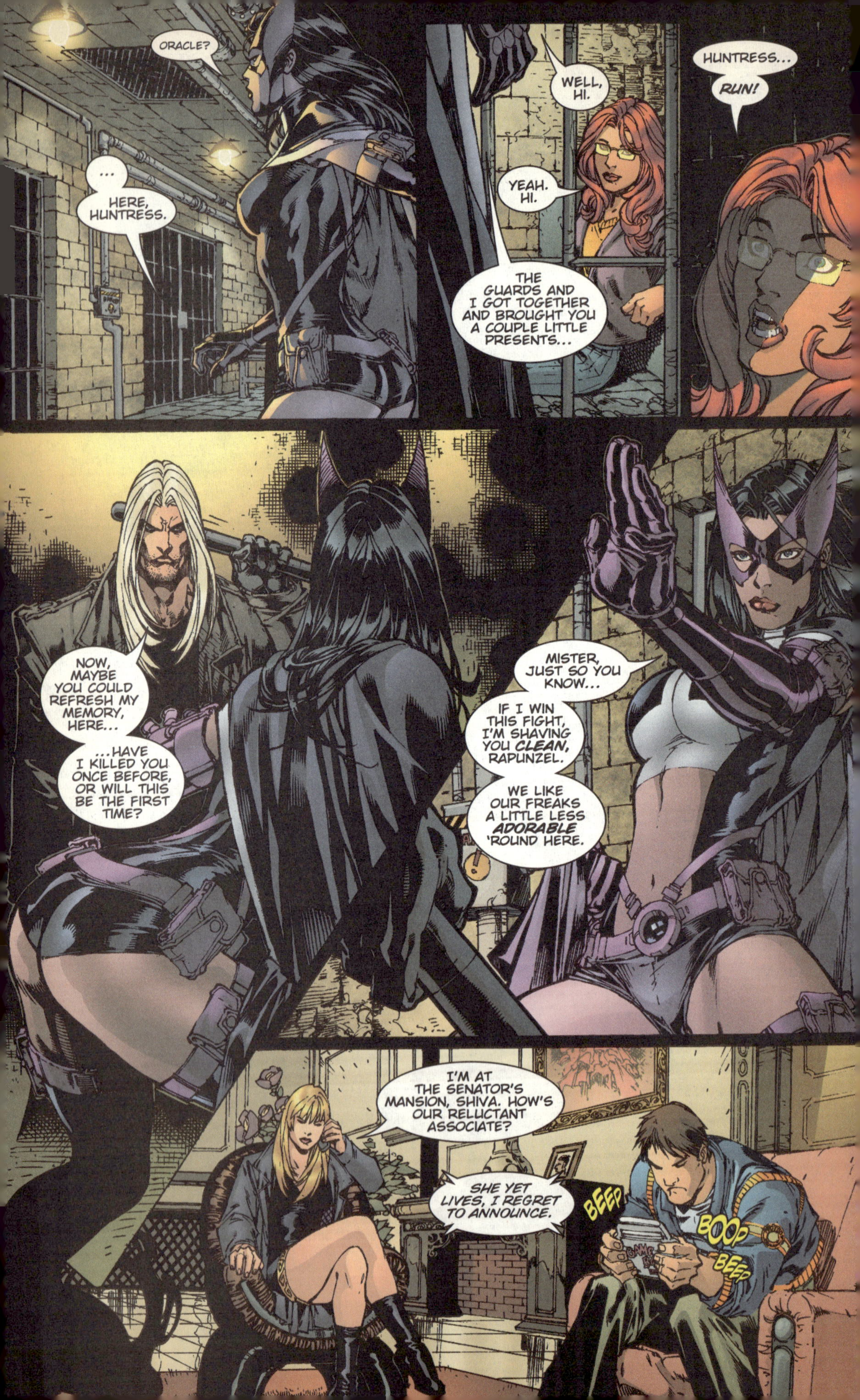
ORACLE?
...HERE, HUNTRESS.
WELL, HI.
YEAH. HI.
THE GUARDS AND I GOT TOGETHER AND BROUGHT YOU A COUPLE LITTLE PRESENTS...
HUNTRESS... RUN!
NOW, MAYBE YOU COULD REFRESH MY MEMORY, HERE...
...HAVE I KILLED YOU ONCE BEFORE, OR WILL THIS BE THE FIRST TIME?
MISTER, JUST SO YOU KNOW...
IF I WIN THIS FIGHT, I'M SHAVING YOU CLEAN, RAPUNZEL.
WE LIKE OUR FREAKS A LITTLE LESS ADORABLE 'ROUND HERE.
I'M AT THE SENATOR'S MANSION, SHIVA. HOW'S OUR RELUCTANT ASSOCIATE?
SHE YET LIVES, I REGRET TO ANNOUNCE.
BEEP
BOOP
BEEP

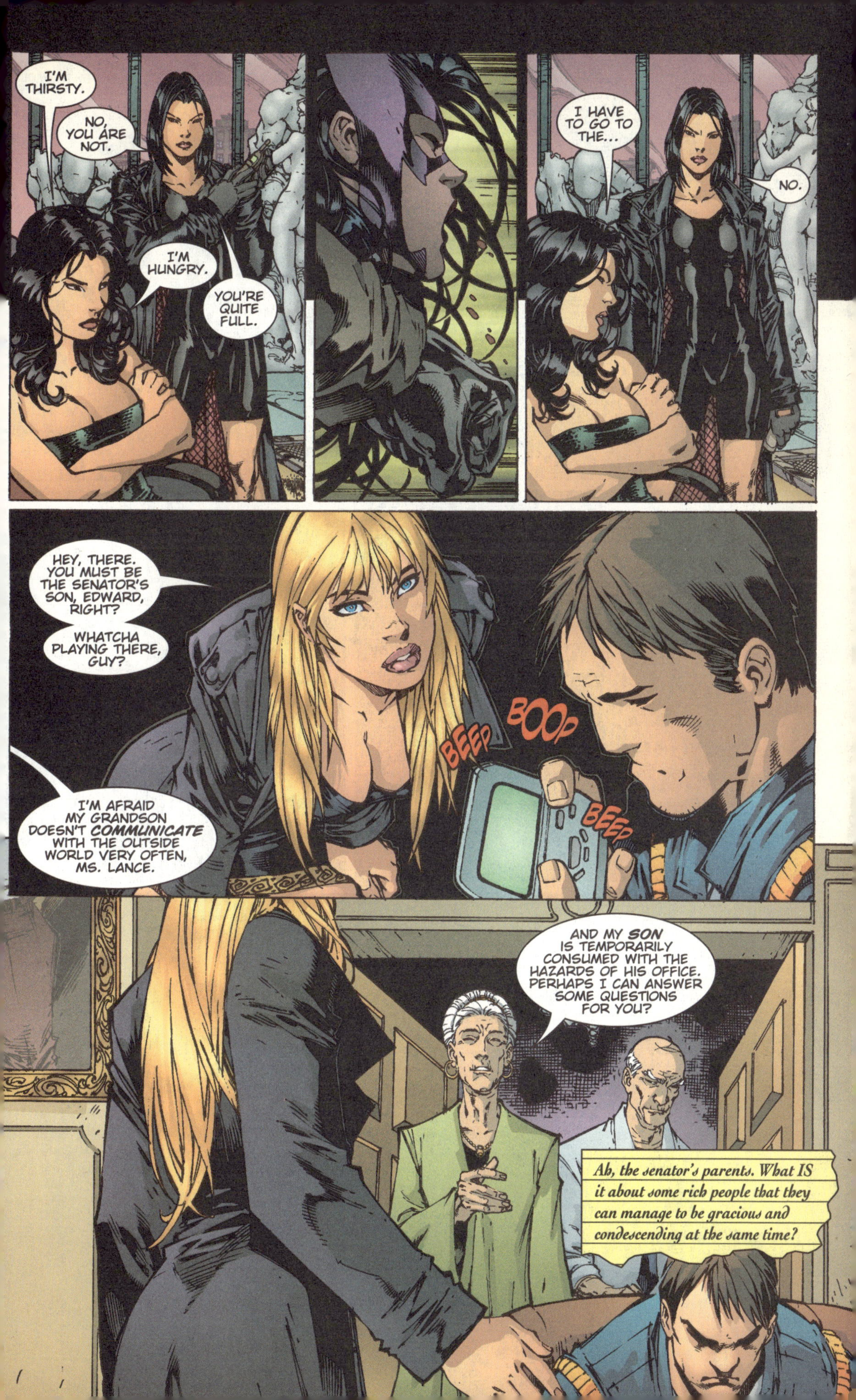
I'M THIRSTY.
NO, YOU ARE NOT.
I'M HUNGRY.
YOU'RE QUITE FULL.
I HAVE TO GO TO THE...
NO.
HEY, THERE. YOU MUST BE THE SENATOR'S SON, EDWARD, RIGHT?
WHATCHA PLAYING THERE, GUY?
BEEP
BOOP
BEEP
I'M AFRAID MY GRANDSON DOESN'T COMMUNICATE WITH THE OUTSIDE WORLD VERY OFTEN, MS. LANCE.
AND MY SON IS TEMPORARILY CONSUMED WITH THE HAZARDS OF HIS OFFICE. PERHAPS I CAN ANSWER SOME QUESTIONS FOR YOU?
Ah, the senator's parents. What IS it about some rich people that they can manage to be gracious and condescending at the same time?

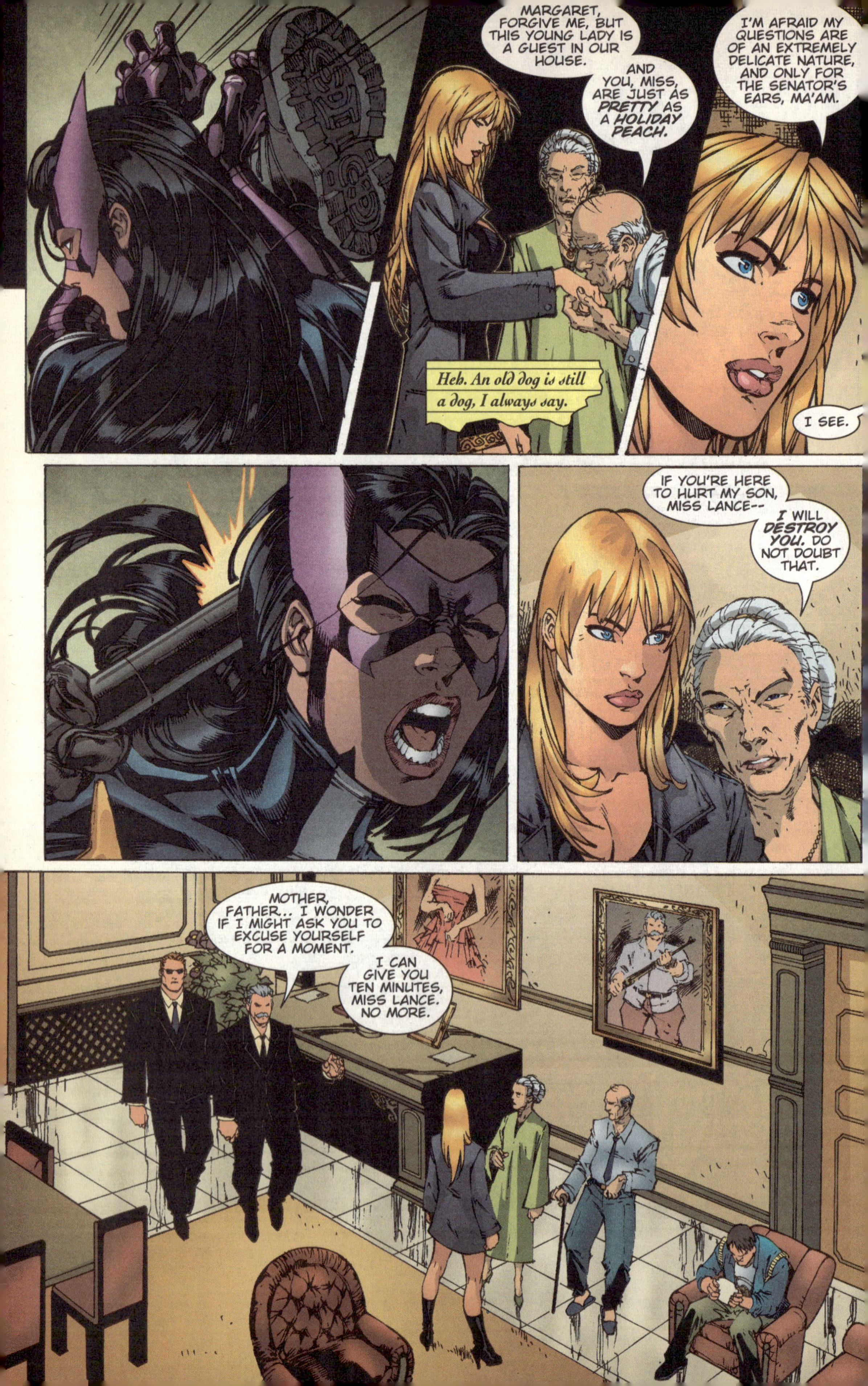
MARGARET, FORGIVE ME, BUT THIS YOUNG LADY IS A GUEST IN OUR HOUSE.
AND YOU, MISS, ARE JUST AS PRETTY AS A HOLIDAY PEACH.
Heh. An old dog is still a dog, I always say.
I'M AFRAID MY QUESTIONS ARE OF AN EXTREMELY DELICATE NATURE, AND ONLY FOR THE SENATOR'S EARS, MA'AM.
I SEE.
IF YOU'RE HERE TO HURT MY SON, MISS LANCE--
I WILL DESTROY YOU. DO NOT DOUBT THAT.
MOTHER, FATHER... I WONDER IF I MIGHT ASK YOU TO EXCUSE YOURSELF FOR A MOMENT.
I CAN GIVE YOU TEN MINUTES, MISS LANCE. NO MORE.

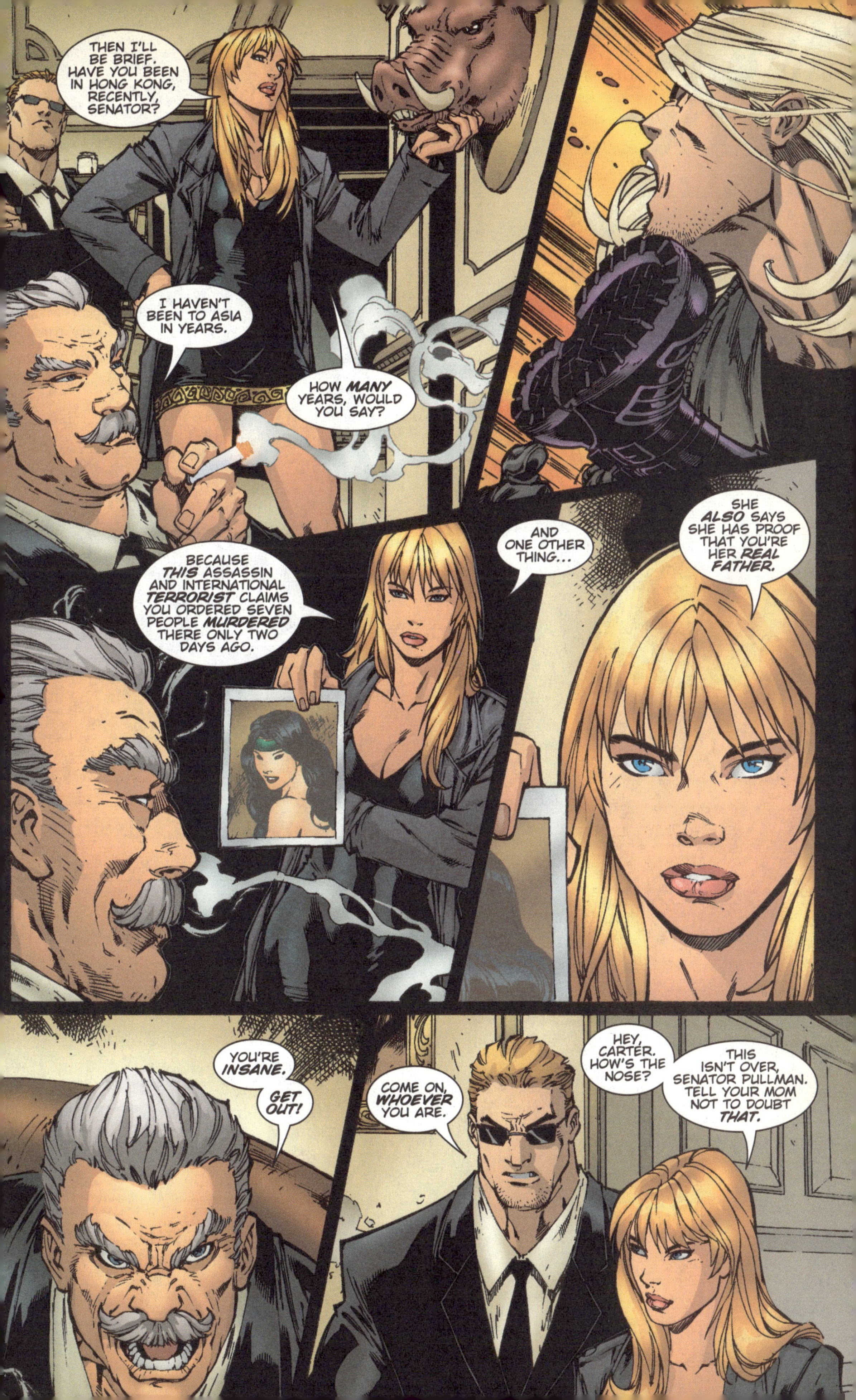
THEN I'LL BE BRIEF. HAVE YOU BEEN IN HONG KONG, RECENTLY, SENATOR?
I HAVEN'T BEEN TO ASIA IN YEARS.
HOW *MANY* YEARS, WOULD YOU SAY?
BECAUSE *THIS* ASSASSIN AND INTERNATIONAL *TERRORIST* CLAIMS YOU ORDERED SEVEN PEOPLE *MURDERED* THERE ONLY TWO DAYS AGO.
AND ONE OTHER THING...
SHE *ALSO* SAYS SHE HAS PROOF THAT YOU'RE HER *REAL FATHER.*
YOU'RE *INSANE.*
GET OUT!
COME ON, *WHOEVER* YOU ARE.
HEY, CARTER. HOW'S THE NOSE?
THIS ISN'T OVER, SENATOR PULLMAN. TELL YOUR MOM NOT TO DOUBT *THAT.*

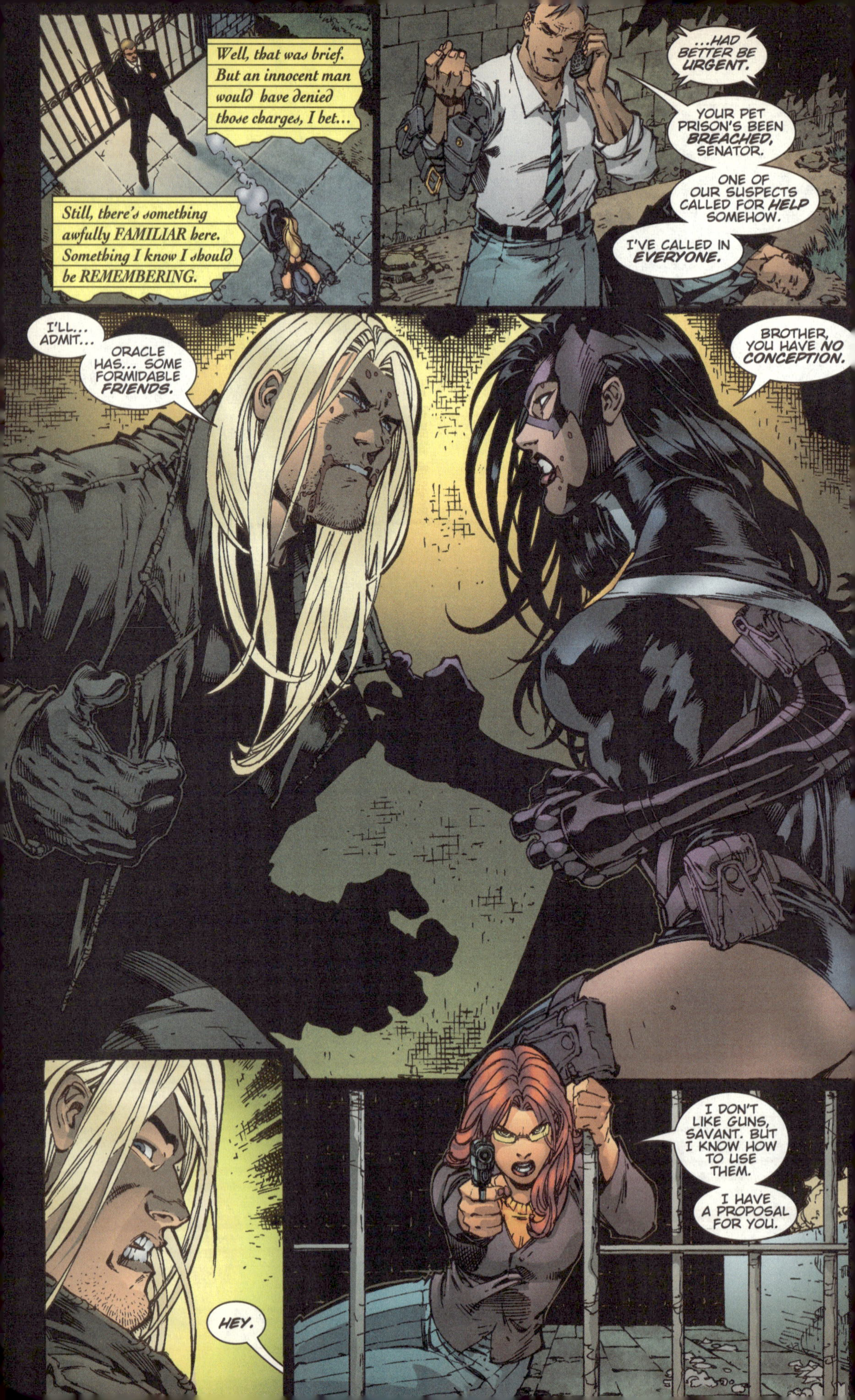
Well, that was brief. But an innocent man would have denied those charges, I bet...
Still, there's something awfully FAMILIAR here. Something I know I should be REMEMBERING.
...HAD BETTER BE URGENT.
YOUR PET PRISON'S BEEN BREACHED, SENATOR.
ONE OF OUR SUSPECTS CALLED FOR HELP SOMEHOW.
I'VE CALLED IN EVERYONE.
I'LL... ADMIT...
ORACLE HAS... SOME FORMIDABLE FRIENDS.
BROTHER, YOU HAVE NO CONCEPTION.
HEY.
I DON'T LIKE GUNS, SAVANT. BUT I KNOW HOW TO USE THEM.
I HAVE A PROPOSAL FOR YOU.

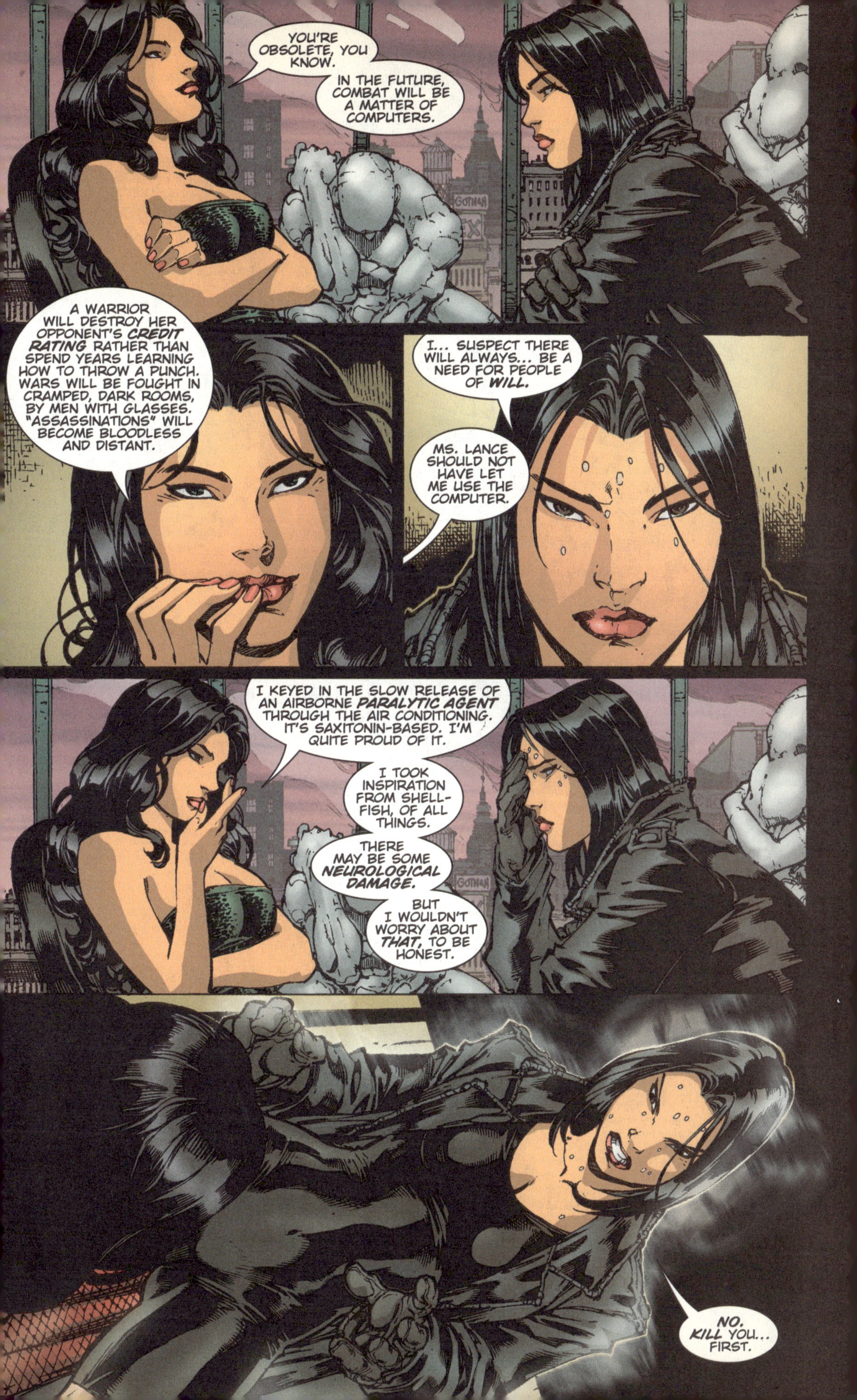
YOU'RE OBSOLETE, YOU KNOW.
IN THE FUTURE, COMBAT WILL BE A MATTER OF COMPUTERS.
A WARRIOR WILL DESTROY HER OPPONENT'S *CREDIT RATING* RATHER THAN SPEND YEARS LEARNING HOW TO THROW A PUNCH. WARS WILL BE FOUGHT IN CRAMPED, DARK ROOMS, BY MEN WITH GLASSES. "ASSASSINATIONS" WILL BECOME BLOODLESS AND DISTANT.
I... SUSPECT THERE WILL ALWAYS... BE A NEED FOR PEOPLE OF *WILL.*
MS. LANCE SHOULD NOT HAVE LET ME USE THE COMPUTER.
I KEYED IN THE SLOW RELEASE OF AN AIRBORNE *PARALYTIC AGENT* THROUGH THE AIR CONDITIONING. IT'S SAXITONIN-BASED. I'M QUITE PROUD OF IT.
I TOOK INSPIRATION FROM SHELL-FISH, OF ALL THINGS.
THERE MAY BE SOME *NEUROLOGICAL DAMAGE.*
BUT I WOULDN'T WORRY ABOUT *THAT,* TO BE HONEST.
NO. KILL YOU... FIRST.

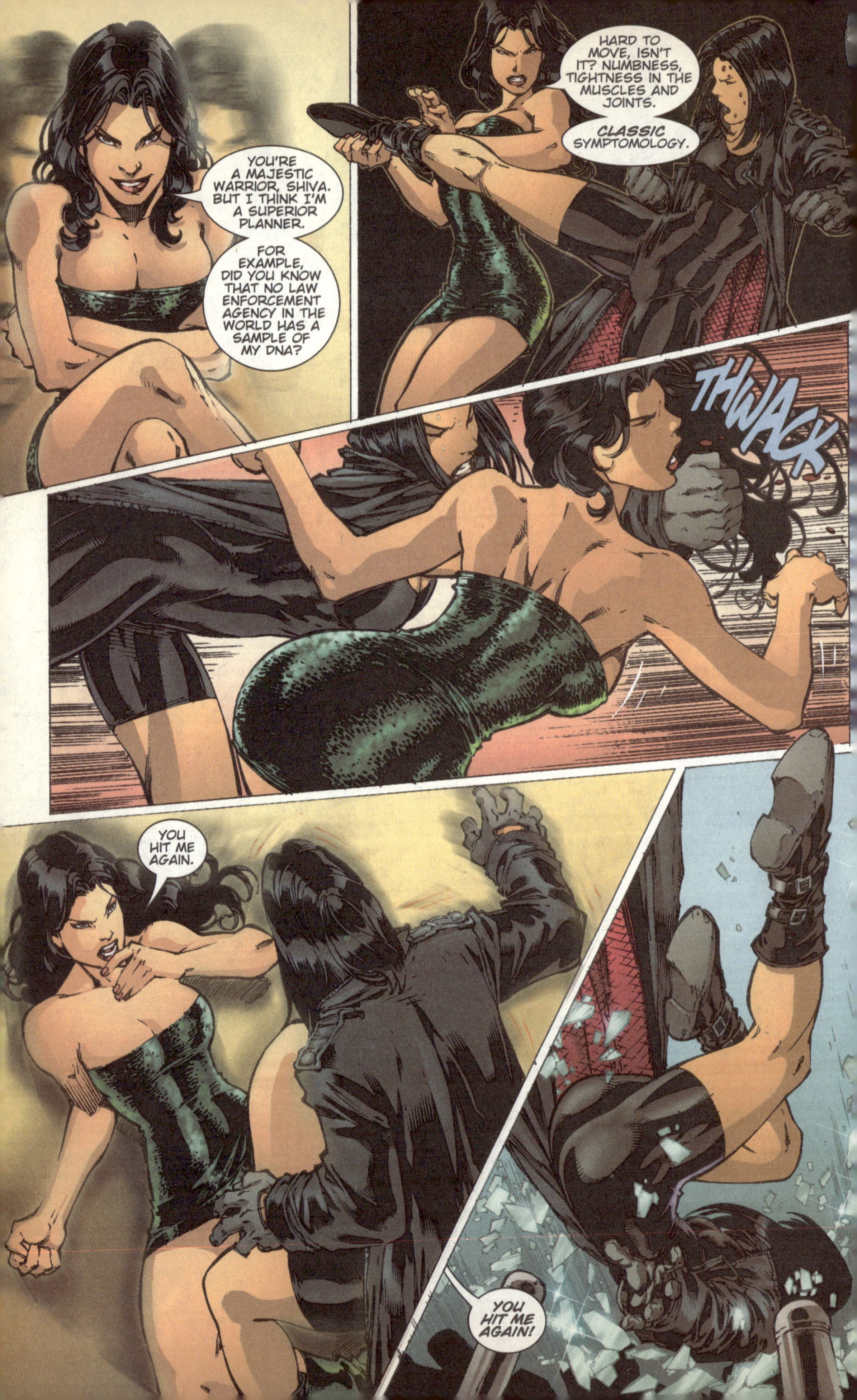

YOU'RE A MAJESTIC WARRIOR, SHIVA. BUT I THINK I'M A SUPERIOR PLANNER.
FOR EXAMPLE, DID YOU KNOW THAT NO LAW ENFORCEMENT AGENCY IN THE WORLD HAS A SAMPLE OF MY DNA?
HARD TO MOVE, ISN'T IT? NUMBNESS, TIGHTNESS IN THE MUSCLES AND JOINTS.
CLASSIC SYMPTOMOLOGY.
THWACK
YOU HIT ME AGAIN.
YOU HIT ME AGAIN!

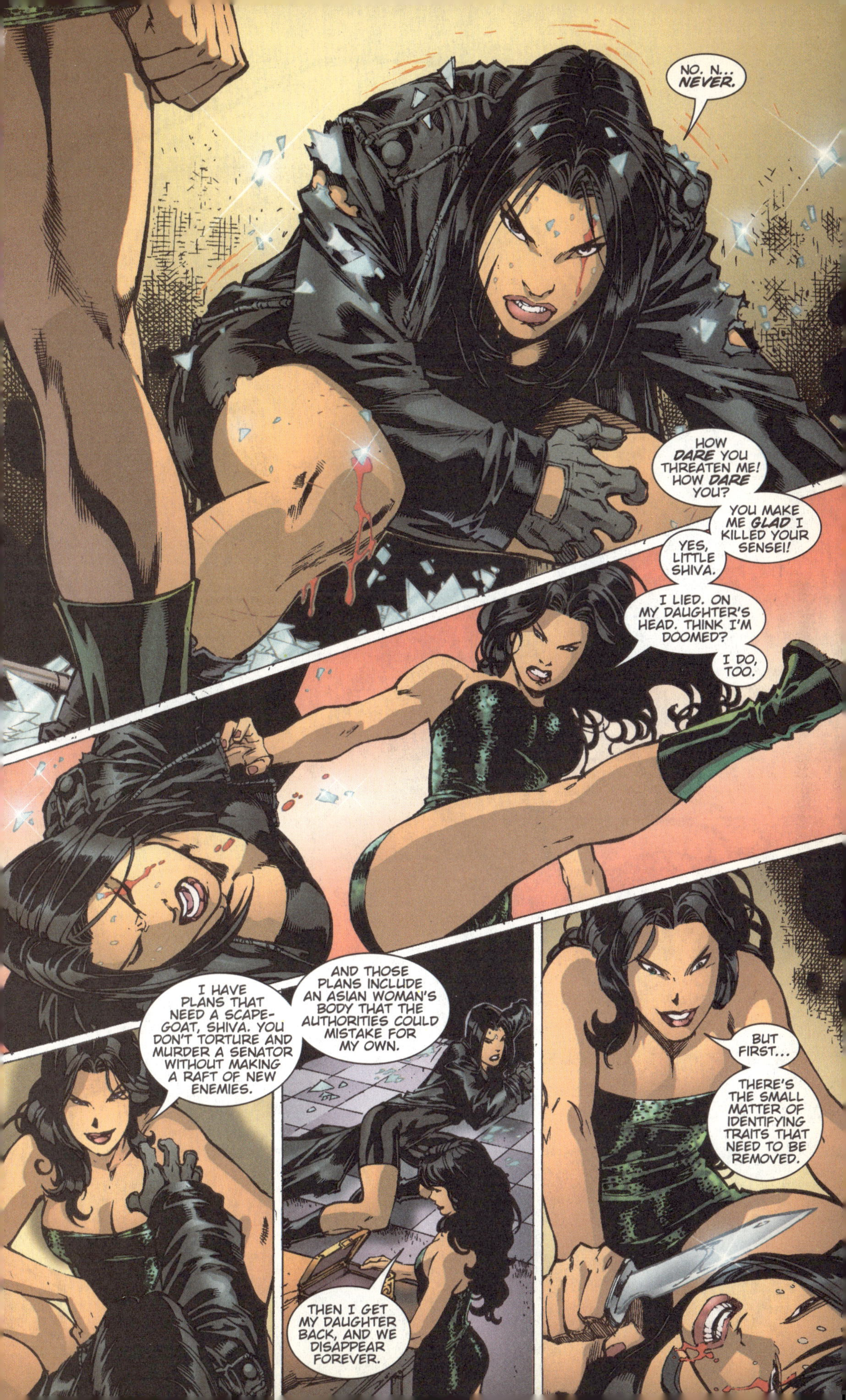

NO. N... NEVER.
HOW DARE YOU THREATEN ME! HOW DARE YOU?
YOU MAKE ME GLAD I KILLED YOUR SENSEI!
YES, LITTLE SHIVA.
I LIED. ON MY DAUGHTER'S HEAD. THINK I'M DOOMED?
I DO, TOO.
I HAVE PLANS THAT NEED A SCAPE-GOAT, SHIVA. YOU DON'T TORTURE AND MURDER A SENATOR WITHOUT MAKING A RAFT OF NEW ENEMIES.
AND THOSE PLANS INCLUDE AN ASIAN WOMAN'S BODY THAT THE AUTHORITIES COULD MISTAKE FOR MY OWN.
THEN I GET MY DAUGHTER BACK, AND WE DISAPPEAR FOREVER.
BUT FIRST...
THERE'S THE SMALL MATTER OF IDENTIFYING TRAITS THAT NEED TO BE REMOVED.

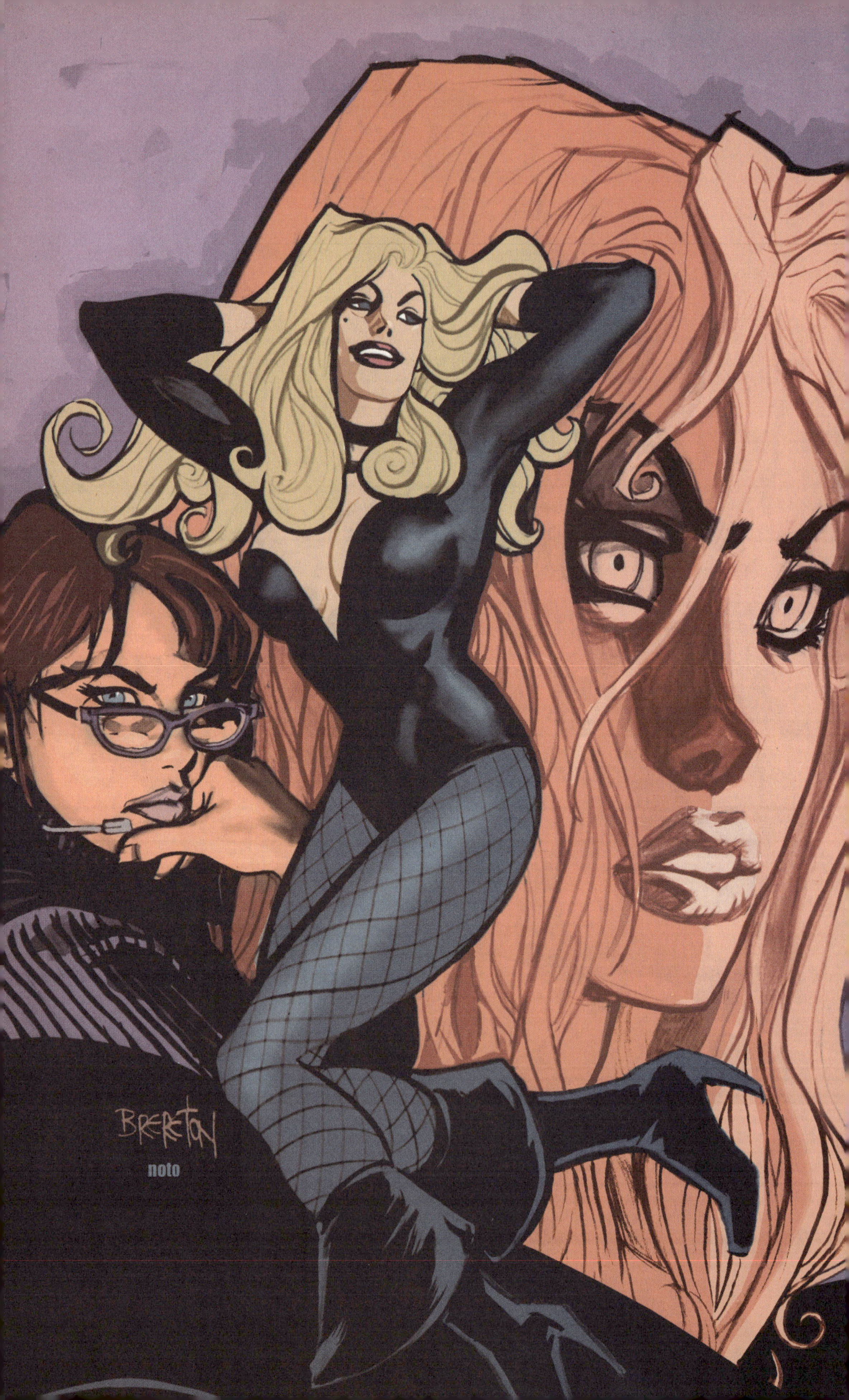
BRERETON
noto

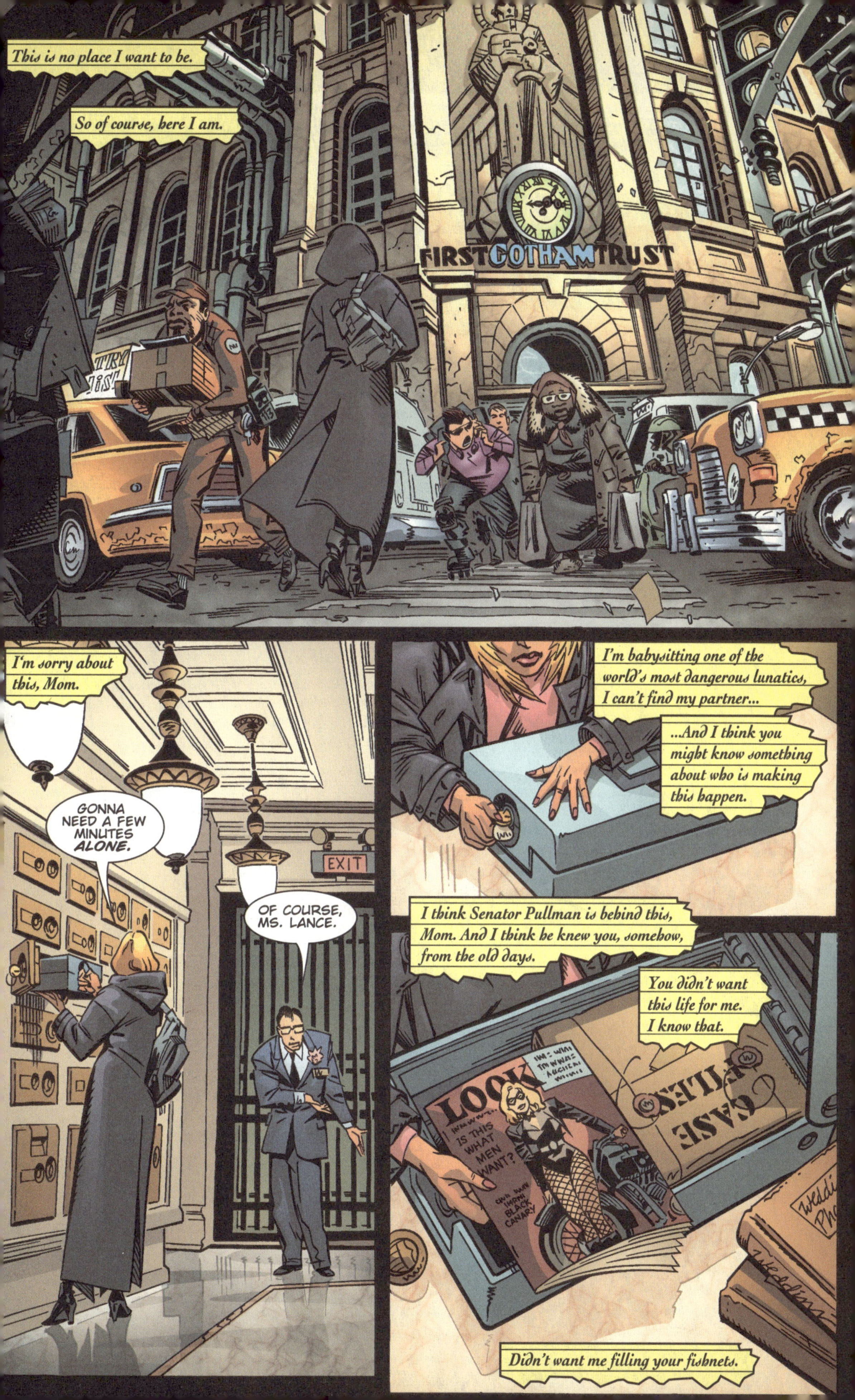
This is no place I want to be.
So of course, here I am.
FIRST GOTHAM TRUST
I'm sorry about this, Mom.
GONNA NEED A FEW MINUTES ALONE.
EXIT
OF COURSE, MS. LANCE.
I'm babysitting one of the world's most dangerous lunatics, I can't find my partner...
...And I think you might know something about who is making this happen.
I think Senator Pullman is behind this, Mom. And I think he knew you, somehow, from the old days.
You didn't want this life for me. I know that.
LOOK
IS THIS WHAT MEN WANT?
BLACK CANARY
CASE FILES
Didn't want me filling your fishnets.

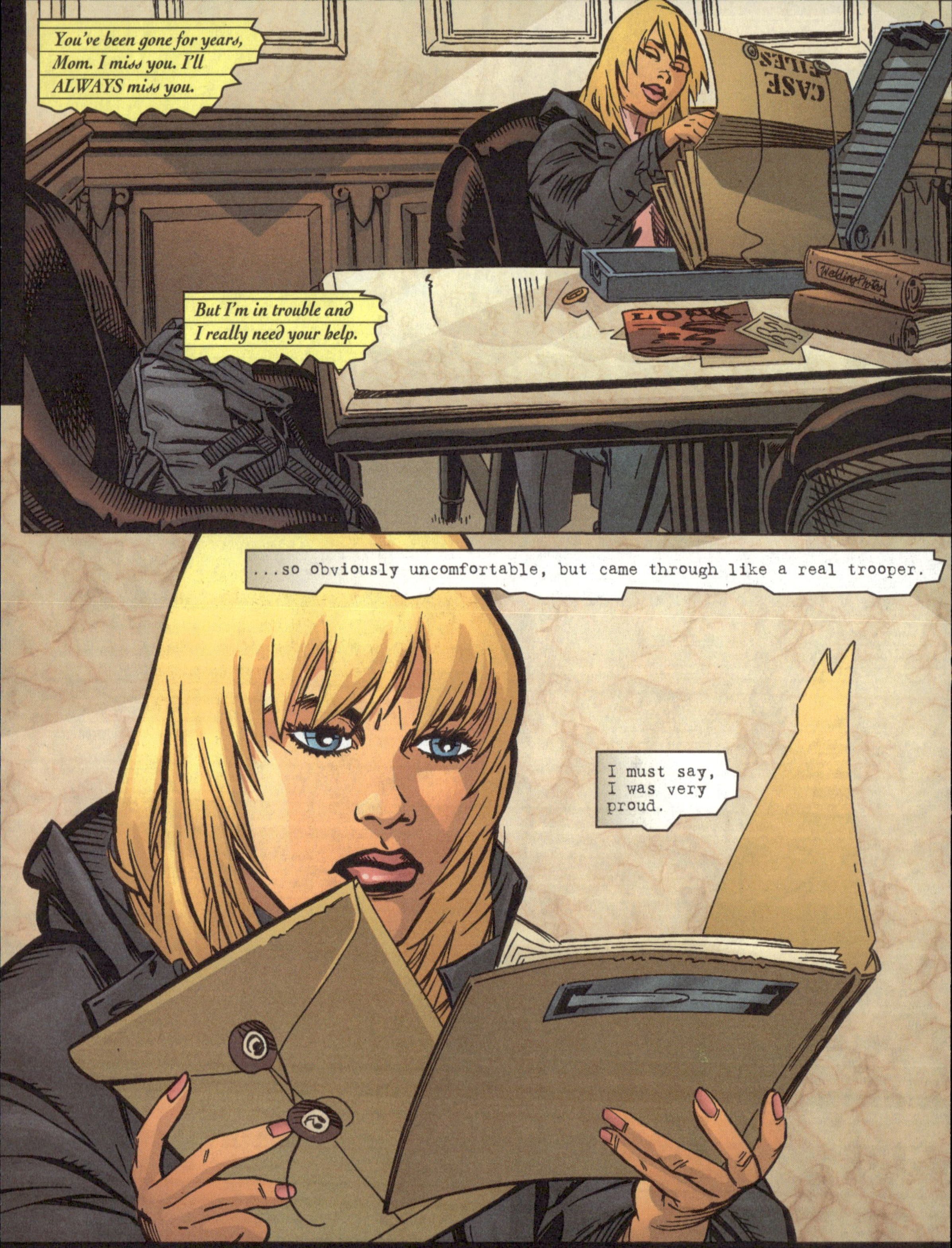
You've been gone for years, Mom. I miss you. I'll ALWAYS miss you.
But I'm in trouble and I really need your help.
CASE FILES
...so obviously uncomfortable, but came through like a real trooper.
I must say, I was very proud.

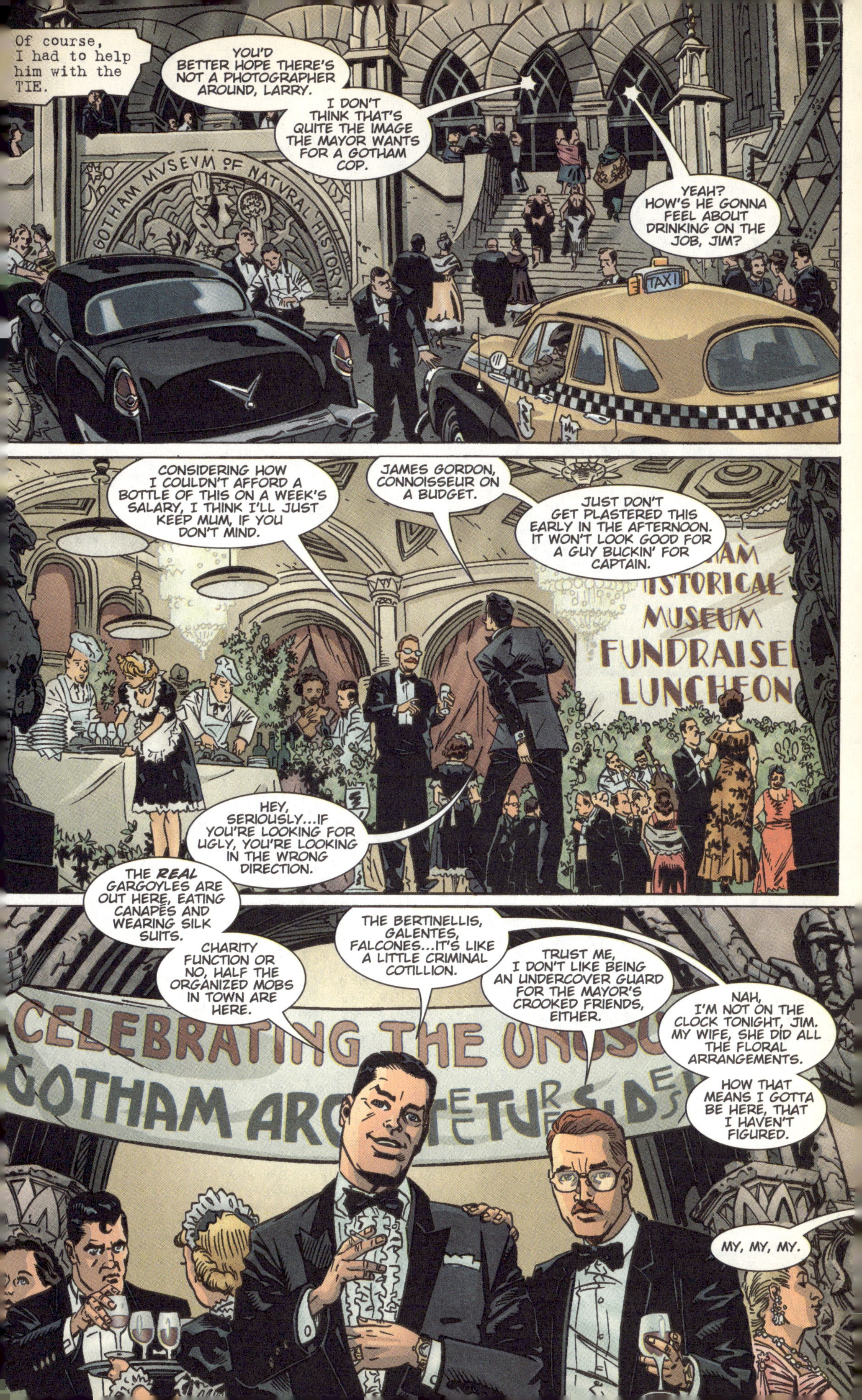
Of course, I had to help him with the TIE.
YOU'D BETTER HOPE THERE'S NOT A PHOTOGRAPHER AROUND, LARRY.
I DON'T THINK THAT'S QUITE THE IMAGE THE MAYOR WANTS FOR A GOTHAM COP.
GOTHAM MUSEUM OF NATURAL HISTORY
YEAH? HOW'S HE GONNA FEEL ABOUT DRINKING ON THE JOB, JIM?
TAXI
CONSIDERING HOW I COULDN'T AFFORD A BOTTLE OF THIS ON A WEEK'S SALARY, I THINK I'LL JUST KEEP MUM, IF YOU DON'T MIND.
JAMES GORDON, CONNOISSEUR ON A BUDGET.
JUST DON'T GET PLASTERED THIS EARLY IN THE AFTERNOON. IT WON'T LOOK GOOD FOR A GUY BUCKIN' FOR CAPTAIN.
HEY, SERIOUSLY...IF YOU'RE LOOKING FOR UGLY, YOU'RE LOOKING IN THE WRONG DIRECTION.
THE *REAL* GARGOYLES ARE OUT HERE, EATING CANAPÉS AND WEARING SILK SUITS.
CHARITY FUNCTION OR NO, HALF THE ORGANIZED MOBS IN TOWN ARE HERE.
THE BERTINELLIS, GALENTES, FALCONES...IT'S LIKE A LITTLE CRIMINAL COTILLION.
TRUST ME, I DON'T LIKE BEING AN UNDERCOVER GUARD FOR THE MAYOR'S CROOKED FRIENDS, EITHER.
NAH, I'M NOT ON THE CLOCK TONIGHT, JIM. MY WIFE, SHE DID ALL THE FLORAL ARRANGEMENTS.
HOW THAT MEANS I GOTTA BE HERE, THAT I HAVEN'T FIGURED.
MY, MY, MY.

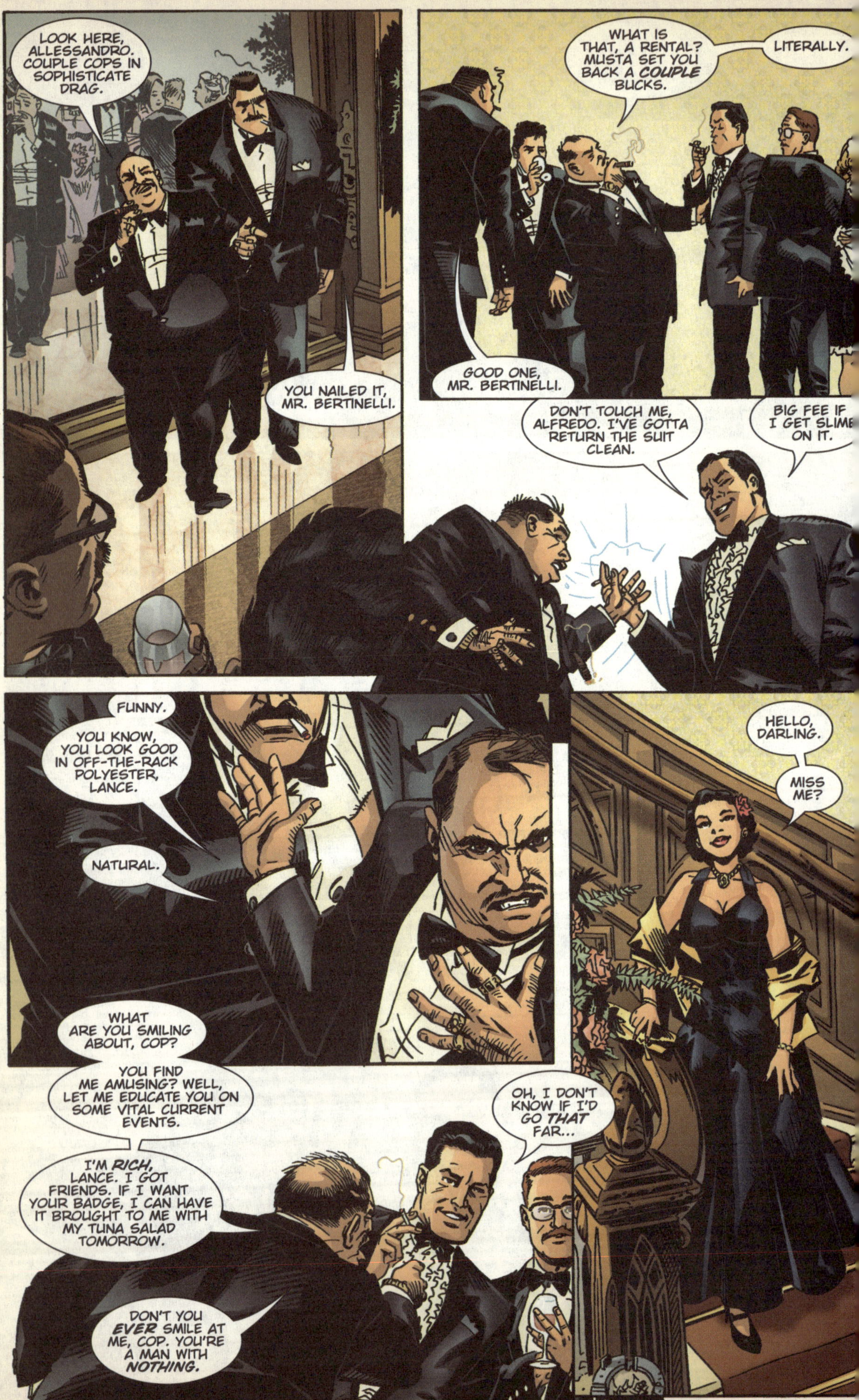

LOOK HERE, ALLESSANDRO. COUPLE COPS IN SOPHISTICATE DRAG.
YOU NAILED IT, MR. BERTINELLI.
WHAT IS THAT, A RENTAL? MUSTA SET YOU BACK A COUPLE BUCKS.
LITERALLY.
GOOD ONE, MR. BERTINELLI.
DON'T TOUCH ME, ALFREDO. I'VE GOTTA RETURN THE SUIT CLEAN.
BIG FEE IF I GET SLIME ON IT.
FUNNY.
YOU KNOW, YOU LOOK GOOD IN OFF-THE-RACK POLYESTER, LANCE.
NATURAL.
WHAT ARE YOU SMILING ABOUT, COP?
YOU FIND ME AMUSING? WELL, LET ME EDUCATE YOU ON SOME VITAL CURRENT EVENTS.
I'M RICH, LANCE. I GOT FRIENDS. IF I WANT YOUR BADGE, I CAN HAVE IT BROUGHT TO ME WITH MY TUNA SALAD TOMORROW.
DON'T YOU EVER SMILE AT ME, COP. YOU'RE A MAN WITH NOTHING.
OH, I DON'T KNOW IF I'D GO THAT FAR...
HELLO, DARLING.
MISS ME?

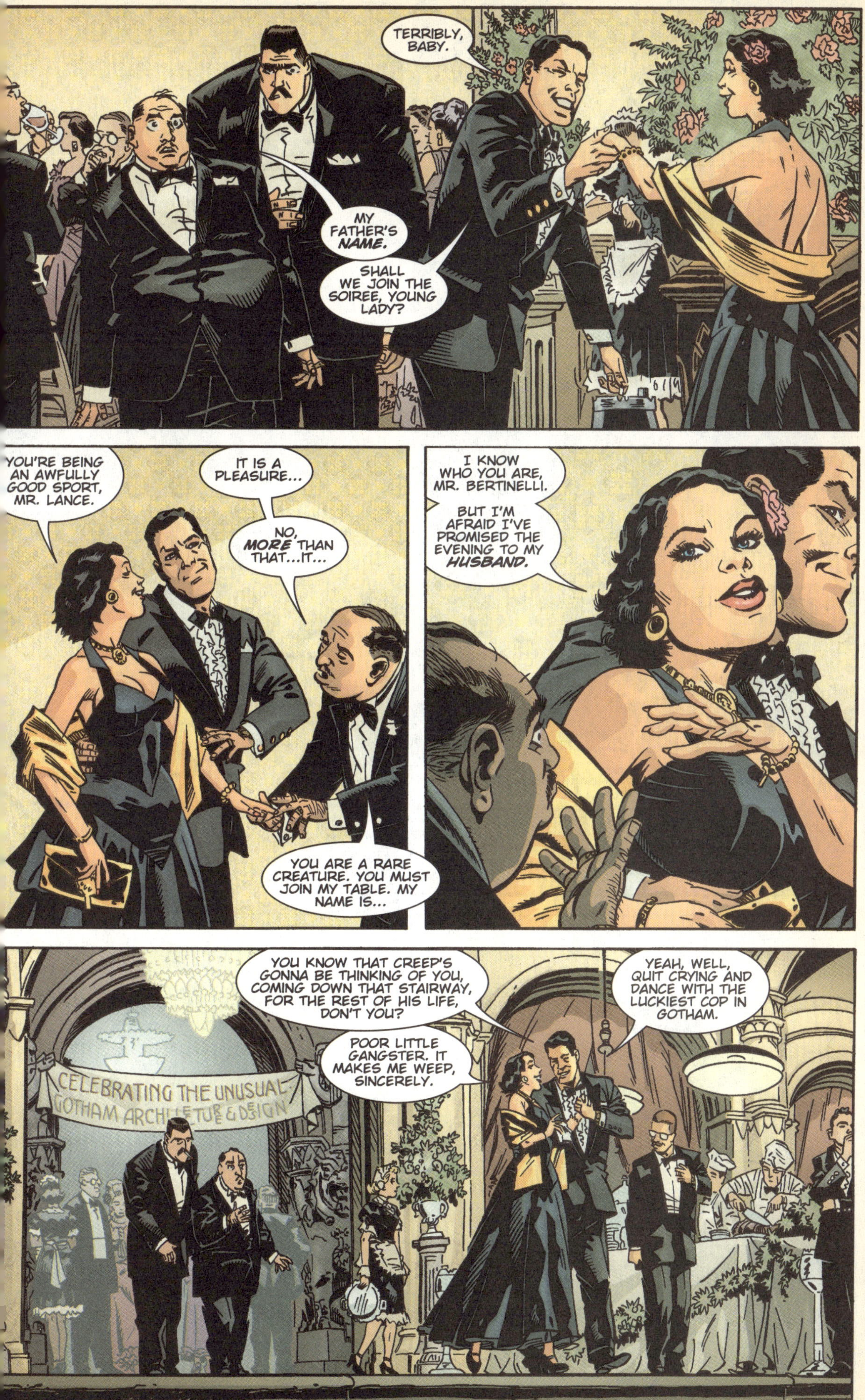
TERRIBLY, BABY.
MY FATHER'S NAME.
SHALL WE JOIN THE SOIREE, YOUNG LADY?
YOU'RE BEING AN AWFULLY GOOD SPORT, MR. LANCE.
IT IS A PLEASURE...
NO, MORE THAN THAT...IT...
YOU ARE A RARE CREATURE. YOU MUST JOIN MY TABLE. MY NAME IS...
I KNOW WHO YOU ARE, MR. BERTINELLI.
BUT I'M AFRAID I'VE PROMISED THE EVENING TO MY HUSBAND.
CELEBRATING THE UNUSUAL: GOTHAM ARCHITECTURE & DESIGN
YOU KNOW THAT CREEP'S GONNA BE THINKING OF YOU, COMING DOWN THAT STAIRWAY, FOR THE REST OF HIS LIFE, DON'T YOU?
POOR LITTLE GANGSTER. IT MAKES ME WEEP, SINCERELY.
YEAH, WELL, QUIT CRYING AND DANCE WITH THE LUCKIEST COP IN GOTHAM.

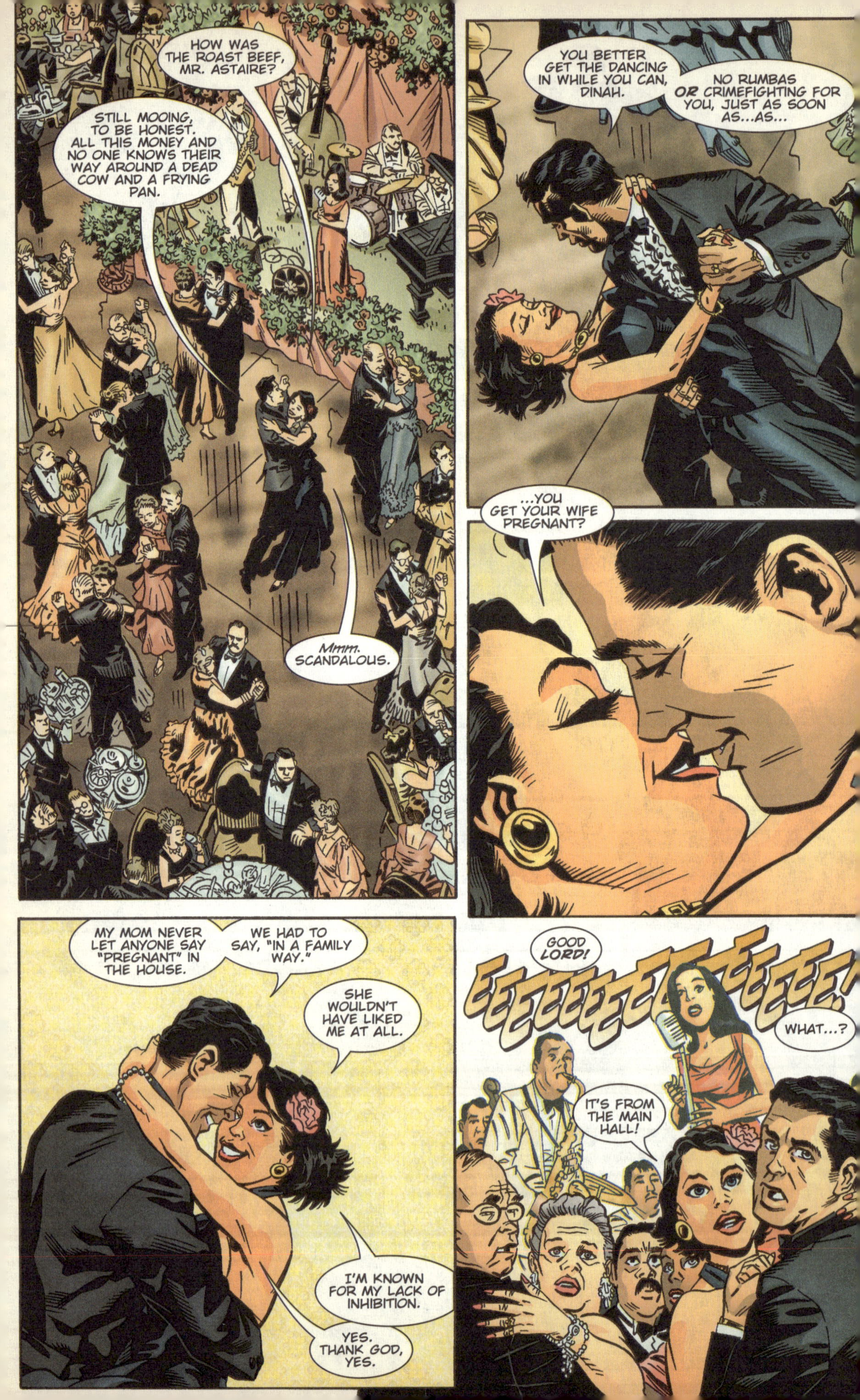
HOW WAS THE ROAST BEEF, MR. ASTAIRE?
STILL MOOING, TO BE HONEST. ALL THIS MONEY AND NO ONE KNOWS THEIR WAY AROUND A DEAD COW AND A FRYING PAN.
Mmm. SCANDALOUS.
YOU BETTER GET THE DANCING IN WHILE YOU CAN, DINAH.
NO RUMBAS OR CRIMEFIGHTING FOR YOU, JUST AS SOON AS...AS...
...YOU GET YOUR WIFE PREGNANT?
MY MOM NEVER LET ANYONE SAY "PREGNANT" IN THE HOUSE.
WE HAD TO SAY, "IN A FAMILY WAY."
SHE WOULDN'T HAVE LIKED ME AT ALL.
I'M KNOWN FOR MY LACK OF INHIBITION.
YES. THANK GOD, YES.
GOOD LORD!
EEEEEEEEEEEEEEE!
WHAT...?
IT'S FROM THE MAIN HALL!

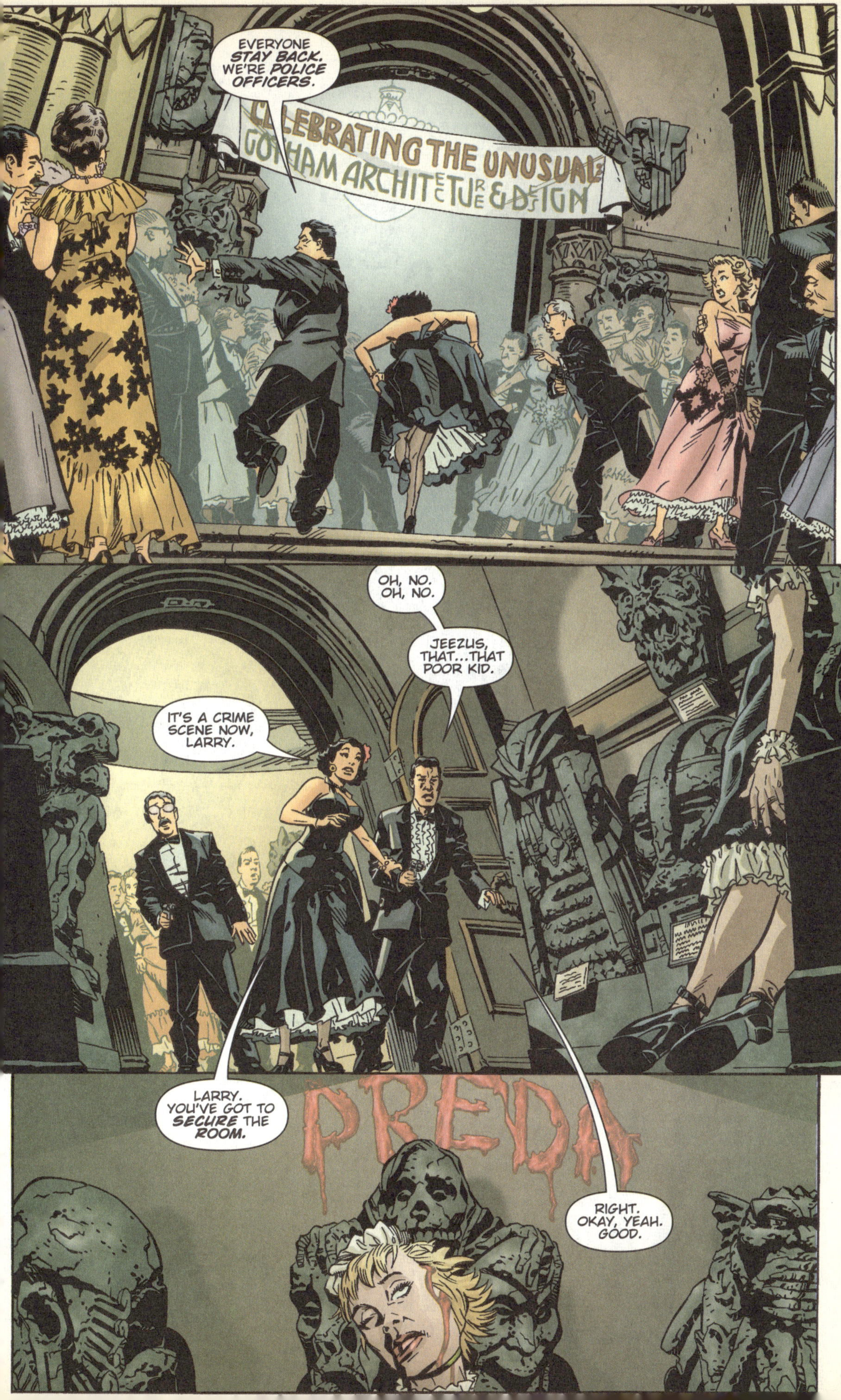
EVERYONE STAY BACK. WE'RE POLICE OFFICERS.
CELEBRATING THE UNUSUAL: GOTHAM ARCHITECTURE & DESIGN
OH, NO. OH, NO.
JEEZUS, THAT...THAT POOR KID.
IT'S A CRIME SCENE NOW, LARRY.
LARRY. YOU'VE GOT TO SECURE THE ROOM.
RIGHT. OKAY, YEAH. GOOD.
PREDA

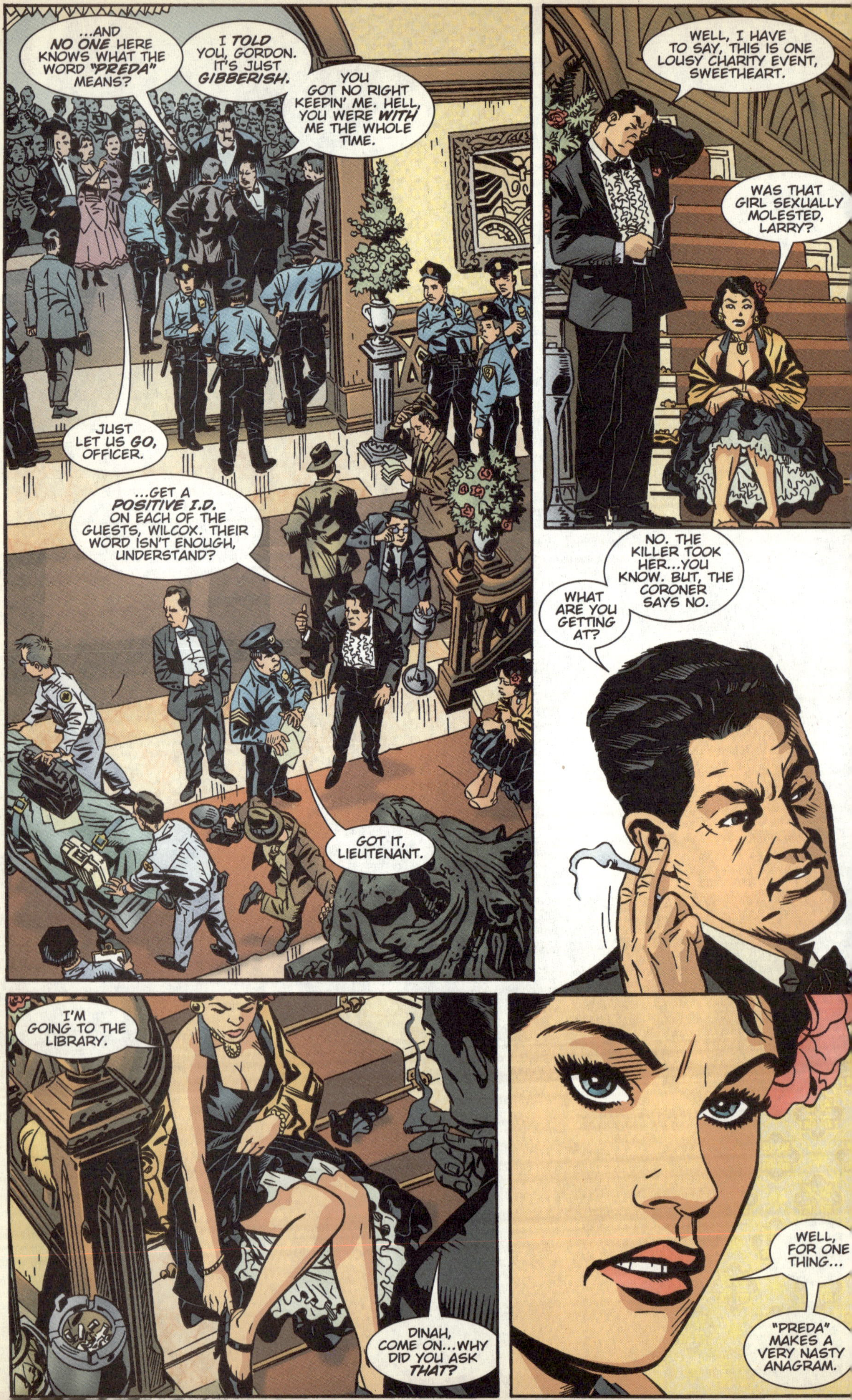
...AND NO ONE HERE KNOWS WHAT THE WORD "PREDA" MEANS?
I TOLD YOU, GORDON. IT'S JUST GIBBERISH.
YOU GOT NO RIGHT KEEPIN' ME. HELL, YOU WERE WITH ME THE WHOLE TIME.
JUST LET US GO, OFFICER.
...GET A POSITIVE I.D. ON EACH OF THE GUESTS, WILCOX. THEIR WORD ISN'T ENOUGH, UNDERSTAND?
GOT IT, LIEUTENANT.
WELL, I HAVE TO SAY, THIS IS ONE LOUSY CHARITY EVENT, SWEETHEART.
WAS THAT GIRL SEXUALLY MOLESTED, LARRY?
NO. THE KILLER TOOK HER...YOU KNOW. BUT, THE CORONER SAYS NO.
WHAT ARE YOU GETTING AT?
I'M GOING TO THE LIBRARY.
DINAH, COME ON...WHY DID YOU ASK THAT?
WELL, FOR ONE THING...
"PREDA" MAKES A VERY NASTY ANAGRAM.

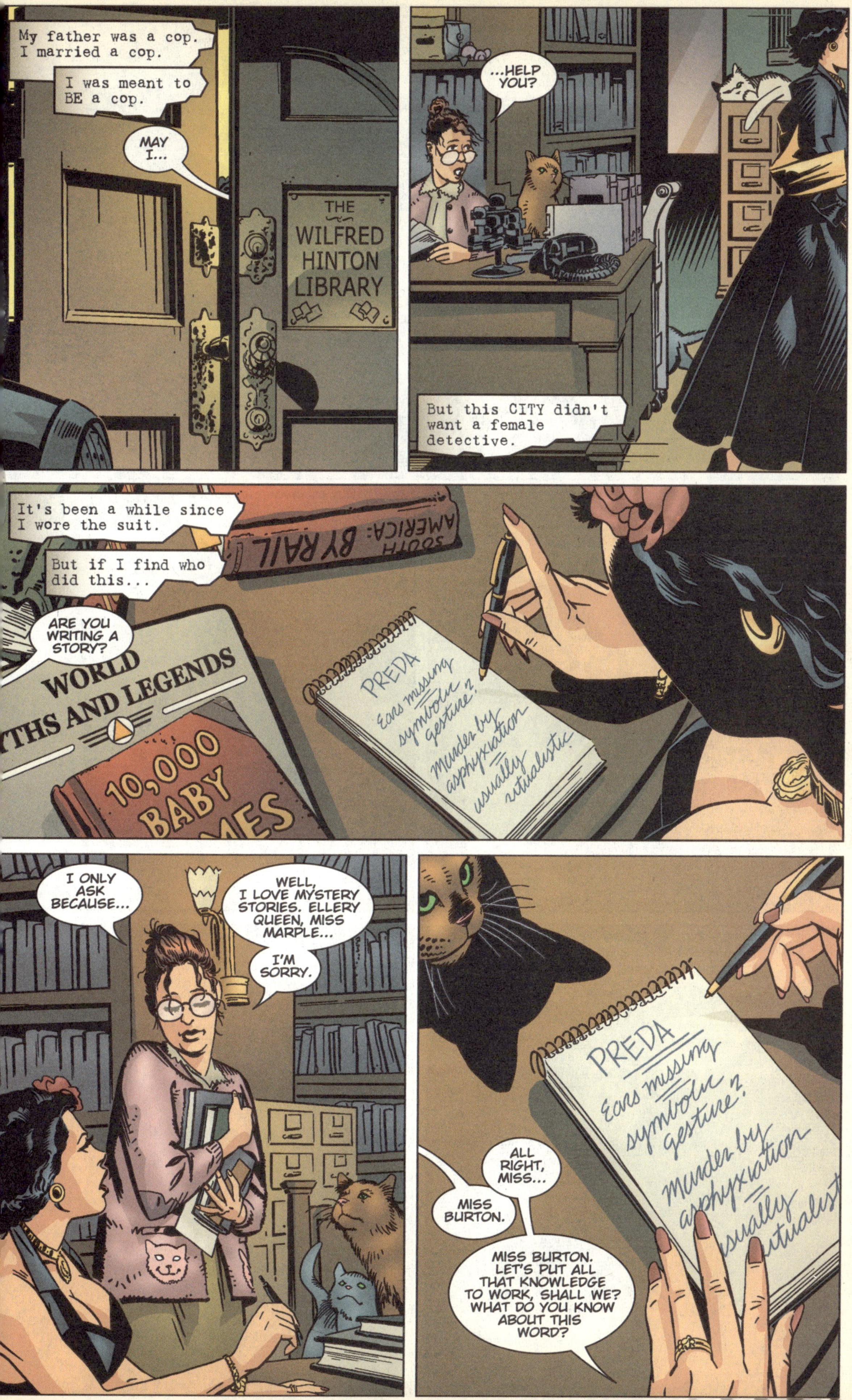

My father was a cop. I married a cop.
I was meant to BE a cop.
MAY I...
THE WILFRED HINTON LIBRARY
...HELP YOU?
But this CITY didn't want a female detective.
It's been a while since I wore the suit.
But if I find who did this...
ARE YOU WRITING A STORY?
SOUTH AMERICA: BY RAIL
WORLD MYTHS AND LEGENDS
10,000 BABY
PREDA
Ears missing
symbolic gesture?
murder by asphyxiation
usually ritualistic
I ONLY ASK BECAUSE...
WELL, I LOVE MYSTERY STORIES. ELLERY QUEEN, MISS MARPLE...
I'M SORRY.
PREDA
Ears missing
symbolic gesture?
murder by asphyxiation
usually ritualist
ALL RIGHT, MISS...
MISS BURTON.
MISS BURTON. LET'S PUT ALL THAT KNOWLEDGE TO WORK, SHALL WE? WHAT DO YOU KNOW ABOUT THIS WORD?

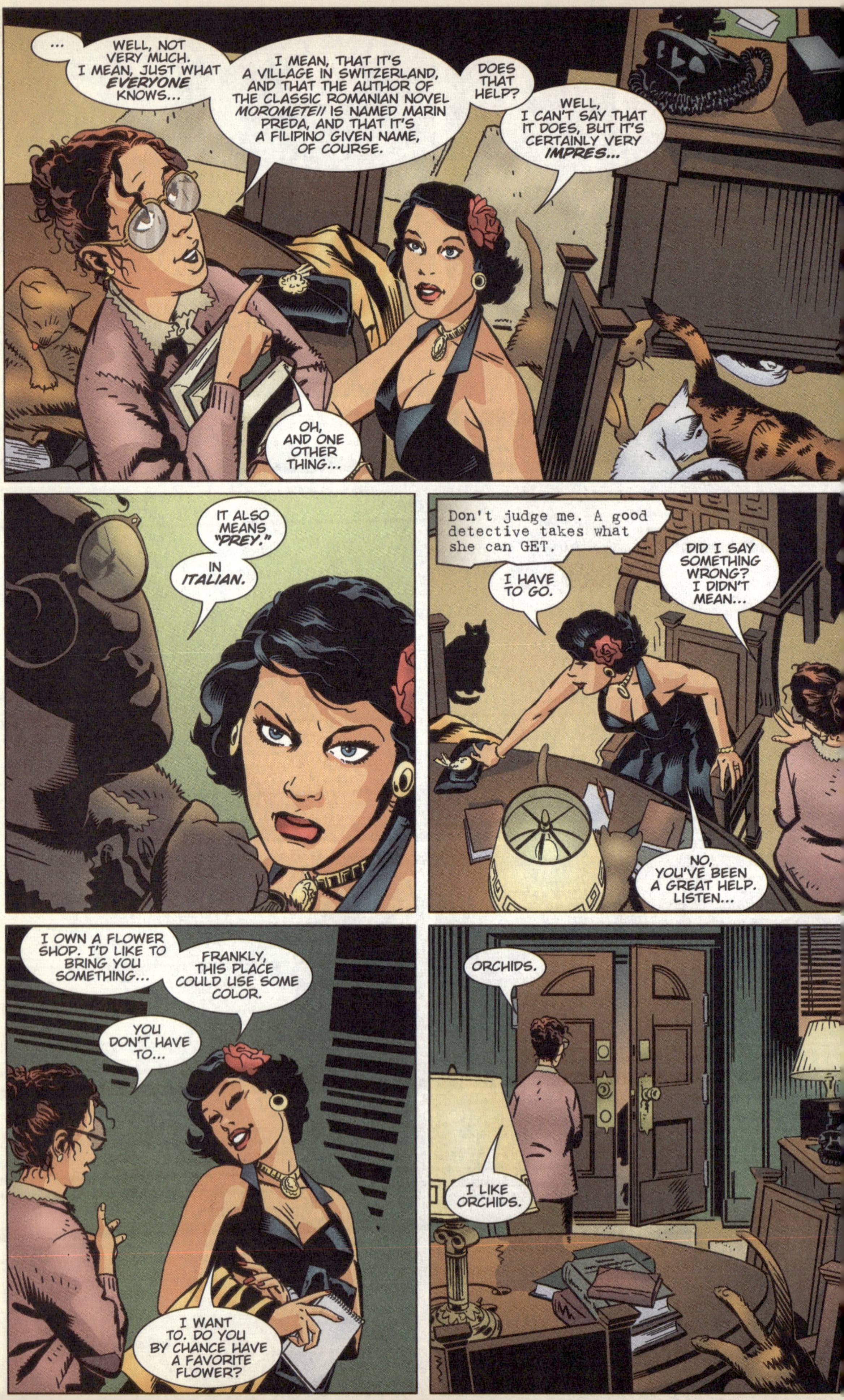
...
WELL, NOT VERY MUCH. I MEAN, JUST WHAT EVERYONE KNOWS...
I MEAN, THAT IT'S A VILLAGE IN SWITZERLAND, AND THAT THE AUTHOR OF THE CLASSIC ROMANIAN NOVEL MOROMETEII IS NAMED MARIN PREDA, AND THAT IT'S A FILIPINO GIVEN NAME, OF COURSE.
DOES THAT HELP?
WELL, I CAN'T SAY THAT IT DOES, BUT IT'S CERTAINLY VERY IMPRES...
OH, AND ONE OTHER THING...
IT ALSO MEANS "PREY."
IN ITALIAN.
Don't judge me. A good detective takes what she can GET.
I HAVE TO GO.
DID I SAY SOMETHING WRONG? I DIDN'T MEAN...
NO, YOU'VE BEEN A GREAT HELP. LISTEN...
I OWN A FLOWER SHOP. I'D LIKE TO BRING YOU SOMETHING...
FRANKLY, THIS PLACE COULD USE SOME COLOR.
YOU DON'T HAVE TO...
I WANT TO. DO YOU BY CHANCE HAVE A FAVORITE FLOWER?
ORCHIDS.
I LIKE ORCHIDS.

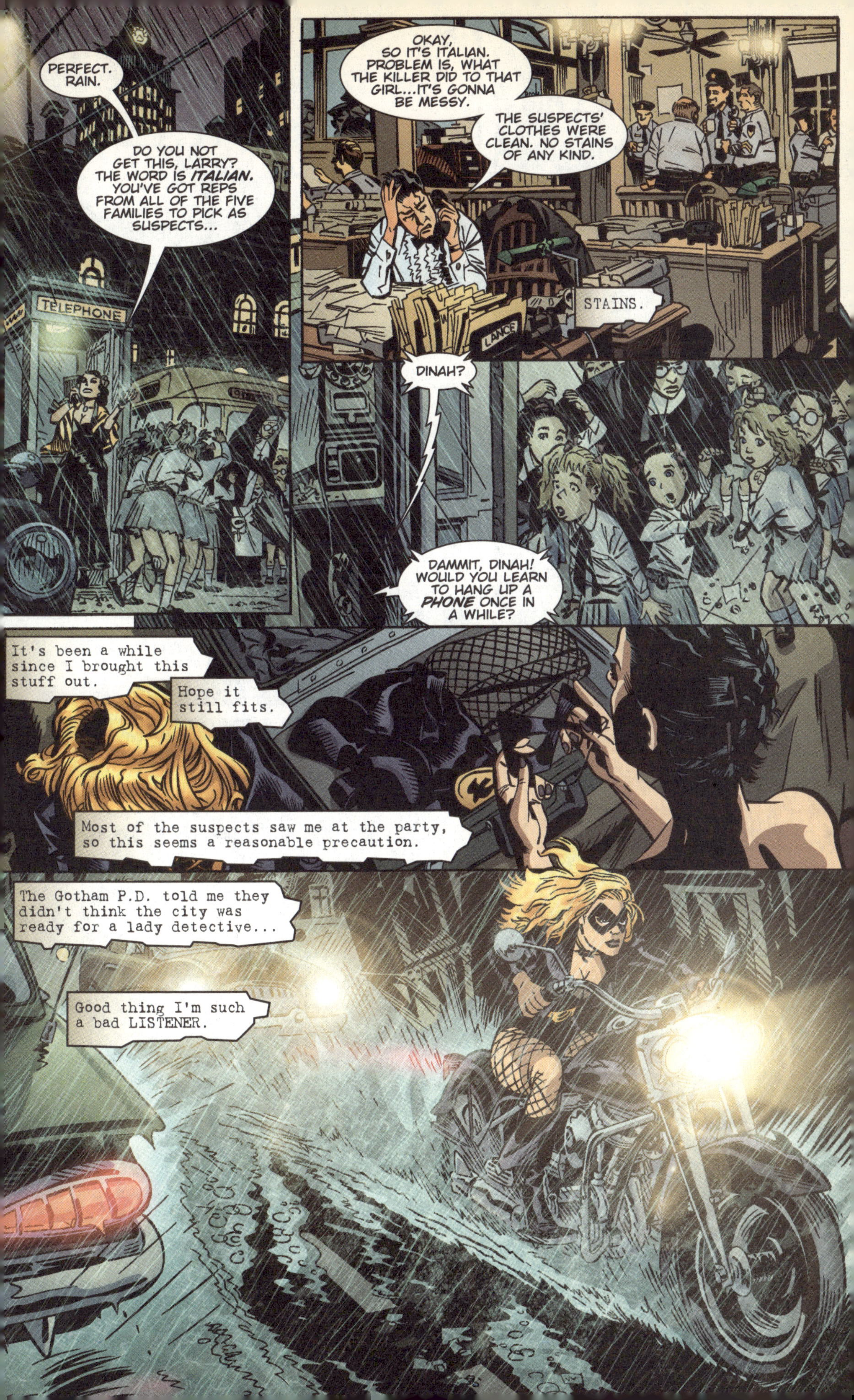

PERFECT. RAIN.
DO YOU NOT GET THIS, LARRY? THE WORD IS *ITALIAN.* YOU'VE GOT REPS FROM ALL OF THE FIVE FAMILIES TO PICK AS SUSPECTS...
OKAY, SO IT'S ITALIAN. PROBLEM IS, WHAT THE KILLER DID TO THAT GIRL...IT'S GONNA BE MESSY.
THE SUSPECTS' CLOTHES WERE CLEAN. NO STAINS OF ANY KIND.
STAINS.
LANCE
TELEPHONE
DINAH?
DAMMIT, DINAH! WOULD YOU LEARN TO HANG UP A *PHONE* ONCE IN A WHILE?
It's been a while since I brought this stuff out.
Hope it still fits.
Most of the suspects saw me at the party, so this seems a reasonable precaution.
The Gotham P.D. told me they didn't think the city was ready for a lady detective...
Good thing I'm such a bad LISTENER.

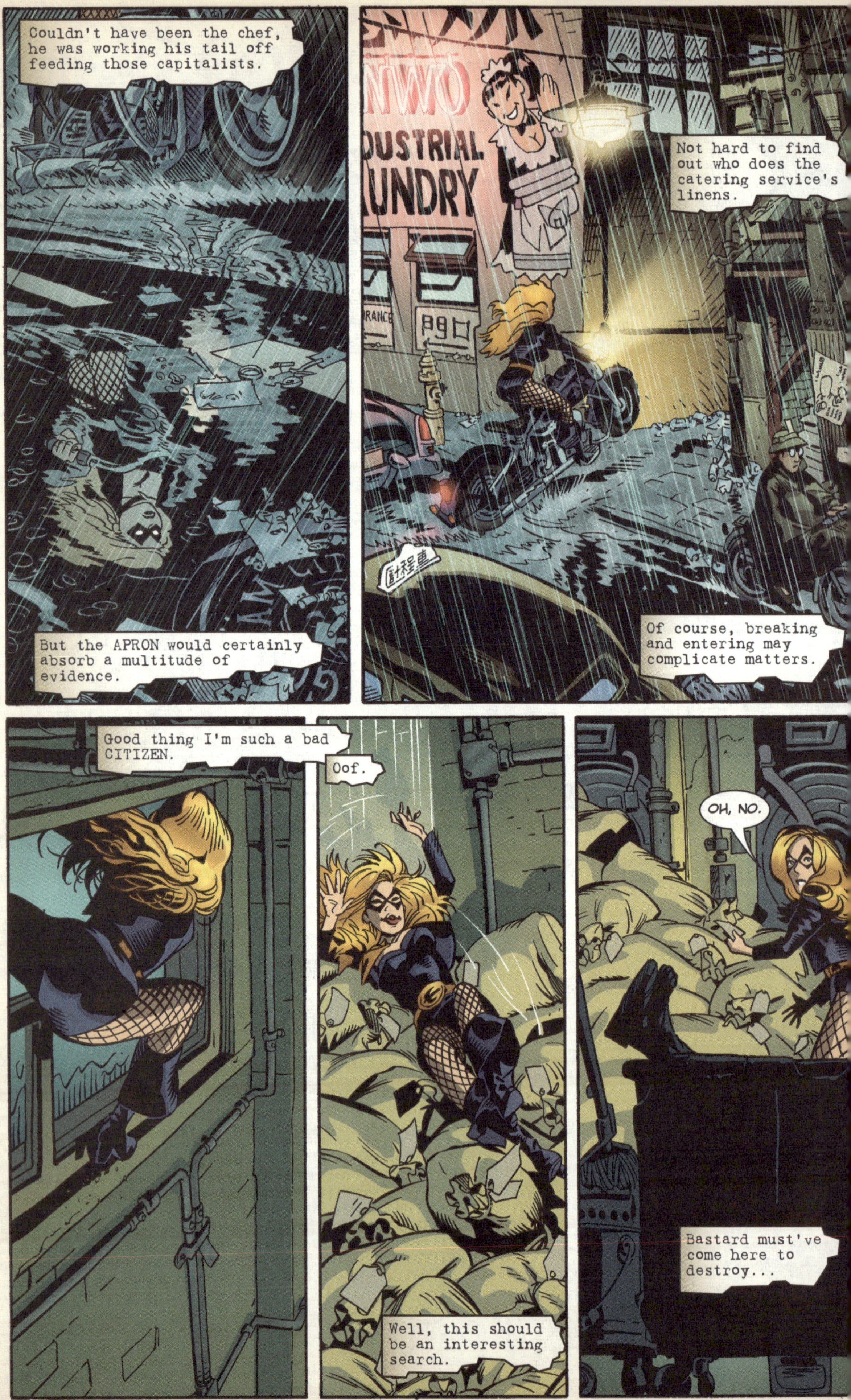

Couldn't have been the chef, he was working his tail off feeding those capitalists.
But the APRON would certainly absorb a multitude of evidence.
USTRIAL
UNDRY
Not hard to find out who does the catering service's linens.
Of course, breaking and entering may complicate matters.
Good thing I'm such a bad CITIZEN.
Oof.
Well, this should be an interesting search.
OH, NO.
Bastard must've come here to destroy...

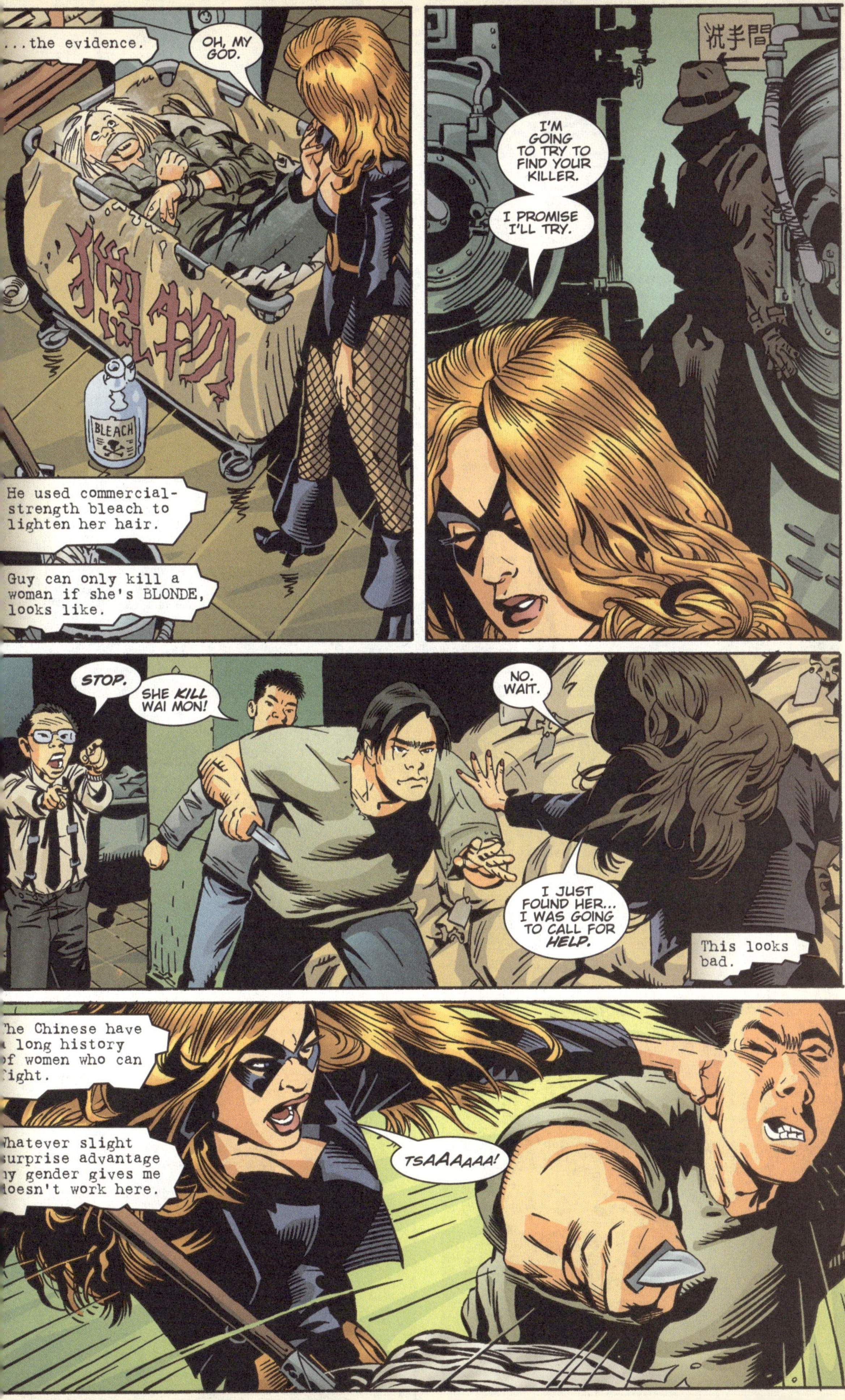

...the evidence.
OH, MY GOD.
He used commercial-strength bleach to lighten her hair.
Guy can only kill a woman if she's BLONDE, looks like.
BLEACH
I'M GOING TO TRY TO FIND YOUR KILLER.
I PROMISE I'LL TRY.
STOP.
SHE KILL WAI MON!
NO. WAIT.
I JUST FOUND HER... I WAS GOING TO CALL FOR HELP.
This looks bad.
The Chinese have a long history of women who can fight.
Whatever slight surprise advantage my gender gives me doesn't work here.
TSAAAAAAA!

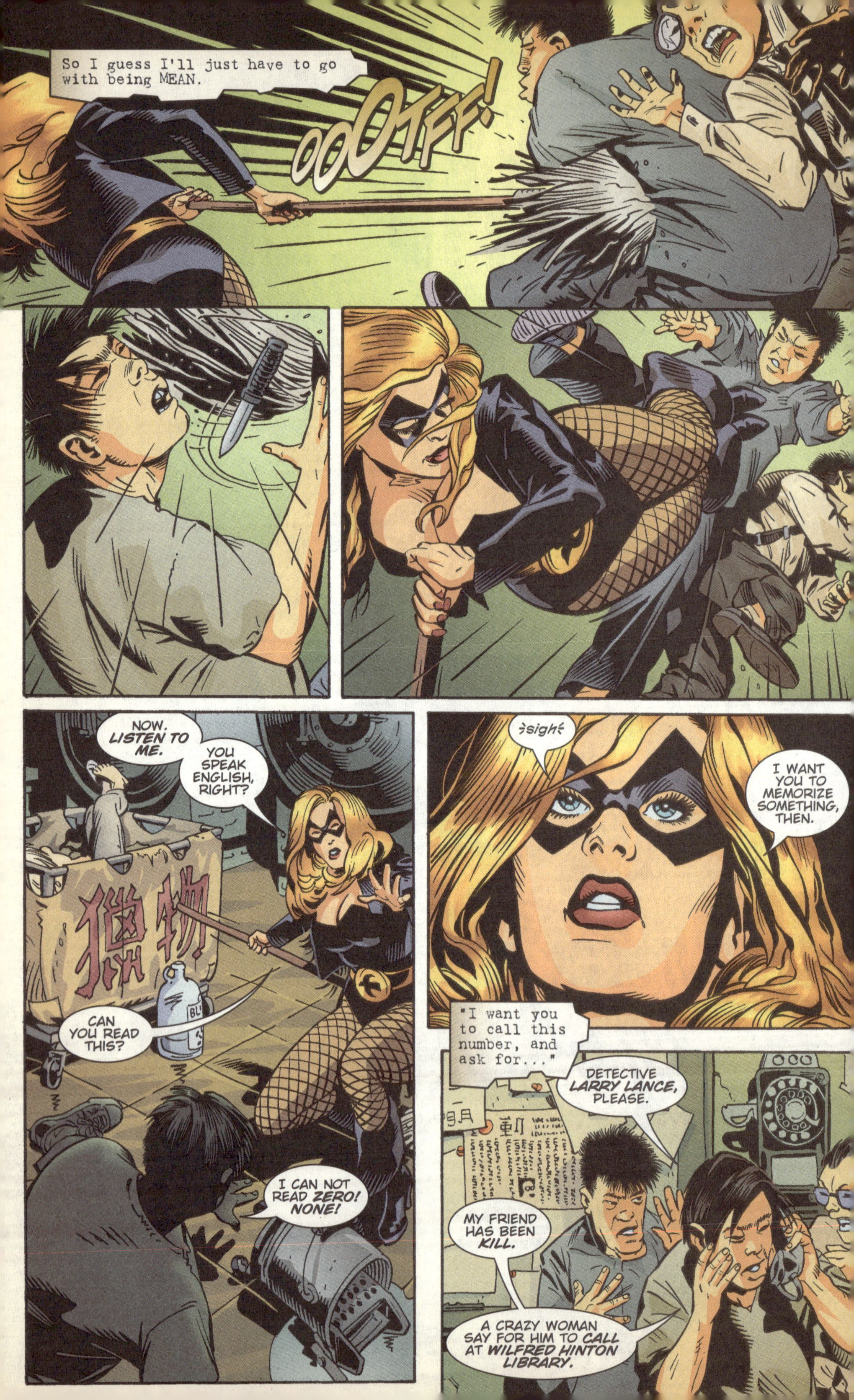
So I guess I'll just have to go with being MEAN.
OOOTFF!
NOW. LISTEN TO ME.
YOU SPEAK ENGLISH, RIGHT?
CAN YOU READ THIS?
I CAN NOT READ ZERO! NONE!
sigh
I WANT YOU TO MEMORIZE SOMETHING, THEN.
"I want you to call this number, and ask for..."
DETECTIVE LARRY LANCE, PLEASE.
MY FRIEND HAS BEEN KILL.
A CRAZY WOMAN SAY FOR HIM TO CALL AT WILFRED HINTON LIBRARY.

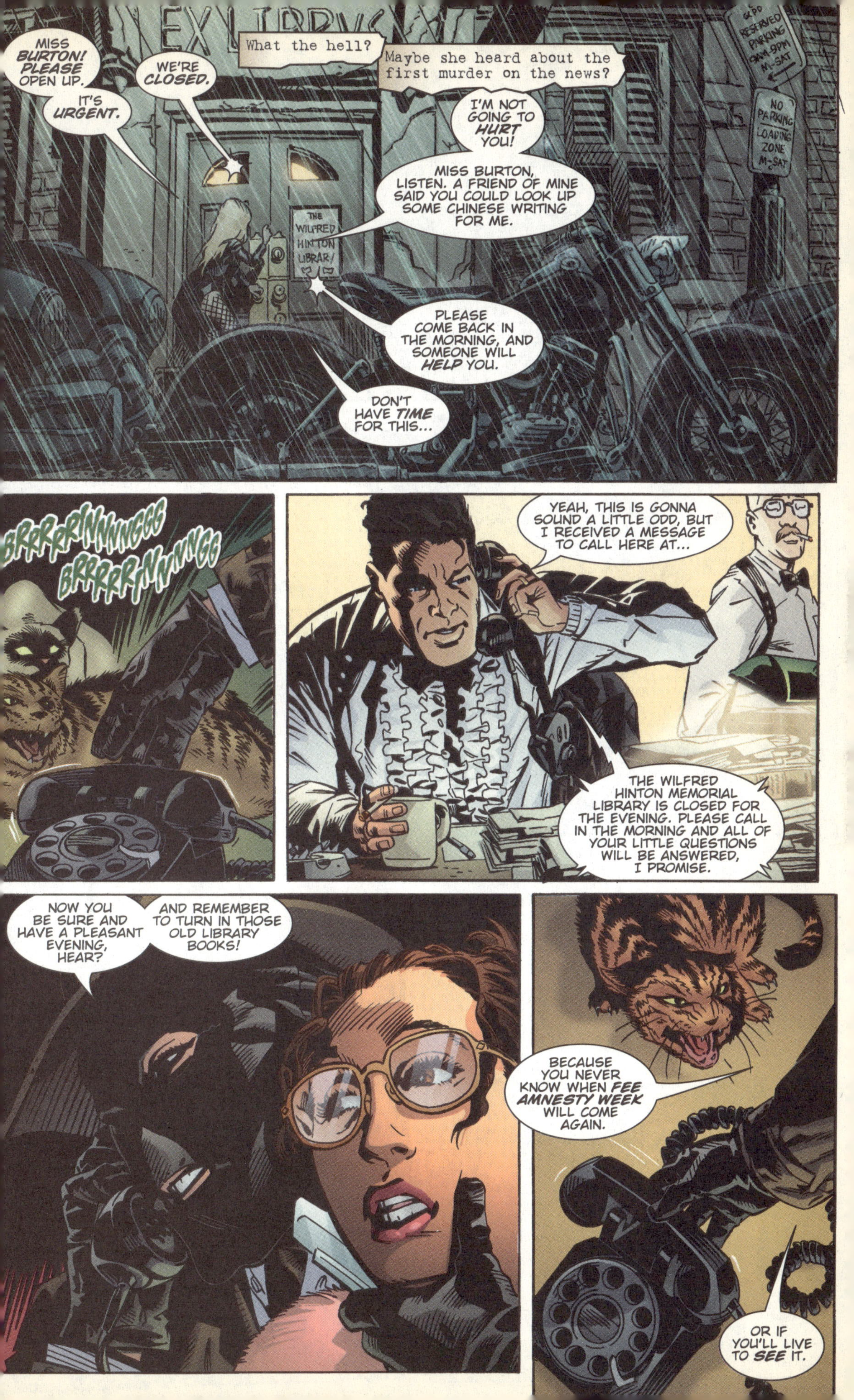

MISS BURTON! PLEASE OPEN UP.
IT'S URGENT.
WE'RE CLOSED.
What the hell?
Maybe she heard about the first murder on the news?
I'M NOT GOING TO HURT YOU!
MISS BURTON, LISTEN. A FRIEND OF MINE SAID YOU COULD LOOK UP SOME CHINESE WRITING FOR ME.
THE WILFRED HINTON LIBRARY!
PLEASE COME BACK IN THE MORNING, AND SOMEONE WILL HELP YOU.
DON'T HAVE TIME FOR THIS...
NO PARKING LOADING ZONE M-SAT
BRRRRRINNNNGGG
BRRRRRINNNNGG
YEAH, THIS IS GONNA SOUND A LITTLE ODD, BUT I RECEIVED A MESSAGE TO CALL HERE AT...
THE WILFRED HINTON MEMORIAL LIBRARY IS CLOSED FOR THE EVENING. PLEASE CALL IN THE MORNING AND ALL OF YOUR LITTLE QUESTIONS WILL BE ANSWERED, I PROMISE.
NOW YOU BE SURE AND HAVE A PLEASANT EVENING, HEAR?
AND REMEMBER TO TURN IN THOSE OLD LIBRARY BOOKS!
BECAUSE YOU NEVER KNOW WHEN FEE AMNESTY WEEK WILL COME AGAIN.
OR IF YOU'LL LIVE TO SEE IT.

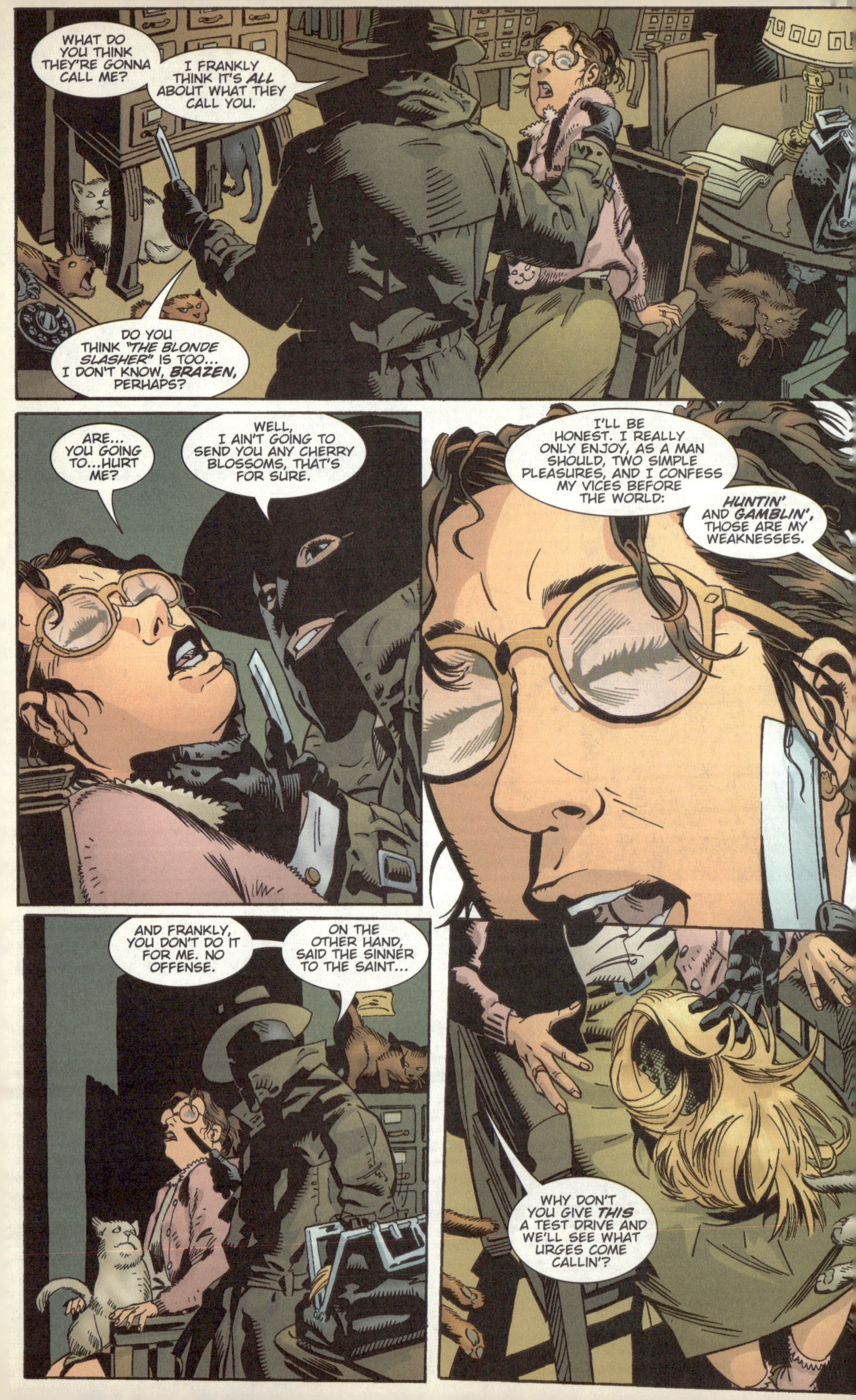
WHAT DO YOU THINK THEY'RE GONNA CALL ME?
I FRANKLY THINK IT'S ALL ABOUT WHAT THEY CALL YOU.
DO YOU THINK "THE BLONDE SLASHER" IS TOO... I DON'T KNOW, BRAZEN, PERHAPS?
ARE... YOU GOING TO...HURT ME?
WELL, I AIN'T GOING TO SEND YOU ANY CHERRY BLOSSOMS, THAT'S FOR SURE.
I'LL BE HONEST. I REALLY ONLY ENJOY, AS A MAN SHOULD, TWO SIMPLE PLEASURES, AND I CONFESS MY VICES BEFORE THE WORLD:
HUNTIN' AND GAMBLIN', THOSE ARE MY WEAKNESSES.
AND FRANKLY, YOU DON'T DO IT FOR ME. NO OFFENSE.
ON THE OTHER HAND, SAID THE SINNER TO THE SAINT...
WHY DON'T YOU GIVE THIS A TEST DRIVE AND WE'LL SEE WHAT URGES COME CALLIN'?

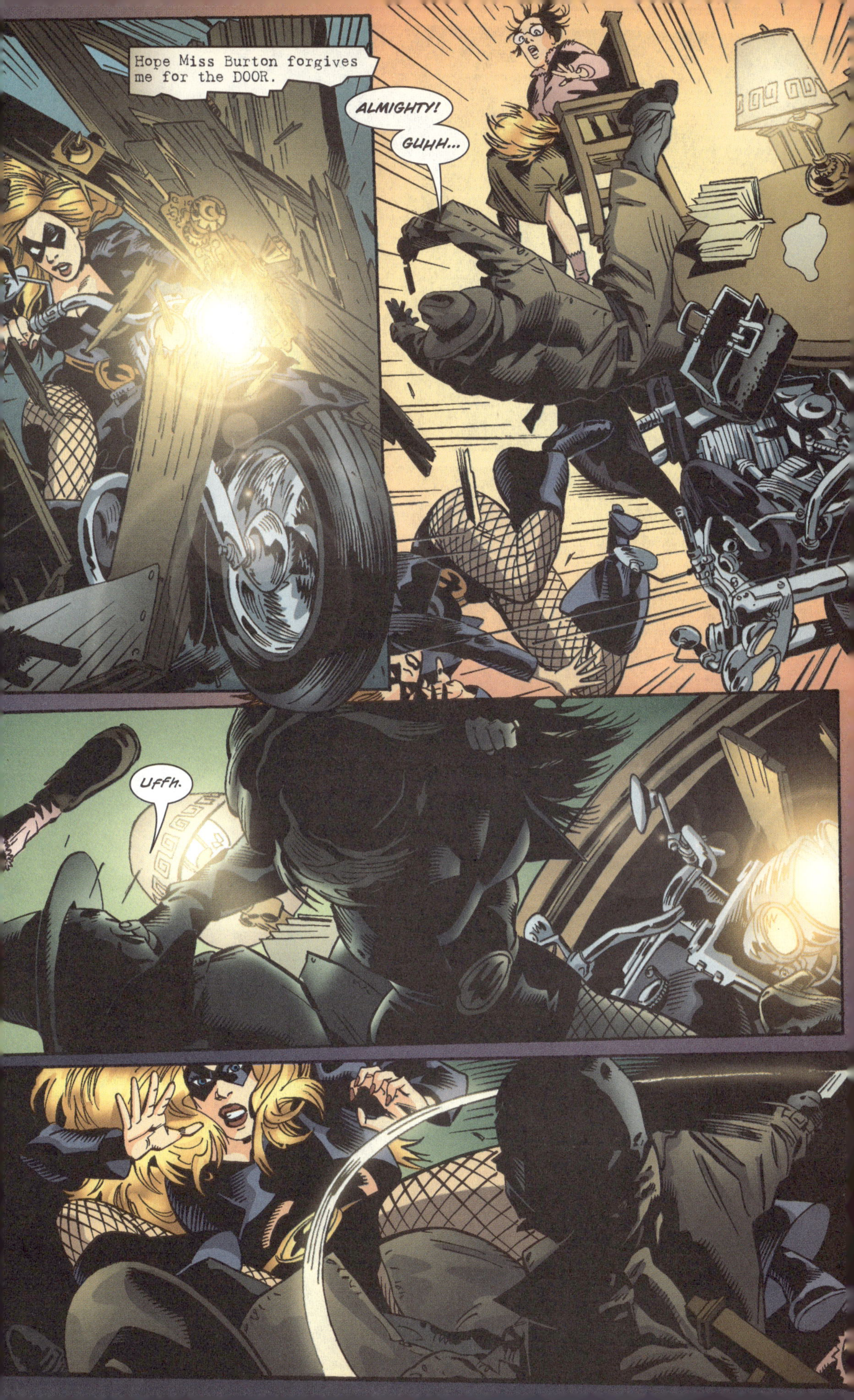
Hope Miss Burton forgives me for the DOOR.
ALMIGHTY!
GUHH...
Uffh.

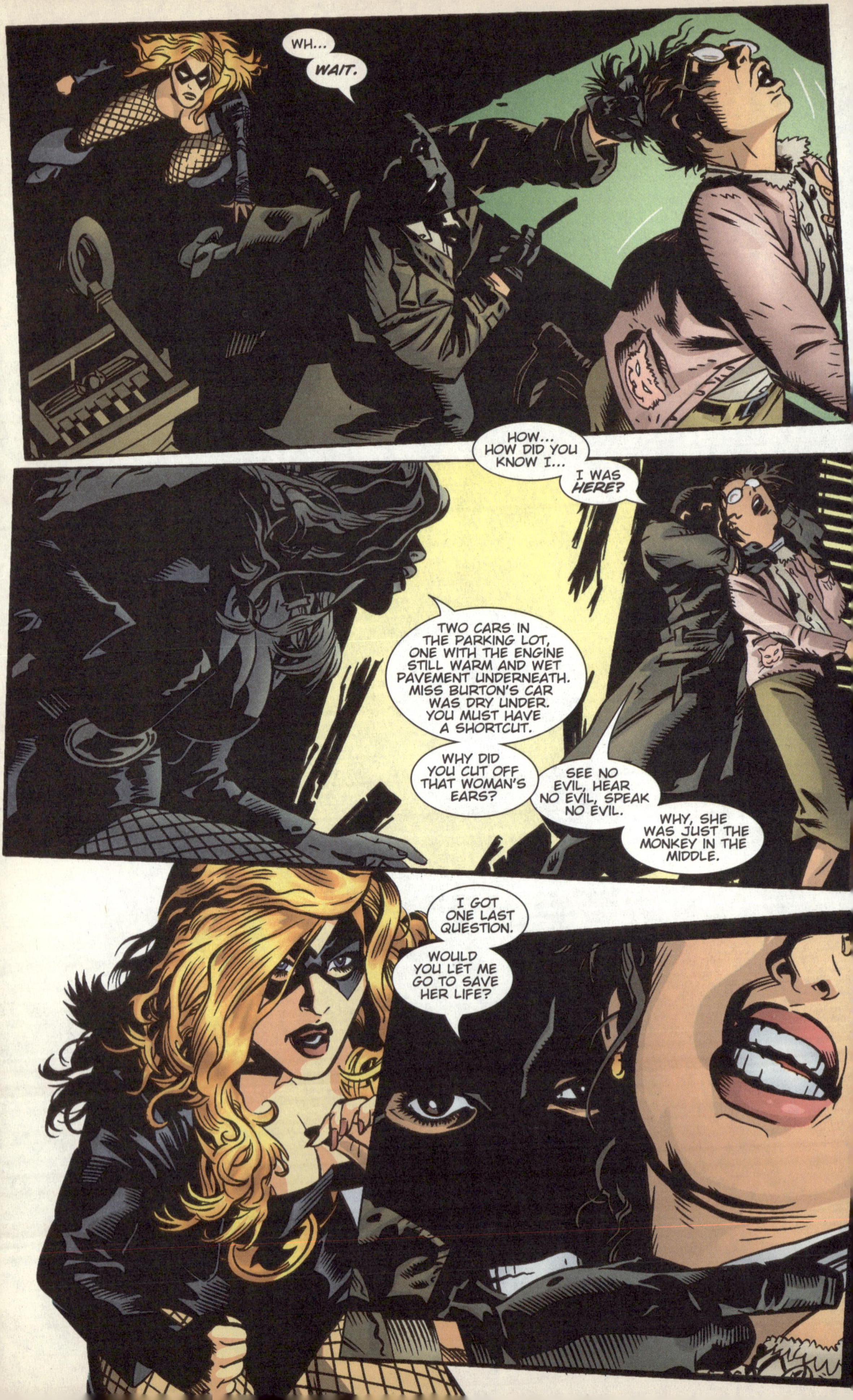
WH...
WAIT.
HOW... HOW DID YOU KNOW I...
I WAS HERE?
TWO CARS IN THE PARKING LOT, ONE WITH THE ENGINE STILL WARM AND WET PAVEMENT UNDERNEATH. MISS BURTON'S CAR WAS DRY UNDER. YOU MUST HAVE A SHORTCUT.
WHY DID YOU CUT OFF THAT WOMAN'S EARS?
SEE NO EVIL, HEAR NO EVIL, SPEAK NO EVIL.
WHY, SHE WAS JUST THE MONKEY IN THE MIDDLE.
I GOT ONE LAST QUESTION.
WOULD YOU LET ME GO TO SAVE HER LIFE?

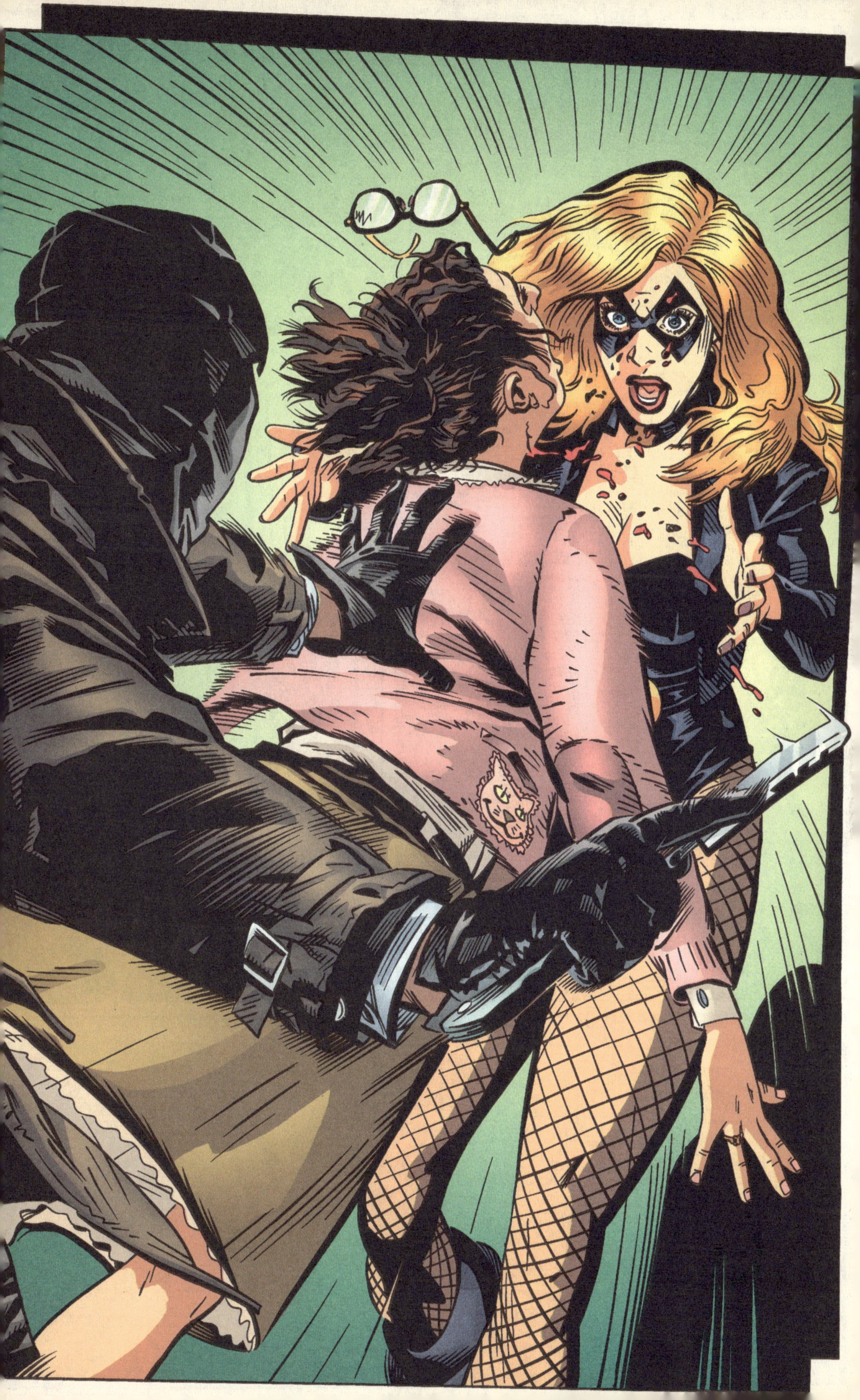

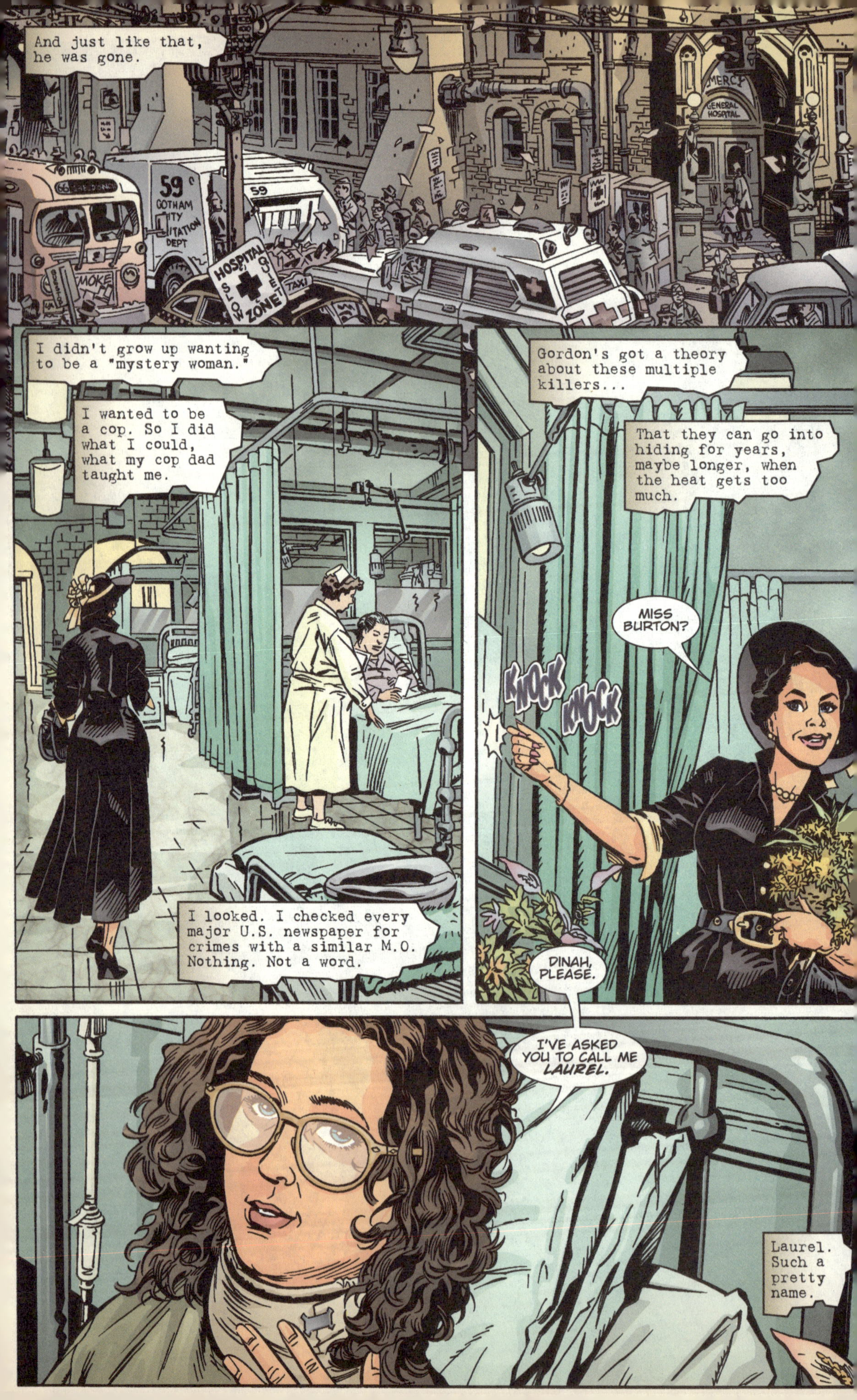
And just like that, he was gone.
MERCY GENERAL HOSPITAL
59 GOTHAM CITY SANITATION DEPT
HOSPITAL SLOW QUIET ZONE
TAXI
I didn't grow up wanting to be a "mystery woman."
I wanted to be a cop. So I did what I could, what my cop dad taught me.
I looked. I checked every major U.S. newspaper for crimes with a similar M.O. Nothing. Not a word.
Gordon's got a theory about these multiple killers...
That they can go into hiding for years, maybe longer, when the heat gets too much.
MISS BURTON?
KNOCK KNOCK
DINAH, PLEASE.
I'VE ASKED YOU TO CALL ME LAUREL.
Laurel. Such a pretty name.

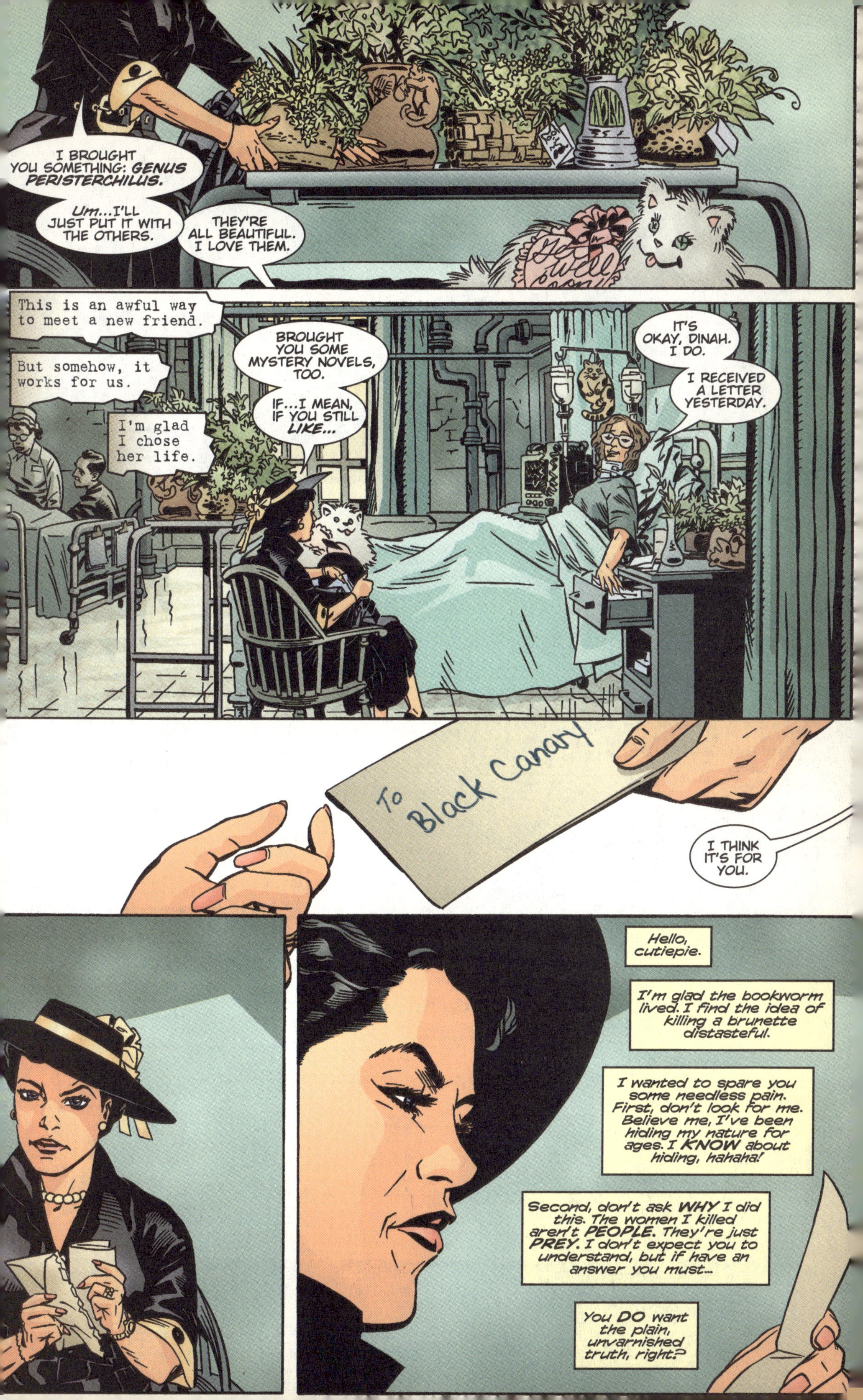

I BROUGHT YOU SOMETHING: **GENUS PERISTERCHILUS.**
UM...I'LL JUST PUT IT WITH THE OTHERS.
THEY'RE ALL BEAUTIFUL. I LOVE THEM.
This is an awful way to meet a new friend.
But somehow, it works for us.
I'm glad I chose her life.
BROUGHT YOU SOME MYSTERY NOVELS, TOO.
IF...I MEAN, IF YOU STILL **LIKE...**
IT'S OKAY, DINAH. I DO.
I RECEIVED A LETTER YESTERDAY.
To Black Canary
I THINK IT'S FOR YOU.
Hello, cutiepie.
I'm glad the bookworm lived. I find the idea of killing a brunette distasteful.
I wanted to spare you some needless pain. First, don't look for me. Believe me, I've been hiding my nature for ages. I **KNOW** about hiding, hahaha!
Second, don't ask **WHY** I did this. The women I killed aren't **PEOPLE.** They're just **PREY.** I don't expect you to understand, but if have an answer you must...
You **DO** want the plain, unvarnished truth, right?

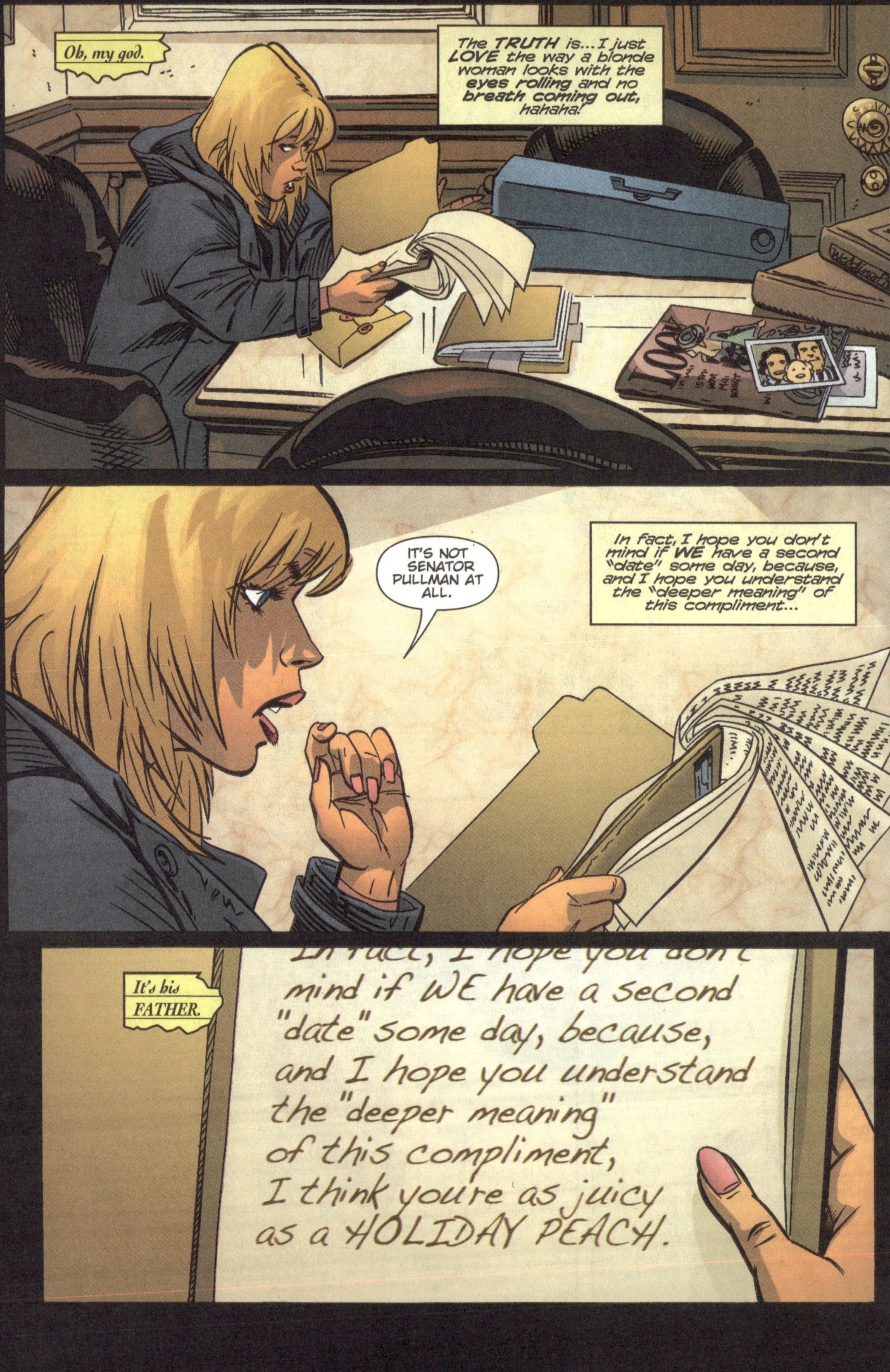
Oh, my god.
The TRUTH is... I just LOVE the way a blonde woman looks with the eyes rolling and no breath coming out, hahaha!
IT'S NOT SENATOR PULLMAN AT ALL.
In fact, I hope you don't mind if WE have a second "date" some day, because, and I hope you understand the "deeper meaning" of this compliment...
It's his FATHER.
mind if WE have a second "date" some day, because, and I hope you understand the "deeper meaning" of this compliment, I think you're as juicy as a HOLIDAY PEACH.

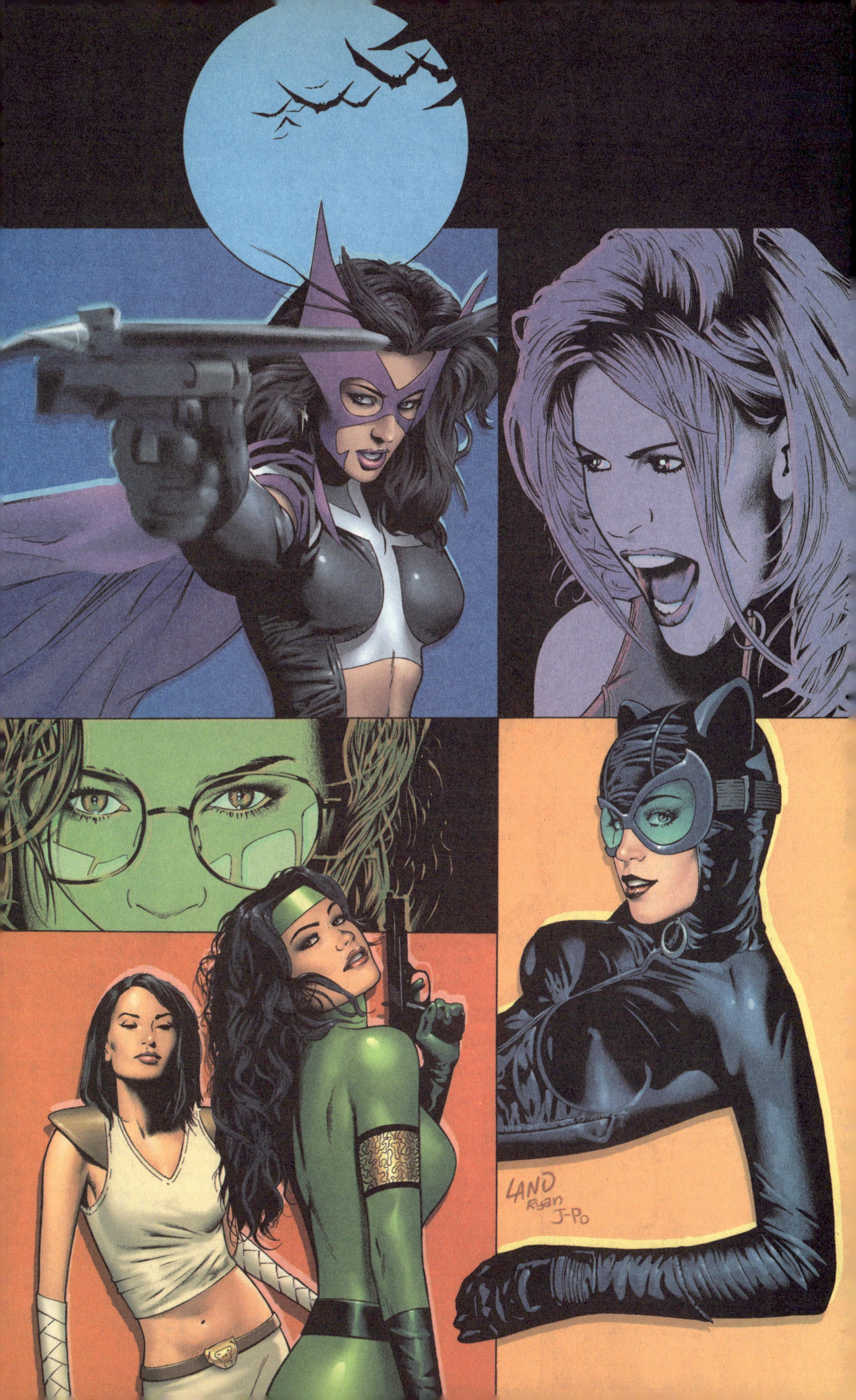
LAND
Ryan
J-Po

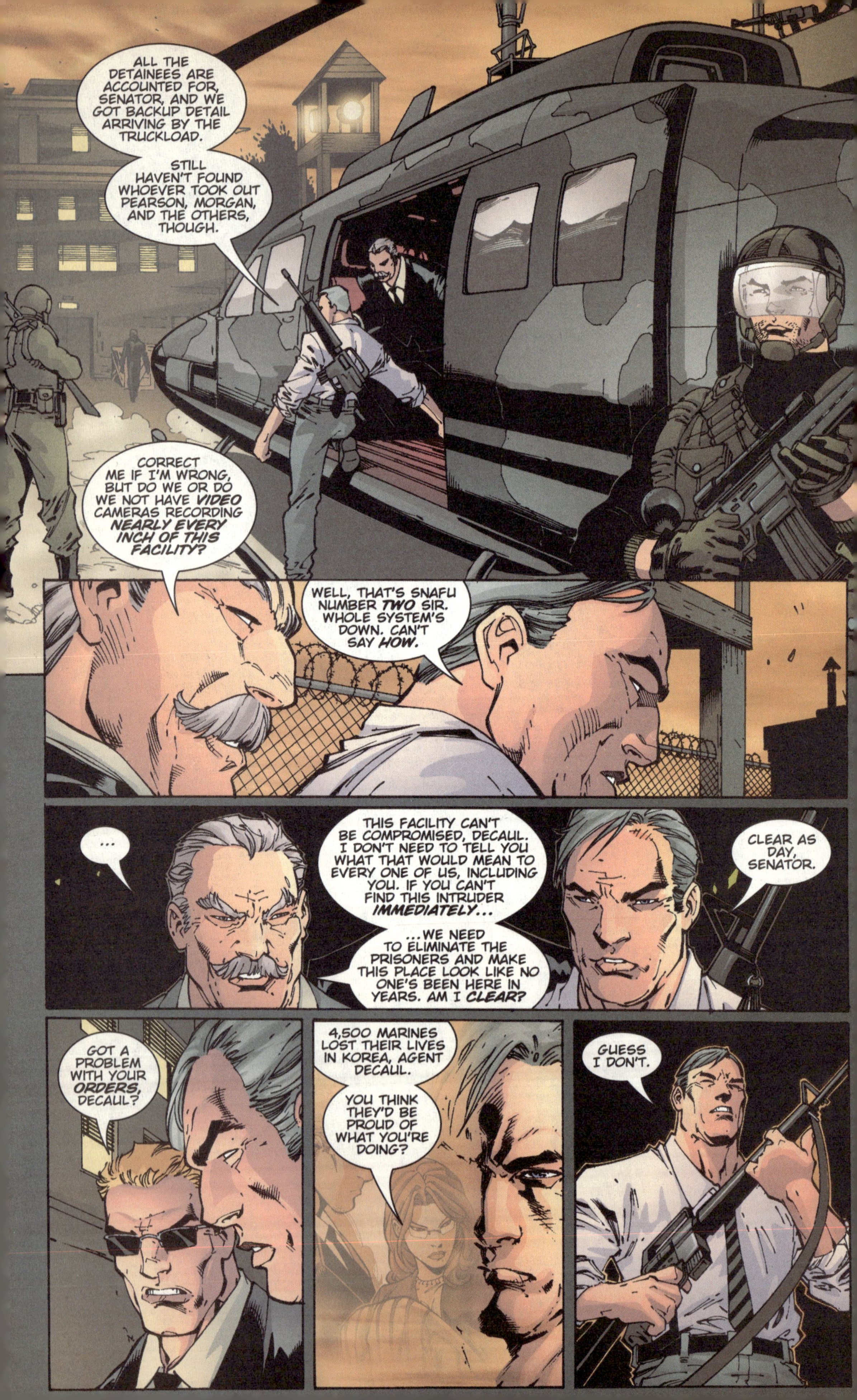
ALL THE DETAINEES ARE ACCOUNTED FOR, SENATOR, AND WE GOT BACKUP DETAIL ARRIVING BY THE TRUCKLOAD.
STILL HAVEN'T FOUND WHOEVER TOOK OUT PEARSON, MORGAN, AND THE OTHERS, THOUGH.
CORRECT ME IF I'M WRONG, BUT DO WE OR DO WE NOT HAVE VIDEO CAMERAS RECORDING NEARLY EVERY INCH OF THIS FACILITY?
WELL, THAT'S SNAFU NUMBER TWO SIR. WHOLE SYSTEM'S DOWN. CAN'T SAY HOW.
...
THIS FACILITY CAN'T BE COMPROMISED, DECAUL. I DON'T NEED TO TELL YOU WHAT THAT WOULD MEAN TO EVERY ONE OF US, INCLUDING YOU. IF YOU CAN'T FIND THIS INTRUDER IMMEDIATELY...
...WE NEED TO ELIMINATE THE PRISONERS AND MAKE THIS PLACE LOOK LIKE NO ONE'S BEEN HERE IN YEARS. AM I CLEAR?
CLEAR AS DAY, SENATOR.
GOT A PROBLEM WITH YOUR ORDERS, DECAUL?
4,500 MARINES LOST THEIR LIVES IN KOREA, AGENT DECAUL.
YOU THINK THEY'D BE PROUD OF WHAT YOU'RE DOING?
GUESS I DON'T.

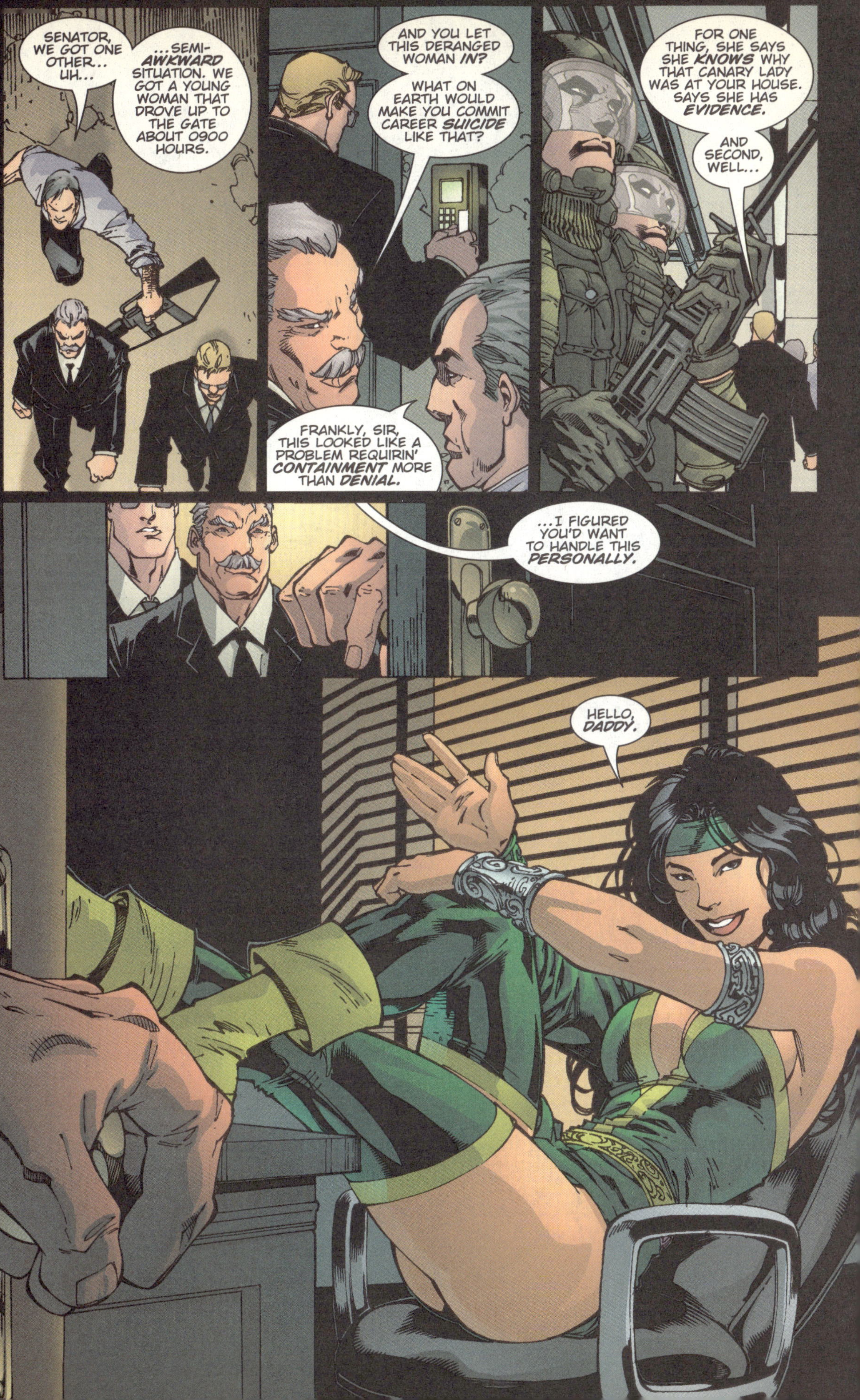
SENATOR, WE GOT ONE OTHER... UH...
...SEMI-AWKWARD SITUATION. WE GOT A YOUNG WOMAN THAT DROVE UP TO THE GATE ABOUT 0900 HOURS.
AND YOU LET THIS DERANGED WOMAN IN?
WHAT ON EARTH WOULD MAKE YOU COMMIT CAREER SUICIDE LIKE THAT?
FRANKLY, SIR, THIS LOOKED LIKE A PROBLEM REQUIRIN' CONTAINMENT MORE THAN DENIAL.
FOR ONE THING, SHE SAYS SHE KNOWS WHY THAT CANARY LADY WAS AT YOUR HOUSE. SAYS SHE HAS EVIDENCE.
AND SECOND, WELL...
...I FIGURED YOU'D WANT TO HANDLE THIS PERSONALLY.
HELLO, DADDY.

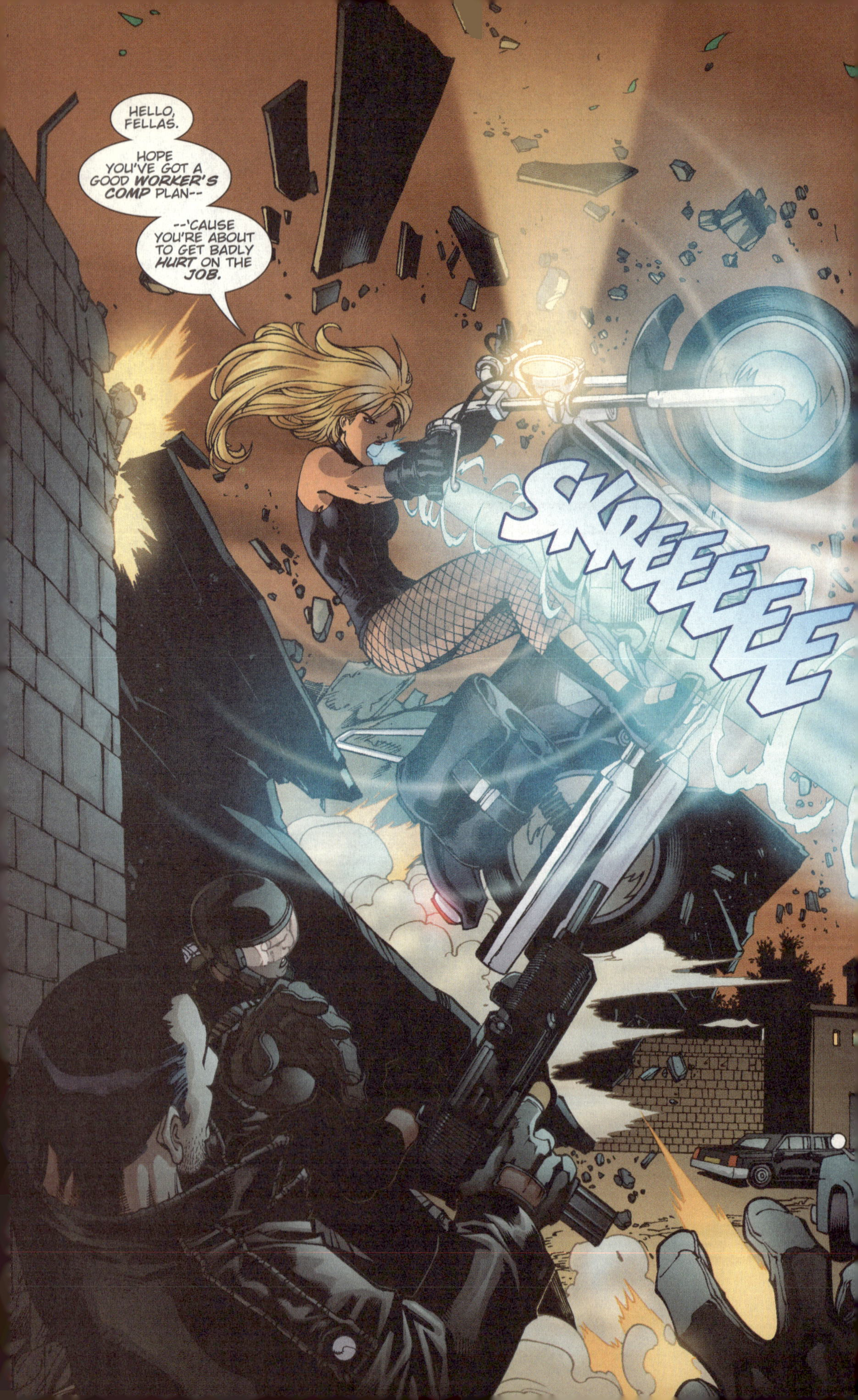
HELLO, FELLAS.
HOPE YOU'VE GOT A GOOD **WORKER'S COMP** PLAN--
--'CAUSE YOU'RE ABOUT TO GET BADLY **HURT** ON THE **JOB.**
SKREEEEEE

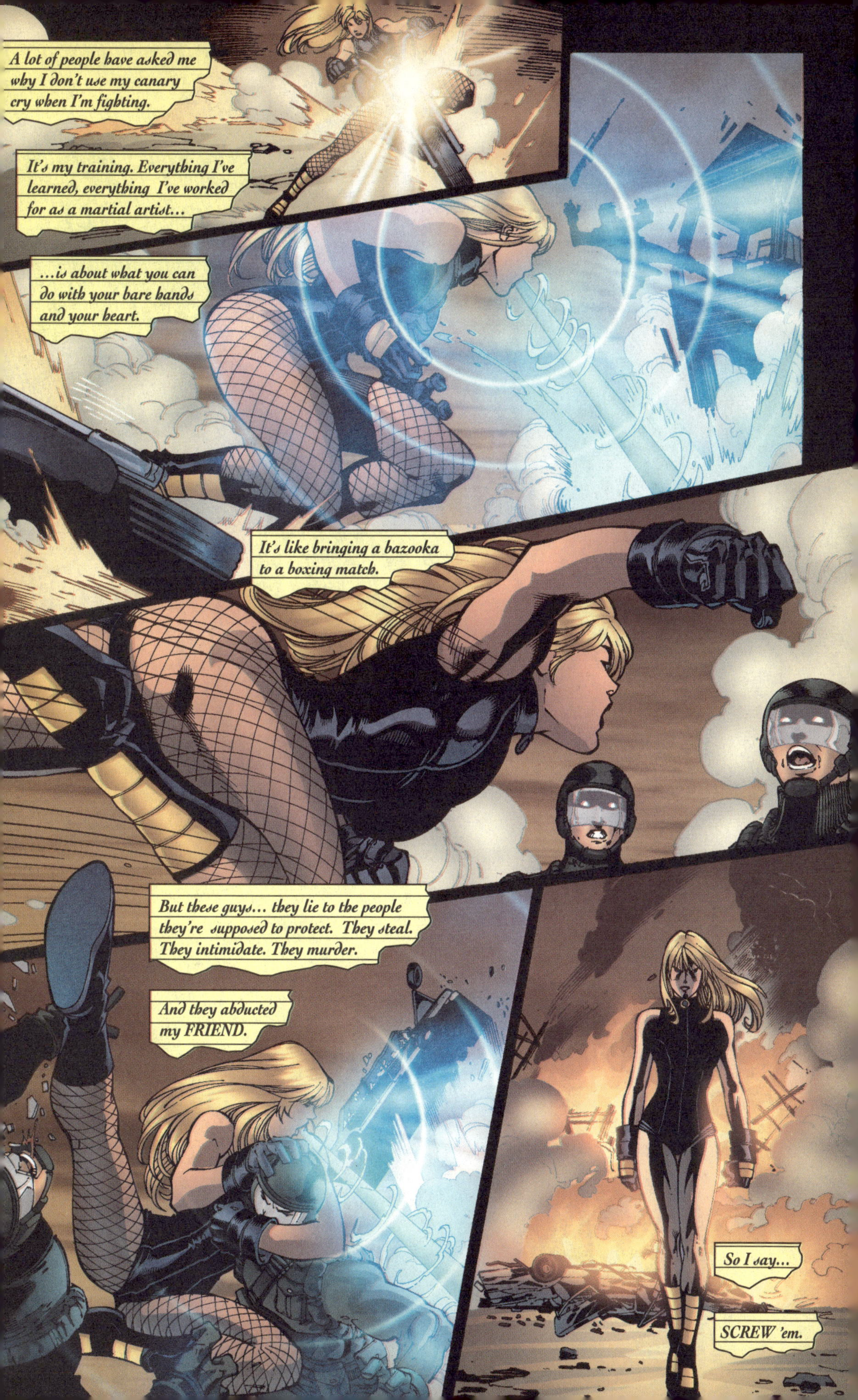
A lot of people have asked me why I don't use my canary cry when I'm fighting.
It's my training. Everything I've learned, everything I've worked for as a martial artist...
...is about what you can do with your bare hands and your heart.
It's like bringing a bazooka to a boxing match.
But these guys... they lie to the people they're supposed to protect. They steal. They intimidate. They murder.
And they abducted my FRIEND.
So I say...
SCREW 'em.

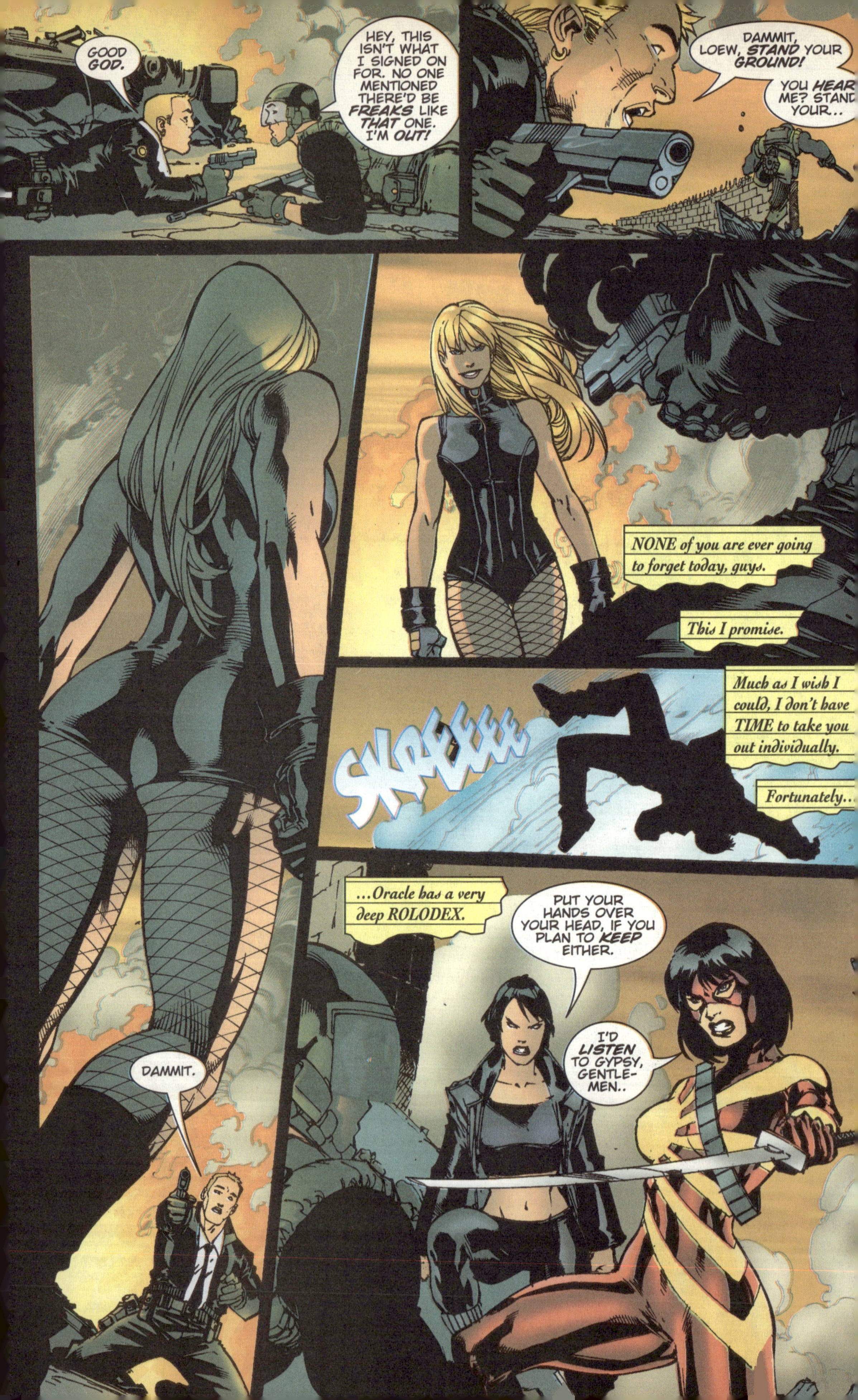
GOOD GOD.
HEY, THIS ISN'T WHAT I SIGNED ON FOR. NO ONE MENTIONED THERE'D BE FREAKS LIKE THAT ONE. I'M OUT!
DAMMIT, LOEW, STAND YOUR GROUND!
YOU HEAR ME? STAND YOUR...
NONE of you are ever going to forget today, guys.
This I promise.
Much as I wish I could, I don't have TIME to take you out individually.
SKREEEE
Fortunately...
...Oracle has a very deep ROLODEX.
PUT YOUR HANDS OVER YOUR HEAD, IF YOU PLAN TO KEEP EITHER.
I'D LISTEN TO GYPSY, GENTLE-MEN..
DAMMIT.

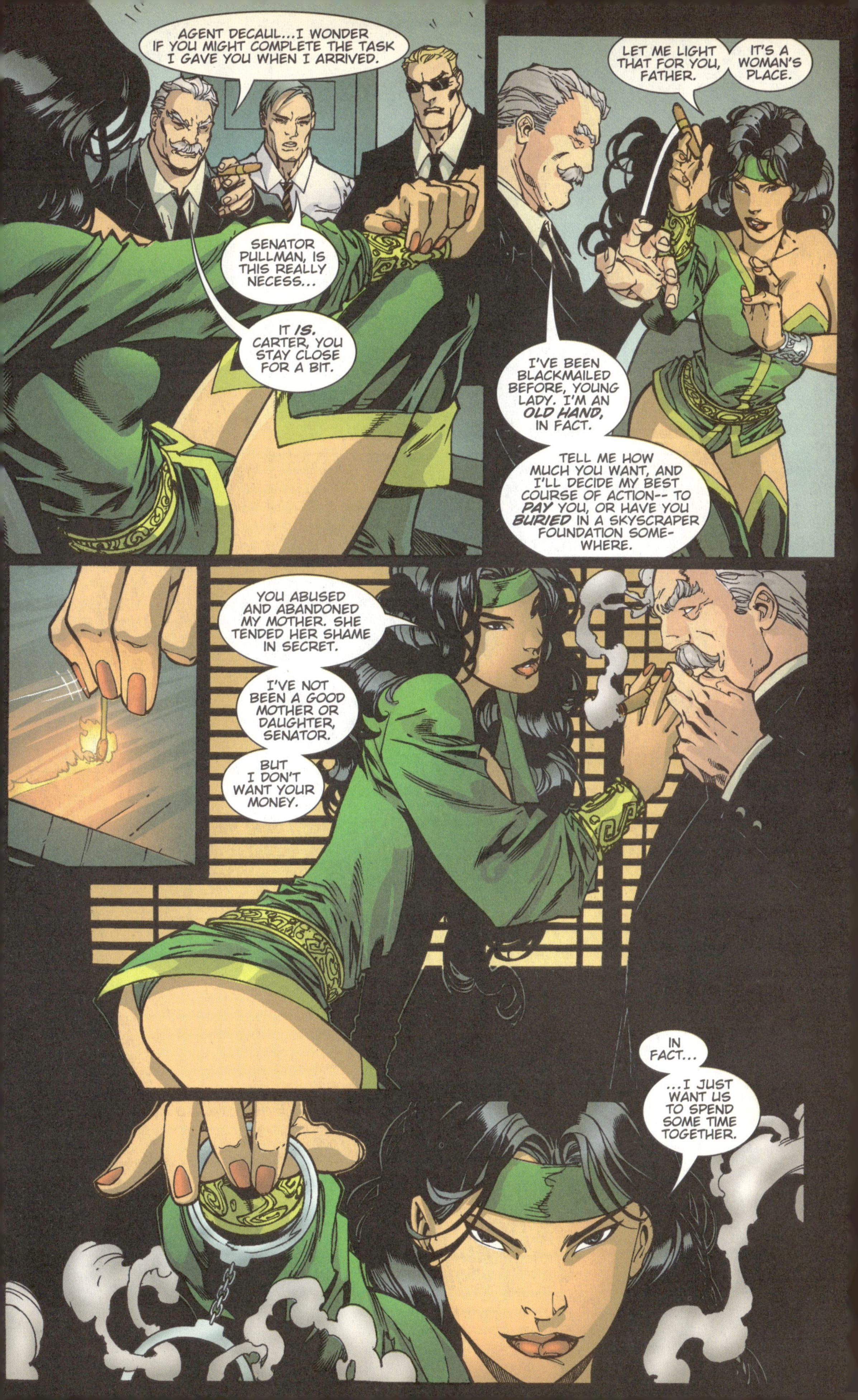
AGENT DECAUL...I WONDER IF YOU MIGHT COMPLETE THE TASK I GAVE YOU WHEN I ARRIVED.
SENATOR PULLMAN, IS THIS REALLY NECESS...
IT *IS.* CARTER, YOU STAY CLOSE FOR A BIT.
LET ME LIGHT THAT FOR YOU, FATHER.
IT'S A WOMAN'S PLACE.
I'VE BEEN BLACKMAILED BEFORE, YOUNG LADY. I'M AN *OLD HAND,* IN FACT.
TELL ME HOW MUCH YOU WANT, AND I'LL DECIDE MY BEST COURSE OF ACTION-- TO *PAY* YOU, OR HAVE YOU *BURIED* IN A SKYSCRAPER FOUNDATION SOMEWHERE.
YOU ABUSED AND ABANDONED MY MOTHER. SHE TENDED HER SHAME IN SECRET.
I'VE NOT BEEN A GOOD MOTHER OR DAUGHTER, SENATOR.
BUT I DON'T WANT YOUR MONEY.
IN FACT...
...I JUST WANT US TO SPEND SOME TIME TOGETHER.

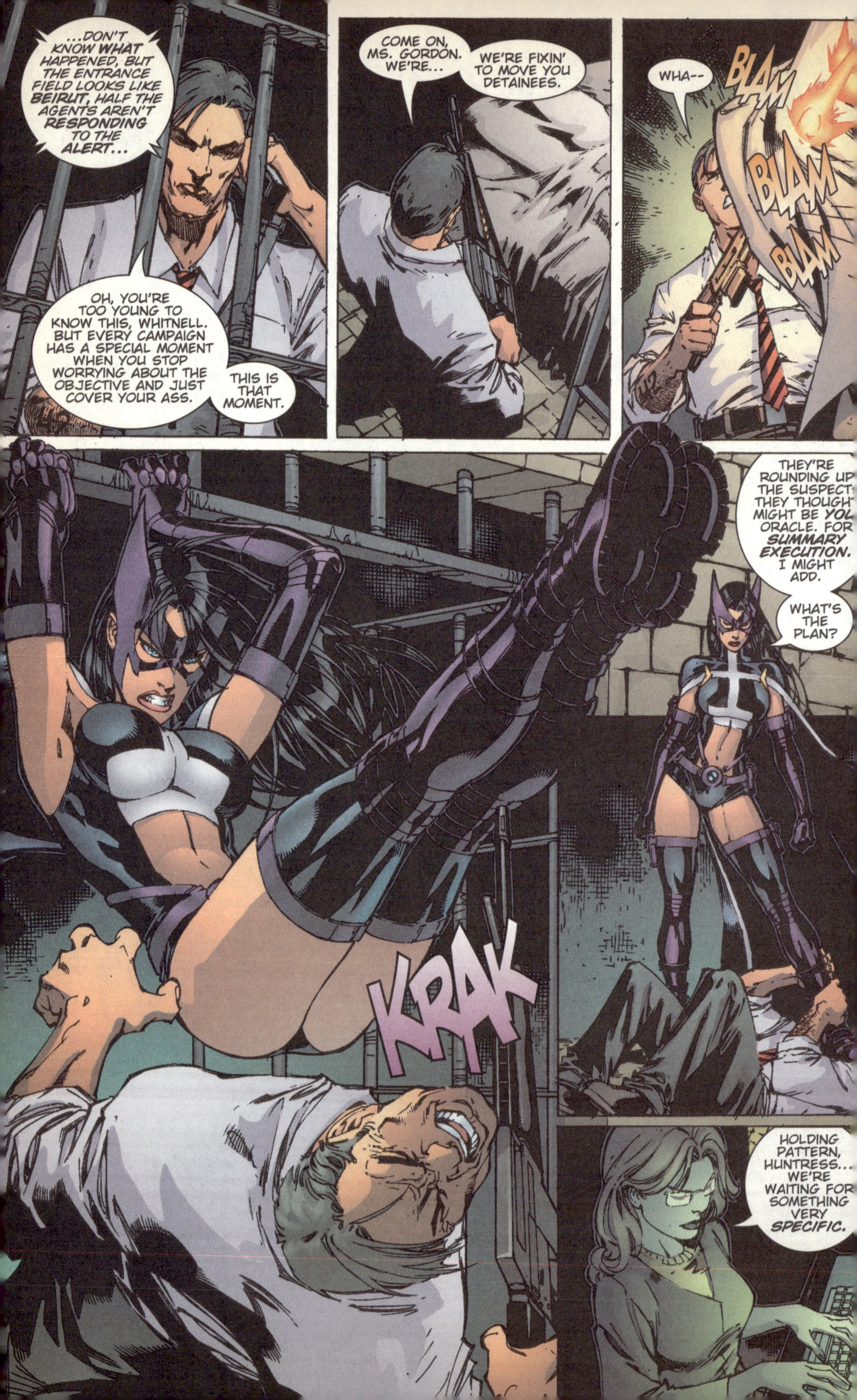

...DON'T KNOW WHAT HAPPENED, BUT THE ENTRANCE FIELD LOOKS LIKE BEIRUT, HALF THE AGENTS AREN'T RESPONDING TO THE ALERT...
OH, YOU'RE TOO YOUNG TO KNOW THIS, WHITNELL. BUT EVERY CAMPAIGN HAS A SPECIAL MOMENT WHEN YOU STOP WORRYING ABOUT THE OBJECTIVE AND JUST COVER YOUR ASS.
THIS IS THAT MOMENT.
COME ON, MS. GORDON. WE'RE...
WE'RE FIXIN' TO MOVE YOU DETAINEES.
WHA--
BLAM
BLAM
BLAM
KRAK
THEY'RE ROUNDING UP THE SUSPECTS THEY THOUGHT MIGHT BE YOU, ORACLE. FOR SUMMARY EXECUTION, I MIGHT ADD.
WHAT'S THE PLAN?
HOLDING PATTERN, HUNTRESS... WE'RE WAITING FOR SOMETHING VERY SPECIFIC.

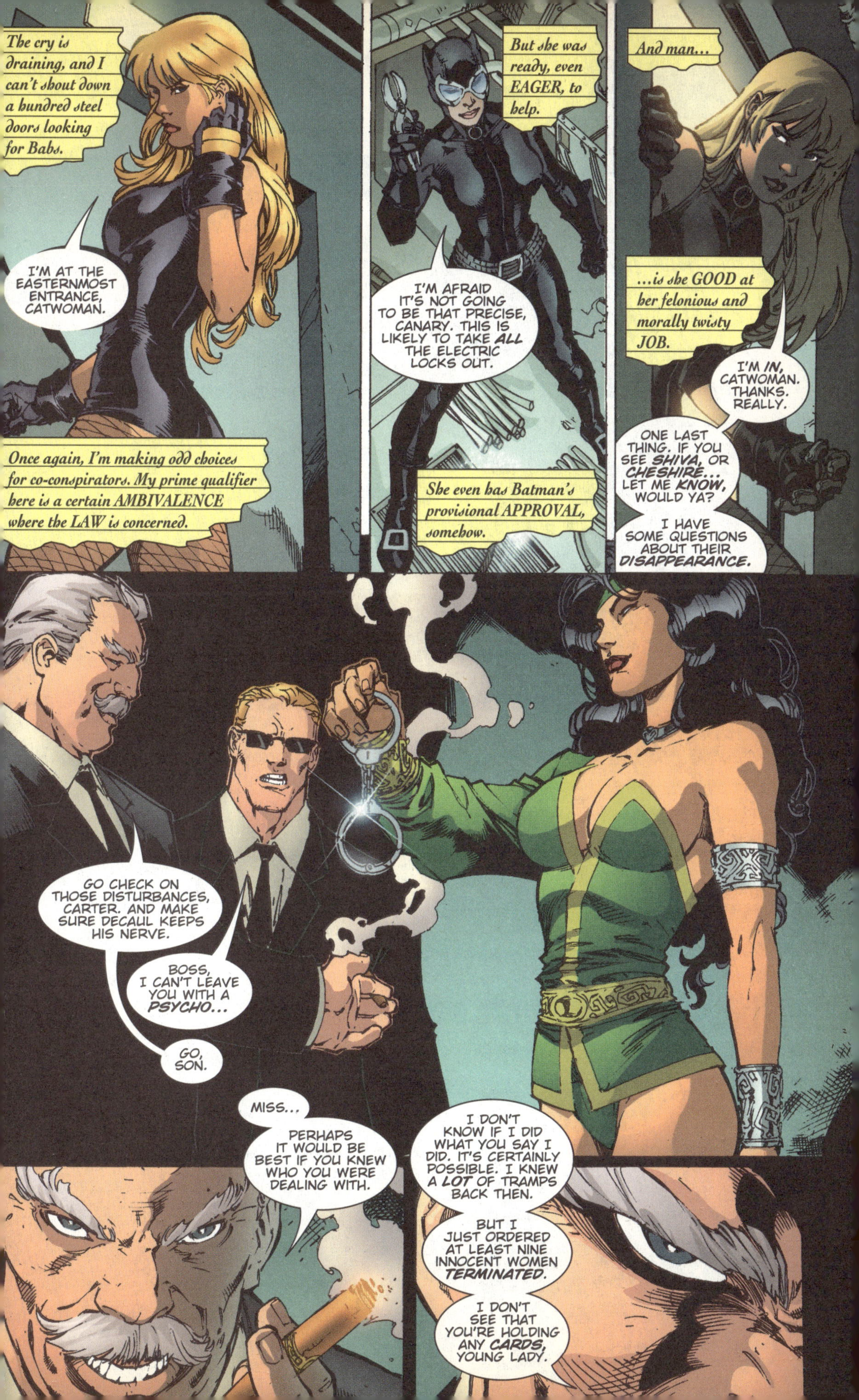
The cry is draining, and I can't shout down a hundred steel doors looking for Babs.
I'M AT THE EASTERNMOST ENTRANCE, CATWOMAN.
Once again, I'm making odd choices for co-conspirators. My prime qualifier here is a certain AMBIVALENCE where the LAW is concerned.
But she was ready, even EAGER, to help.
I'M AFRAID IT'S NOT GOING TO BE THAT PRECISE, CANARY. THIS IS LIKELY TO TAKE ALL THE ELECTRIC LOCKS OUT.
She even has Batman's provisional APPROVAL, somehow.
And man...
...is she GOOD at her felonious and morally twisty JOB.
I'M IN, CATWOMAN. THANKS. REALLY.
ONE LAST THING. IF YOU SEE SHIVA, OR CHESHIRE... LET ME KNOW, WOULD YA?
I HAVE SOME QUESTIONS ABOUT THEIR DISAPPEARANCE.
GO CHECK ON THOSE DISTURBANCES, CARTER. AND MAKE SURE DECAUL KEEPS HIS NERVE.
BOSS, I CAN'T LEAVE YOU WITH A PSYCHO...
GO, SON.
MISS...
PERHAPS IT WOULD BE BEST IF YOU KNEW WHO YOU WERE DEALING WITH.
I DON'T KNOW IF I DID WHAT YOU SAY I DID. IT'S CERTAINLY POSSIBLE. I KNEW A LOT OF TRAMPS BACK THEN.
BUT I JUST ORDERED AT LEAST NINE INNOCENT WOMEN TERMINATED.
I DON'T SEE THAT YOU'RE HOLDING ANY CARDS, YOUNG LADY.

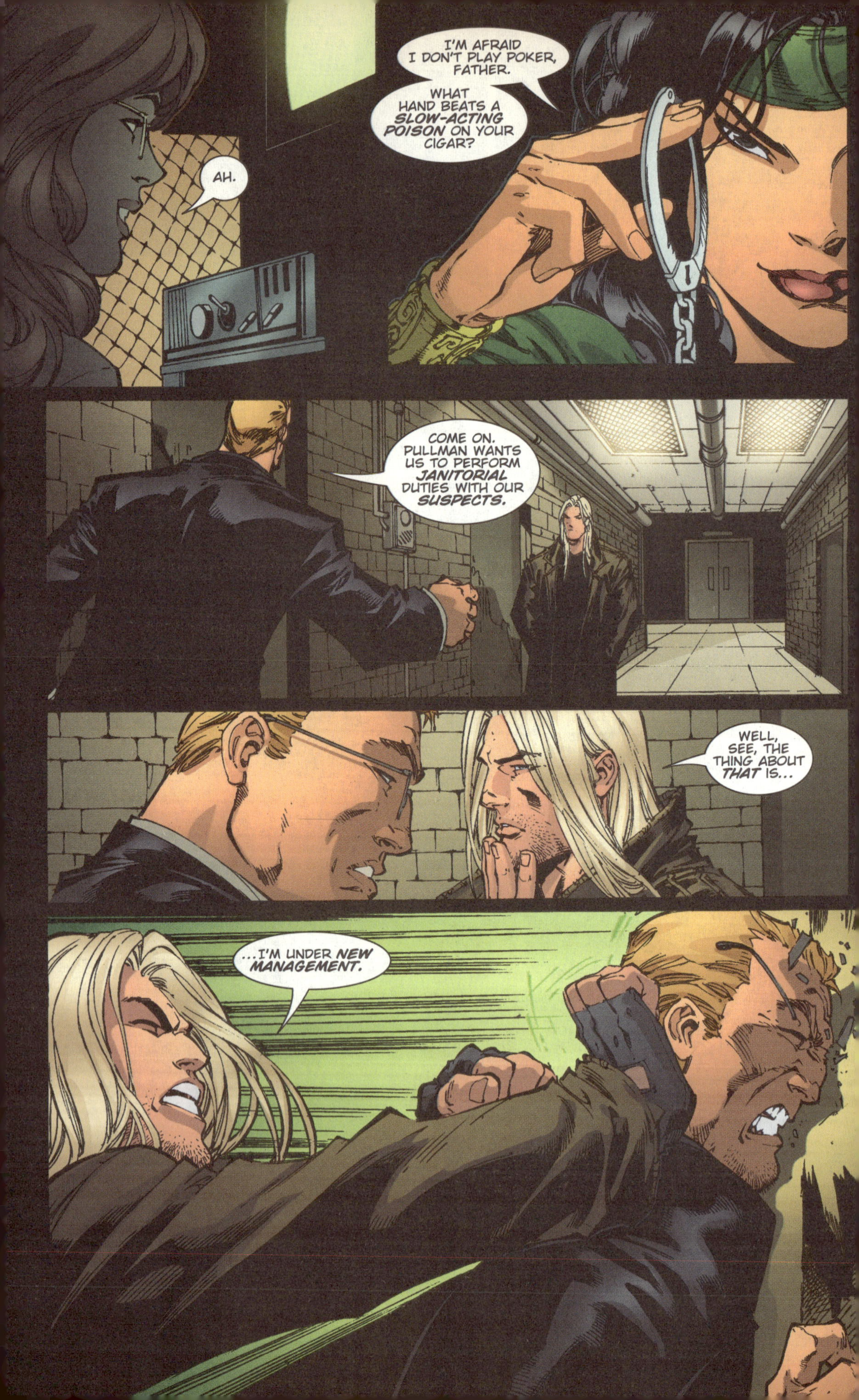
AH.
I'M AFRAID I DON'T PLAY POKER, FATHER.
WHAT HAND BEATS A SLOW-ACTING POISON ON YOUR CIGAR?
COME ON. PULLMAN WANTS US TO PERFORM JANITORIAL DUTIES WITH OUR SUSPECTS.
WELL, SEE, THE THING ABOUT THAT IS...
...I'M UNDER NEW MANAGEMENT.

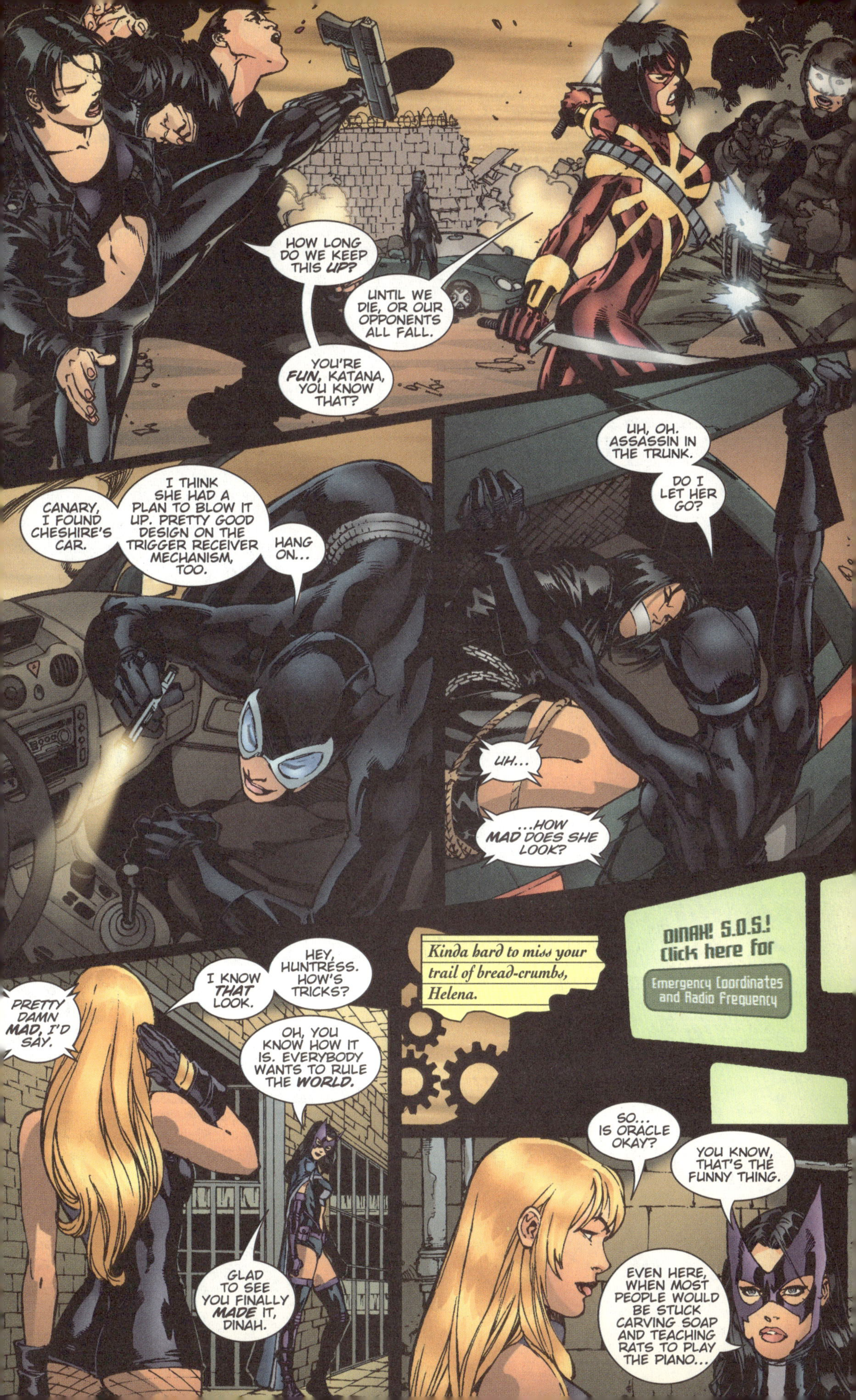
HOW LONG DO WE KEEP THIS UP?
UNTIL WE DIE, OR OUR OPPONENTS ALL FALL.
YOU'RE FUN, KATANA, YOU KNOW THAT?
CANARY, I FOUND CHESHIRE'S CAR.
I THINK SHE HAD A PLAN TO BLOW IT UP. PRETTY GOOD DESIGN ON THE TRIGGER RECEIVER MECHANISM, TOO.
HANG ON...
UH, OH. ASSASSIN IN THE TRUNK.
DO I LET HER GO?
UH...
...HOW MAD DOES SHE LOOK?
PRETTY DAMN MAD, I'D SAY.
I KNOW THAT LOOK.
HEY, HUNTRESS. HOW'S TRICKS?
OH, YOU KNOW HOW IT IS. EVERYBODY WANTS TO RULE THE WORLD.
GLAD TO SEE YOU FINALLY MADE IT, DINAH.
Kinda hard to miss your trail of bread-crumbs, Helena.
DINAH! S.O.S.! Click here for
Emergency Coordinates and Radio Frequency
SO... IS ORACLE OKAY?
YOU KNOW, THAT'S THE FUNNY THING.
EVEN HERE, WHEN MOST PEOPLE WOULD BE STUCK CARVING SOAP AND TEACHING RATS TO PLAY THE PIANO...

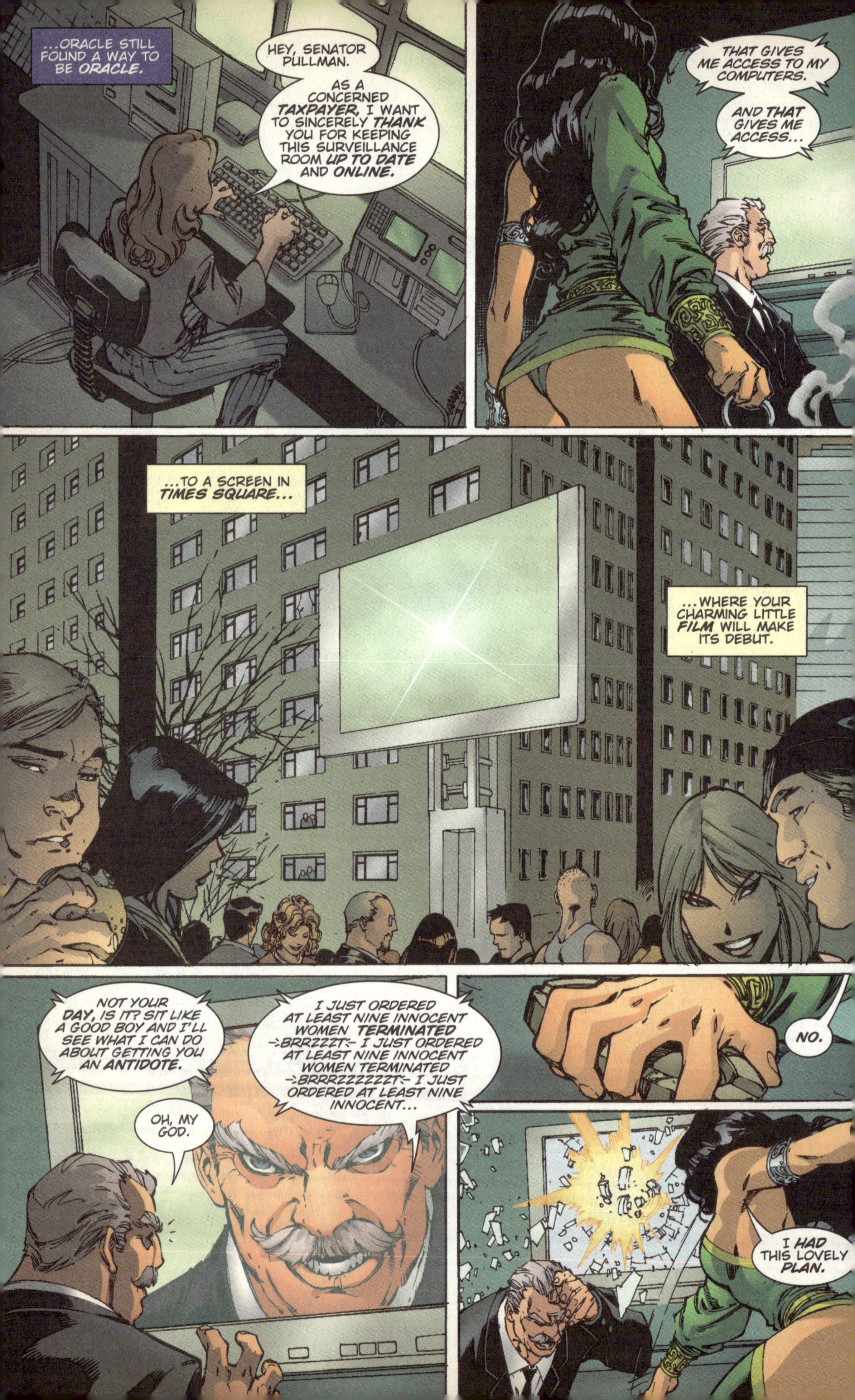
...ORACLE STILL FOUND A WAY TO BE ORACLE.
HEY, SENATOR PULLMAN.
AS A CONCERNED TAXPAYER, I WANT TO SINCERELY THANK YOU FOR KEEPING THIS SURVEILLANCE ROOM UP TO DATE AND ONLINE.
THAT GIVES ME ACCESS TO MY COMPUTERS.
AND THAT GIVES ME ACCESS...
...TO A SCREEN IN TIMES SQUARE...
...WHERE YOUR CHARMING LITTLE FILM WILL MAKE ITS DEBUT.
NOT YOUR DAY, IS IT? SIT LIKE A GOOD BOY AND I'LL SEE WHAT I CAN DO ABOUT GETTING YOU AN ANTIDOTE.
I JUST ORDERED AT LEAST NINE INNOCENT WOMEN TERMINATED -BRRZZZT- I JUST ORDERED AT LEAST NINE INNOCENT WOMEN TERMINATED -BRRRZZZZZZT- I JUST ORDERED AT LEAST NINE INNOCENT...
OH, MY GOD.
NO.
I HAD THIS LOVELY PLAN.

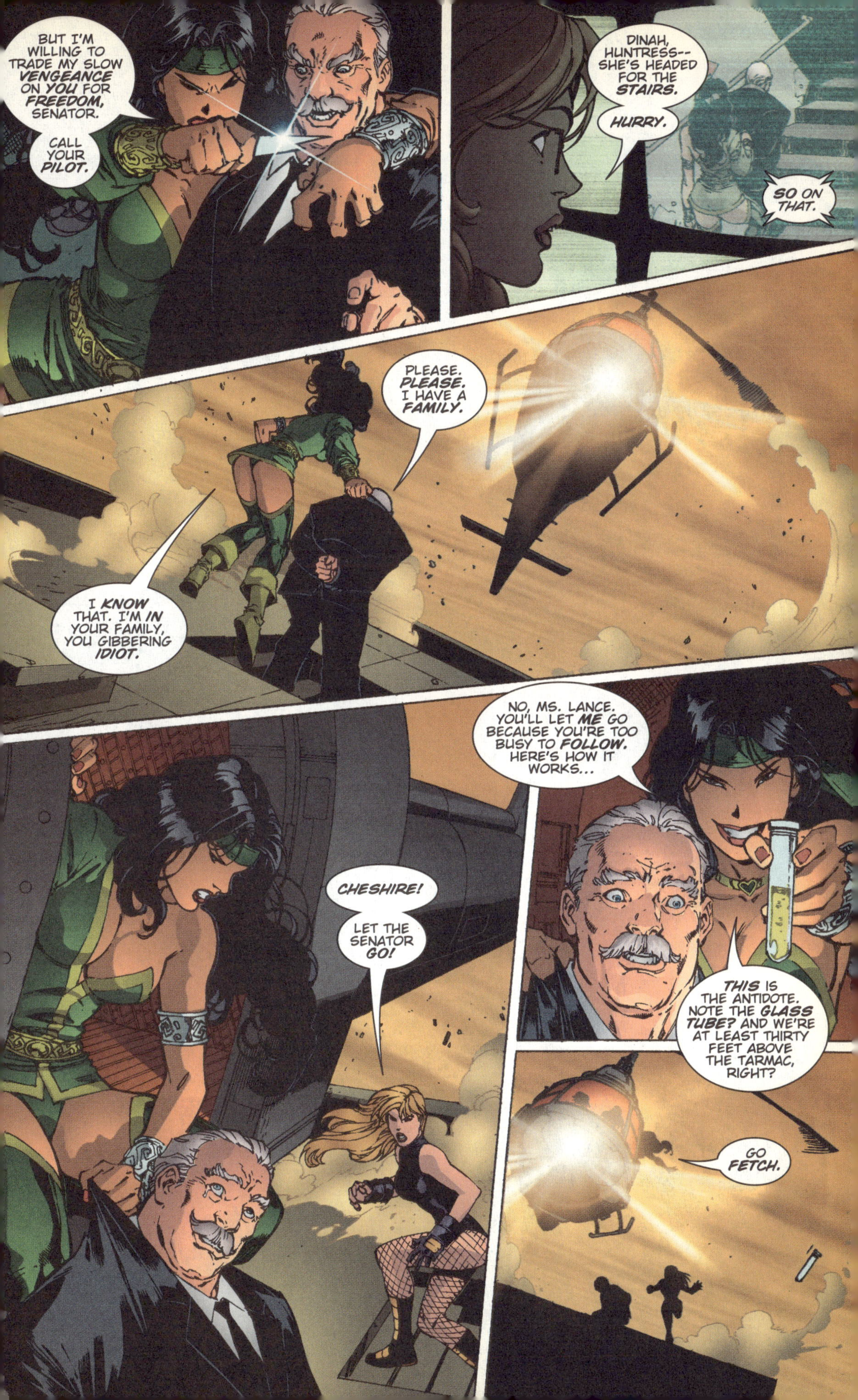
BUT I'M WILLING TO TRADE MY SLOW VENGEANCE ON YOU FOR FREEDOM, SENATOR.
CALL YOUR PILOT.
DINAH, HUNTRESS-- SHE'S HEADED FOR THE STAIRS.
HURRY.
SO ON THAT.
PLEASE. PLEASE. I HAVE A FAMILY.
I KNOW THAT. I'M IN YOUR FAMILY, YOU GIBBERING IDIOT.
CHESHIRE!
LET THE SENATOR GO!
NO, MS. LANCE. YOU'LL LET ME GO BECAUSE YOU'RE TOO BUSY TO FOLLOW. HERE'S HOW IT WORKS...
THIS IS THE ANTIDOTE. NOTE THE GLASS TUBE? AND WE'RE AT LEAST THIRTY FEET ABOVE THE TARMAC, RIGHT?
GO FETCH.

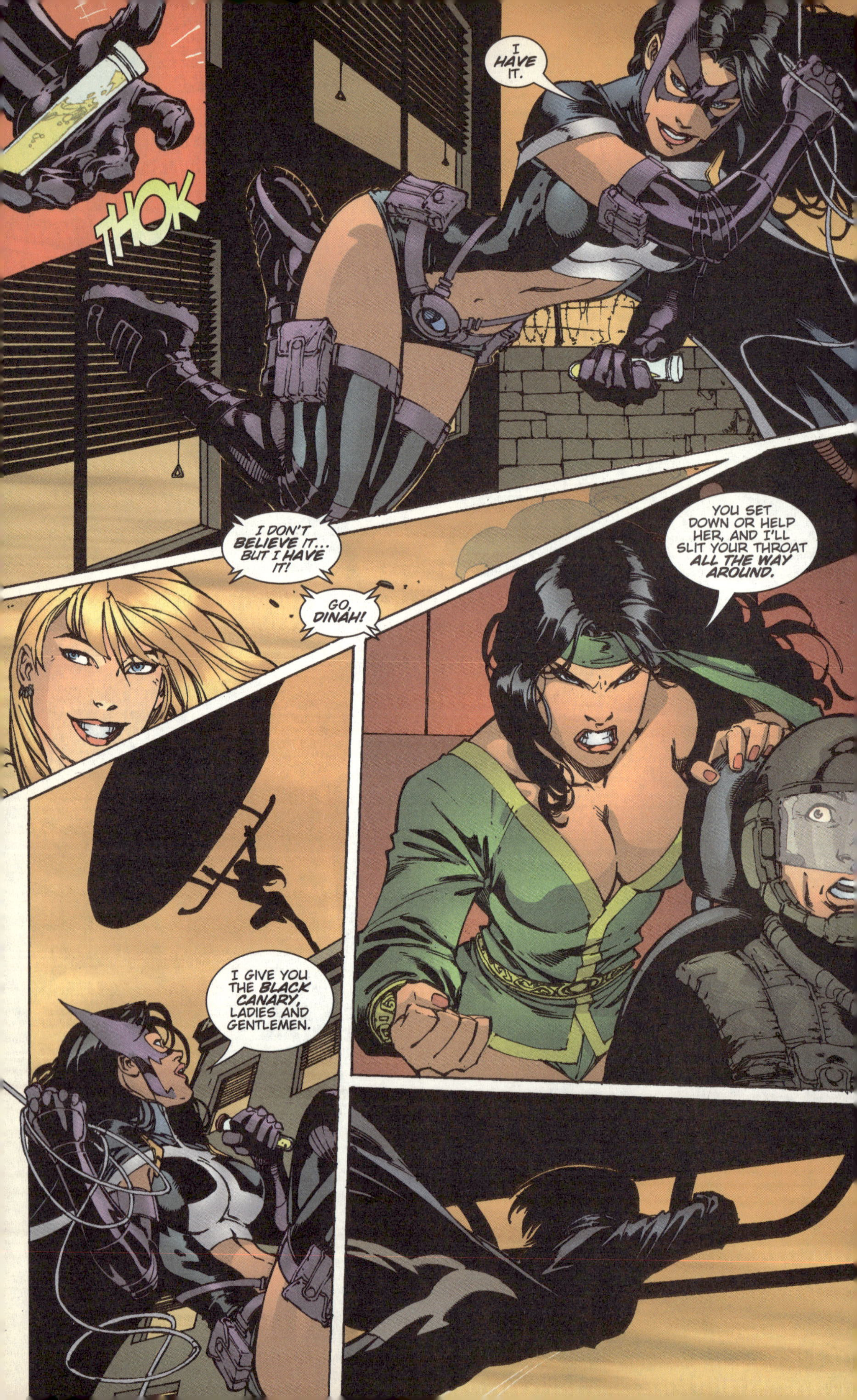
THOK
I HAVE IT.
I DON'T BELIEVE IT... BUT I HAVE IT!
GO, DINAH!
YOU SET DOWN OR HELP HER, AND I'LL SLIT YOUR THROAT ALL THE WAY AROUND.
I GIVE YOU THE BLACK CANARY, LADIES AND GENTLEMEN.

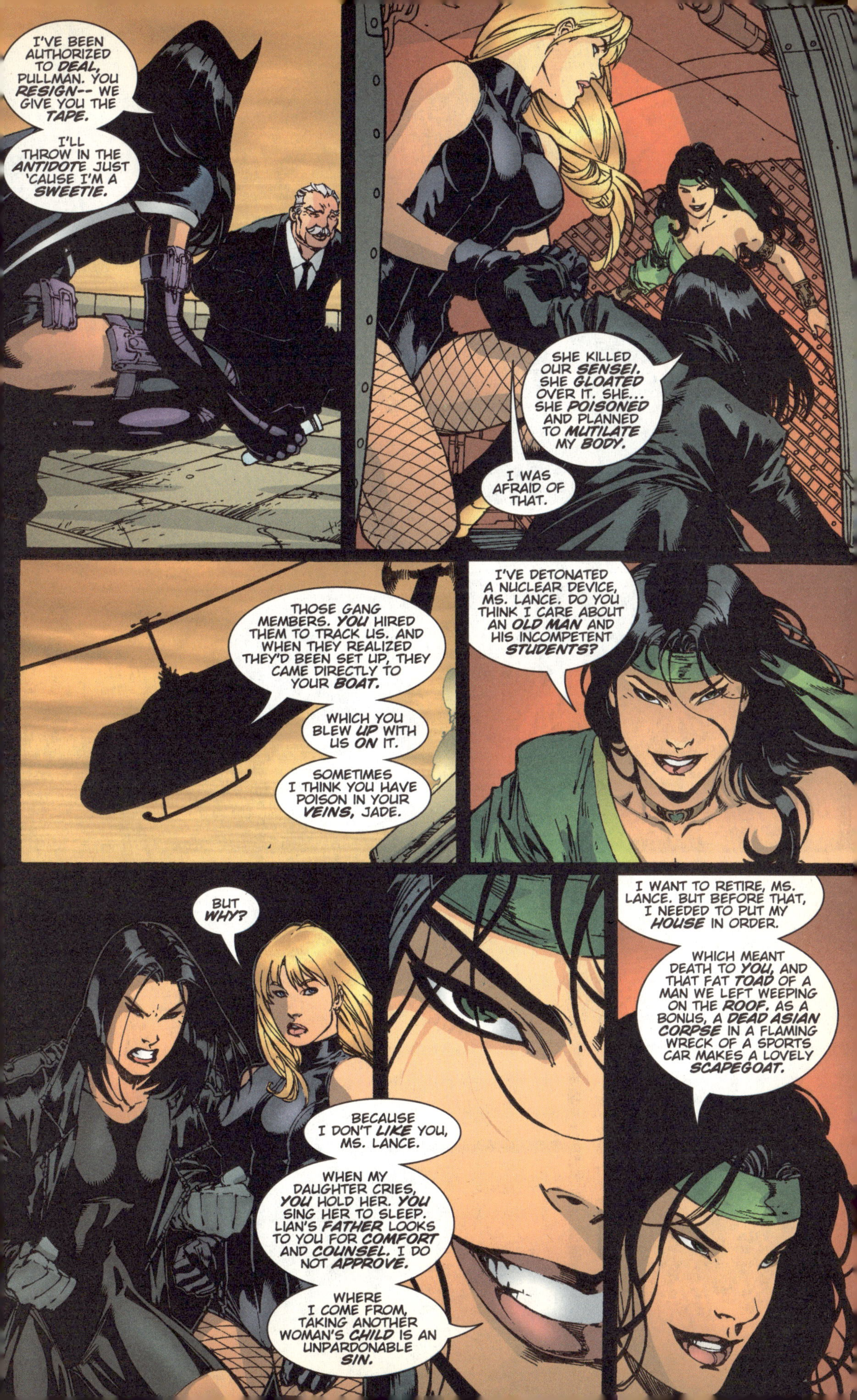
I'VE BEEN AUTHORIZED TO DEAL, PULLMAN. YOU RESIGN-- WE GIVE YOU THE TAPE.
I'LL THROW IN THE ANTIDOTE JUST 'CAUSE I'M A SWEETIE.
SHE KILLED OUR SENSEI. SHE GLOATED OVER IT. SHE... SHE POISONED AND PLANNED TO MUTILATE MY BODY.
I WAS AFRAID OF THAT.
THOSE GANG MEMBERS. YOU HIRED THEM TO TRACK US. AND WHEN THEY REALIZED THEY'D BEEN SET UP, THEY CAME DIRECTLY TO YOUR BOAT.
WHICH YOU BLEW UP WITH US ON IT.
SOMETIMES I THINK YOU HAVE POISON IN YOUR VEINS, JADE.
I'VE DETONATED A NUCLEAR DEVICE, MS. LANCE. DO YOU THINK I CARE ABOUT AN OLD MAN AND HIS INCOMPETENT STUDENTS?
BUT WHY?
BECAUSE I DON'T LIKE YOU, MS. LANCE.
WHEN MY DAUGHTER CRIES, YOU HOLD HER. YOU SING HER TO SLEEP. LIAN'S FATHER LOOKS TO YOU FOR COMFORT AND COUNSEL. I DO NOT APPROVE.
WHERE I COME FROM, TAKING ANOTHER WOMAN'S CHILD IS AN UNPARDONABLE SIN.
I WANT TO RETIRE, MS. LANCE. BUT BEFORE THAT, I NEEDED TO PUT MY HOUSE IN ORDER.
WHICH MEANT DEATH TO YOU, AND THAT FAT TOAD OF A MAN WE LEFT WEEPING ON THE ROOF. AS A BONUS, A DEAD ASIAN CORPSE IN A FLAMING WRECK OF A SPORTS CAR MAKES A LOVELY SCAPEGOAT.

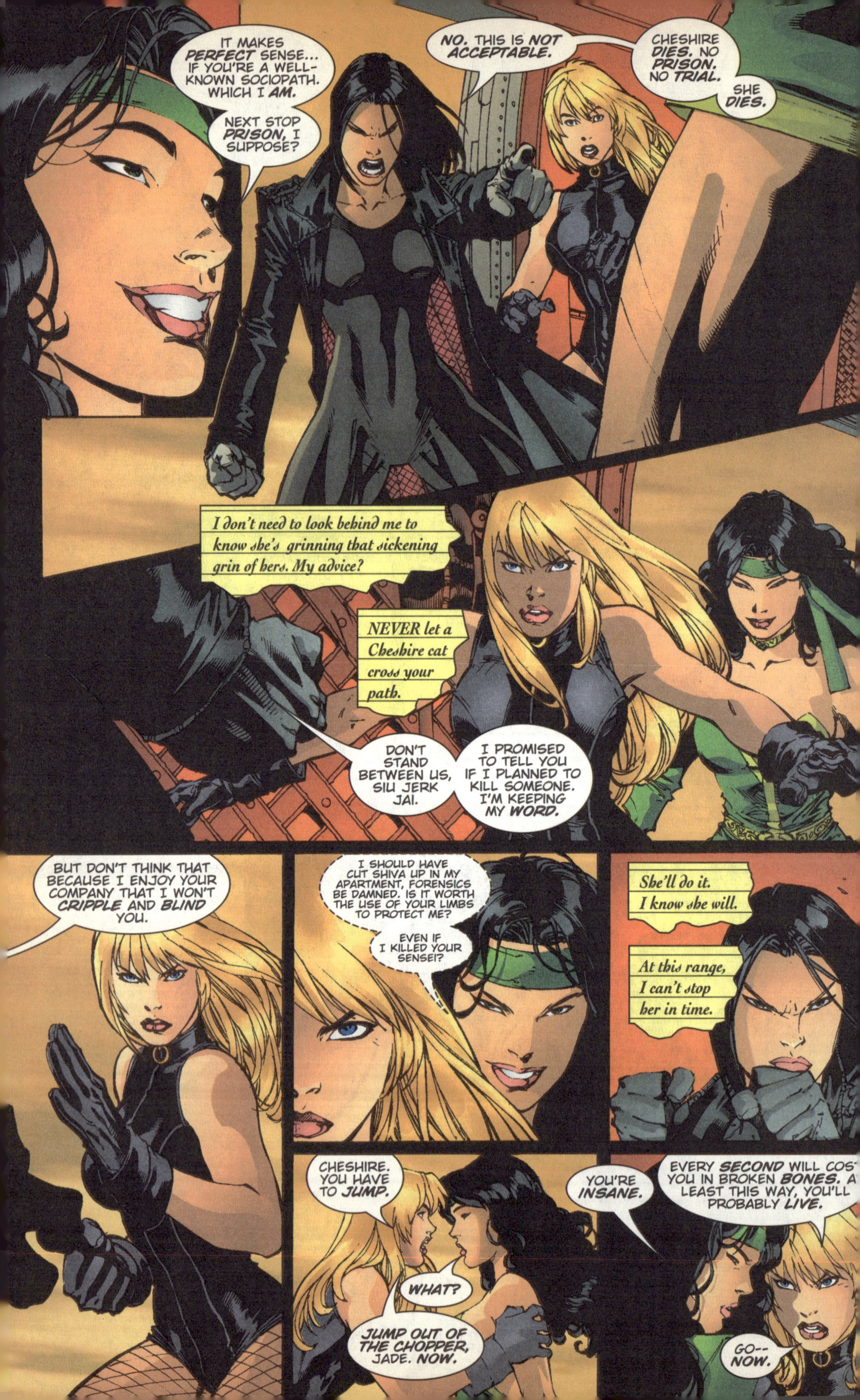
IT MAKES PERFECT SENSE... IF YOU'RE A WELL-KNOWN SOCIOPATH. WHICH I AM.
NEXT STOP PRISON, I SUPPOSE?
NO. THIS IS NOT ACCEPTABLE.
CHESHIRE DIES. NO PRISON. NO TRIAL.
SHE DIES.
I don't need to look behind me to know she's grinning that sickening grin of hers. My advice?
NEVER let a Cheshire cat cross your path.
DON'T STAND BETWEEN US, SIU JERK JAI.
I PROMISED TO TELL YOU IF I PLANNED TO KILL SOMEONE. I'M KEEPING MY WORD.
BUT DON'T THINK THAT BECAUSE I ENJOY YOUR COMPANY THAT I WON'T CRIPPLE AND BLIND YOU.
I SHOULD HAVE CUT SHIVA UP IN MY APARTMENT, FORENSICS BE DAMNED. IS IT WORTH THE USE OF YOUR LIMBS TO PROTECT ME?
EVEN IF I KILLED YOUR SENSEI?
She'll do it. I know she will.
At this range, I can't stop her in time.
CHESHIRE. YOU HAVE TO JUMP.
WHAT?
JUMP OUT OF THE CHOPPER, JADE. NOW.
YOU'RE INSANE.
EVERY SECOND WILL COST YOU IN BROKEN BONES. AT LEAST THIS WAY, YOU'LL PROBABLY LIVE.
GO--NOW.

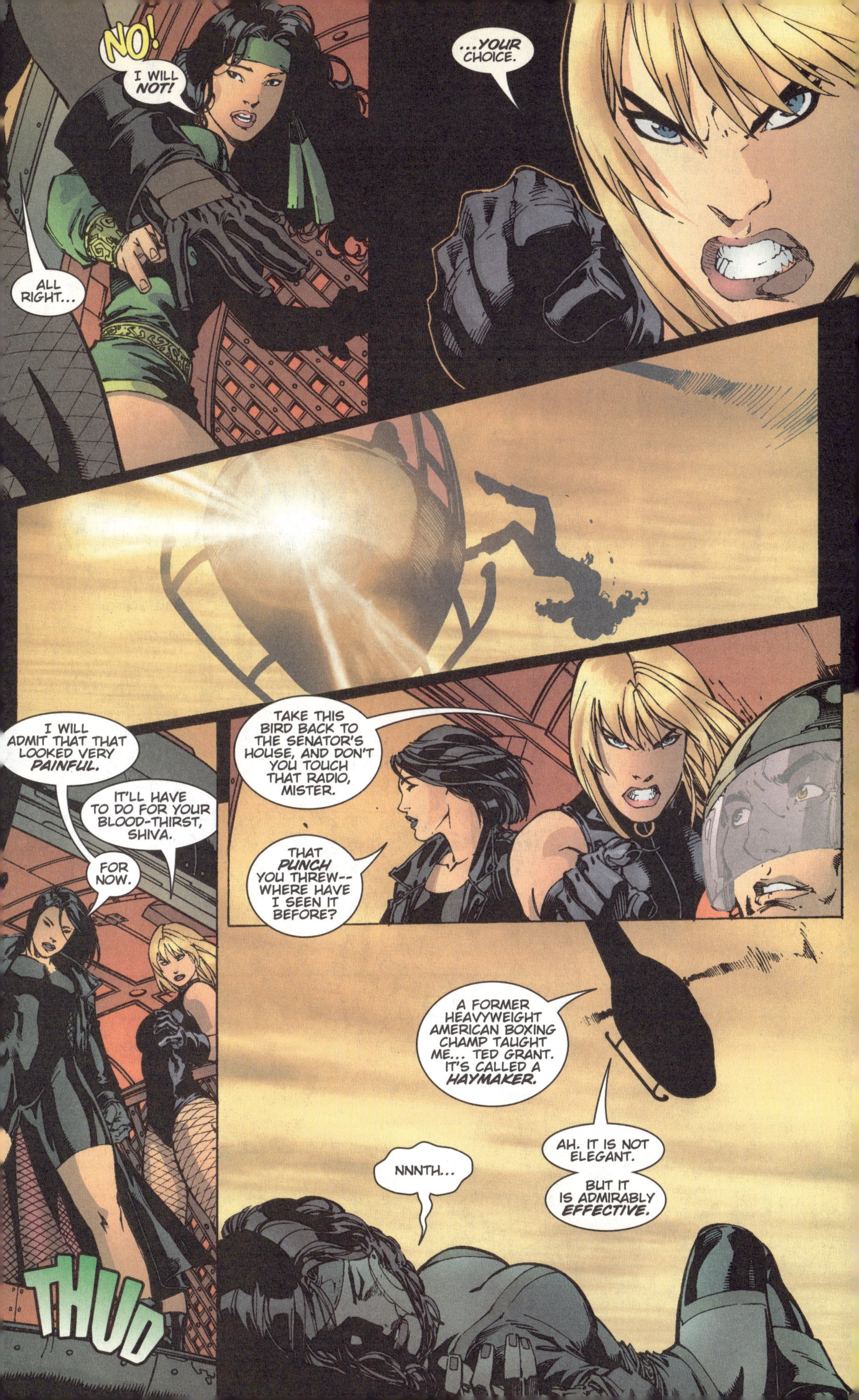
NO!
I WILL NOT!
ALL RIGHT...
...YOUR CHOICE.
I WILL ADMIT THAT THAT LOOKED VERY PAINFUL.
IT'LL HAVE TO DO FOR YOUR BLOOD-THIRST, SHIVA.
FOR NOW.
TAKE THIS BIRD BACK TO THE SENATOR'S HOUSE, AND DON'T YOU TOUCH THAT RADIO, MISTER.
THAT PUNCH YOU THREW-- WHERE HAVE I SEEN IT BEFORE?
A FORMER HEAVYWEIGHT AMERICAN BOXING CHAMP TAUGHT ME... TED GRANT. IT'S CALLED A HAYMAKER.
AH. IT IS NOT ELEGANT.
BUT IT IS ADMIRABLY EFFECTIVE.
NNNTH...
THUD

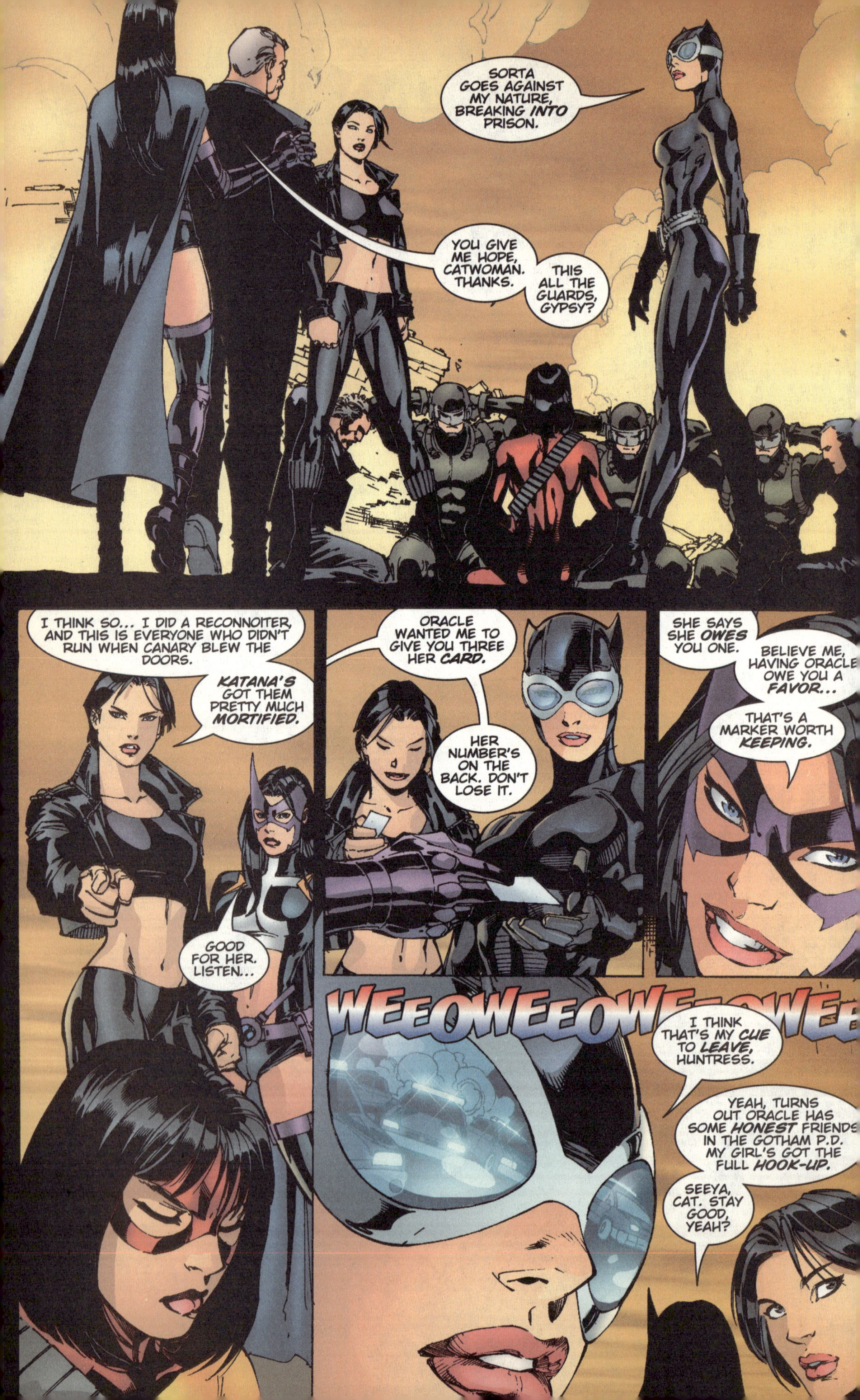

SORTA GOES AGAINST MY NATURE, BREAKING INTO PRISON.
YOU GIVE ME HOPE, CATWOMAN. THANKS.
THIS ALL THE GUARDS, GYPSY?
I THINK SO... I DID A RECONNOITER, AND THIS IS EVERYONE WHO DIDN'T RUN WHEN CANARY BLEW THE DOORS.
KATANA'S GOT THEM PRETTY MUCH MORTIFIED.
GOOD FOR HER. LISTEN...
ORACLE WANTED ME TO GIVE YOU THREE HER CARD.
HER NUMBER'S ON THE BACK. DON'T LOSE IT.
SHE SAYS SHE OWES YOU ONE.
BELIEVE ME, HAVING ORACLE OWE YOU A FAVOR...
THAT'S A MARKER WORTH KEEPING.
WEEEOWEEEOWE
I THINK THAT'S MY CUE TO LEAVE, HUNTRESS.
YEAH, TURNS OUT ORACLE HAS SOME HONEST FRIENDS IN THE GOTHAM P.D. MY GIRL'S GOT THE FULL HOOK-UP.
SEEYA, CAT. STAY GOOD, YEAH?

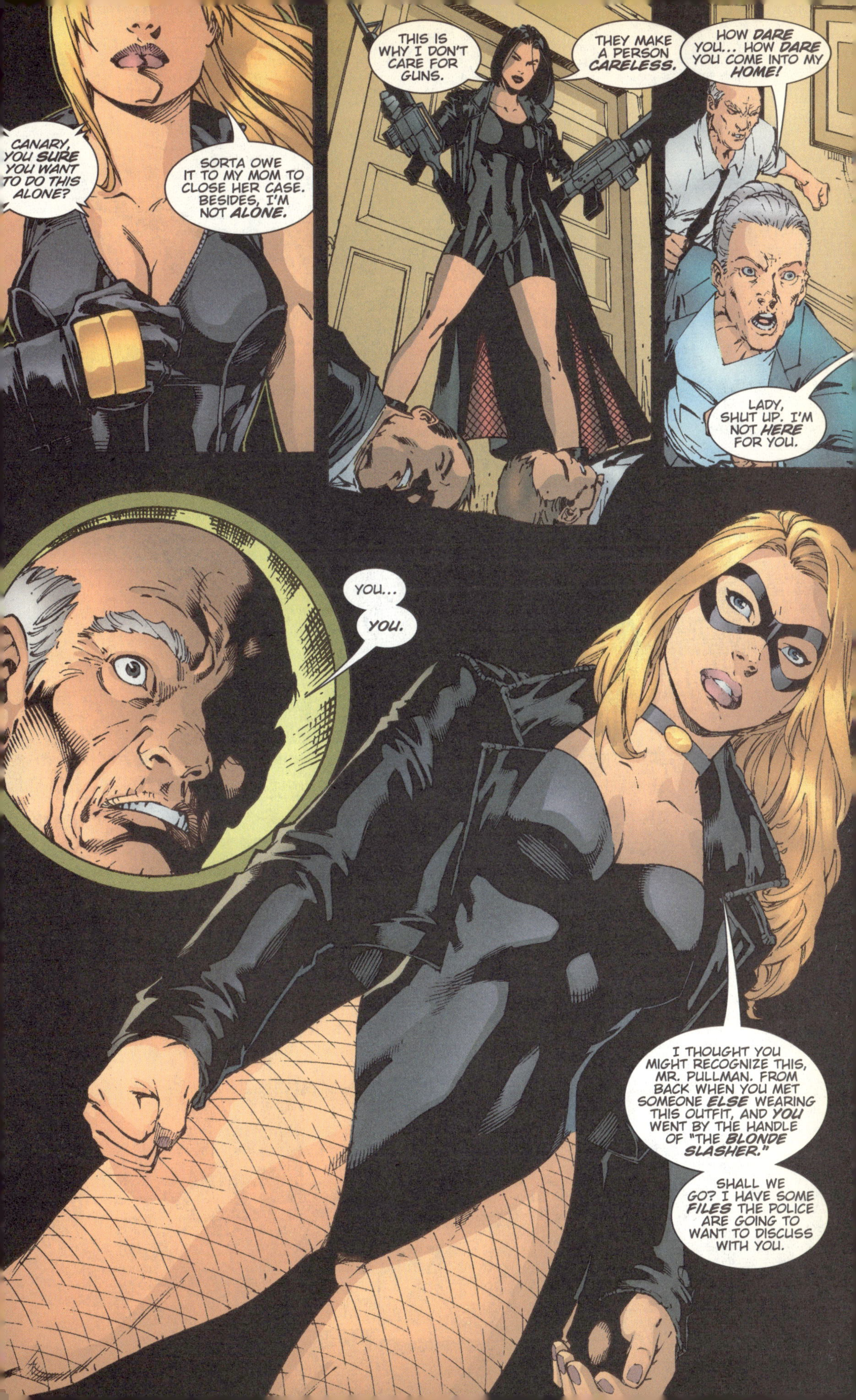
CANARY, YOU SURE YOU WANT TO DO THIS ALONE?
SORTA OWE IT TO MY MOM TO CLOSE HER CASE. BESIDES, I'M NOT ALONE.
THIS IS WHY I DON'T CARE FOR GUNS.
THEY MAKE A PERSON CARELESS.
HOW DARE YOU... HOW DARE YOU COME INTO MY HOME!
LADY, SHUT UP. I'M NOT HERE FOR YOU.
YOU... YOU.
I THOUGHT YOU MIGHT RECOGNIZE THIS, MR. PULLMAN. FROM BACK WHEN YOU MET SOMEONE ELSE WEARING THIS OUTFIT, AND YOU WENT BY THE HANDLE OF "THE BLONDE SLASHER."
SHALL WE GO? I HAVE SOME FILES THE POLICE ARE GOING TO WANT TO DISCUSS WITH YOU.

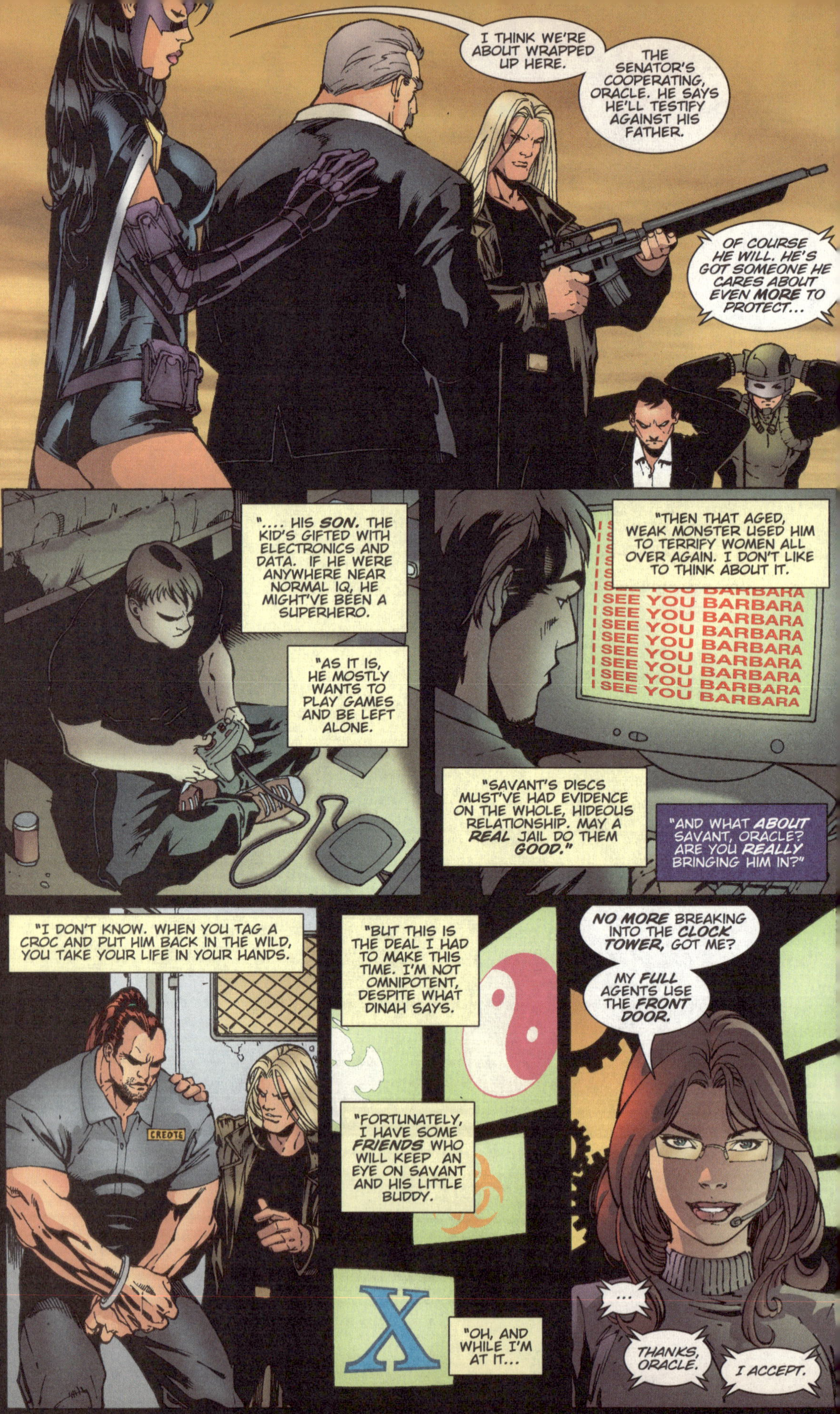
I THINK WE'RE ABOUT WRAPPED UP HERE.
THE SENATOR'S COOPERATING, ORACLE. HE SAYS HE'LL TESTIFY AGAINST HIS FATHER.
OF COURSE HE WILL. HE'S GOT SOMEONE HE CARES ABOUT EVEN MORE TO PROTECT...
"... HIS SON. THE KID'S GIFTED WITH ELECTRONICS AND DATA. IF HE WERE ANYWHERE NEAR NORMAL IQ, HE MIGHT'VE BEEN A SUPERHERO.
"AS IT IS, HE MOSTLY WANTS TO PLAY GAMES AND BE LEFT ALONE.
"THEN THAT AGED, WEAK MONSTER USED HIM TO TERRIFY WOMEN ALL OVER AGAIN. I DON'T LIKE TO THINK ABOUT IT.
I SEE YOU BARBARA
"SAVANT'S DISCS MUST'VE HAD EVIDENCE ON THE WHOLE, HIDEOUS RELATIONSHIP. MAY A REAL JAIL DO THEM GOOD."
"AND WHAT ABOUT SAVANT, ORACLE? ARE YOU REALLY BRINGING HIM IN?"
"I DON'T KNOW. WHEN YOU TAG A CROC AND PUT HIM BACK IN THE WILD, YOU TAKE YOUR LIFE IN YOUR HANDS.
CREOTE
"BUT THIS IS THE DEAL I HAD TO MAKE THIS TIME. I'M NOT OMNIPOTENT, DESPITE WHAT DINAH SAYS.
"FORTUNATELY, I HAVE SOME FRIENDS WHO WILL KEEP AN EYE ON SAVANT AND HIS LITTLE BUDDY.
X
"OH, AND WHILE I'M AT IT...
NO MORE BREAKING INTO THE CLOCK TOWER, GOT ME?
MY FULL AGENTS USE THE FRONT DOOR.
...
THANKS, ORACLE.
I ACCEPT.

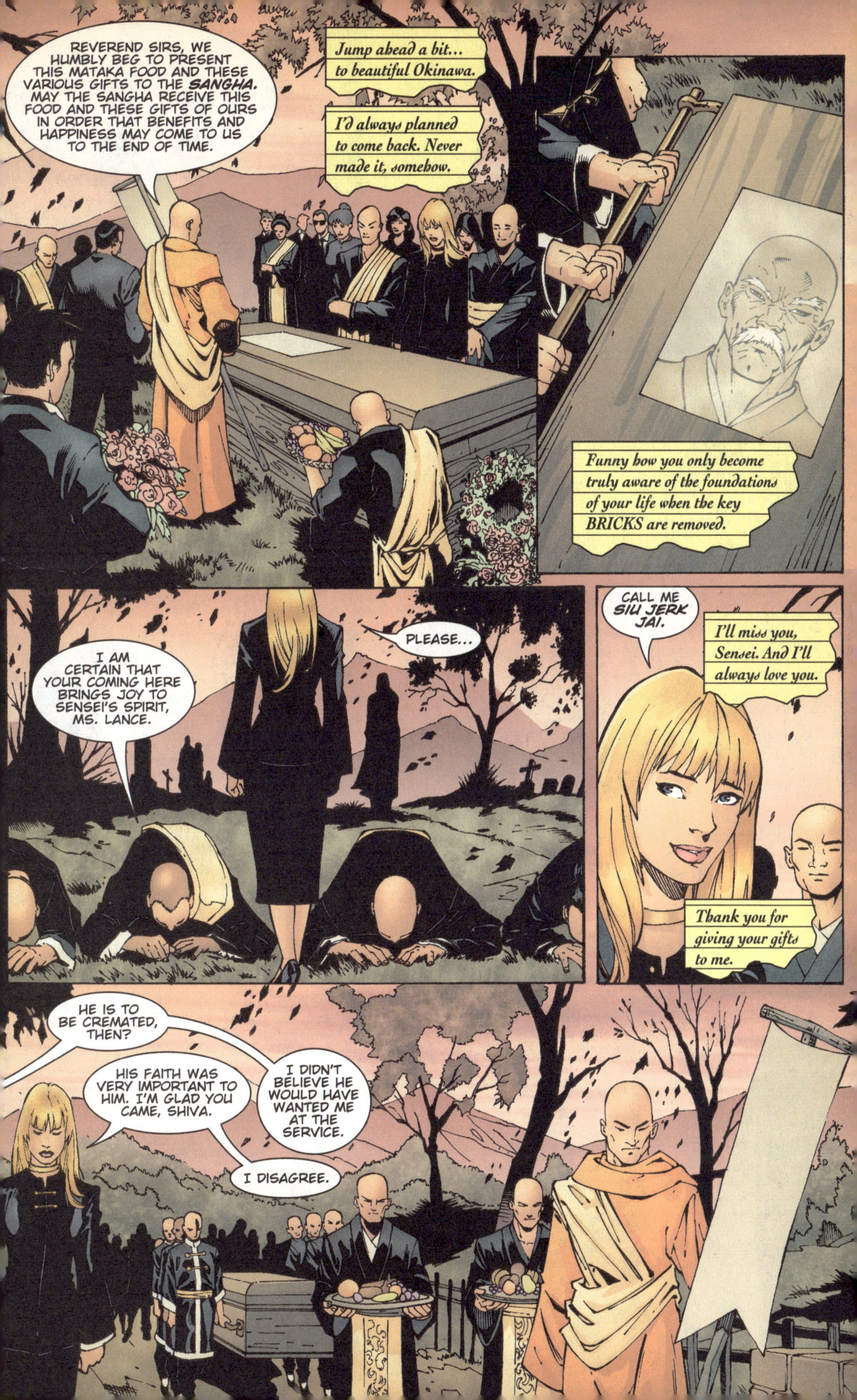
REVEREND SIRS, WE HUMBLY BEG TO PRESENT THIS MATAKA FOOD AND THESE VARIOUS GIFTS TO THE SANGHA. MAY THE SANGHA RECEIVE THIS FOOD AND THESE GIFTS OF OURS IN ORDER THAT BENEFITS AND HAPPINESS MAY COME TO US TO THE END OF TIME.
Jump ahead a bit... to beautiful Okinawa.
I'd always planned to come back. Never made it, somehow.
Funny how you only become truly aware of the foundations of your life when the key BRICKS are removed.
I AM CERTAIN THAT YOUR COMING HERE BRINGS JOY TO SENSEI'S SPIRIT, MS. LANCE.
PLEASE...
CALL ME SIU JERK JAI.
I'll miss you, Sensei. And I'll always love you.
Thank you for giving your gifts to me.
HE IS TO BE CREMATED, THEN?
I DIDN'T BELIEVE HE WOULD HAVE WANTED ME AT THE SERVICE.
HIS FAITH WAS VERY IMPORTANT TO HIM. I'M GLAD YOU CAME, SHIVA.
I DISAGREE.

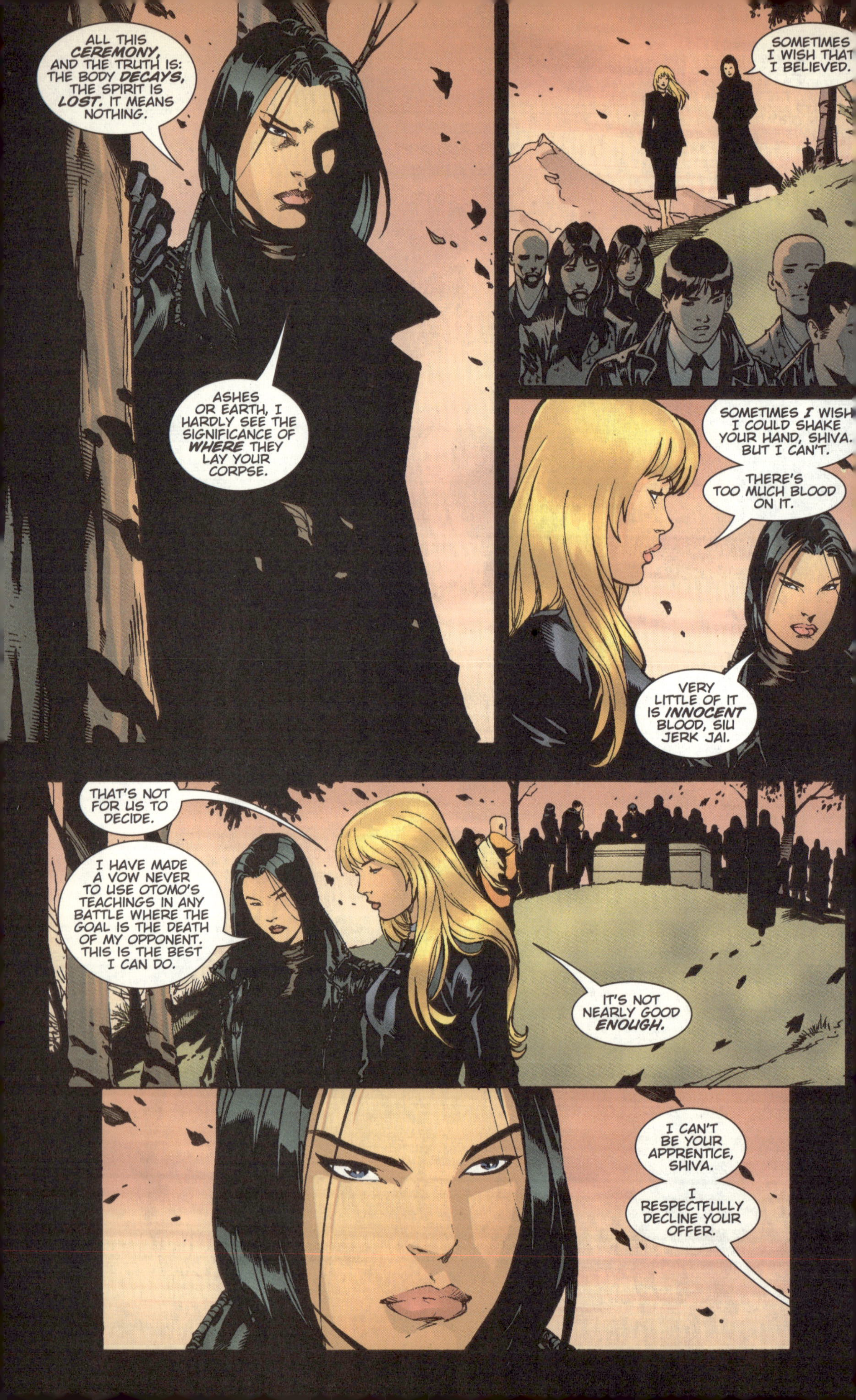
ALL THIS CEREMONY, AND THE TRUTH IS: THE BODY DECAYS, THE SPIRIT IS LOST. IT MEANS NOTHING.
ASHES OR EARTH, I HARDLY SEE THE SIGNIFICANCE OF WHERE THEY LAY YOUR CORPSE.
SOMETIMES I WISH THAT I BELIEVED.
SOMETIMES I WISH I COULD SHAKE YOUR HAND, SHIVA. BUT I CAN'T.
THERE'S TOO MUCH BLOOD ON IT.
VERY LITTLE OF IT IS INNOCENT BLOOD, SIU JERK JAI.
THAT'S NOT FOR US TO DECIDE.
I HAVE MADE A VOW NEVER TO USE OTOMO'S TEACHINGS IN ANY BATTLE WHERE THE GOAL IS THE DEATH OF MY OPPONENT. THIS IS THE BEST I CAN DO.
IT'S NOT NEARLY GOOD ENOUGH.
I CAN'T BE YOUR APPRENTICE, SHIVA.
I RESPECTFULLY DECLINE YOUR OFFER.

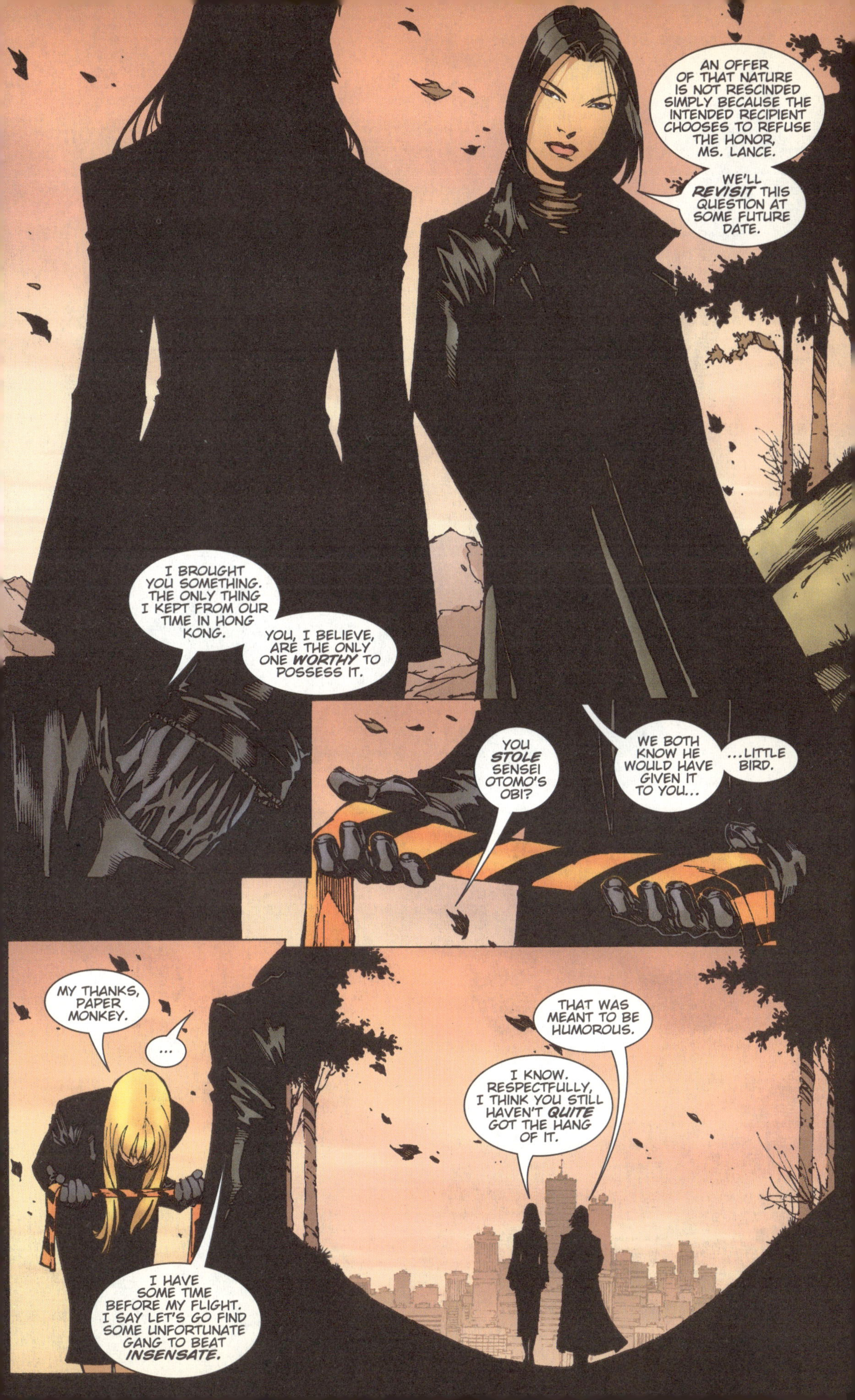
AN OFFER OF THAT NATURE IS NOT RESCINDED SIMPLY BECAUSE THE INTENDED RECIPIENT CHOOSES TO REFUSE THE HONOR, MS. LANCE.
WE'LL ***REVISIT*** THIS QUESTION AT SOME FUTURE DATE.
I BROUGHT YOU SOMETHING. THE ONLY THING I KEPT FROM OUR TIME IN HONG KONG.
YOU, I BELIEVE, ARE THE ONLY ONE ***WORTHY*** TO POSSESS IT.
YOU ***STOLE*** SENSEI OTOMO'S OBI?
WE BOTH KNOW HE WOULD HAVE GIVEN IT TO YOU...
...LITTLE BIRD.
MY THANKS, PAPER MONKEY.
...
I HAVE SOME TIME BEFORE MY FLIGHT. I SAY LET'S GO FIND SOME UNFORTUNATE GANG TO BEAT ***INSENSATE.***
THAT WAS MEANT TO BE HUMOROUS.
I KNOW. RESPECTFULLY, I THINK YOU STILL HAVEN'T ***QUITE*** GOT THE HANG OF IT.

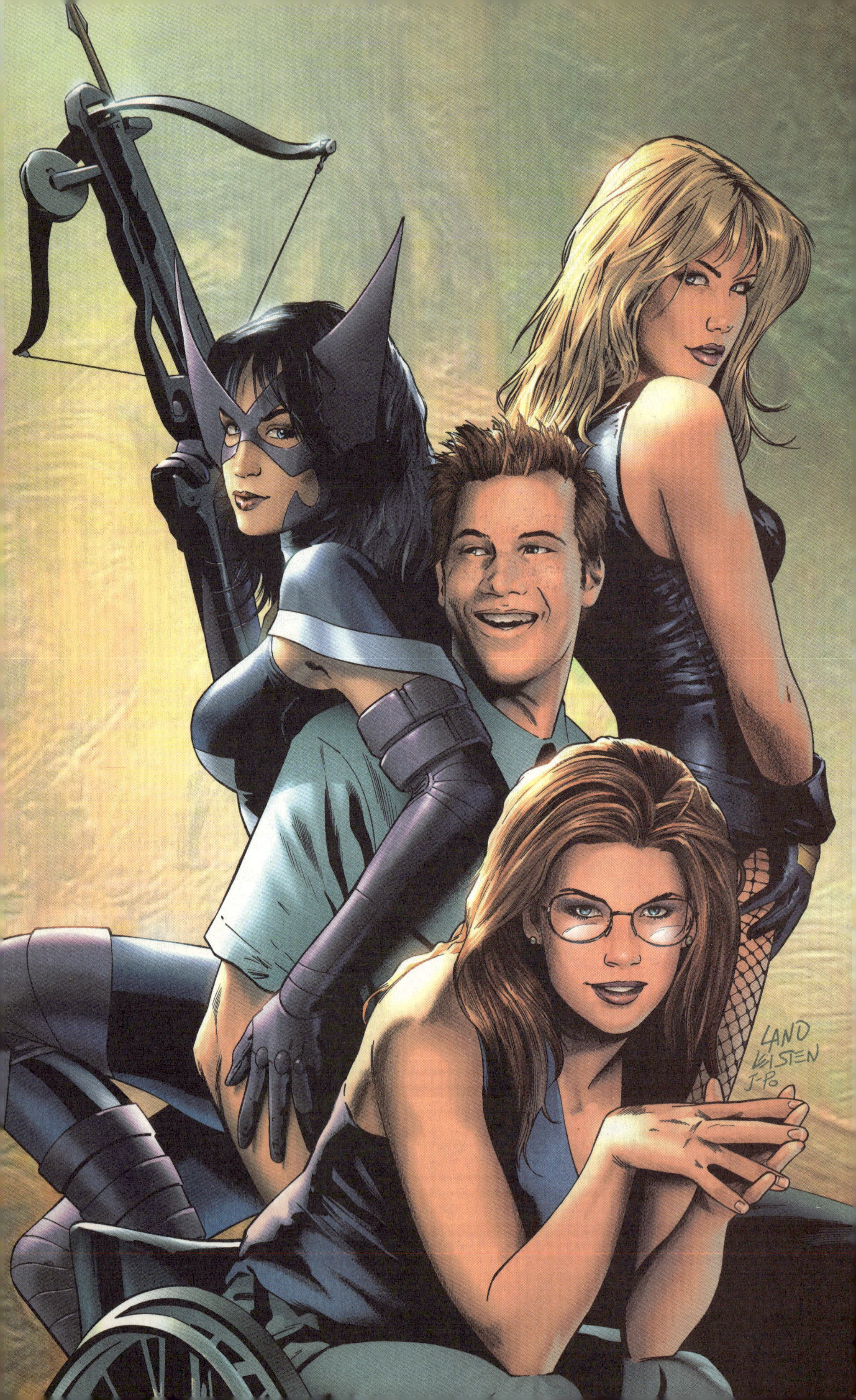
LAND
LEISTEN
J-Po

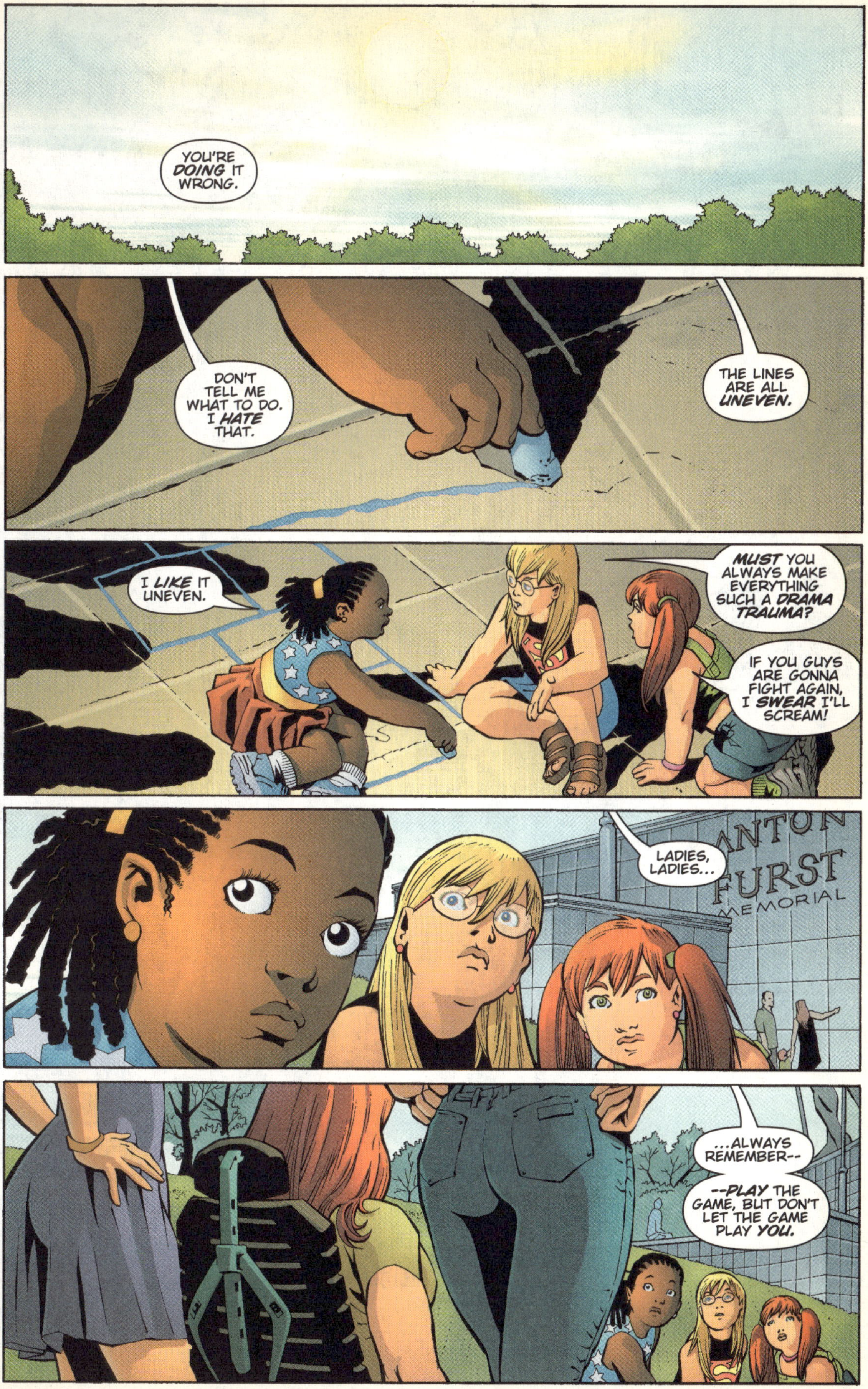
YOU'RE DOING IT WRONG.
DON'T TELL ME WHAT TO DO. I HATE THAT.
THE LINES ARE ALL UNEVEN.
I LIKE IT UNEVEN.
MUST YOU ALWAYS MAKE EVERYTHING SUCH A DRAMA TRAUMA?
IF YOU GUYS ARE GONNA FIGHT AGAIN, I SWEAR I'LL SCREAM!
LADIES, LADIES...
ANTON FURST MEMORIAL
...ALWAYS REMEMBER--
--PLAY THE GAME, BUT DON'T LET THE GAME PLAY YOU.

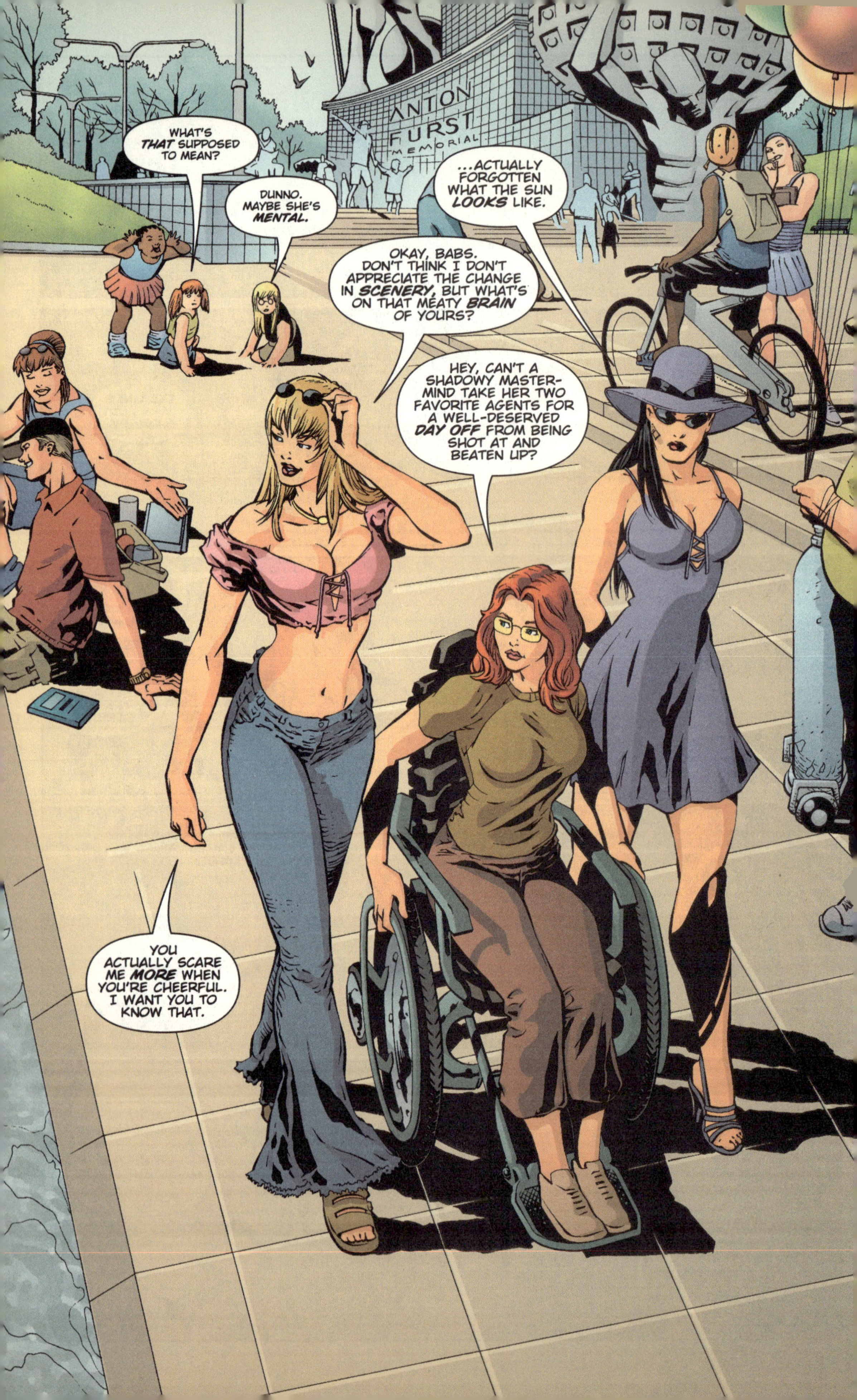
ANTON FURST MEMORIAL
WHAT'S THAT SUPPOSED TO MEAN?
DUNNO. MAYBE SHE'S MENTAL.
OKAY, BABS. DON'T THINK I DON'T APPRECIATE THE CHANGE IN SCENERY, BUT WHAT'S ON THAT MEATY BRAIN OF YOURS?
...ACTUALLY FORGOTTEN WHAT THE SUN LOOKS LIKE.
HEY, CAN'T A SHADOWY MASTER-MIND TAKE HER TWO FAVORITE AGENTS FOR A WELL-DESERVED DAY OFF FROM BEING SHOT AT AND BEATEN UP?
YOU ACTUALLY SCARE ME MORE WHEN YOU'RE CHEERFUL. I WANT YOU TO KNOW THAT.

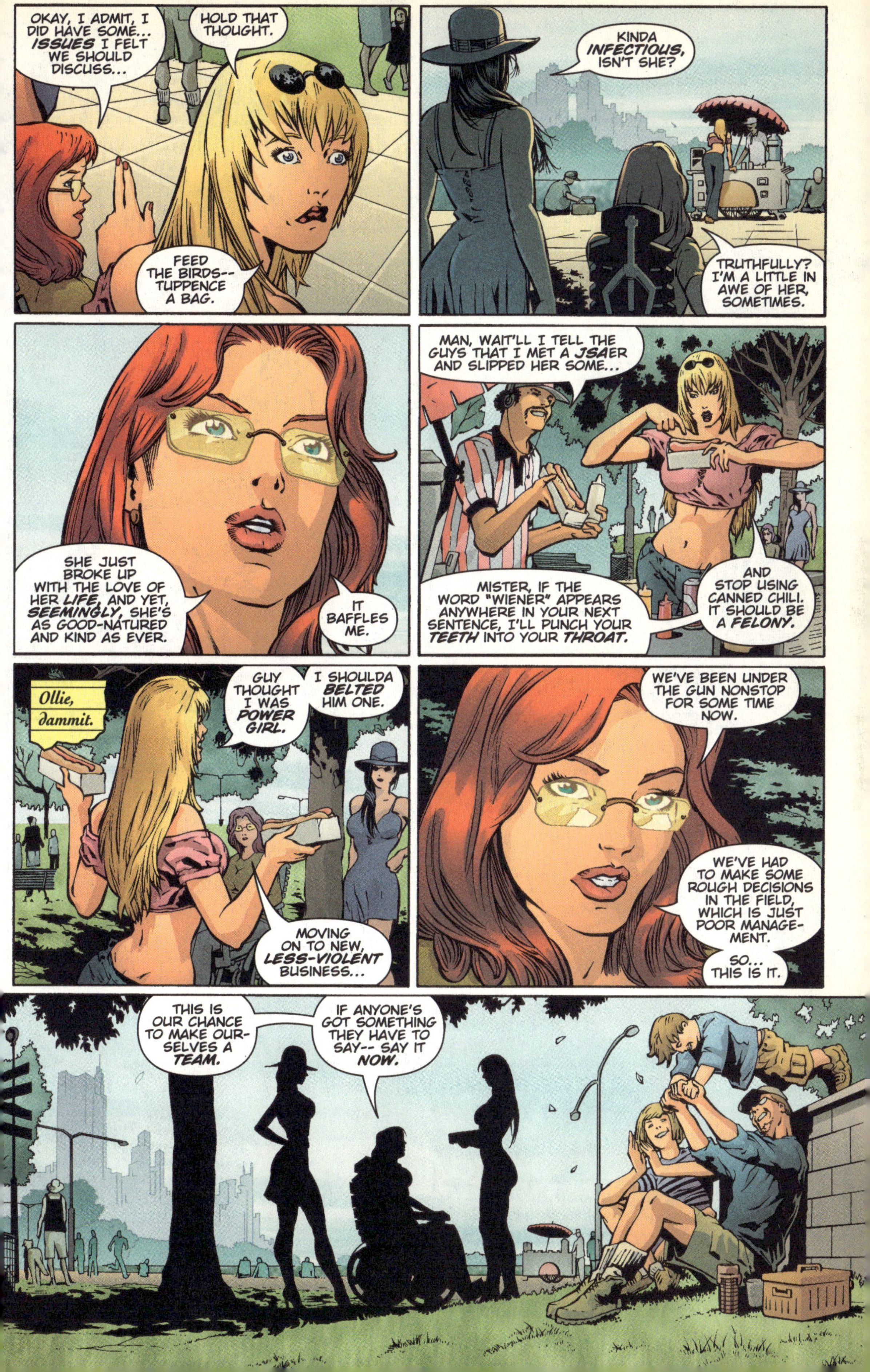

OKAY, I ADMIT, I DID HAVE SOME... ISSUES I FELT WE SHOULD DISCUSS...
HOLD THAT THOUGHT.
FEED THE BIRDS-- TUPPENCE A BAG.
KINDA INFECTIOUS, ISN'T SHE?
TRUTHFULLY? I'M A LITTLE IN AWE OF HER, SOMETIMES.
SHE JUST BROKE UP WITH THE LOVE OF HER LIFE, AND YET, SEEMINGLY, SHE'S AS GOOD-NATURED AND KIND AS EVER.
IT BAFFLES ME.
MAN, WAIT'LL I TELL THE GUYS THAT I MET A JSAer AND SLIPPED HER SOME...
MISTER, IF THE WORD "WIENER" APPEARS ANYWHERE IN YOUR NEXT SENTENCE, I'LL PUNCH YOUR TEETH INTO YOUR THROAT.
AND STOP USING CANNED CHILI. IT SHOULD BE A FELONY.
Ollie, dammit.
GUY THOUGHT I WAS POWER GIRL.
I SHOULDA BELTED HIM ONE.
MOVING ON TO NEW, LESS-VIOLENT BUSINESS...
WE'VE BEEN UNDER THE GUN NONSTOP FOR SOME TIME NOW.
WE'VE HAD TO MAKE SOME ROUGH DECISIONS IN THE FIELD, WHICH IS JUST POOR MANAGE-MENT.
SO... THIS IS IT.
THIS IS OUR CHANCE TO MAKE OUR-SELVES A TEAM.
IF ANYONE'S GOT SOMETHING THEY HAVE TO SAY-- SAY IT NOW.

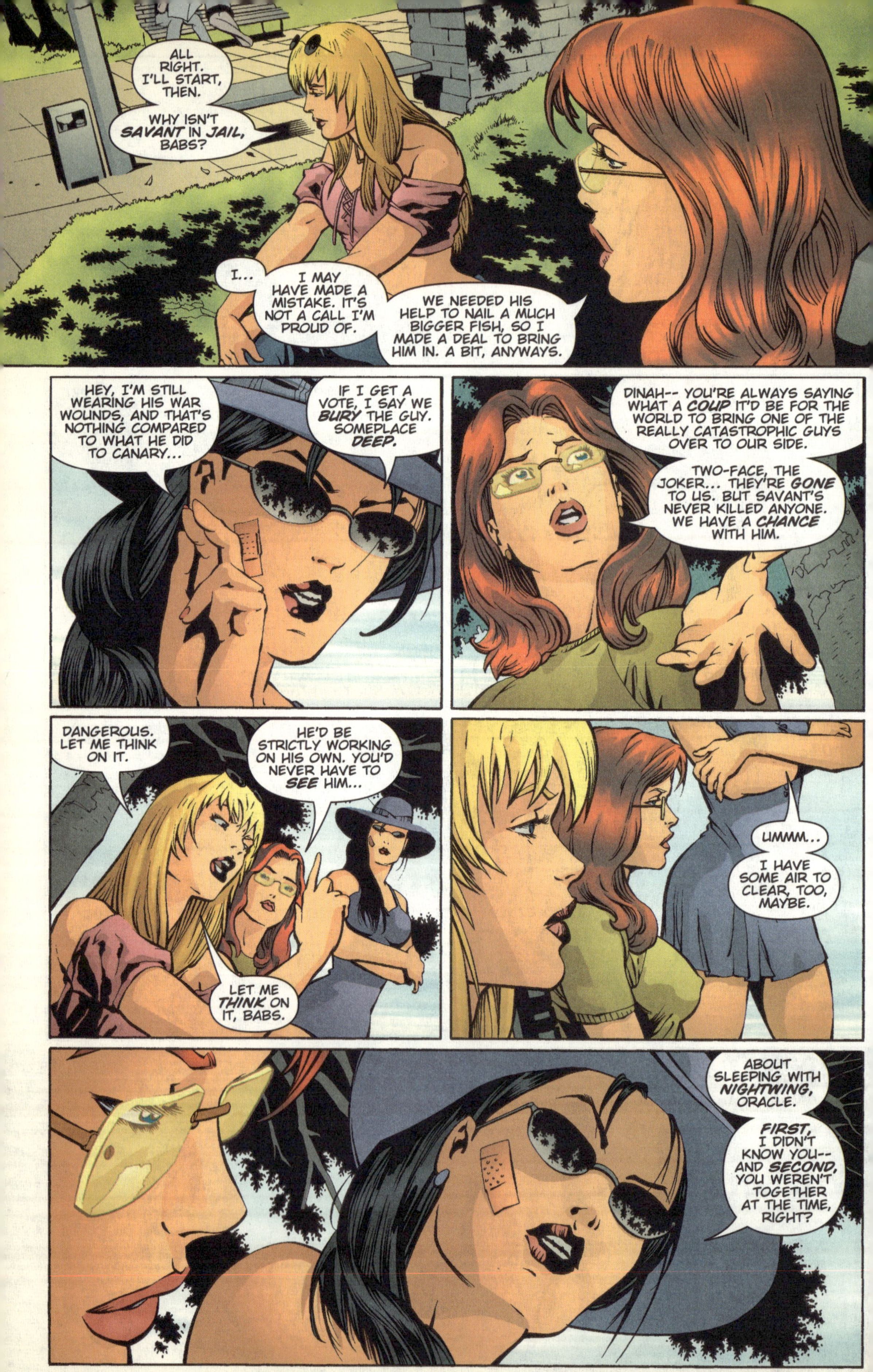
ALL RIGHT. I'LL START, THEN.
WHY ISN'T SAVANT IN JAIL, BABS?
I...
I MAY HAVE MADE A MISTAKE. IT'S NOT A CALL I'M PROUD OF.
WE NEEDED HIS HELP TO NAIL A MUCH BIGGER FISH, SO I MADE A DEAL TO BRING HIM IN. A BIT, ANYWAYS.
HEY, I'M STILL WEARING HIS WAR WOUNDS, AND THAT'S NOTHING COMPARED TO WHAT HE DID TO CANARY...
IF I GET A VOTE, I SAY WE BURY THE GUY. SOMEPLACE DEEP.
DINAH-- YOU'RE ALWAYS SAYING WHAT A COUP IT'D BE FOR THE WORLD TO BRING ONE OF THE REALLY CATASTROPHIC GUYS OVER TO OUR SIDE.
TWO-FACE, THE JOKER... THEY'RE GONE TO US. BUT SAVANT'S NEVER KILLED ANYONE. WE HAVE A CHANCE WITH HIM.
DANGEROUS. LET ME THINK ON IT.
HE'D BE STRICTLY WORKING ON HIS OWN. YOU'D NEVER HAVE TO SEE HIM...
LET ME THINK ON IT, BABS.
UMMM...
I HAVE SOME AIR TO CLEAR, TOO, MAYBE.
ABOUT SLEEPING WITH NIGHTWING, ORACLE.
FIRST, I DIDN'T KNOW YOU-- AND SECOND, YOU WEREN'T TOGETHER AT THE TIME, RIGHT?

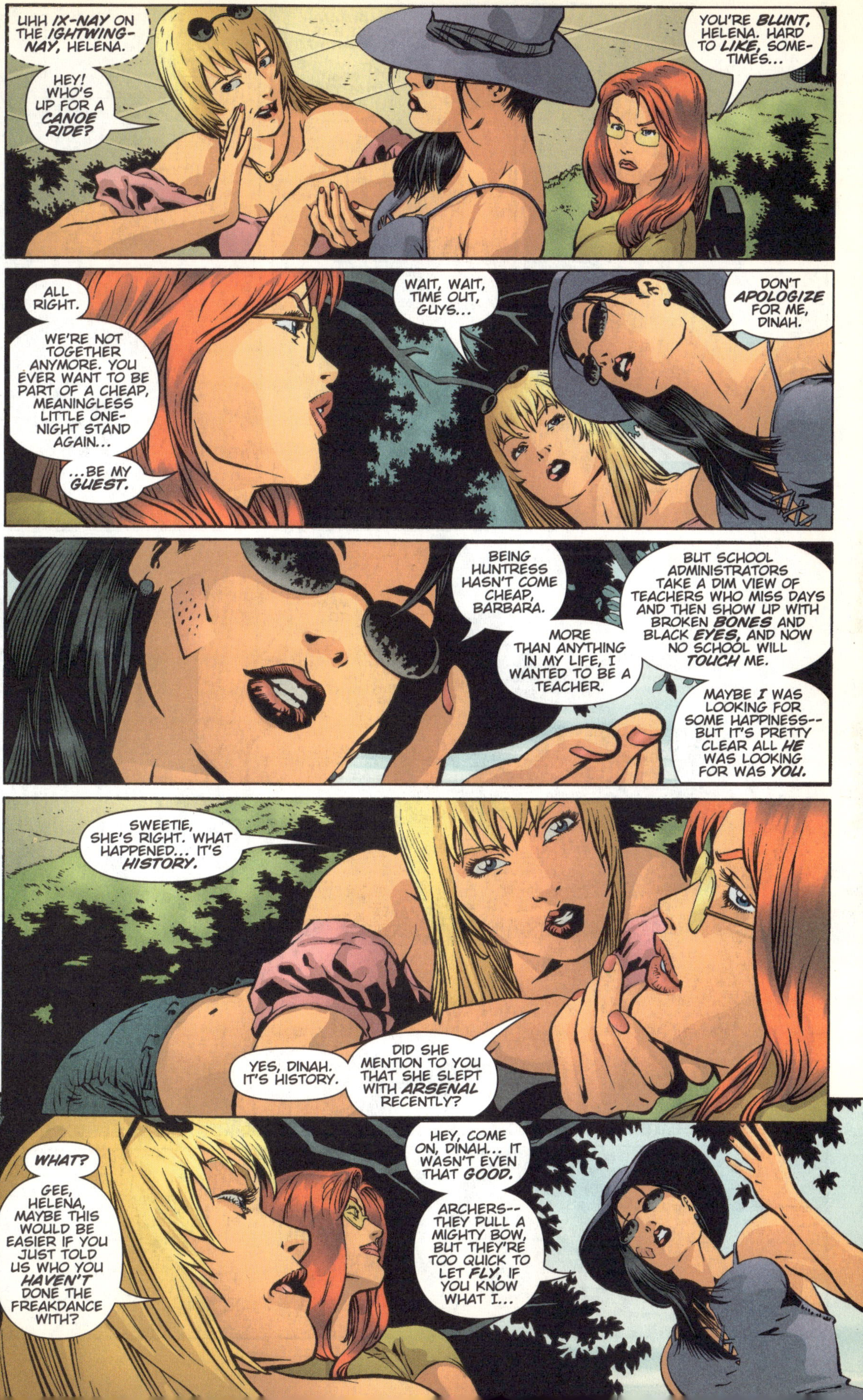
UHH IX-NAY ON THE IGHTWING-NAY, HELENA.
HEY! WHO'S UP FOR A CANOE RIDE?
YOU'RE BLUNT, HELENA. HARD TO LIKE, SOMETIMES...
ALL RIGHT.
WE'RE NOT TOGETHER ANYMORE. YOU EVER WANT TO BE PART OF A CHEAP, MEANINGLESS LITTLE ONE-NIGHT STAND AGAIN...
...BE MY GUEST.
WAIT, WAIT, TIME OUT, GUYS...
DON'T APOLOGIZE FOR ME, DINAH.
BEING HUNTRESS HASN'T COME CHEAP, BARBARA.
MORE THAN ANYTHING IN MY LIFE, I WANTED TO BE A TEACHER.
BUT SCHOOL ADMINISTRATORS TAKE A DIM VIEW OF TEACHERS WHO MISS DAYS AND THEN SHOW UP WITH BROKEN BONES AND BLACK EYES, AND NOW NO SCHOOL WILL TOUCH ME.
MAYBE I WAS LOOKING FOR SOME HAPPINESS-- BUT IT'S PRETTY CLEAR ALL HE WAS LOOKING FOR WAS YOU.
SWEETIE, SHE'S RIGHT. WHAT HAPPENED... IT'S HISTORY.
YES, DINAH. IT'S HISTORY.
DID SHE MENTION TO YOU THAT SHE SLEPT WITH ARSENAL RECENTLY?
WHAT?
GEE, HELENA, MAYBE THIS WOULD BE EASIER IF YOU JUST TOLD US WHO YOU HAVEN'T DONE THE FREAKDANCE WITH?
HEY, COME ON, DINAH... IT WASN'T EVEN THAT GOOD.
ARCHERS-- THEY PULL A MIGHTY BOW, BUT THEY'RE TOO QUICK TO LET FLY, IF YOU KNOW WHAT I...

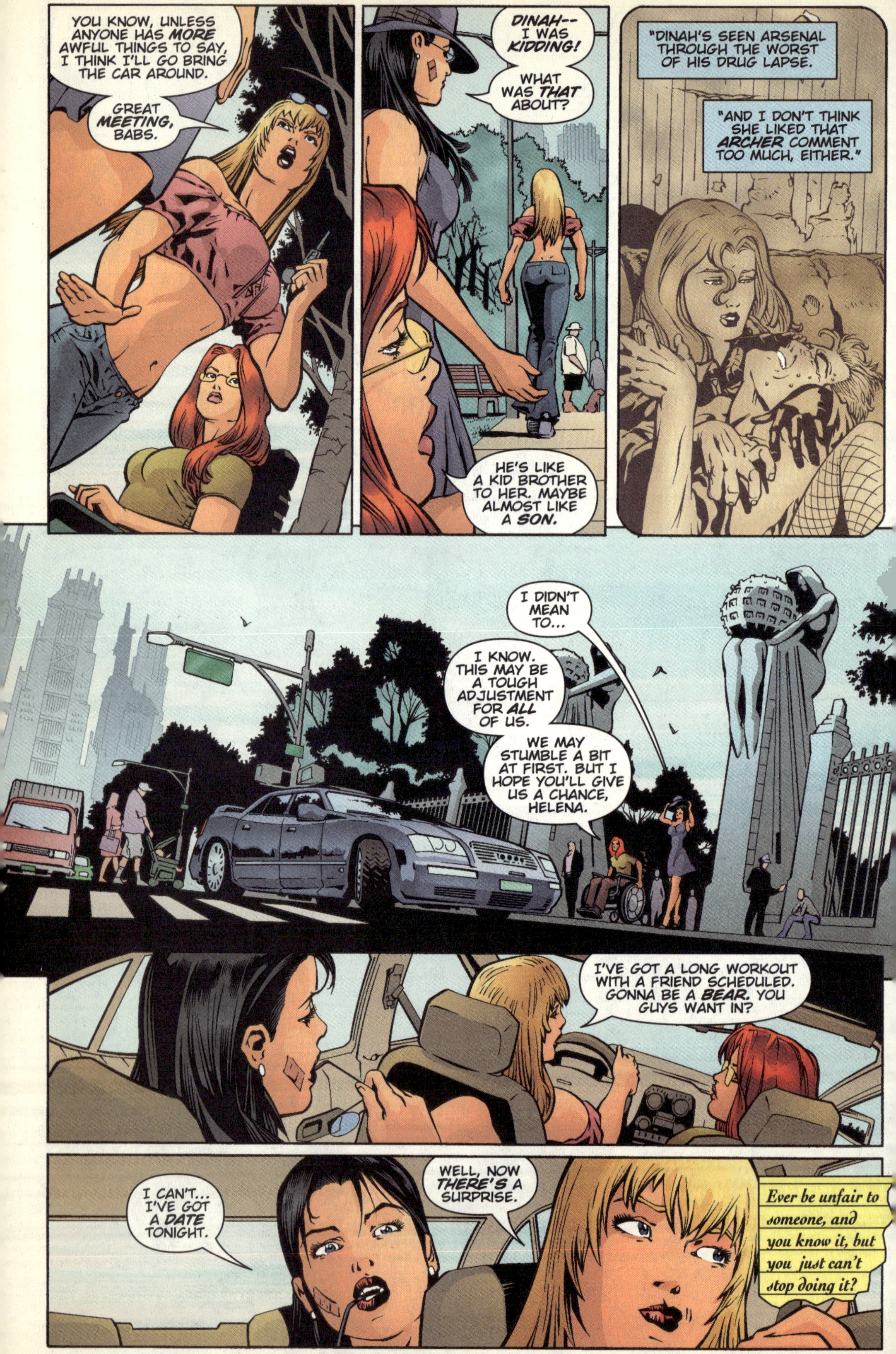
YOU KNOW, UNLESS ANYONE HAS **MORE** AWFUL THINGS TO SAY, I THINK I'LL GO BRING THE CAR AROUND.
GREAT **MEETING,** BABS.
DINAH-- I WAS **KIDDING!**
WHAT WAS **THAT** ABOUT?
HE'S LIKE A KID BROTHER TO HER. MAYBE ALMOST LIKE A **SON.**
"DINAH'S SEEN ARSENAL THROUGH THE WORST OF HIS DRUG LAPSE.
"AND I DON'T THINK SHE LIKED THAT **ARCHER** COMMENT TOO MUCH, EITHER."
I DIDN'T MEAN TO...
I KNOW. THIS MAY BE A TOUGH ADJUSTMENT FOR **ALL** OF US.
WE MAY STUMBLE A BIT AT FIRST. BUT I HOPE YOU'LL GIVE US A CHANCE, HELENA.
I'VE GOT A LONG WORKOUT WITH A FRIEND SCHEDULED. GONNA BE A **BEAR.** YOU GUYS WANT IN?
I CAN'T... I'VE GOT A **DATE** TONIGHT.
WELL, NOW **THERE'S** A SURPRISE.
Ever be unfair to someone, and you know it, but you just can't stop doing it?

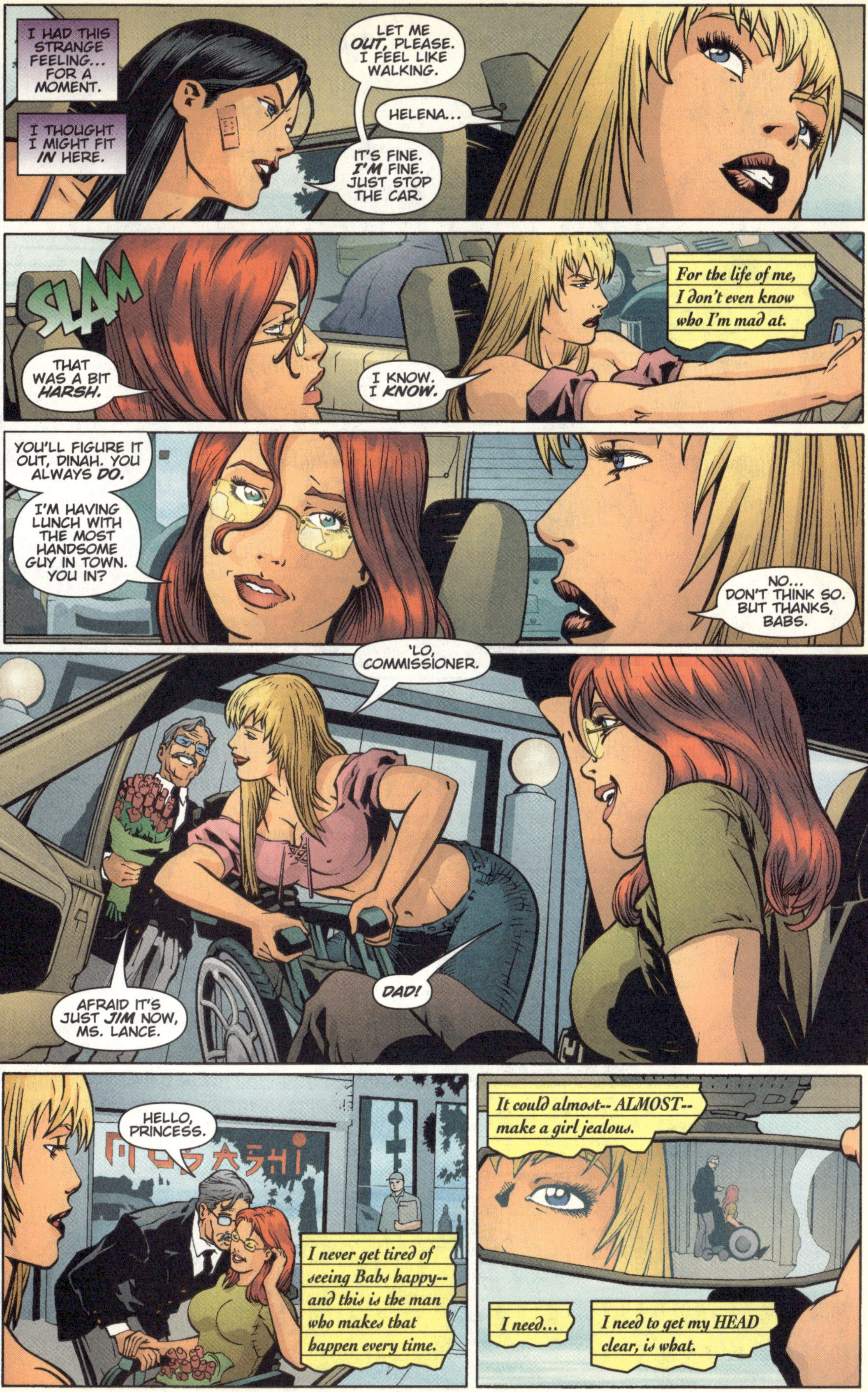
I HAD THIS STRANGE FEELING... FOR A MOMENT.
I THOUGHT I MIGHT FIT IN HERE.
LET ME OUT, PLEASE. I FEEL LIKE WALKING.
HELENA...
IT'S FINE. I'M FINE. JUST STOP THE CAR.
SLAM
For the life of me, I don't even know who I'm mad at.
THAT WAS A BIT HARSH.
I KNOW. I KNOW.
YOU'LL FIGURE IT OUT, DINAH. YOU ALWAYS DO.
I'M HAVING LUNCH WITH THE MOST HANDSOME GUY IN TOWN. YOU IN?
NO... DON'T THINK SO. BUT THANKS, BABS.
'LO, COMMISSIONER.
AFRAID IT'S JUST JIM NOW, MS. LANCE.
DAD!
HELLO, PRINCESS.
I never get tired of seeing Babs happy-- and this is the man who makes that happen every time.
It could almost-- ALMOST-- make a girl jealous.
I need...
I need to get my HEAD clear, is what.

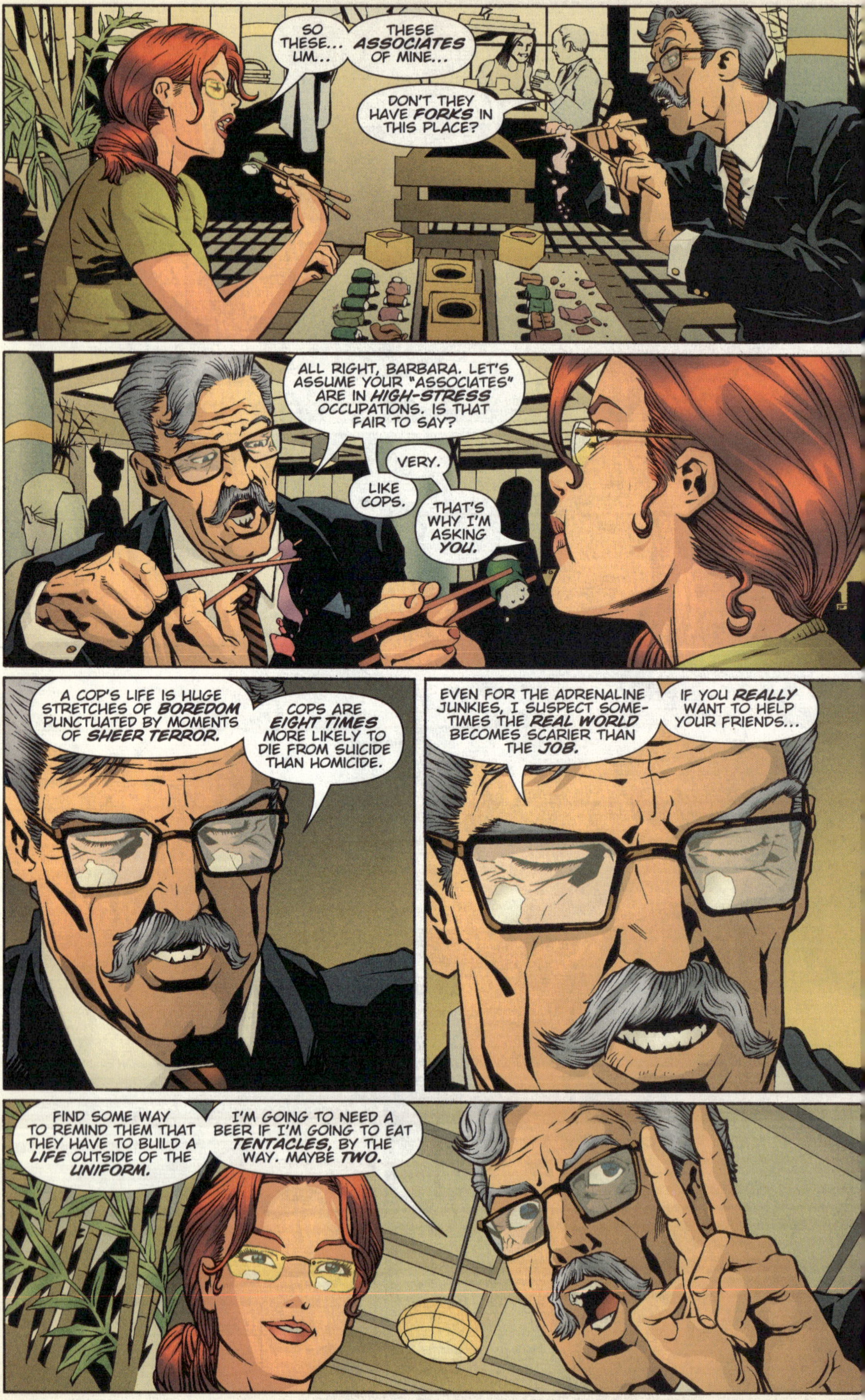
SO THESE... UM...
THESE ASSOCIATES OF MINE...
DON'T THEY HAVE FORKS IN THIS PLACE?
ALL RIGHT, BARBARA. LET'S ASSUME YOUR "ASSOCIATES" ARE IN HIGH-STRESS OCCUPATIONS. IS THAT FAIR TO SAY?
VERY.
LIKE COPS.
THAT'S WHY I'M ASKING YOU.
A COP'S LIFE IS HUGE STRETCHES OF BOREDOM PUNCTUATED BY MOMENTS OF SHEER TERROR.
COPS ARE EIGHT TIMES MORE LIKELY TO DIE FROM SUICIDE THAN HOMICIDE.
EVEN FOR THE ADRENALINE JUNKIES, I SUSPECT SOMETIMES THE REAL WORLD BECOMES SCARIER THAN THE JOB.
IF YOU REALLY WANT TO HELP YOUR FRIENDS...
FIND SOME WAY TO REMIND THEM THAT THEY HAVE TO BUILD A LIFE OUTSIDE OF THE UNIFORM.
I'M GOING TO NEED A BEER IF I'M GOING TO EAT TENTACLES, BY THE WAY. MAYBE TWO.

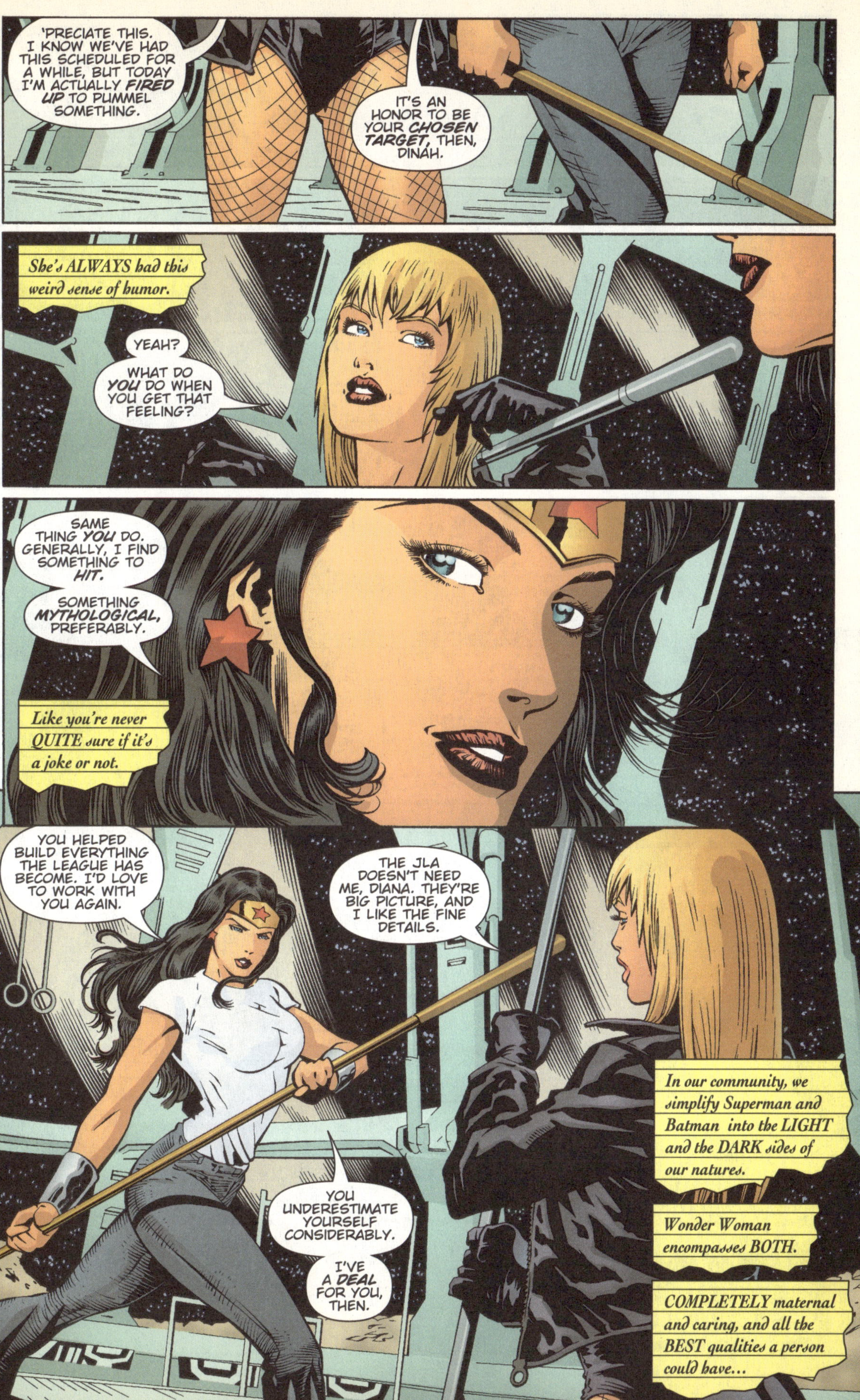
'PRECIATE THIS. I KNOW WE'VE HAD THIS SCHEDULED FOR A WHILE, BUT TODAY I'M ACTUALLY FIRED UP TO PUMMEL SOMETHING.
IT'S AN HONOR TO BE YOUR CHOSEN TARGET, THEN, DINAH.
She's ALWAYS had this weird sense of humor.
YEAH? WHAT DO YOU DO WHEN YOU GET THAT FEELING?
SAME THING YOU DO. GENERALLY, I FIND SOMETHING TO HIT.
SOMETHING MYTHOLOGICAL, PREFERABLY.
Like you're never QUITE sure if it's a joke or not.
YOU HELPED BUILD EVERYTHING THE LEAGUE HAS BECOME. I'D LOVE TO WORK WITH YOU AGAIN.
THE JLA DOESN'T NEED ME, DIANA. THEY'RE BIG PICTURE, AND I LIKE THE FINE DETAILS.
YOU UNDERESTIMATE YOURSELF CONSIDERABLY.
I'VE A DEAL FOR YOU, THEN.
In our community, we simplify Superman and Batman into the LIGHT and the DARK sides of our natures.
Wonder Woman encompasses BOTH.
COMPLETELY maternal and caring, and all the BEST qualities a person could have...

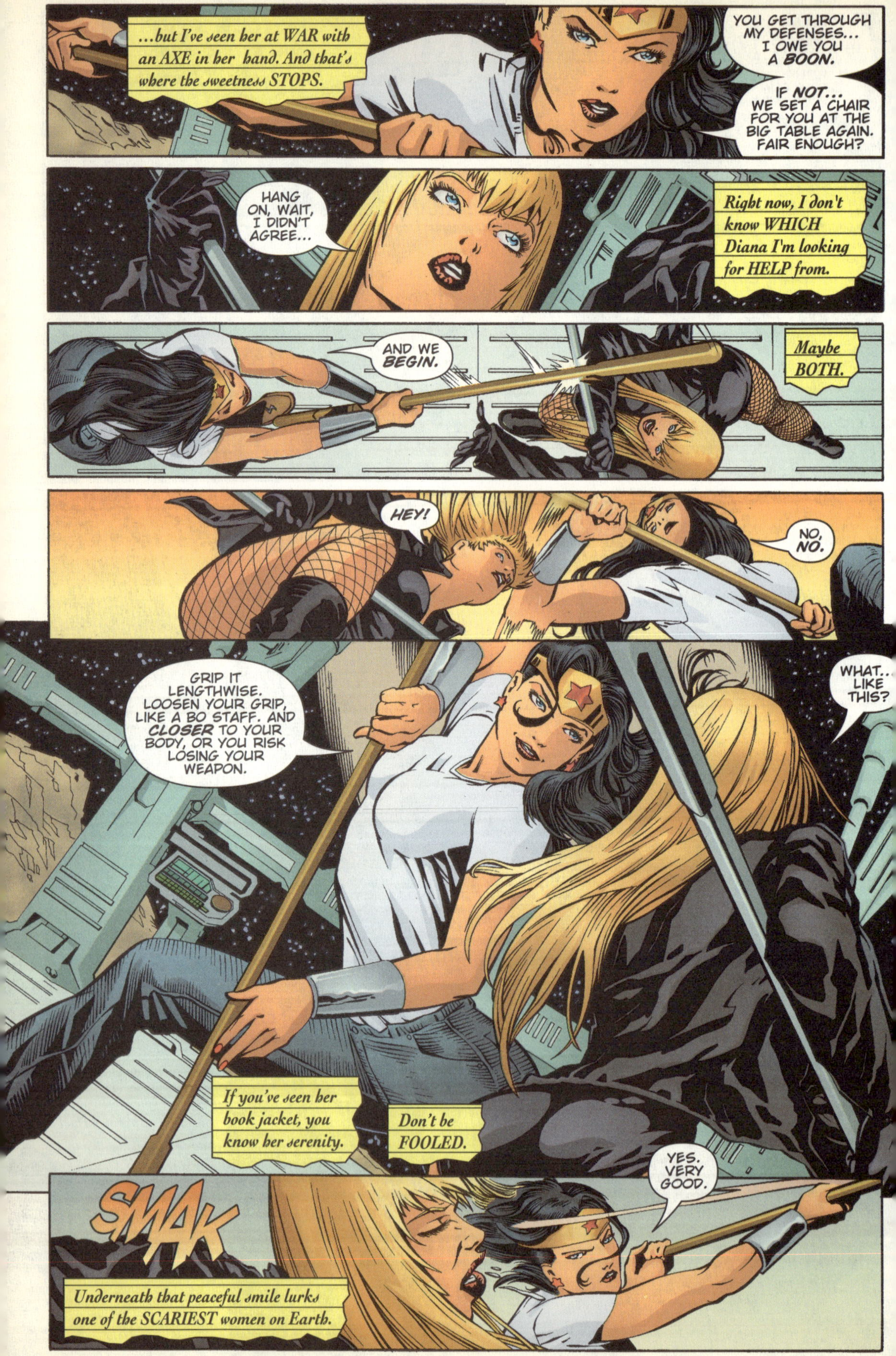
...but I've seen her at WAR with an AXE in her hand. And that's where the sweetness STOPS.
YOU GET THROUGH MY DEFENSES... I OWE YOU A BOON.
IF NOT... WE SET A CHAIR FOR YOU AT THE BIG TABLE AGAIN. FAIR ENOUGH?
HANG ON, WAIT, I DIDN'T AGREE...
Right now, I don't know WHICH Diana I'm looking for HELP from.
AND WE BEGIN.
Maybe BOTH.
HEY!
NO, NO.
GRIP IT LENGTHWISE. LOOSEN YOUR GRIP, LIKE A BO STAFF. AND CLOSER TO YOUR BODY, OR YOU RISK LOSING YOUR WEAPON.
WHAT... LIKE THIS?
If you've seen her book jacket, you know her serenity.
Don't be FOOLED.
SMAK
YES. VERY GOOD.
Underneath that peaceful smile lurks one of the SCARIEST women on Earth.

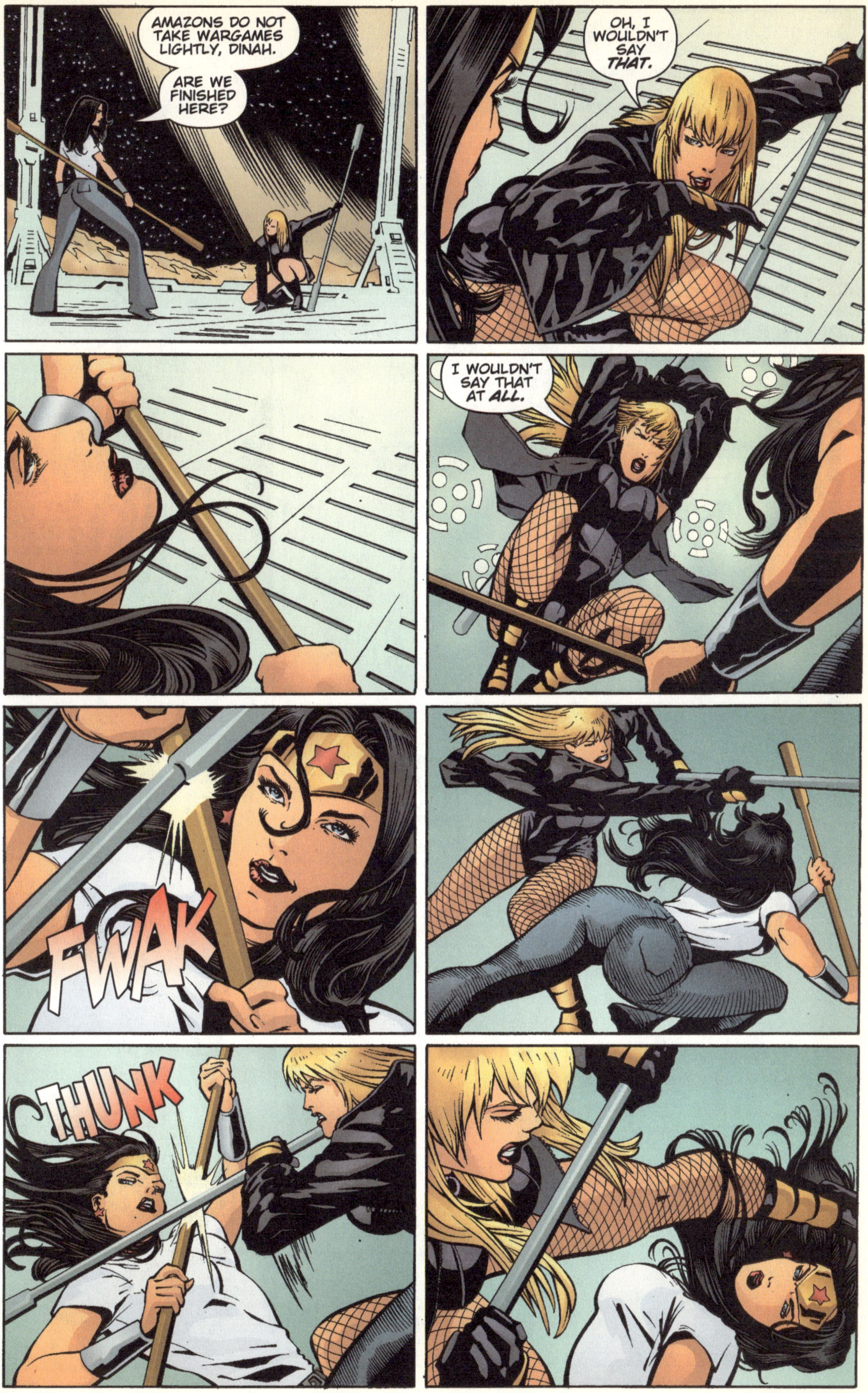
AMAZONS DO NOT TAKE WARGAMES LIGHTLY, DINAH.
ARE WE FINISHED HERE?
OH, I WOULDN'T SAY THAT.
I WOULDN'T SAY THAT AT ALL.
FWAK
THUNK

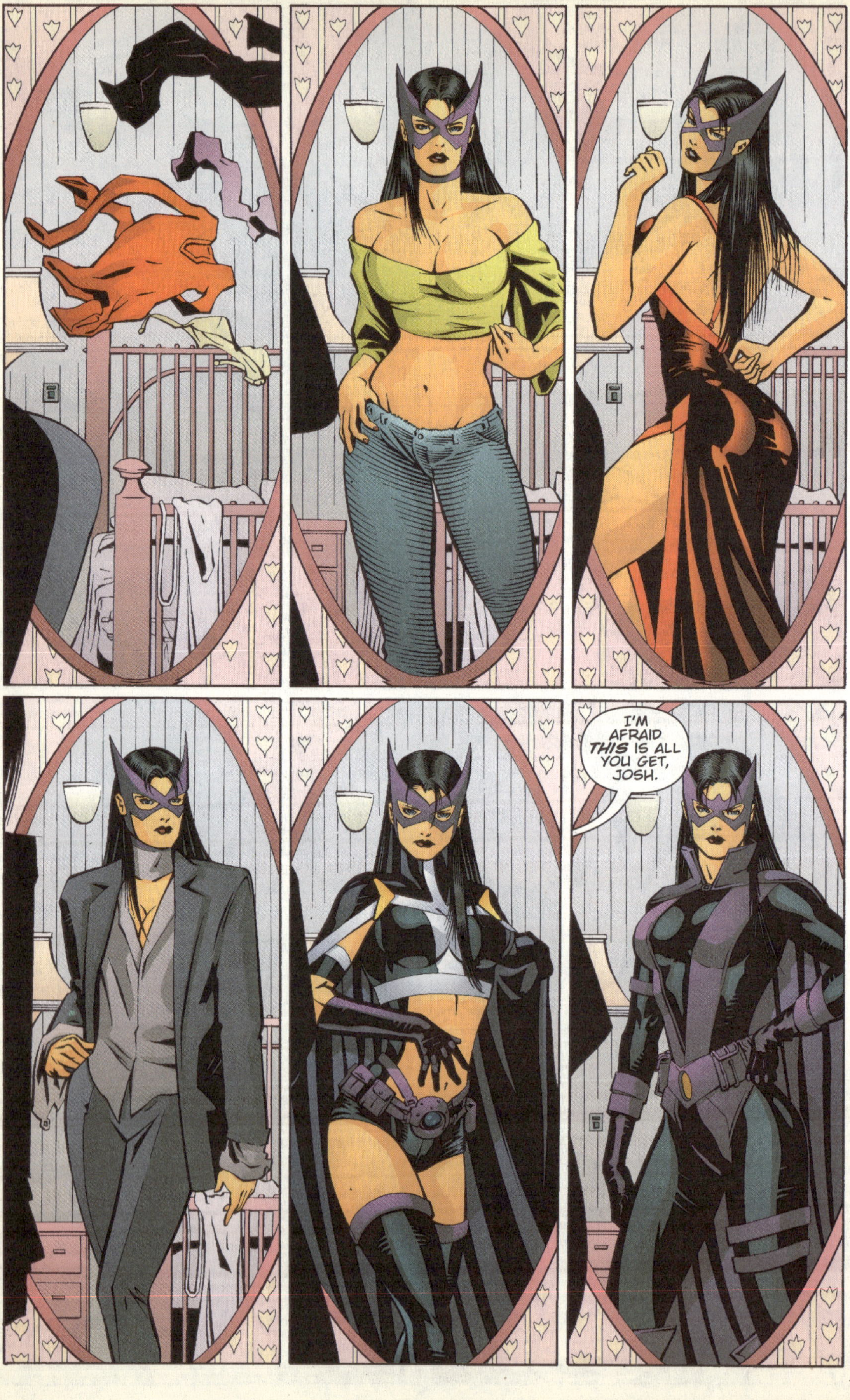
I'M AFRAID THIS IS ALL YOU GET, JOSH.

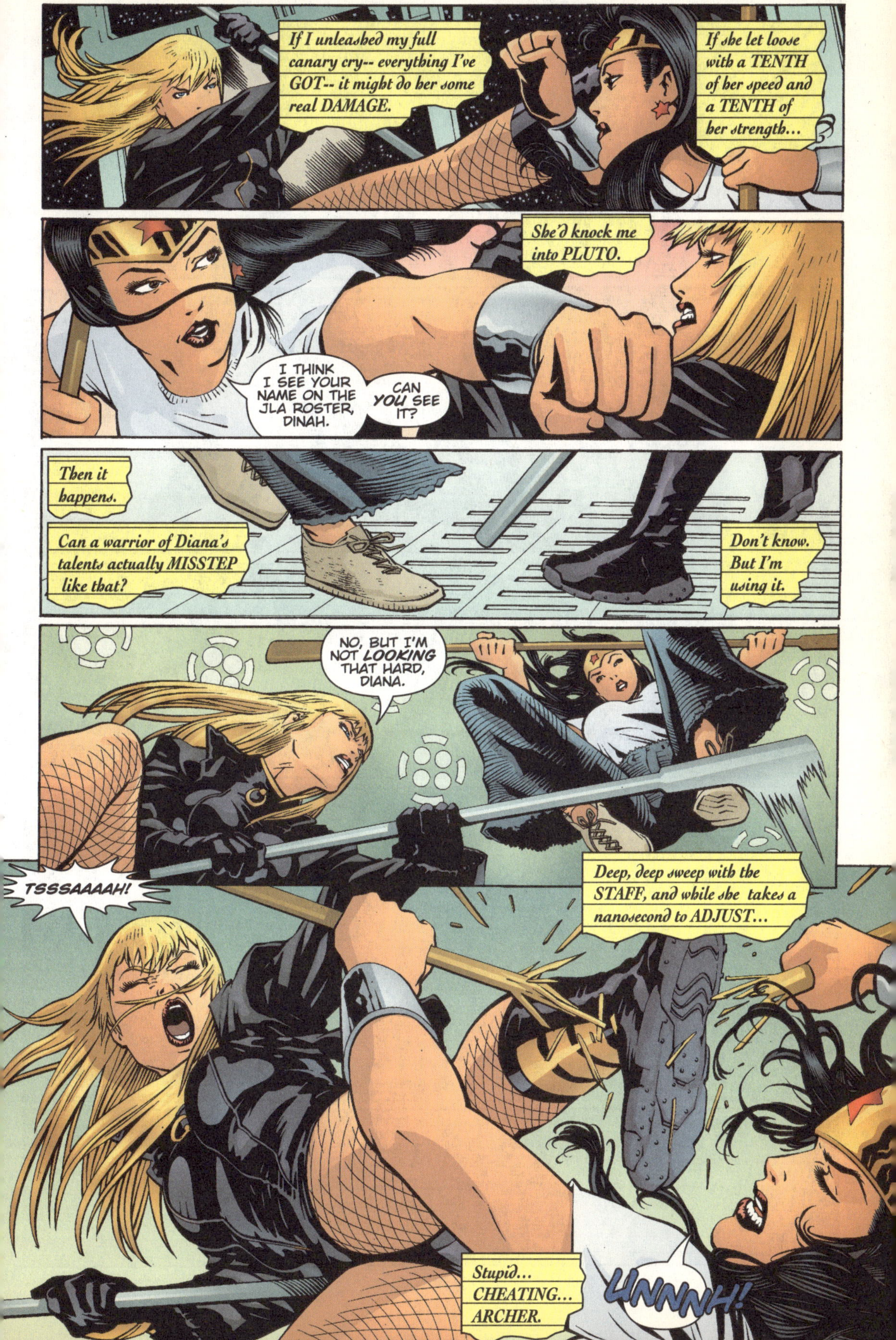
If I unleashed my full canary cry-- everything I've GOT-- it might do her some real DAMAGE.
If she let loose with a TENTH of her speed and a TENTH of her strength...
She'd knock me into PLUTO.
I THINK I SEE YOUR NAME ON THE JLA ROSTER, DINAH.
CAN YOU SEE IT?
Then it happens.
Can a warrior of Diana's talents actually MISSTEP like that?
Don't know. But I'm using it.
NO, BUT I'M NOT LOOKING THAT HARD, DIANA.
TSSSAAAAH!
Deep, deep sweep with the STAFF, and while she takes a nanosecond to ADJUST...
Stupid... CHEATING... ARCHER.
UNNNH!

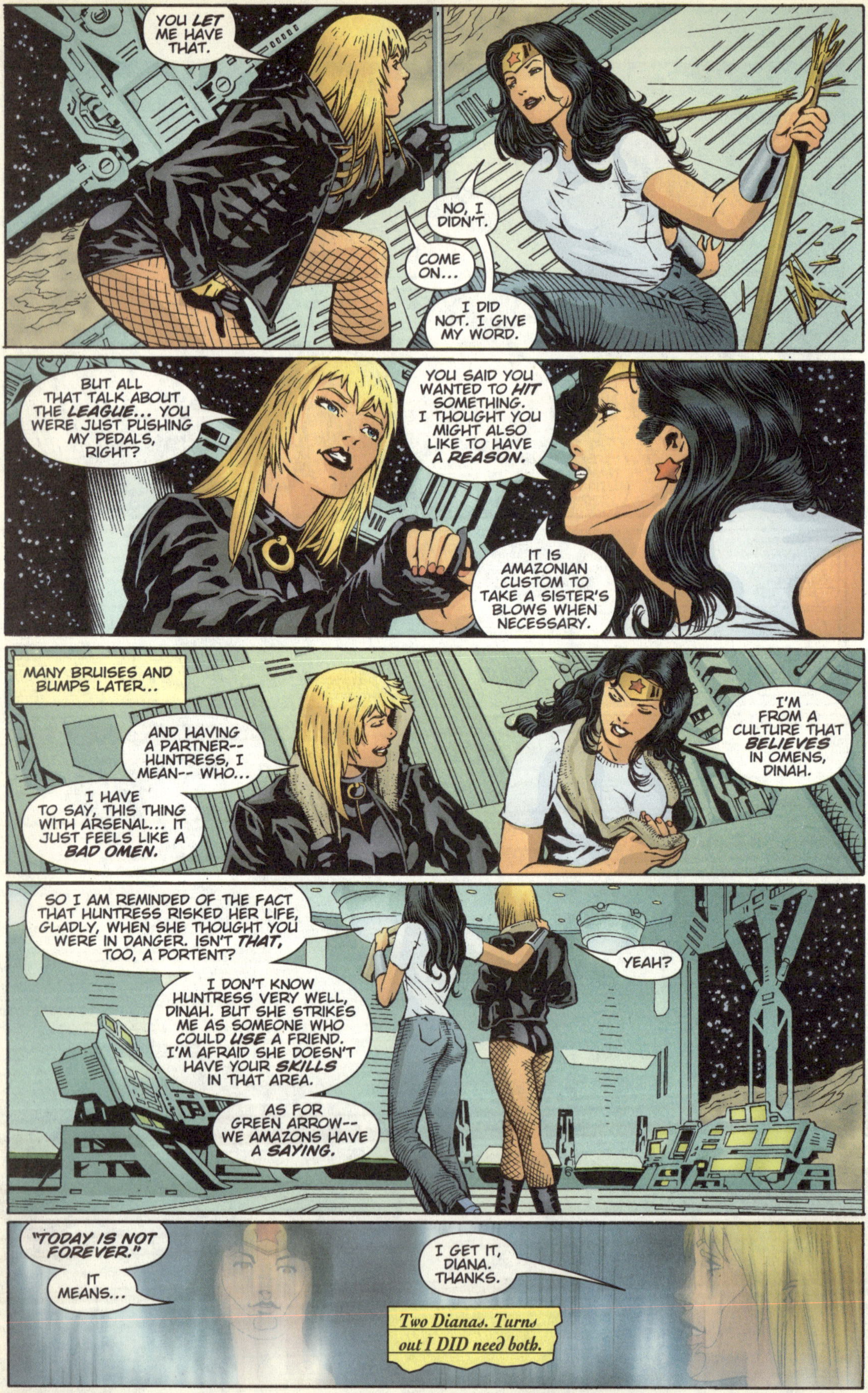
YOU LET ME HAVE THAT.
NO, I DIDN'T.
COME ON...
I DID NOT. I GIVE MY WORD.
BUT ALL THAT TALK ABOUT THE LEAGUE... YOU WERE JUST PUSHING MY PEDALS, RIGHT?
YOU SAID YOU WANTED TO HIT SOMETHING. I THOUGHT YOU MIGHT ALSO LIKE TO HAVE A REASON.
IT IS AMAZONIAN CUSTOM TO TAKE A SISTER'S BLOWS WHEN NECESSARY.
MANY BRUISES AND BUMPS LATER..
AND HAVING A PARTNER-- HUNTRESS, I MEAN-- WHO...
I HAVE TO SAY, THIS THING WITH ARSENAL... IT JUST FEELS LIKE A BAD OMEN.
I'M FROM A CULTURE THAT BELIEVES IN OMENS, DINAH.
SO I AM REMINDED OF THE FACT THAT HUNTRESS RISKED HER LIFE, GLADLY, WHEN SHE THOUGHT YOU WERE IN DANGER. ISN'T THAT, TOO, A PORTENT?
YEAH?
I DON'T KNOW HUNTRESS VERY WELL, DINAH. BUT SHE STRIKES ME AS SOMEONE WHO COULD USE A FRIEND. I'M AFRAID SHE DOESN'T HAVE YOUR SKILLS IN THAT AREA.
AS FOR GREEN ARROW-- WE AMAZONS HAVE A SAYING.
"TODAY IS NOT FOREVER."
IT MEANS...
I GET IT, DIANA. THANKS.
Two Dianas. Turns out I DID need both.

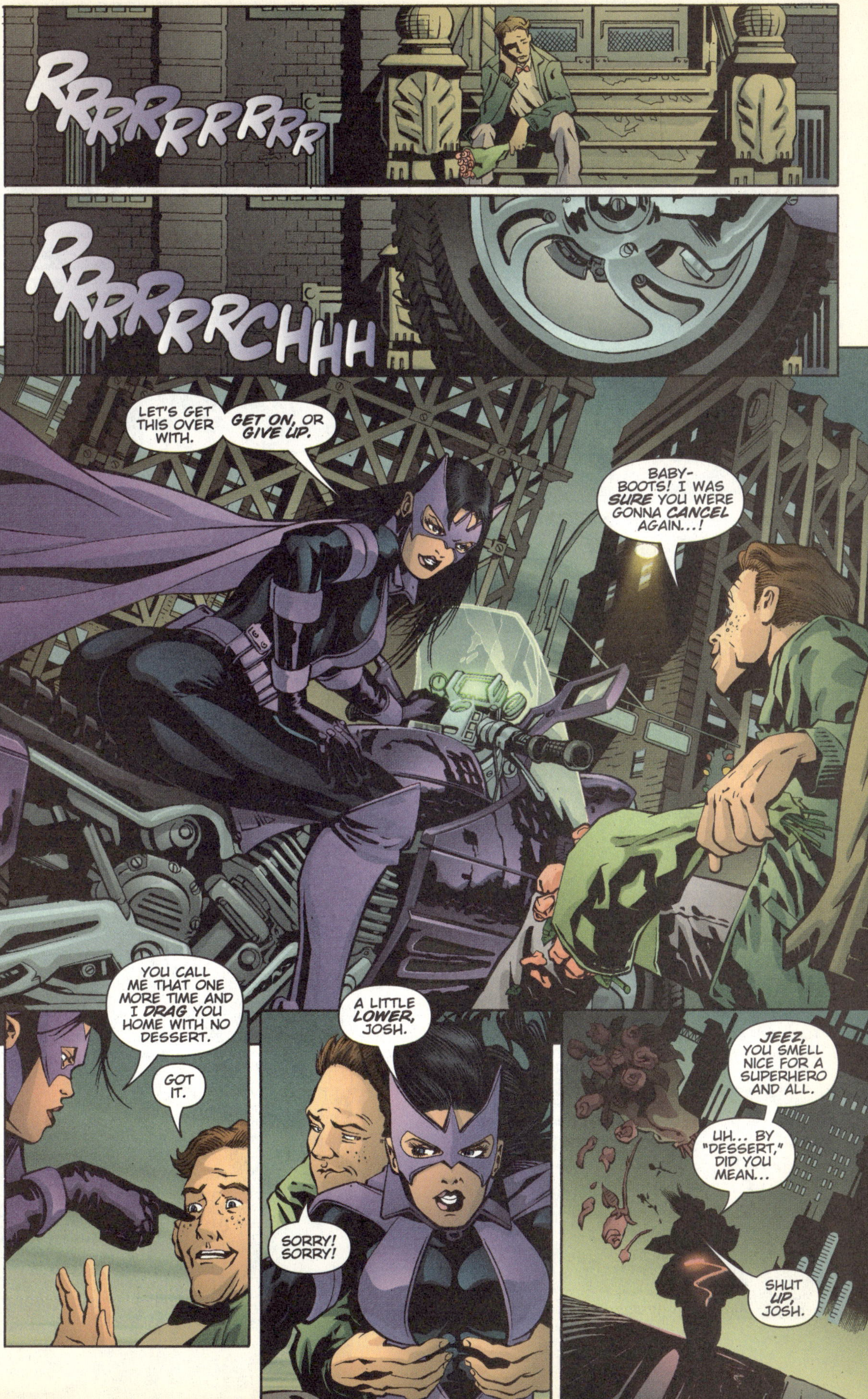
RRRRRRRRRR
RRRRRRRCHHH
LET'S GET THIS OVER WITH.
GET ON, OR GIVE UP.
BABY-BOOTS! I WAS SURE YOU WERE GONNA CANCEL AGAIN...!
YOU CALL ME THAT ONE MORE TIME AND I DRAG YOU HOME WITH NO DESSERT.
GOT IT.
A LITTLE LOWER, JOSH.
SORRY! SORRY!
JEEZ, YOU SMELL NICE FOR A SUPERHERO AND ALL.
UH... BY "DESSERT," DID YOU MEAN...
SHUT UP, JOSH.

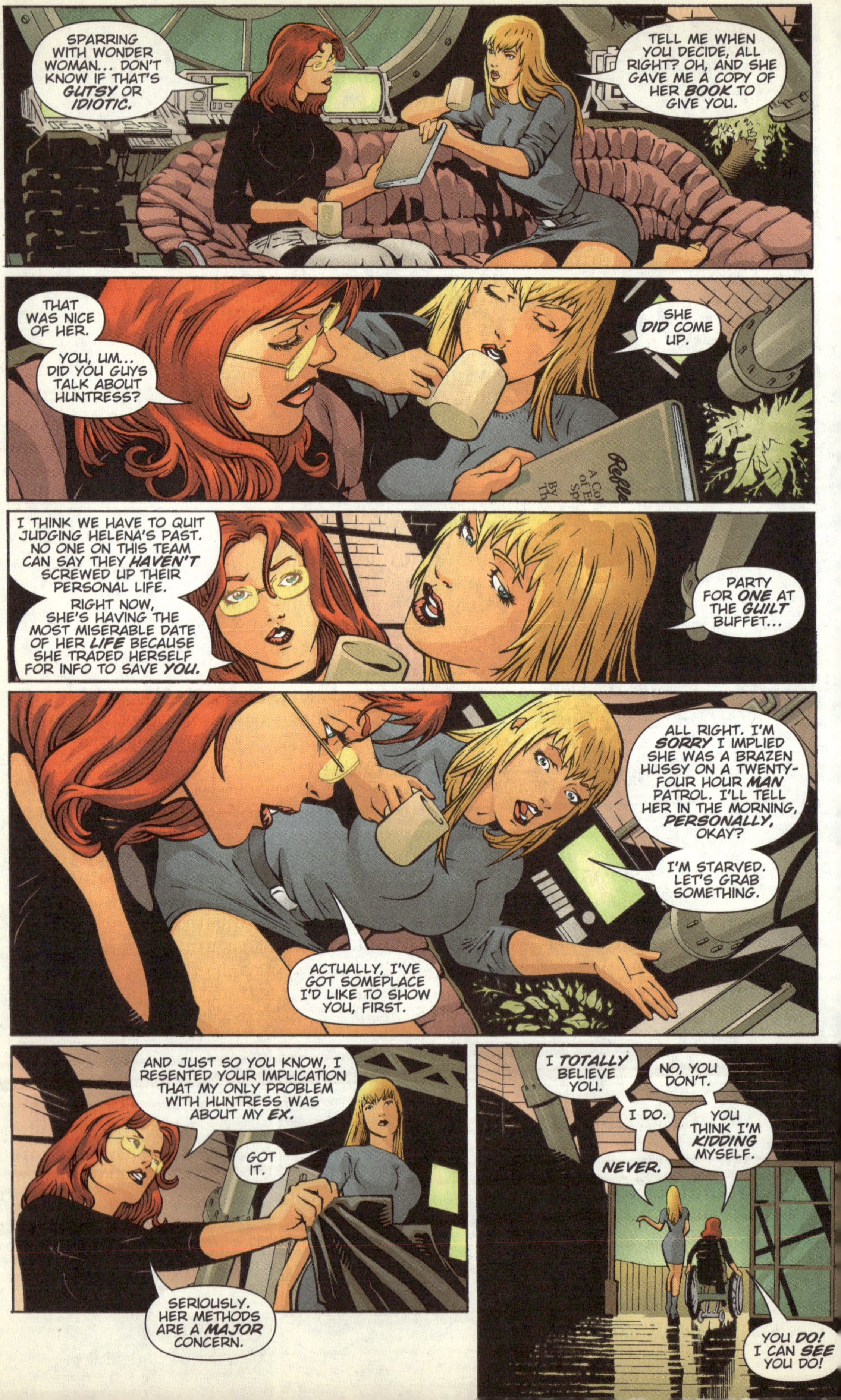
SPARRING WITH WONDER WOMAN... DON'T KNOW IF THAT'S GUTSY OR IDIOTIC.
TELL ME WHEN YOU DECIDE, ALL RIGHT? OH, AND SHE GAVE ME A COPY OF HER BOOK TO GIVE YOU.
THAT WAS NICE OF HER.
YOU, UM... DID YOU GUYS TALK ABOUT HUNTRESS?
SHE DID COME UP.
I THINK WE HAVE TO QUIT JUDGING HELENA'S PAST. NO ONE ON THIS TEAM CAN SAY THEY HAVEN'T SCREWED UP THEIR PERSONAL LIFE.
RIGHT NOW, SHE'S HAVING THE MOST MISERABLE DATE OF HER LIFE BECAUSE SHE TRADED HERSELF FOR INFO TO SAVE YOU.
PARTY FOR ONE AT THE GUILT BUFFET...
ALL RIGHT. I'M SORRY I IMPLIED SHE WAS A BRAZEN HUSSY ON A TWENTY-FOUR HOUR MAN PATROL. I'LL TELL HER IN THE MORNING, PERSONALLY, OKAY?
I'M STARVED. LET'S GRAB SOMETHING.
ACTUALLY, I'VE GOT SOMEPLACE I'D LIKE TO SHOW YOU, FIRST.
AND JUST SO YOU KNOW, I RESENTED YOUR IMPLICATION THAT MY ONLY PROBLEM WITH HUNTRESS WAS ABOUT MY EX.
GOT IT.
SERIOUSLY. HER METHODS ARE A MAJOR CONCERN.
I TOTALLY BELIEVE YOU.
NO, YOU DON'T.
I DO.
YOU THINK I'M KIDDING MYSELF.
NEVER.
YOU DO! I CAN SEE YOU DO!

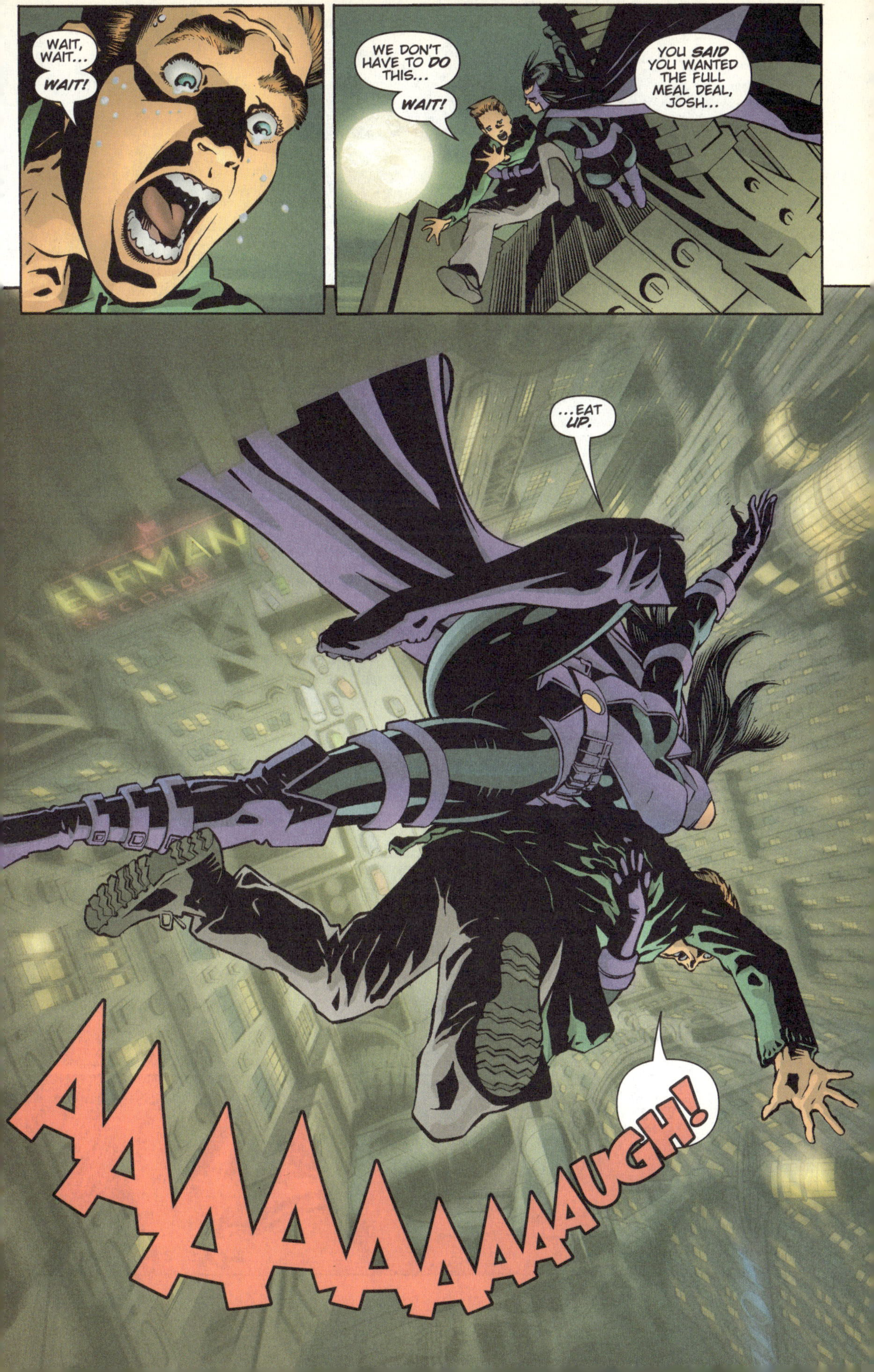
WAIT, WAIT... WAIT!
WE DON'T HAVE TO DO THIS... WAIT!
YOU SAID YOU WANTED THE FULL MEAL DEAL, JOSH...
...EAT UP.
ELFMAN RECORDS
AAAAAAAAAAUGH!

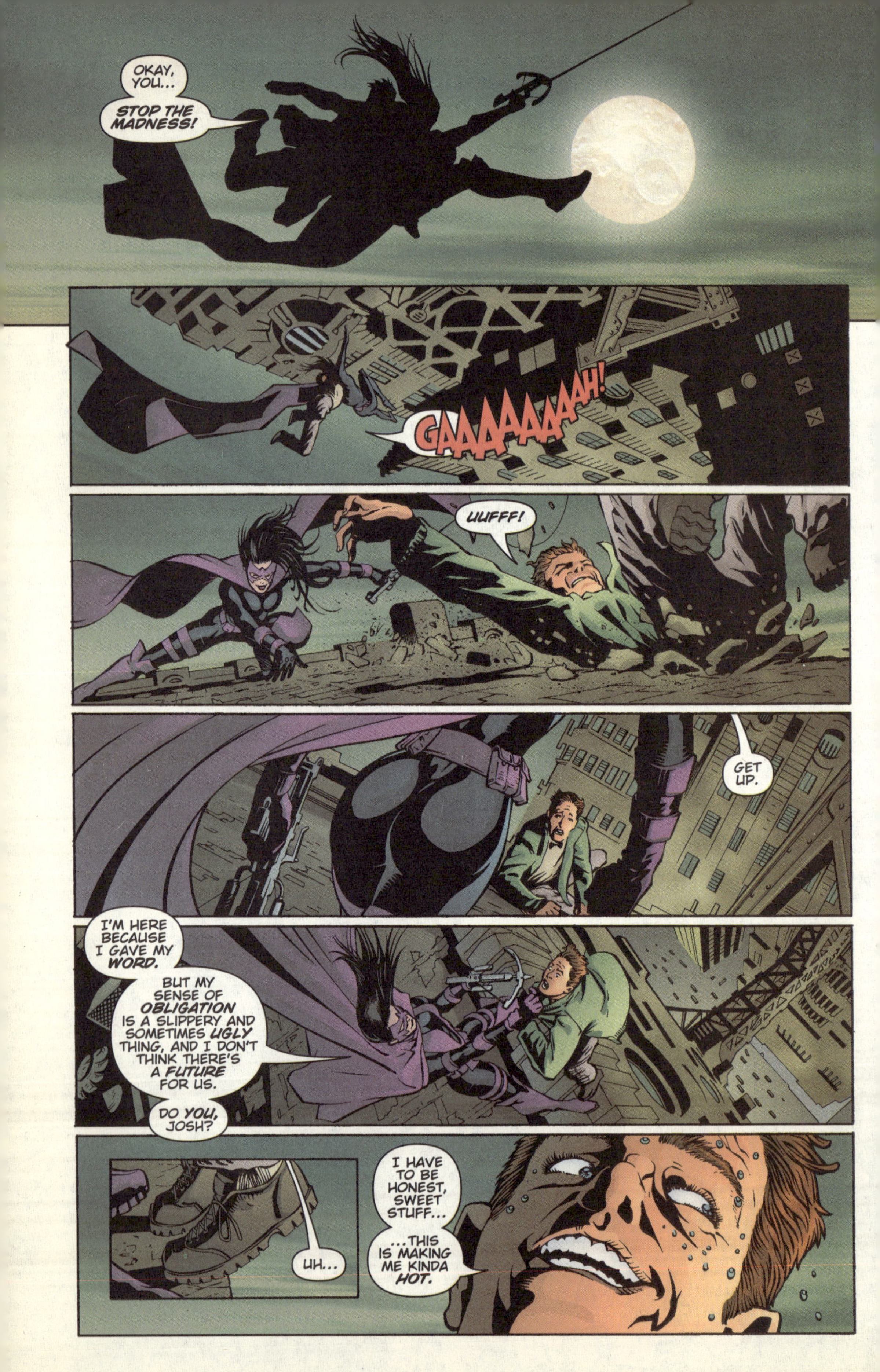
OKAY, YOU... STOP THE MADNESS!
GAAAAAAAAH!
UUFFF!
GET UP.
I'M HERE BECAUSE I GAVE MY WORD.
BUT MY SENSE OF OBLIGATION IS A SLIPPERY AND SOMETIMES UGLY THING, AND I DON'T THINK THERE'S A FUTURE FOR US.
DO YOU, JOSH?
UH...
I HAVE TO BE HONEST, SWEET STUFF...
...THIS IS MAKING ME KINDA HOT.

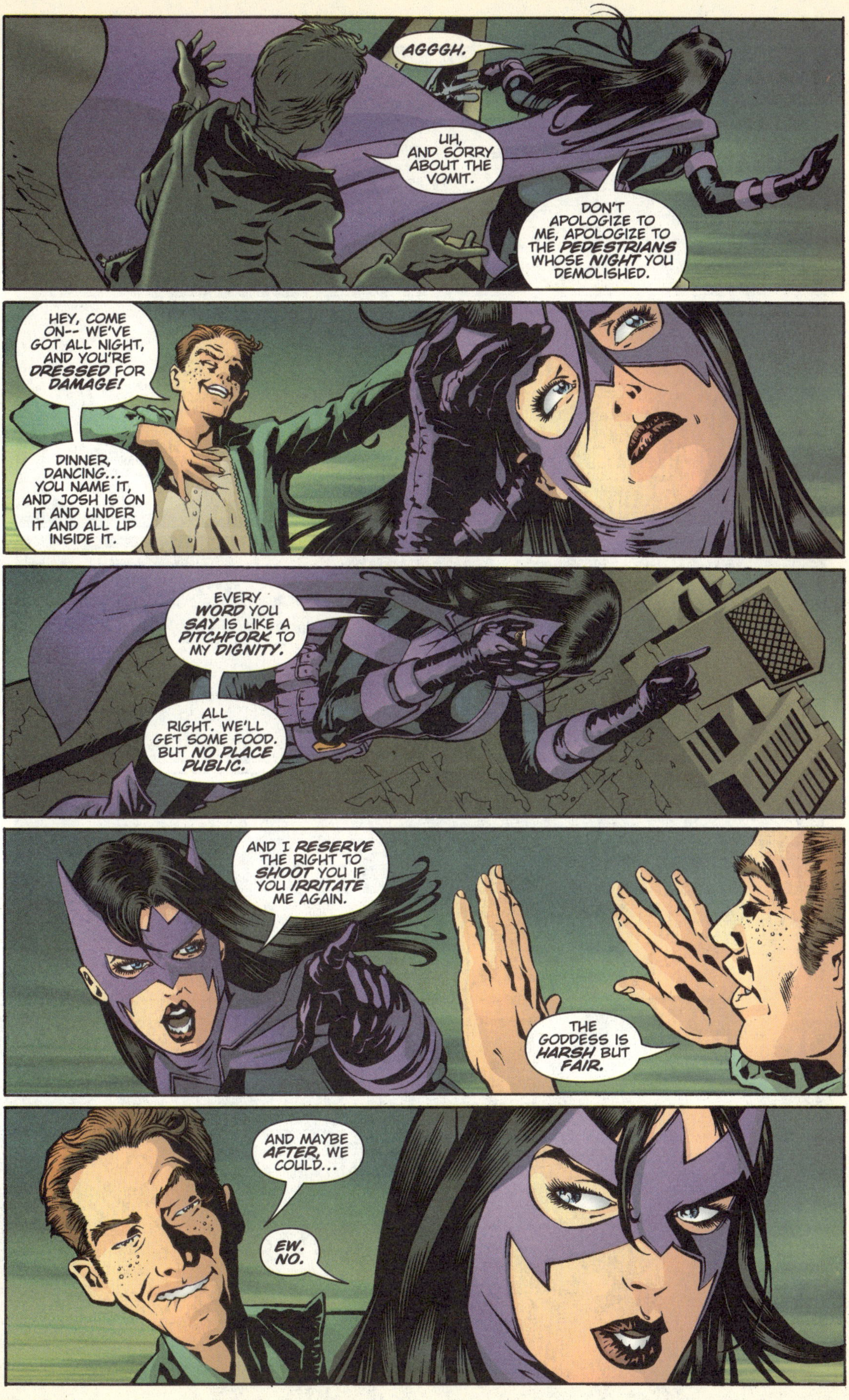
AGGGH.
UH, AND SORRY ABOUT THE VOMIT.
DON'T APOLOGIZE TO ME, APOLOGIZE TO THE PEDESTRIANS WHOSE NIGHT YOU DEMOLISHED.
HEY, COME ON-- WE'VE GOT ALL NIGHT, AND YOU'RE DRESSED FOR DAMAGE!
DINNER, DANCING... YOU NAME IT, AND JOSH IS ON IT AND UNDER IT AND ALL UP INSIDE IT.
EVERY WORD YOU SAY IS LIKE A PITCHFORK TO MY DIGNITY.
ALL RIGHT. WE'LL GET SOME FOOD. BUT NO PLACE PUBLIC.
AND I RESERVE THE RIGHT TO SHOOT YOU IF YOU IRRITATE ME AGAIN.
THE GODDESS IS HARSH BUT FAIR.
AND MAYBE AFTER, WE COULD...
EW. NO.

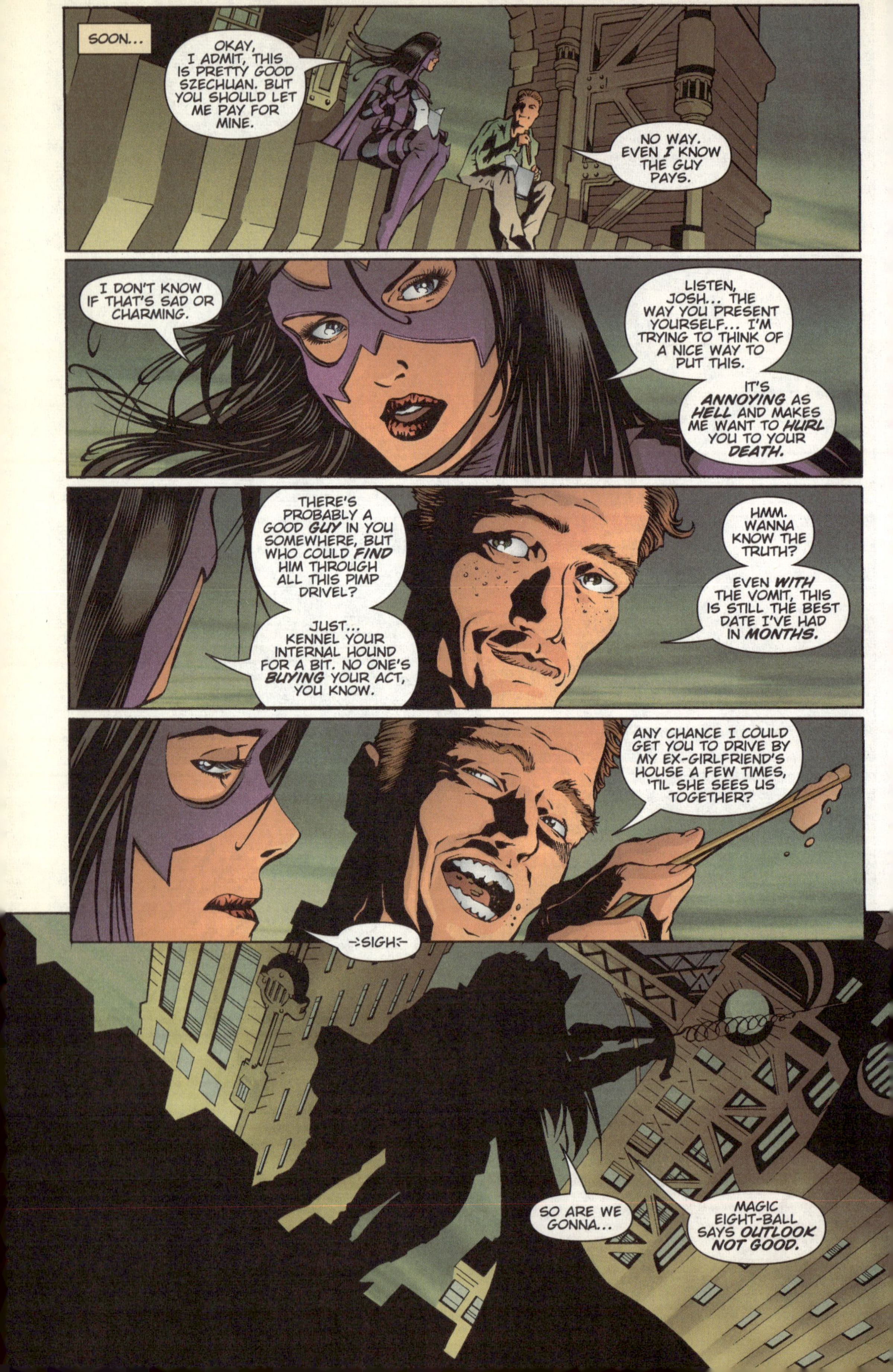
SOON...
OKAY, I ADMIT, THIS IS PRETTY GOOD SZECHUAN. BUT YOU SHOULD LET ME PAY FOR MINE.
NO WAY. EVEN I KNOW THE GUY PAYS.
I DON'T KNOW IF THAT'S SAD OR CHARMING.
LISTEN, JOSH... THE WAY YOU PRESENT YOURSELF... I'M TRYING TO THINK OF A NICE WAY TO PUT THIS.
IT'S ANNOYING AS HELL AND MAKES ME WANT TO HURL YOU TO YOUR DEATH.
THERE'S PROBABLY A GOOD GUY IN YOU SOMEWHERE, BUT WHO COULD FIND HIM THROUGH ALL THIS PIMP DRIVEL?
JUST... KENNEL YOUR INTERNAL HOUND FOR A BIT. NO ONE'S BUYING YOUR ACT, YOU KNOW.
HMM. WANNA KNOW THE TRUTH?
EVEN WITH THE VOMIT, THIS IS STILL THE BEST DATE I'VE HAD IN MONTHS.
ANY CHANCE I COULD GET YOU TO DRIVE BY MY EX-GIRLFRIEND'S HOUSE A FEW TIMES, 'TIL SHE SEES US TOGETHER?
-SIGH-
SO ARE WE GONNA...
MAGIC EIGHT-BALL SAYS OUTLOOK NOT GOOD.

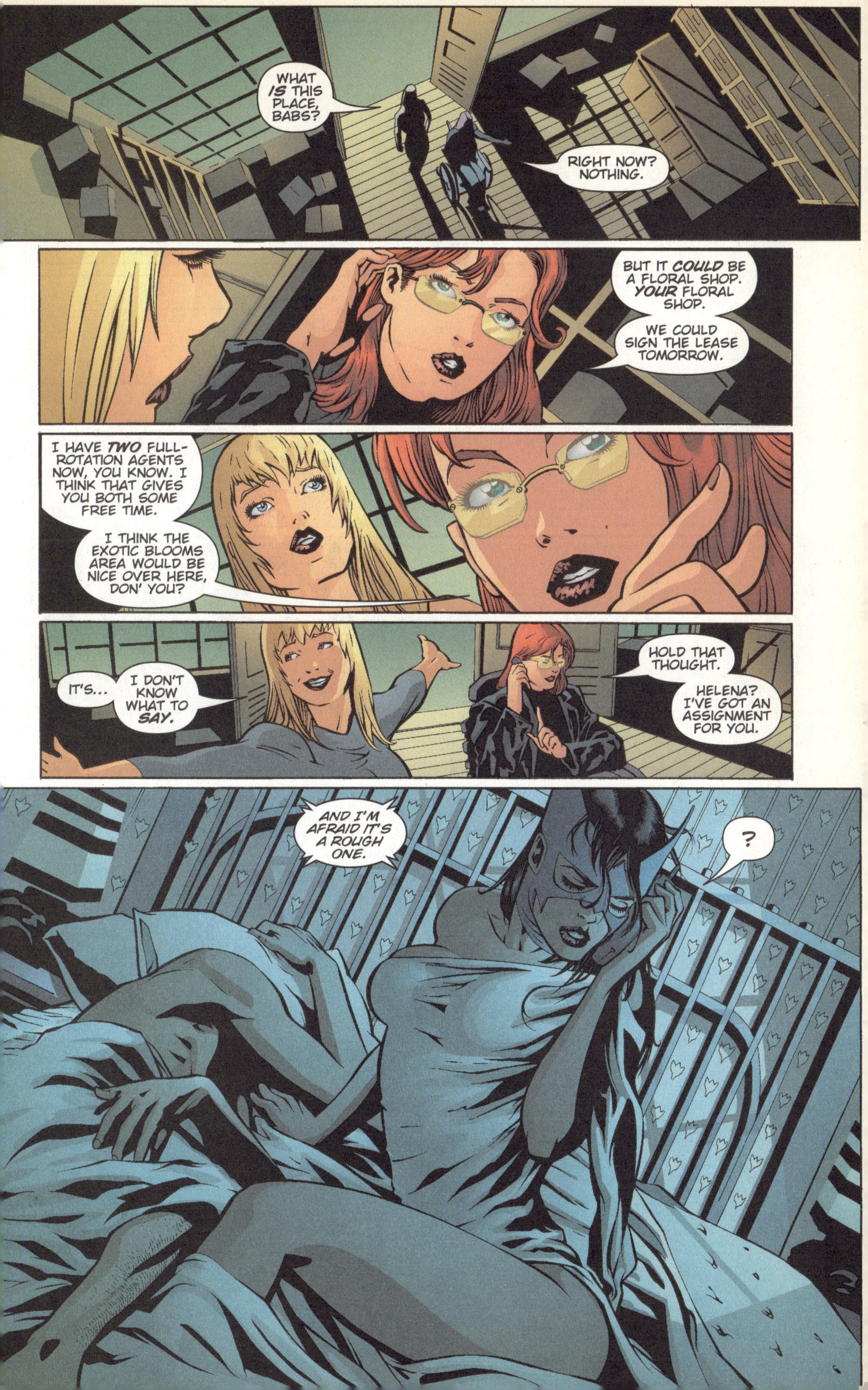
WHAT *IS* THIS PLACE, BABS?
RIGHT NOW? NOTHING.
BUT IT *COULD* BE A FLORAL SHOP. *YOUR* FLORAL SHOP.
WE COULD SIGN THE LEASE TOMORROW.
I HAVE *TWO* FULL-ROTATION AGENTS NOW, YOU KNOW. I THINK THAT GIVES YOU BOTH SOME FREE TIME.
I THINK THE EXOTIC BLOOMS AREA WOULD BE NICE OVER HERE, DON' YOU?
IT'S...
I DON'T KNOW WHAT TO *SAY.*
HOLD THAT THOUGHT.
HELENA? I'VE GOT AN ASSIGNMENT FOR YOU.
AND I'M AFRAID IT'S A ROUGH ONE.
?

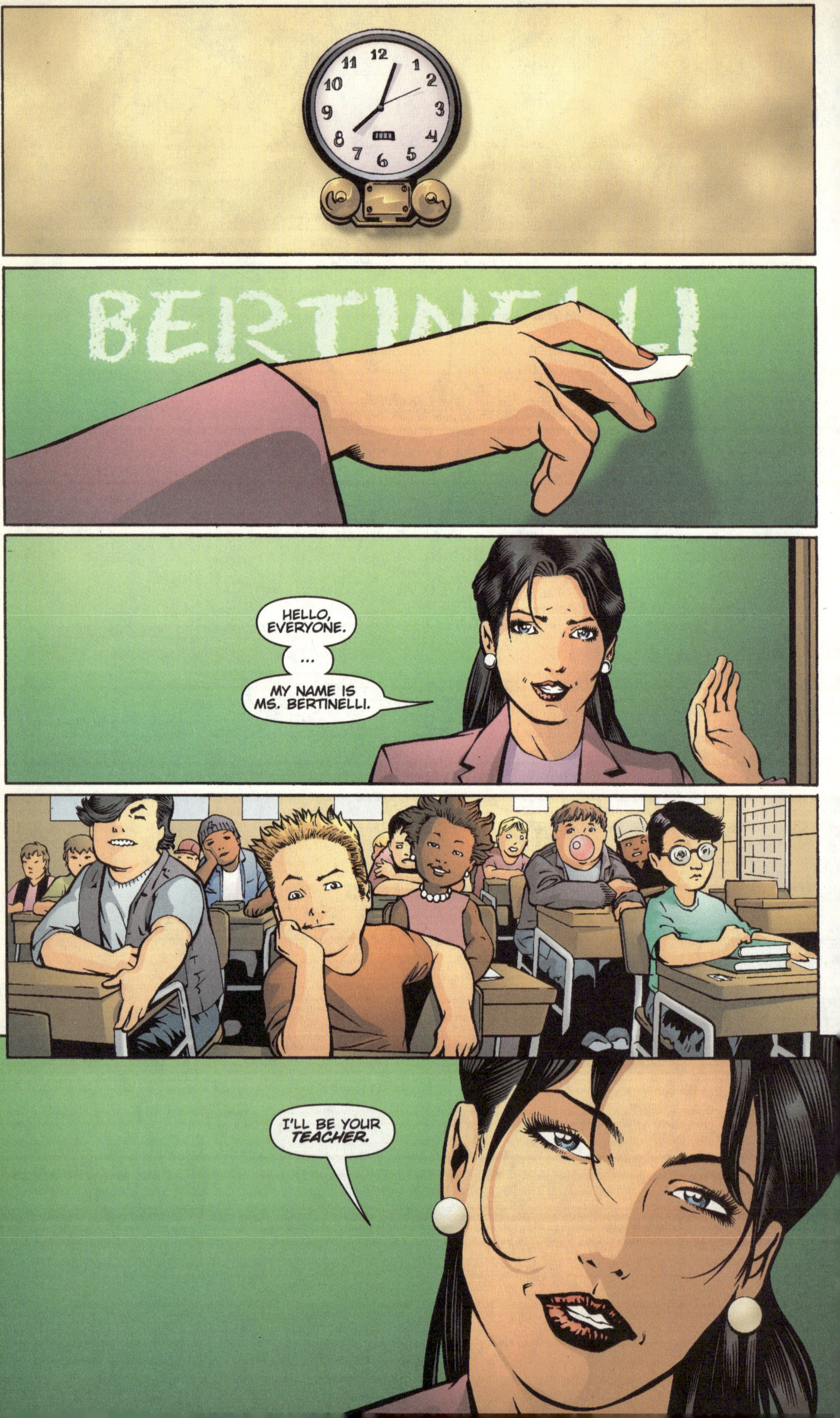
BERTINELLI
HELLO, EVERYONE.
...
MY NAME IS MS. BERTINELLI.
I'LL BE YOUR TEACHER.

DON'T MISS THESE OTHER GREAT TITLES FROM AROUND THE DCU!

SUPERMAN: BIRTHRIGHT

**MARK WAID
LEINIL FRANCIS YU
GERRY ALANGUILAN**

BATMAN: DARK VICTORY

**JEPH LOEB
TIM SALE**

WONDER WOMAN: GODS AND MORTALS
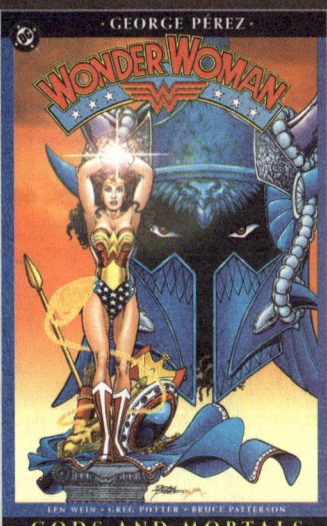
**GEORGE PÉREZ
LEN WEIN/GREG POTTER
BRUCE PATTERSON**

GREEN LANTERN: NO FEAR

**GEOFF JOHNS
CARLOS PACHECO
ETHAN VAN SCIVER**

GREEN ARROW: QUIVER
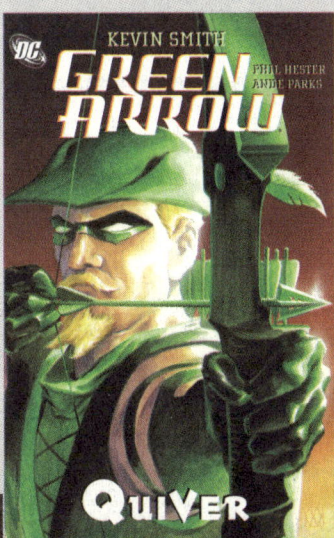
**KEVIN SMITH
PHIL HESTER
ANDE PARKS**

TEEN TITANS: A KID'S GAME
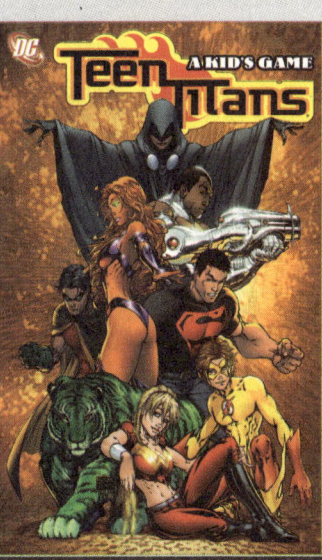
**GEOFF JOHNS
MIKE McKONE**

SEARCH THE GRAPHIC NOVELS SECTION OF
WWW.DCCOMICS.COM
FOR ART AND INFORMATION ON ALL OF OUR BOOKS!

READ MORE ADVENTURES OF YOUR FAVORITE HEROES IN THESE COLLECTIONS FROM DC COMICS:

KINGDOM COME

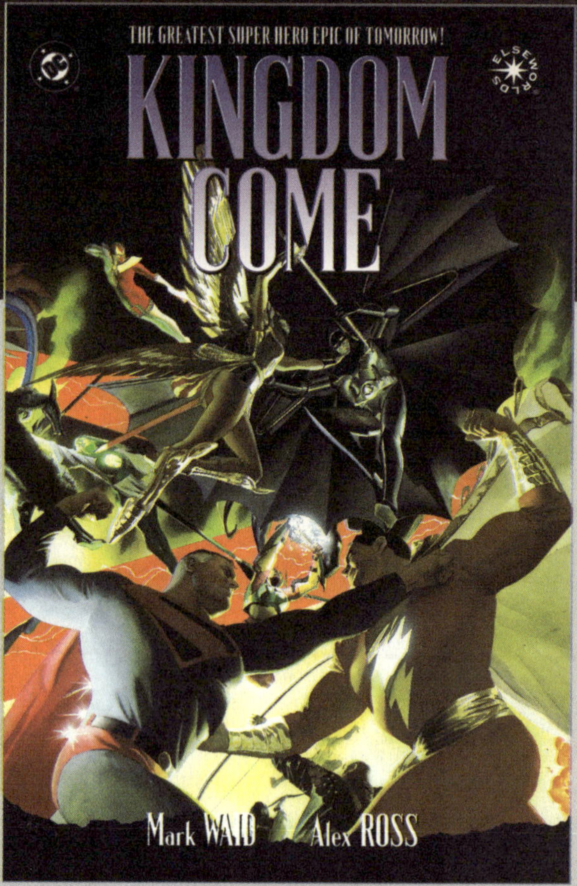
THE GREATEST SUPER HERO EPIC OF TOMORROW!
KINGDOM COME
Mark WAID
Alex ROSS

Mark Waid and **Alex Ross** deliver a grim tale of youth versus experience, tradition versus change and what defines a hero. KINGDOM COME is a riveting story pitting the old guard — Superman, Batman, Wonder Woman and their peers — against a new uncompromising generation.

WINNER OF FIVE EISNER AND HARVEY AWARDS, INCLUDING BEST LIMITED SERIES AND BEST ARTIST

IDENTITY CRISIS

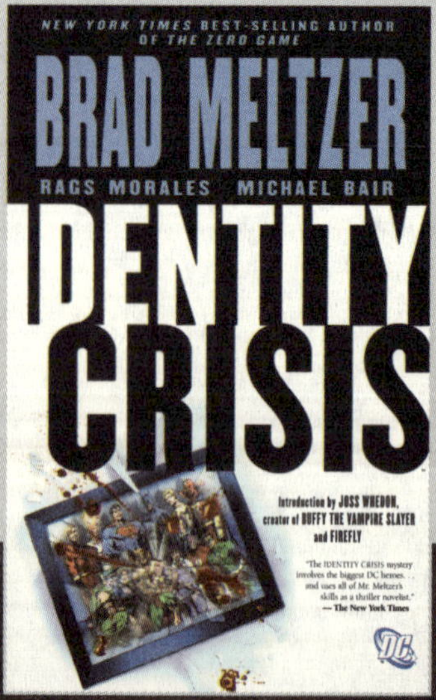
NEW YORK TIMES BEST-SELLING AUTHOR OF THE ZERO GAME
BRAD MELTZER
RAGS MORALES MICHAEL BAIR
IDENTITY CRISIS
Introduction by JOSS WHEDON, creator of BUFFY THE VAMPIRE SLAYER and FIREFLY

BRAD MELTZER
RAGS MORALES
MICHAEL BAIR

CRISIS ON INFINITE EARTHS

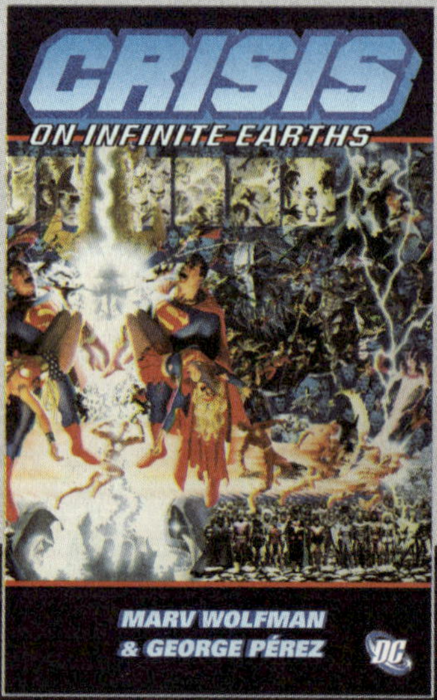
CRISIS
ON INFINITE EARTHS
MARV WOLFMAN & GEORGE PÉREZ

MARV WOLFMAN
GEORGE PÉREZ

DC: THE NEW FRONTIER VOLUME 1

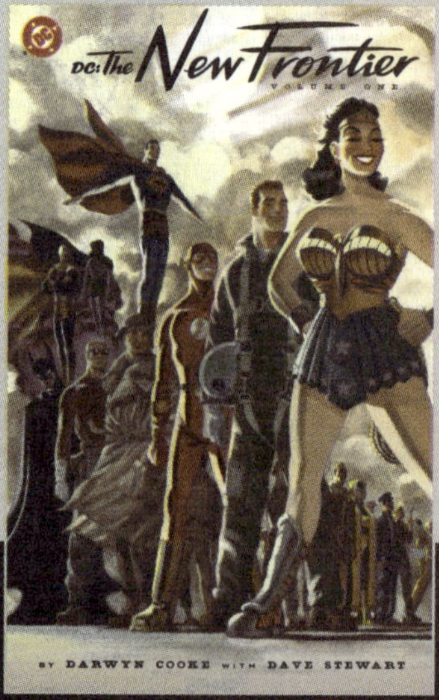
DC: The New Frontier
VOLUME ONE
BY DARWYN COOKE WITH DAVE STEWART

DARWYN COOKE
DAVE STEWART